Stories with a Moral

MICHAEL E. PRICE

Stories with a Moral

Literature and Society in Nineteenth-Century Georgia

THE UNIVERSITY OF GEORGIA PRESS
Athens & London

© 2000 by the University of Georgia Press
Athens, Georgia 30602
All rights reserved
Designed by Walton Harris
Set in 10.5 on 13 Minion by G&S Typesetters, Inc.
Printed and bound by Maple-Vail
The paper in this book meets the guidelines for permanence and durability of the Committee on Production Guidelines for Book Longevity of the Council on Library Resources.

Printed in the United States of America

04 03 02 01 00 C 5 4 3 2 1

Library of Congress Cataloging-in-Publication Data

Price, Michael E., 1953–
Stories with a moral : literature and society in nineteenth-century Georgia / Michael E. Price.
p. cm.
Includes bibliographical references and index.
ISBN 0-8203-2132-X (alk. paper)
1. American literature—Georgia—History and criticism.
2. Literature and society—Georgia—History—19th century.
3. American literature—19th century—History and criticism.
4. Didactic literature, American—History and criticism.
5. Georgia—Intellectual life—19th century. 6. Georgia—Moral conditions. 7. Ethics in literature. I. Title.
PS266.G4P75 2000
810.9′9758′09034—dc21 99-25524

British Library Cataloging-in-Publication Data available

To Vivian

CONTENTS

ACKNOWLEDGMENTS

Finally bringing into publication one's first book provides a welcome opportunity to acknowledge long-overdue debts. One of the high points of my undergraduate years at Kansas State University was being introduced to my future craft by a remarkable group of historians who had gathered together in Eisenhower Hall during the early 1970s. Though some have subsequently moved on to other universities, belated thanks to Robert H. Zieger, Donald G. Nieman, Jacob W. Kipp, George M. Kren, Burton I. Kaufman, Donald J. Mrozek, and Albert N. Hamscher.

While I was a student in the Department of History at the University of Georgia in the late 1970s, Numan V. Bartley and William F. Holmes guided my master's thesis on the Highlander Folk School to successful completion. Professor Bartley endured my pugnacious learning style in his various courses on the modern South with remarkable grace and good humor. During my subsequent career as a teacher, he also provided invaluable assistance on several occasions during the decade that it took me to complete my doctoral dissertation. I learned more about doing southern history during two years as a research assistant for Professor Holmes than I will ever put into practice. Michael J. Cassity, Charles Crowe, Aubrey C. Land, and Alf Andrew Heggoy all made a lasting impact on my subsequent development as a historian. Dan Woods and David and Julie Potenziani helped to make being an impoverished graduate student enjoyable and memorable.

It is impossible to express my full gratitude to Marion J. Rice of the Department of Social Science Education at the University of Georgia, to whom I owe the original idea for this manuscript. Professor Rice was a wonderful mentor who allowed me to devote most of my time as a graduate assistant to my own research, but he should not be held accountable for my ideological orientation or interpretation of Georgia history. Special thanks are also in order for Donald O. Schneider for taking over as my major professor upon Dr. Rice's retirement and helping me bring my dissertation to completion. Louis De Vorsey and Phinizy Spalding helped to refine my understanding of the landscape and history of early Georgia. I have also drawn repeatedly upon what I learned from James E. Kibler Jr. during an intensive initiation into the mysteries of southern literature. Thanks as well to A. Guy Larkins and Robert Cohen for serving on my dissertation committee.

This manuscript is largely a product of the Georgia Room in the Hargrett Rare Books and Manuscript Library at the University of Georgia. The staff tolerated my lurking presence almost daily from June 1991 through August 1992, providing well-appreciated assistance on numerous occasions. I have also made good use of the excellent holdings in southern history and literature at Emory University, Duke University, the University of South Carolina, Vanderbilt University, Georgia Southern University, and the Georgia Historical Society in Savannah. Special thanks are also in order for my friends on the library staff at Armstrong Atlantic State University. A grant from the Georgia Endowment for the Humanities in 1984 and a Teacher-Scholar Award from the National Endowment for the Humanities in 1991 made this study possible. Professor Bartley and Dr. Kathryn Hugg of the Clarke County School District wrote wonderfully effective letters in support of my NEH award. The Clarke County School District in Athens, Georgia, also provided financial support for my year of sabbatical leave during the 1991–92 school year. Armstrong Atlantic State University contributed a timely research grant that enabled me to complete my library research in 1997.

Parts of chapters 2, 4, and 6 were published previously as "Stories with a Moral: Augustus Baldwin Longstreet, William Tappan Thompson, and Other Literary Defenders of Plantation Society in Antebellum Georgia," *Atlanta History: A Journal of Georgia and the South* 39 (1995), 23–45; "'Such Are the Changes of Life': The Literary Response on the Georgia Homefront to the Civil War," *Journal of the Georgia Association of Historians* 15 (1994), 162–91; and "Back to the Briar Patch: Joel Chandler Harris and the Literary Defense of Paternalism," *Georgia Historical Quarterly* 81 (1997), 686–712. I am grateful for permission to reprint this work here.

I would also like to express my appreciation to John C. Inscoe, Bradley R. Rice, Mark K. Bauman, Carol Andrews, Chris Hendricks, Nancy A. White, Jean E. Friedman, Henry Robertson, David Rachels, and John Mayfield for reading portions or all of this manuscript. My colleague Mark Finlay is a demanding in-house editor who has given freely of his time on numerous occasions to make this a better book. No author could ask for more valuable critiques than were provided by my anonymous reader and Mart A. Stewart for the University of Georgia Press. My editor Malcolm Call displayed incredible patience while waiting for me to complete my revisions after the manuscript was initially contracted. My copy editor Debbie Winter has my undying appreciation for guiding me through the tedious process of final revision. Courtney Denney, Stephanie Hansen, Erin Kelly, and the rest of the staff at the University of Georgia Press who had a hand in this project also have my gratitude.

Special thanks as well to all of the boisterous yet incredibly gifted students who participated in my history classes at Cedar Shoals High School in Athens, Georgia, from 1984 to 1993. They taught me more about writing and history than they will ever know. My students and colleagues at Armstrong Atlantic State University make me glad that I decided to become a professional historian in 1993. Evangeline Wallace and Durward E. Price have my love and gratitude for all of the support they have given over the years. Without the love, wisdom, and encouragement of George A. Rogers and Vivian Rogers-Price and the patience of Jessica, John, and Amanda, I would have quit the backcountry a long time ago.

PROLOGUE

Georgia Scenes Revisited

Travels through the Backcountry of the Southern Literary Imagination in Search of Ideological Significance

This study builds upon the assumption that literature illuminates past social reality. Viewed in such a light, traveler accounts, diaries and journals, family letters, short stories, poetry, and novels become significant primary sources in historical study. Through its wealth of descriptive, anecdotal, and ideological detail, literature communicates the richness of the human experience. In fact, one might well begin a study of southern history by turning first to the literary record. Nevertheless, the nature of the relationship between history and literature continues to generate much debate. Scholars have explored the literary heritage of nineteenth-century Georgia selectively, but there existed until now no comprehensive study of its historical significance. Indeed, the sheer volume of Georgia's literary record and its thematic diversity are daunting without an underlying theme to provide interpretive order.

Stories with a Moral: Literature and Society in Nineteenth-Century Georgia is a study of the impact of the rise, fall, and resurrection of King Cotton on the literary imagination of the time. Although plantation slavery was well established along the rice coast by the time of the American Revolution, it was the expansion of cotton production into the backcountry in the early decades of the nineteenth century that firmly enthroned the plantation economy as the ruling force in Georgia until recent times. Those who wrote in the nineteenth century about life in Georgia ranged far and wide in their selection of literary themes and topics, but plantation society delineated the broad parameters of their creative universe.

When I began this study in the spring of 1983, I had no idea where I was going or how long it would take me to get there. Initially, I concentrated on gathering literary passages that shed light on life in rural Georgia, past and present. The next year Marion J. Rice and I received a grant from the Georgia Endowment for the Humanities to organize a series of community forums throughout the state around the theme of changing images of the Georgia landscape. By the time the Life on the Land program ended in 1985, I knew a lot more about Georgia history and literature, but my research still lacked direction. After several more years of wandering through the backcountry of the southern literary imagination, I finally began to develop a feel for the historical significance of my research when I narrowed my focus to the relationships among social development, literary expression, and the process of ideological formation, transformation, and communication.

My travels through Georgia's literary past evolved thereafter into a search for an understanding of the ways that contemporary literary expression makes known the dynamics of social change and persistence. Though I do not profess to offer a comprehensive model of culture in this study, the literary record illustrates dramatically the ways in which the social relations of production, reproduction, and governance, which I define loosely as how people make a living and who benefits, how gender constructions affect social relations, and how power is exercised in the public and private arenas, shaped artistic expression in Georgia during the nineteenth century. This is not to argue that class, race, gender, and politics determined artistic expression, but simply to assert that people tended to write, sing, paint, build, and talk with great frequency about what they deemed significant in their social relations. It follows that fundamental changes and continuities in social relations can be tracked with good effect by examining patterns in literary expression.[1]

The South is unique in American history because of its commitment to slavery and the proslavery ideology long after the rest of the nation had taken a different road of social and cultural development. In consequence, an old theoretical problem has shaped my thinking about nineteenth-century Georgia. Specifically, what is the relation between literature and society? How does social change and cultural persistence affect the literary imagination, and vice versa? Literary sources are vital to the study of social history because they reveal that the relationship between social change and cultural persistence is seldom linear even when fundamental patterns of linearity become evident in retrospect. It is therefore important when emphasizing the continuity of plantation agriculture in nineteenth-century Georgia not to overlook the social revolution that divided the Old and New Souths.

Considered within a larger perspective, this is also a study of the capitalist transformation of the Georgia countryside. Raymond Williams has written that the "one vital lesson" learned by the nineteenth century was that "the basic economic organization could not be separated from its moral and intellectual concerns." The fundamental problem that complicates the picture is that capitalism generates a continuous cultural crisis by constantly redefining the structure of society. This in turn impedes the proper working of traditional cultural agencies for incorporating new experiences into consciousness because they are the creations of the society under transformation. Those in the forefront of social change generated from above, who stand to benefit the most from the process, rely upon ideological communication to implant the "right" ideas into the population. But as Williams notes: "Communication is not only transmission; it is also reception and response." Time and again throughout the nineteenth century, the capitalist transformation of Georgia was shaped by the cultural heritage of plantation slavery, even after the Civil War destroyed the peculiar institution. As the conflation of the New South creed into the Lost Cause ideology at the end of the century makes abundantly clear, in a transitional culture "the whole sum of experience will reassert itself, and inhabit its own world." To borrow a phrase from C. Vann Woodward, the burden of Georgia history existed long before the bulldozer revolution leveled the plantation system in the second half of the twentieth century.[2]

The phenomenal material accomplishments of the market revolution in the nineteenth century repeatedly exposed plantation society to great danger. In response, southern writers, like agrarians elsewhere in the Atlantic world, fashioned a pastoral defense of their way of life. In the words of Karl Polanyi, "In literary romanticism Nature had made its alliance with the Past; in the agrarian movement of the nineteenth century feudalism was trying not unsuccessfully to recover its past by presenting itself as the guardian of man's natural habitat, the soil. If the danger had not been genuine, the stratagem could not have worked." That many southerners in the late twentieth century continue to buy into the agrarian critique of capitalist development speaks volumes to the lasting significance of ideological transmission.[3]

To borrow a key concept from Williams, art speaks directly from the prevalent way of life or structure of feeling of any given era. Thus it follows that a close reading of literary evidence can be used to piece together a richer understanding of capitalist social development in the nineteenth century. As Williams notes in *Culture and Society,* "the art of a period is closely and necessarily related to the generally prevalent 'way of life,' and . . . in consequence, aesthetic, moral and social judgements are closely interrelated." Speaking of English society in a later work, Williams observed that attitudes toward the country exerted such a powerful hold on the literary imagination that "even in the twentieth century in an urban and industrial land, forms of the older ideas and experiences" persist as a standard by which to critique the ongoing impact of capitalist development. Williams nonetheless cautions against accepting at face value either the progressive nature of social change or the moral economy of an idealized agrarian past, a warning that applies with particular force to the American South.[4]

Williams also stresses that the nineteenth-century city in Britain and elsewhere was the creation of industrial capitalism. Yet because Georgia was first and foremost an agricultural society, its literary record understandably focuses on rural life. Town development and urbanization will thus be examined primarily within the context of their relationship to the countryside. Throughout the Atlantic world and beyond in the nineteenth century, however, the countryside was slowly drawn into closer association with urban economic centers. Such change came late to Georgia, but northern traveler descriptions of Atlanta rising phoenix-like from the ashes of defeat speak directly to yet another "case of a capital city drawing the character of an economy and a society" toward itself. That almost all Georgia writers portrayed the city's relationship with rural society in negative terms is a strong reminder that agrarian resistance to urban capitalism has deep roots. Significantly, one of the best-selling novels of the twentieth century, *Gone with the Wind,* is as much a critical exploration of the rise of Atlanta as a glorification of antebellum plantation society.[5]

The myth of a lost golden age appealed to all segments of white society in the nineteenth century, especially during the decades following the Civil War. In the past, for example, there had been enough upward mobility in plantation society that the nonslaveholding white yeomanry had bought into the proslavery ideology. Even after the yeomanry as a class began its downward descent into tenancy and sharecropping, dispossessed white farmers continued to identify with the landlord class. With tragic consequences, the white majority thus perceived the destruction of slavery and Reconstruction as a personal loss and vented its collective anger over its parallel loss of social status racially rather than toward the landed elite. If the rising tide of racist violence that engulfed Georgia in the late nineteenth century is a guide, the loss of the garden was not something to be taken lightly.[6]

One of the consistent responses by Georgia writers to the ongoing chaos wrought by nineteenth-century capitalist development was to emphasize the need for moral regeneration. But as one historian has written, the morality advocated by agrarian critics seldom accords with the newer arrangements that follow the intrusion of market relationships into traditional societies and thus brings neither human happiness, progress, nor riches. Romantic calls for moral regeneration at best provide temporary respite from the demands of the present by appealing to a way of life that had "somehow proved its validity in the past." Within the pastoral world view that was shared alike by antebellum and postbellum Georgia writers, the organic life of the countryside was considered "superior to the atomized and disintegrating world of modern science and modern urban civilization." In light of the real dislocation in the countryside that accompanied modernization, it is not surprising that nineteenth-century readers responded favorably to clarion calls for a return to rural virtue.[7]

In fashioning a literature of resistance to outside domination, Georgia authors also relied extensively on binary oppositions to construct identity archetypes of dominance and submission. Literary portrayals of social pariahs such as drunkards, fallen women, violent rednecks, and black beasts, as well as sober citizens, good wives, sturdy yeoman, and loyal servants like Uncle Remus, played an important auxiliary role in the formation and maintenance of socially acceptable identity archetypes. The varied categories of public and private identity constructed, contested, and reconstructed by Georgia authors in the nineteenth century in response to outside challenges illustrate the process of ideological transmission in plantation society. Although this narrative focuses primarily on the process of ideological communication from above, the ambiguities and hints of subversion in the literary record reveal the ongoing struggle inherent in the exercise of power in American society in the nineteenth century.

The ideological significance of literary archetypes becomes evident when one recalls Raymond Williams's statement that "meaning is always *pro-*

duced; it is never simply expressed." As observed by V. N. Volosinov seven decades ago, "*Without signs there is no ideology.*" A sign is more than simply a part of reality; it "reflects and refracts another reality." Individuals learn to comprehend new signs by locating them in relation with signs already internalized, a dialogic activity that Volosinov likened to an unbroken chain. Simply stated, language consists of a series of signs drawn from a given system of social relations deeply rooted in the past. Once internalized, signs thereafter remain subject to further modification through historical time. The key point of emphasis is that the ideological chain is born of discourse.[8]

The act of linguistic formation and transformation also reflects and refracts fundamental power relations in a given historical era that are primarily constructed as weighted binary oppositions between the dominant and the other. Because there are always a multitude of oppositions of power at work, the dialogue is multi-voiced and as such in conflict. Whereas the purpose of ideology is to impose order on what would otherwise be a chaotic situation, the key to successful ideological communication lies within the concept of legitimization. An other can always be controlled by brute force if necessary, but this is hardly an efficient means of maximizing the various forms of social production. Effective ideological communication thus depends upon the existence of enough shared ground so that a consensus can take shape that mutes or channels the fundamental sources of conflict that might otherwise threaten the social advantage of the dominant group. When dominance is firm, a state of cultural hegemony can be said to exist.[9]

Perhaps the most effective way for a dominant group to maintain its position of social privilege is to tolerate, reinforce, or encourage a measure of conflict between the various categories of others that exist within its social domain. In nineteenth-century Georgia, for example, the white landed elite exploited with frequent but not always conscious intent the class, racial, and gender divisions of plantation society to its advantage, although it is important to remember that such conflict could get out of hand. The language of identity, the system of signs that all Georgians relied upon to define their individual and social sense of self, was weighted from the outset in favor of the dominant class. Thus the memory of the past, what really happened and what people came to believe happened, was enlisted in the service of the status quo, particularly during times of crisis when ideological challenges appeared.

The shifting landscape of power in a changing nation in which sectional elites found themselves in conflict with one another and with the various social groups under their individual or shared governance necessitated an ongoing process of ideological adjustment throughout the nineteenth century. The major way that language serves the cause of social stability is that it enables the dominant group to define the parameters of discourse. Yet because the social reality that underlies the sign system engenders perpetual conflict and flux, language itself can become contested terrain as competing groups struggle over the meaning of key words encoded with special significance. In particular, cultural resistance to structural change creates the vital space necessary to prevent the political and linguistic systems from becoming completely closed. In other words, the power of language is no more absolute than the power of any individual group; a dialogic process is at work in both cases.[10]

It should come as no surprise that every social group that rises or attempts to rise to dominance during a period of social change relies upon ideological communication to legitimize its power. It is equally important to remember that the processes involved are neither deterministic in any absolute sense nor strictly speaking linear except in retrospect. In the protean universe of social relations and cultural expression, there are always lost or forgotten alternatives—roads not taken, choices not made, or roads taken and choices made and subsequently forgotten or silenced in the common memory. Simply stated, the potential for agency always exists among all social groups and individuals. Nevertheless, because all of the binary oppositions that underpin any social structure are also weighted relations, the dice are loaded toward dominance.

The vital contribution that linguistic theorists have made to our understanding of the social development of the American South within the world capitalist system has been to draw attention to the dynamics of ideological communication. To state it differently, linguistic theory is tedious business, but it alerts us to the truth that language is vital to the exercise of power and resistance alike. This in itself legitimizes the use of literary sources as primary sources in historical discourse. Moreover, it is precisely because literary sources are impressionistic and subjective that they are fundamental to the study of culture and society. The truth of the old adage that knowledge is power lies in the realization that discourse is the vehicle by which real people act, interact, and react in society.[11]

But what is ideology? Terry Eagleton describes ideology as a text "woven of a whole tissue of different conceptual strands" that resists precise definition. Among its various meanings, ideology can be understood as the process of production of meanings, signs, and values in social life; a body of ideas characteristic of a particular social group or class; ideas and false ideas that help to legitimate a dominant political power; forms of thought motivated by social interests; identity thinking; the conjuncture of discourse and power; the medium in which conscious social actors make sense of their world; and the indispensable medium in which individuals live out their relations to a social structure. In sum, ideology can be defined "as any kind of intersection between belief systems and political power." As defined by Eagleton, the test of ideology amounts to "who is saying what to whom for what purposes."[12]

Ideological messages transmitted from above must be put into practice, but everyday people are not empty vessels waiting to be filled at the whim of the powerful. Ruling imperatives that do not accord significantly with lived experience are rarely successful. Moreover, Eagleton distinguishes between normative (I agree this is right) and pragmatic acceptance (I do not buy your ideology but as a member of a subaltern group see no realistic alternative to acceptance). A good illustration of the limits of ideological communication can be found in the books published in the late nineteenth century by southern authors. Typically, reluctant testimony to the evils of slavery in the preface was negated later in the text by a vigorous defense of the peculiar institution. Much the same holds true about postbellum southern attitudes toward sectional reconciliation.[13]

One current that runs through the literary record is the underlying tension generated by the compulsion Georgia authors felt to defend a way of life they perceived as being under relentless attack. Men and women who were overwhelmingly wedded to tradition found themselves trying to incorporate new experiences into their conscious existence. It is precisely this broad ideological struggle that gives a political dimension to the varied forms of literary expression. Barrington Moore notes that it is misleading to speak of cultural inertia in a capitalist society because "the transmission of values is a continuous process." Moore also maintains that "reactionary social theories are liable to flourish in a landed upper class that manages to hang onto political power successfully although it is losing out economically or is threatened by a new and strange source of economic power." He concludes that the typical response of the landlord class to the undermining pressures of commercial transformation is to extol the peasant as the "backbone of society." Relative to nineteenth-century Georgia fiction, his point is well taken. Singing the praises of the common folk during the turbulent postwar decades, for example, was an ideological smoke screen that concealed political discontent among rural whites and blacks, which in turn served the status quo by downplaying social unrest from below. Throughout the nineteenth century, Georgia authors employed romantic agrarian themes while shaping a literary defense of plantation society.[14]

In my first three chapters, I examine the portrayal of antebellum plantation society in three distinctive but related literary genres, an admittedly redundant but important exercise necessary to flesh out the contours of the debate over slavery. Chapter one attempts to establish the underlying ideological context by examining the expansion of plantation society along the Georgia frontier as portrayed by visitors in traveler accounts. A unique literary genre spawned by European imperial expansion in the sixteenth century, the traveler accounts are important because they afford insight into the process of social development as plantation society attempted to impose social order on a moving frontier. Though there were more influential forms of public discourse that increased the awareness of white Georgians of their identity as southerners, such as the treatment of sectional issues in the national press, the traveler accounts shaped national and international perceptions of Georgia. White Georgians became increasingly conscious that they lived under a microscope and that their social institutions were at the center of a worldwide dialogue regarding the future of slavery. Although the primitive conditions of frontier travel remained an ongoing topic of interest, by the mid-1820s slavery had taken center stage in the traveler narratives. The ideological dialogue audible in the background of many accounts reveals that leading Georgians were self-conscious of their increasingly negative public image in Europe and the North.

Chapter 2 examines the public literary defense fashioned by Georgia writers in response to outside criticism of plantation society. As do all forms of public expression, fiction reflects the society in which it originates. Initially, antebellum Georgia fiction centered on two primary concerns. The first was the expressed desire to create a realistic literary record of the frontier before it vanished, although the effort was ideologically charged from the beginning. The second was to further the cause of moral reform in plantation society. The tensions engendered by outside criticism of the social arrangements of plantation society and the protracted process of taming the frontier inspired a minor literary awakening. By 1848, however, the explosive debate over slavery had pushed aside other concerns in Georgia fiction, which rapidly became just another shrill voice in the angry war of words over the future of slavery in American life.

After examining two forms of public literary expression, I explore the literature of domesticity, a broad literary genre that had public and private voices. I have christened the private literary voice of domesticity the literature of intimacy to distinguish it from its public sister, domestic fiction. Although I devote considerable attention to the writings of women who resided temporarily in antebellum Georgia, and equal time to one piece of domestic fiction because of its frank exploration of the proslavery defense, the diaries and family letters written by members of leading slaveholding families are the primary focus of this chapter. The literature of intimacy reveals the growing level of class, racial, gender, and sectional identity within antebellum Georgia's leading slaveholding families. United in outlook because of their class assumptions, commitment to domesticity, and shared experiences with slavery, the men and women of the planter elite fashioned a private defense of their way of life. Some engaged in direct dialogue with the outside world from time to time in their journals and letters, but most directed their thoughts toward more private concerns as they went about the business of everyday life. As the authors of journals and letters described the events of their lives to themselves and to one another, they also communicated their basic beliefs and feelings about the society in which they lived and the world at large. For purposes of manageability, I have used a representative sampling of published editions of journals and letters and rely when necessary upon several excellent secondary studies based on extensive work in unpublished manuscripts as an interpretive guide.

Whereas the first three chapters explore the same period from different literary perspectives, the last three chapters adhere loosely to a chronological format that begins with the Civil War. Though they got the part about slavery wrong, I nonetheless follow Charles and Mary Beard and interpret the Civil War as a social revolution and a great turning point in the history of the South and the United States. In chapter 4, I revisit the literature of intimacy, then pause to examine one major domestic novel for what it reveals about the Confederate ideology before shifting back to the letters and diaries of the era. Indicative of the profound changes wrought by the war, the literature of intimacy gradually acquired a public political voice that would continue to be heard for decades to come.[15]

The private and public literary reaction to emancipation and Reconstruction is the theme of chapter 5. Temporarily dethroned, King Cotton found not only his kingdom in ruins but its very future in doubt in an empire not of his own choosing. His armies driven from the field by Yankee roundheads who had the audacity to release his black peasants from their feudal obligations, and the ranks of his nobility and loyal yeomanry decimated by war, he turned his attention toward restoring life to his damaged and neglected fields. Not surprisingly, a rising generation of literary cavaliers in Georgia portrayed the interregnum as a dark and terrible time, an ideologically loaded interpretation frozen in fiction that also dominated the historical literature until recent decades.

To the dismay of planter landlords, the anticipated peace did not come with the removal of the army of occupation and King Cotton's restoration to power. The inner borders of his realm stretched outward with a vengeance during the urban-industrial transformation of the American empire, but disorder spread throughout the land and a series of pretenders laid claim to his throne. The efforts of literary spokespersons to shape a coherent ideological response to New South modernization and the Populist revolt is the subject of chapter 6. In my epilogue, I attempt to explain how everything came together in the Lost Cause ideology at the beginning of the twentieth century and offer a few tentative conclusions.

Some readers may wonder whether *Stories with a Moral* is social history or literary history. It is both. Part of the difficulty reflects my broad definition of literature to include nonfiction and fiction, as well as the nature of the literary evidence available in each chronological period. Whereas the first three chapters are organized around specific types of literary evidence, an approach that some may liken to three blind men trying to describe an elephant by touching different parts of his anatomy, the remaining chapters focus on the efforts of Georgia authors to piece together a jigsaw puzzle with some of the pieces missing, several strange new pieces added, and nothing to guide them but their memory of the original picture. Well over a decade after beginning this study, I remain more convinced than ever that the literary record is vital to the historical study of the American South. I still do not understand fully the tangled relationship between literature and society in nineteenth-century Georgia, but the ride has been enjoyable and at times enlightening.

PART ONE

In the Realm of King Cotton

CHAPTER ONE

Breaking New Ground

Traveler Perceptions of Antebellum Georgia

Having completed "an ample apprenticeship" in one of Glasgow's leading textile manufacturing houses, John Melish set sail for Savannah, where he arrived after a disagreeable passage of sixty-one days on 12 May 1806. Cotton had lured the enterprising Scot to Georgia, where he hoped to establish himself in the lucrative trade opening in the interior. Noting upon his arrival the "sallow appearance of the inhabitants and the extreme warmth of the weather," Melish set out to familiarize himself with the city's unique layout and its bustling commercial district along the Savannah River. Leaving his new export business under the care of a trusted assistant, Melish purchased a horse and saddle in late June and joined a man bound for Augusta, brushing aside the warning that the creeks were up and the bridges down. Swimming their horses across several creeks, Melish and his traveling companion eventually arrived at Hely's Inn, where they caught up with the Augusta stage that had departed earlier that day from Savannah. After arranging for the care of their horses, Melish and his companion joined the passengers around a common table to dine on a hearty fare of fowls, bacon, eggs, butter, wheat bread, "Indian" corn bread, cherry brandy, and a dish new to him called "homony." Continuing his journey, Melish came upon a spot some two miles later where two slaves had been executed for killing an overseer. One had been hanged, the other burned alive, a mode of punishment for flagrant crimes said "to deprive them of the mental consolation arising from a hope that they will after death return to their own country." Observing that such treatment might be "good policy as respects the blacks," Melish was nonetheless horror-struck at the sight of the scorched tree and the bone fragments at its foot.[1]

At the inn where Melish stopped to take his afternoon meal the next day, he observed a slave girl carding cotton while the landlord's daughter was spinning thread on a large wheel. The mistress informed him that all of the families in the area spun cotton year round, then wove the yarn into a wide variety of useful domestic articles such as sheeting, shirts, towels, petticoats, and aprons. Examining the yarns, cloth, and finished goods, Melish found them substantial, describing them as durable, neatly manufactured, and often quite handsome. Meeting a family "independent of commerce" pleased Melish, although he recognized that domestic manufacturing militated against his interests as an exporter of raw materials and importer of British goods. As he later reminded the readers of his *Travels through the United States of America,* "Self-interest is a proper principle, but it should be regulated as not to blunt the feelings of humanity, nor make us repine at the well-being of others."[2]

Stopping at a grocery store two miles down the road to quench his thirst, Melish met a lady from Savannah who had abandoned the unhealthy city for the healthier pine barrens to protect her sole remaining child after losing her other two children. Melish wrote that "Georgia ladies appear to be very fond of their children, and, in the country at least, they seem to be sufficiently prolific," but he also recognized that the hardships of frontier life aged women prematurely. "We hardly ever passed a house without seeing a cluster of young ones," yet he observed many nursing mothers "whom, judging from the external appearance, I would have reckoned past child-bearing."[3]

Veering off the Augusta road toward Waynesboro, Melish noticed that the soil improved and "natural woods" of oak and hickory began to appear among the seemingly omnipresent pines. He also passed a Methodist church, which led to reflections on the "excessive enthusiasm" displayed at camp meetings. Melish believed that the Methodists had done much good on the frontier but described camp meetings as "a species of 'holy fair' at which 'grace' is not the only commodity to be purchased; and from the mode in which they are frequented by the profane and the profligate, it is questionable whether the evil attending them does not overbalance the good." Melish also described the Baptists as being numerous, influential, and austere, although he "did not hear of any excesses in their camp meetings or churches."[4]

After remaining one day in Waynesboro, where he duly noted the presence of several wealthy planters and a considerable trade in dry goods and groceries, Melish departed early on the first of July for Louisville, then the capital of Georgia. Five miles out of Waynesboro he came to a fine spring where he heard the sound of several mills. "The sound of machinery is always grateful to my ear," he wrote, "and the view of the stones excited no small degree of interest; being the first that I had seen in the United States." Although the Ogeechee River "marsh effluvia" made the locale rather unhealthy, Melish was much taken with the little town of Louisville, which he described as having about one hundred dwellings, ten dry goods and one grocery store, a substantial inland trade, and a population of 550, nearly half slave. The region was well-cultivated and supported a civil, well-bred society. When he came down with a bad fever, a local doctor and his wife invited him to recuperate in their home, an invitation he gladly accepted to escape the mosquito-infested tavern.[5]

By the Fourth of July, Melish's health had recovered enough for him to take a walk to the state-house, a good brick building that also housed the land office. Even though it was Independence Day, he observed a flurry of activity at the land office because of the recent purchase from "one of the Indian tribes" of the lands between the Oconee and Ocmulgee rivers. Melish expressed his disapproval of the land lottery as a means of distributing public lands, however, suggesting instead that selling the lands at market value would provide much-needed funds for roads and bridges, improving navigation on rivers, and marsh drainage.[6]

Several militia companies were also on hand to salute the occasion with their great guns. Melish joined the celebration and accepted an invitation to dine that afternoon with an artillery company. The meal was followed by toasts of Madeira to each state in the young nation, as well as to celebrated heroes of the Revolution such as George Washington and Benjamin Franklin. Each toast was followed by a discharge of artillery and "a number of excellent songs were sung." All told, "the afternoon was spent with great conviviality and good humour." Melish wrote that when he returned that evening, the "cordial drop" had elevated "the animal spirits" of the company and several officers high in command were present. When his turn came around, Melish toasted Mr. Fox and the independent Whigs of Britain and reconciliation between the two nations.[7]

The widespread enthusiasm for republicanism that he encountered in the backcountry made a strong impression on Melish. Deeming it unfair to judge the United States by its coastal commercial centers, he stated that the true character of the American people was to be found in the interior, where "the inhabitants have a spirit of independence, and will brook no superiority." Each man, he continued, was conscious of his own political importance, an awareness that pervaded all ranks of American society and was "probably the best guarantee for the continuance of the liberty and independence of the country."[8]

Melish departed Louisville for Augusta on 5 July, stopping en route at Richmond Springs to rejuvenate himself at a limestone springs resort operated by a Mr. Posner. He described the water and food at Mr. Posner's bathing-house as excellent, yet remarked that white women refused to visit the establishment because Mrs. Posner was "a woman of colour." Where the ladies would not go, neither did their men, "so poor Mr. Posner does not get a proper reward for his exertions, and the Georgians lose the benefit of one of the sweetest summer retreats in all the country." He also described Posner as something of a poet, "though his rhymes are not to be compared with those of Pope or Milton." Posner's forte was humorous verse recited "in a dialect that never fails to excite risibility." The old man favored Melish with a copy of verses "addressed to a swindling little Jew" in Savannah who had cheated him. In Melish's words, the stanza that follows "will be sufficient to satisfy the reader of his poetical powers":

> But it surely was a great sin,
> To send me common whiskey in place of Hollands gin.
> The worse remains behind,—
> To send me common Malaga, in place of good Madeira wine.[9]

Melish described Augusta as a town with a mixed free and slave population of about 2,400. Originally settled by emigrants from Scotland and subsequently enriched by an influx of settlers of Irish extraction, Augusta's thriving down-river trade with Savannah and the cotton plantations that dotted the surrounding countryside supported a well-informed society that was "polite and hospitable to strangers." Melish provided his readers with a panoramic view of the fall line: "The falls in the river are three miles above Augusta, and immediately on leaving the town for the westward, the great contrast between this and the low country is seen: in place of swamps, marshes, and sandy deserts, the senses are gratified by high rising ground, rich verdure in the woods, and clear streams of water."[10]

During the return ride to Savannah, he was caught in a sudden storm when the coolness of the air after the day's sultry heat tempted him to chance it rather than seek shelter. To his astonishment, "a stream of electric fluid, apparently as thick as a man's wrist, darted suddenly from a black cloud, almost right over my head, and dividing in a middle of the road, a few yards before me, struck the trees on each side, with a shock which made the whole woods ring. This was instantaneously followed by such a peal of thunder, as made my horse spring two or three feet high." Such storms were a common theme in the traveler accounts and personal correspondence of the era and a clear reminder of how close to nature nineteenth-century Georgians lived.[11]

Shortly after his return to Savannah, Melish boarded a steamship for New York, where he argued against the necessity of revolution with Thomas Paine. He also traveled throughout New England before heading south to Washington, D.C., where he interviewed President Jefferson. In poor health, he sailed for Savannah in late October aboard the *Delight,* but upon his arrival found his assistant dying of fever. Melish spent the winter regaining his own health and putting his business in order. As a merchant on the make, Melish tended to put a bright face on things but the war in Europe had hindered his commercial affairs from the beginning. When the suspension of the Non-Intercourse Act freed up a quantity of his goods, however, he decided to remain in business and departed for England in April 1807.

The war with France, the British Orders in Council, and the Jeffersonian embargo delayed his return to Georgia longer than he intended. When he finally made it back to Savannah in December 1808, Melish discovered that his business had deteriorated badly. With over 185 debtors scattered throughout nearly two hundred square miles of territory, he embarked upon a bill collecting tour, setting out from Savannah on horseback on 2 April 1809. To put it mildly, his account of his second foray into the Georgia backcountry illustrates dramatically the damage done to the international cotton market by the Napoleonic wars.

In small interior towns like Sparta, which had formerly enjoyed a flourishing commerce, Melish discovered that many merchants and country people were simply unable to pay their debts. Turning to the courts to settle his accounts, on the other hand, "produced effects distressing to contemplate." New towns like Madison had been founded since his last expedition to the backcountry, along with so many new settlements that he seldom lost sight of a plantation. Melish next visited his country store in Mount

Vernon in the New Purchase but found the state of economic affairs equally depressed. Stopping in Greensboro during the return ride to Augusta, Melish was surprised to find the inhabitants in a state of general alarm over rumors of a pending slave insurrection.[12]

During the ride to Augusta the next day, Melish and his traveling companion discussed in some detail the prospects of a large-scale slave rebellion. Making inquiry at all of the settlements they visited along the way, Melish discovered that popular attitudes about the danger of slave revolt varied greatly but everyone thought that precautionary measures were appropriate. At this point in the narrative, Melish inserted a rather lengthy discussion of the prospects of a successful slave rebellion in the United States, a topic that he undoubtedly thought would interest his readership. Citing the white population's vast superiority in numbers and arms, the personal affection that often existed between masters and slaves, and the peaceful disposition of the blacks, Melish dismissed the likelihood of such. According to Melish this was in contrast to the prevailing view in Britain, where it was generally assumed that slave rebellion would eventually lead to the destruction of the southern states.[13]

Of greater immediate concern was the depressed economic state of the region. Melish explained that "during this journey to the upper country, I made every inquiry that I could regarding the state of its commercial concerns, and I was satisfied that it had undergone a great revolution since I was in the country before." The staple commodity was still cotton, but "it had fallen in value as to cut off upwards of one third of the income of the country." Interpreting the proliferation of homespun in the interior "and the agreeable employment it afforded to the young women of the country" as evidence that domestic production would soon lead to "nearly the total exclusion of British goods," Melish closed out his commission business in Savannah and sailed for Charleston on the *Delight* in early June.[14]

Events would prove that Melish had misjudged Georgia's long-term prospects, although the instability of Georgia's economy between his departure in 1809 and the publication of his traveler account in 1815 undoubtedly gave him little cause to doubt the accuracy of his judgment. The expansion of Great Britain's dominance at the expense of Napoleonic France, and the concomitant efforts of the United States to develop its own internal market while carving out a limited commercial niche in the international economy, continued to wreak havoc with the young Cotton Kingdom until the Treaty of Ghent signaled a more stable relationship between world demand and southern plantation production. The restoration of peace set the stage for a long cotton boom that dramatically transformed the southern frontier.

John Melish abandoned his commission business in Georgia because he understandably misread the "revolution" he saw in Middle Georgia as a sign of the emergence of an agricultural economy based on small yeoman farms, domestic production, and little direct contact with international market forces. In retrospect it becomes clear that he was actually witnessing the birth of King Cotton in Middle Georgia. Firmly entrenched along the rice coast since the 1750s, slavery and the plantation system were given new vitality by the expansion of short-staple cotton production into the interior. The end of the War of 1812 also made Georgia more attractive to European travelers, a remarkable group of adventurers who left vivid accounts of the transformation of the frontier. Examined in conjunction with the accounts written by visitors from the North, the European traveler narratives reveal much about the social development of nineteenth-century Georgia. In addition to the wealth of information that they preserved about life in Georgia, the traveler accounts played a significant role in the rising debate over the future of slavery in the United States, an ideological debate that forced the defenders of plantation slavery to clarify the assumptions upon which southern society was based. Acutely aware of the South's precarious position and eager to defend their way of life in the court of international public opinion, many white Georgians embraced the opportunity to engage in dialogue with visitors.[15]

This is not to deny the problems inherent in such a body of evidence. Whereas some travelers had prior knowledge of the South, a fairly open mind, and keen powers of observation, others were antislavery propagandists or easily swayed by the proslavery polemics and social attitudes they encountered upon their arrival in Georgia. Moreover, with the exception of a few rare individuals, most travelers moved rather quickly along established routes of transportation. To draw a modern parallel, imagine the picture of contemporary American life today one might paint from the perspective of interstate truckstops, fast food joints, bus and railroad stations, and airport terminals. There was a natural tendency as well for authors to emphasize the exceptional rather than the normal routines of life, possibly to entertain readers and thus increase sales. And because antebellum travel was expensive and time-consuming, travelers were generally wealthy, well-educated, and somewhat elitist, especially those with connections to the European aristocracy. Consequently, most adhered to the class, racial, and gender assumptions common to their social station, although a few remained open to new ideas and experiences. And while some came to Georgia seeking adventure, many travelers were fulfilling professional obligations or pursuing personal pecuniary interests. Bearing all of these caveats in mind, travel literature remains one of the richest sources available to students of Georgia's antebellum frontier.[16]

Thus it is hardly surprising that historians, past and present, have relied so extensively on traveler accounts. Only recently, however, have scholars begun to give much consideration to traveler accounts as a literary genre characterized by distinctive narrative and ideological traditions. In "Scratches on the Face of the Country; or, What Mr. Barrow Saw in the Land of the Bushmen," Mary Louise Pratt describes the characteristic portrait of manners and customs that one encounters in traveler accounts as "a normalizing discourse, whose work is to codify difference, to fix the Other in a timeless present where all 'his' actions and reactions are repetitions of 'his' normal habits." When European travelers visited the "imperial frontier," even former colonial frontiers such as Georgia, they felt compelled to normalize the human and natural landscape so it could be incorporated into the world capitalist system. Indeed, as products of a given dialogic environment who were attempting to define difference within the guidelines of codes derived at "home," travelers were simultaneously vulnerable and expansive, "for nowhere are the notions of normal, familiar action and given systems of difference in greater jeopardy than on the imperial frontier."[17]

What complicated matters for visitors like John Melish was the fact that white Georgians had recently achieved a separate political identity. To be sure, Melish felt a certain attraction toward the republicanism he encountered during his initial foray into the backcountry, although his obvious misgivings about slavery reveal that Melish was never in danger of "going native." Significantly, however, it was not slavery that drove Melish from Georgia, but his conclusion that the backcountry was growing apart from the world capitalist market. Given the course of events that affected his economic endeavors, not to mention the tone of the Jeffersonian republican political discourse that was on the ascendancy during his visits to the United States, it seems hardly surprising in retrospect that Melish would reach such a conclusion.

Travelers on the Georgia frontier ranked high among the "principle producers" of the South for European and northern imaginations. The stories that they told also imparted a measure of ideological coherence to frontier expansion. What muddled the picture in frontier Georgia, as opposed to the European travel literature that dealt with Africa and parts of Asia, was the presence of well-established white "imperialists" who were staunchly committed to plantation slavery in a world capitalist system that was actively searching by the early nineteenth century for a more humane and possibly profitable standard of acceptable labor exploitation. Whereas many visitors clearly saw themselves as advance agents of a higher civilization, and thereby justified the critical stance evident in their observations, others already felt somewhat alienated prior to their arrival in Georgia from "homelands" undergoing industrial transformation. Finding themselves far away from home yet face-to-face with "others" who seemed equally civilized, many visitors fell sway to the pastoral appeals of plantation society.[18]

Pratt also discerns a tendency in traveler accounts to divorce descriptions of the landscape, "the face of the country," from evidence of human presence. While Edenic narratives often seem strange to modern readers who are concerned primarily with recovering a sense of the human dimension of the landscape, pastoral images of beautiful empty spaces also suggested land simply waiting to be taken. Pratt argues that travelers typically concerned themselves more with "scratches" on the surface of the land rather than the people who made them. In the Georgia accounts, real dialogue undoubtedly occurred on the verandas of plantation big houses, inside stagecoaches, or around the common dining tables of taverns and hotels, but the resident speakers usually disappear into the background behind an impenetrable veil of passive voice. Only the traces of human agency remain, like bone fragments at the foot of scorched trees.[19]

The panoramic view that characterizes traveler accounts, such as Melish's description of the fall line at Augusta, also communicates more than aesthetic appreciation. Pratt maintains that such descriptions express a "fantasy of dominance" in which the eye of the traveler takes in all that it sees, enabling the reader at home to experience vicariously the dynamic process of visual conquest and perhaps forming or reinforcing conceptual maps that made later political aggression seem normal, or the natural movement into empty space of a superior culture. Moving rapidly through space and time, such travelers seldom paused to interact with the landscape as they mapped out new terrain for future conquest. Pratt thus describes the claims to objectivity that are characteristic of traveler accounts, the presumably distanced and self-effacing observer simply recording images for their scientific value or popular edification, as a pretense. Such gathering of "information" amounted to "incorporating a particular reality" into a system of aesthetic, geographic, botanical, agricultural, economic, and ethnographic categories, among others. Such catalogues of knowledge enabled readers to join vicariously in the author's daydreams about transforming the landscape being described.[20]

The problem with the "voice of science" approach that dominated traveler accounts throughout the seventeenth and much of the eighteenth century was that readers unaccustomed to the language of natural history often found such narratives boring. In the late eighteenth century a contrasting sentimental style of traveler account appeared, a more entertaining and edifying version of the genre that proved more congenial to the dictates of commercial society. The tradition of the self-effacing traveler was replaced by the traveler as conscious hero as the predominant source of action in the narrative shifted from providing information to recounting individual experience.[21]

An imperial tone is clearly evident in the Georgia traveler accounts, although the voice of reform rather than conquest dominated the narratives throughout the antebellum era. Positioning Georgians like specimens under the glass, the authors of traveler accounts kept whites and blacks alike in their "place" by subjecting their manners, mores, and social customs to constant scrutiny. Ironically, the position that travelers took concerning the social customs and values of plantation society was not really the issue. Whether travelers elected to praise or criticize what they "saw" during their brief forays through the state, their narratives contributed to a pattern of public political discourse that positioned Georgia to be acted upon and kept white Georgians in a defensive posture. Simply stated, slavery made the South appear inferior to many outside observers, an "other" that merited being reformed. Whether intentionally or not, the antebellum traveler accounts helped to condition readers in Europe and the North to become more accepting of arguments for direct political intervention into the internal affairs of the region.[22]

Regardless of their social background or ideological orientation, travelers expressed nearly universal agreement that conditions along the Georgia frontier were primitive, but only the truly narrow-minded expected otherwise. Because of the colonial character of the state's economy and the constant westward migration of population, travel conditions never improved very much even after the maturation of plantation society in the interior. Prior to the railroad expansion of the mid-1840s, visitors were mostly limited to travel by steamship along the coast and navigable rivers, or by stagecoach over terrible roads. Steamship travel was slow and potentially hazardous, but the journey from Charleston to Savannah and Augusta was easily the most comfortable leg of a trip across the state. Perhaps unaware of the hard road ahead, travelers typically complained of the snail's pace, the monotonous landscape along the Savannah River, the nasty passion southerners had for chewing tobacco, and the seemingly incessant talk of cotton and slaves.[23]

By 1830 there were five main stage routes that crossed Georgia, plus many short lines. From Augusta to Columbus, the most common line of travel was the fall-line route through Warrenton, Sparta, Milledgeville, and Talbotton, including a rough section appropriately christened "Shakegut Road." At best, Georgia's roads made for a risky journey. In the words of one historian, the red clay roads in the Piedmont resembled glue in wet weather and "were probably as bad as any on planet earth." The so-called "roads" that traversed the immense pine barrens to the south were little more than trails blazed through the heart of the forest, an experience in travel that Captain Basil Hall of the Royal Navy likened to "navigating by means of the stars over the trackless ocean!" Fortunately, the experienced eyes of the drivers usually saw paths where none seemed to exist.[24]

Although some travelers hired private conveyances, the most common form of overland travel was in high-wheeled stagecoaches, so-called because of regular stops for fresh teams of horses. Uncomfortable and crowded, passengers felt every bump and jolt in the road, often had to shift positions or even walk to keep the vehicle from bogging down, and were expected to exit the coach in the pouring rain when necessary to assist passage through mud or high water. In addition, passengers were boarded in democratic fashion in order of arrival with no regard for class distinctions, although women received preferential seating by common agreement. Europeans of genteel birth found themselves seated next to backwoodsmen and ruffians, antislavery sympathizers like the Reverend George Lewis of Scotland next to slavetraders. In the words of William I. Hair, a Georgia stagecoach "resembled a little ark of humanity, with people of all description journeying together into an uncertain future."[25]

Piloting the ark through the turbulent backcountry was the quintessential "cracker" of frontier lore. Crude, proud, and fiercely independent, the driver's authority on the road was reminiscent of a captain's at sea. Whereas most were apparently dedicated and skilled coachmen, a drunken driver placed the lives of his passengers in danger, as reported by Karl Bernhard, duke of Saxe-Weimar-Eisenbach, during his travels across Georgia in December 1825. Bernhard also infuriated his driver by attempting to prevent the boarding of another passenger. Bernhard wrote that everything he encountered in his travels through Georgia "contributed to give me an unfavourable impression." Significantly, he also told his readers that "the inhabitants of Georgia are regarded in the United States under the character of great barbarians," a reputation he deemed "not unjustly conferred." Bernard's slight did not go unnoticed by the South's ideological defenders. Although the story may be apocryphal, when the South Carolina author William Gilmore Simms traveled by stagecoach through Georgia in 1831, he heard that a sturdy "cracker" driver had threatened to whip "old Saxe Weimar" and the governor too when the duke challenged his authority. A significant shift in the popular meaning of cracker, however, was already discernible. It would not be long before the sturdy, independent citizen of the republic would be transformed in the public mind into a degenerate pariah.[26]

Stagecoaches often depended on government mail contracts to turn a profit and consequently tended to travel at night, a frustrating inconvenience that would-be sightseers and landscape enthusiasts bemoaned because little could be seen beyond the occasional campfire of a party of westward-moving emigrants. After every Indian land cession and throughout the subsequent flush times of Alabama and Mississippi, streams of land-hungry settlers flowed across Georgia. When traveling by day, stages frequently passed caravans of emigrants, bands of dispossessed Native Americans, and gangs of slaves chained together for secure transport to markets in the booming Southwest.[27]

The recollections of C. D. Arfwedson, a Swedish scholar who was en route to New Orleans when he passed through Georgia in 1833, are particularly valuable because his descriptions of a group of slaves and a solitary Indian communicated a powerful ideological message about the human costs of frontier expansion. Traveling after midnight toward Columbus from Macon, Arfwedson unexpectedly found himself on foot after his driver smashed his stage between two trees. Before long he came upon a large fire, around which was seated a group of slaves bound together by shackles who were being transported for sale in New Orleans. Ignoring the slavetrader's efforts to quiet the scene, many were loudly enjoying themselves telling stories, becoming momentarily silent only when a young man from South Carolina described the severe punishment he had once received for trying to escape. Suddenly, a solitary Creek warrior emerged from the dark bushes, characterized by the Swede as a previously noble man now consumed by his passion for whiskey. Recalling the moment for his readers, Arfwedson mourned the sad fate of the dispossessed. "How much more delighted should I have been," he wrote, "had I seen him raise his tomahawk, and foaming with rage, demand the blood of the Whites, instead of begging for a compound which, like slow poison, undermined his constitution, enervated the sinewy arm, and made the free hero an object of contempt, commiserated by none." The next day the Creek's charred corpse was found in the woods.[28]

Arfwedson's short passage reveals much about the conceptual barriers that existed between white slaveholders and his readers in Europe and the North. The image of men in chains trying to make the best of a bad situation by telling stories in the night communicated a powerful critique of slavery. Equally powerful was the Swede's tragic portrayal of the drunken "free hero," an image that communicated well the lost Arcadian spirit of the Romantic era. It is not much of a leap to the conclusion that white slaveholders were murderous savages who would stop at nothing in their quest for new territory and wealth.

The migration of settlers followed close on the heels of Indian removal. By far the most astute observer of the expansion of the plantation system into the interior was the Irish comedian, Tyrone Power, who toured Georgia in December 1834. After four nights of performing before merry and sophisticated audiences in Savannah, Power boarded a steamship for Augusta. December was a busy time in Augusta because of the cotton harvest. The streets were crowded with planters and the suburbs filled with wagons arriving daily from the interior. After a pleasant stay at the Planter's Hotel, Power boarded an overloaded mail stage "with nine other victims" and departed in the rain on the 19th of December. During the night his stage passed several camps of emigrants destined for the rich alluvial lands of Alabama, their campfires burning brightly even in the rain. In Power's words, "The caravan usually consists of from two to four tilt waggons, long and low-roofed; each laden, first with the needful provisions and such household gear as may be considered indispensable; next, over this portion of the freight is stowed the family of the emigrant planter, his wife, and commonly a round squad of white-haired children, with their attendants: on the march these vehicles are preceded and surrounded by the field slaves, varying in numbers from a dozen to fifty or sixty, according to the wealth of the proprietor; a couple of mounted travellers commonly complete the cavalcade, which moves over these roads at the rate of twelve or fifteen miles a day."[29]

Power's description of an emigrant caravan suggests the importance of migration to the plantation system, although historians disagree sharply about the impact on plantation social relations. Much as the wind carries the seeds of the dandelion to distant fields, migration spawned new plantation households across the southern frontier. This is not to suggest, however, that families found westward migration easy. Although the young men of the planter elite apparently welcomed the opportunity to escape the patriarchal authority of their fathers, their wives agonized terribly over the loss of contact with their female kinfolk. While they recognized the necessity of migration to preserve the next generation's favored social position, plantation patriarchs also worried about the impact on their children. When his son was contemplating starting a new plantation on land he had purchased in Baker County, Charles Colcock Jones of Liberty County gave his blessing but later expressed strong reservations about the "godlessness" of Southwest Georgia.[30]

As a rule, most families waited until they had harvested their crops before pulling up stakes and venturing forth to new lands. Not only were travel expenses heavy, a family needed ready cash to begin anew once it reached its final destination. Winter on the Georgia frontier brought cold winds and rain, high water, and miserable roads, which led Power to remark that emigrants must have suffered tremendously. Still, the people he encountered were in remarkably good humor and a holiday spirit prevailed. Like the slaves that Arfwedson met around the campfire, the emigrant families in Power's narrative were determined to make the best of the situation, knowing well the uncertainties that lay ahead. Rewarding opportunities as well as dangers awaited hardworking and lucky families on the cotton frontier, a gamble that Power depicted well: "Thus they crawl onward from day to day, for weeks or months, until they have reached that portion of the forest, or cane-brake, fixed upon for the plantation: and here the enterprising settler has to encounter new toil, and a long series of privations, cheered however by the hope, seldom a delusive one, of ultimate wealth accumulating to the survivors of the party; for, unhappily, health is the sacrifice, I believe, generally paid for the possession of the fat soil lying along these sluggish rivers." No stranger himself to the pleasures and rigors of a wandering life, Power communicated well the magnetic appeal of migration to ambitious families. Nevertheless there were no guarantees of success on the frontier. Power also informed his readers that he met little parties returning in defeat from "the land of promise," including a young widow with five children and a half dozen slaves en route to Virginia after her husband's death.[31]

Those who settled in Middle Georgia soon discovered that the region's climate and rich soil made it ideally suited for large-scale production of staple crops. As Powers and others learned firsthand, the weather was always a force to be reckoned with in Georgia. Because of the subtropical climate, summer travelers came to expect sudden storms and close encounters with lightning frequent the pages of the traveler accounts. The road conditions and slow pace of travel virtually guaranteed that all travelers found themselves warring with the elements sooner or later. Descriptions of such weather-related phenomena as the aftermath of tornadoes in the pine barrens not only illustrated dramatically to readers the awesome power of nature to shape the landscape, they reinforced the prevailing impression that the backcountry was rough and primitive by emphasizing climatic phenomena foreign to many readers. And because Georgia's rivers run north to south, water crossings sometimes presented major problems for westward travelers. To their dismay, travelers frequently discovered that bridges, where they had ever existed, had been vandalized or washed away. To the wonder of many, rivers had to be forded by rope-pulled ferries. Otherwise quiet streams became raging rivers after a storm.[32]

Travelers also understood the entertainment value of recounting their travails with the unpredictable Georgia weather. One of Basil Hall's most vivid descriptions dealt with the crossing of Yam Grandy Creek, a tributary of the Ohoopee River in Emanuel County. When his family reached its banks near present-day Nunez, the creek was at flood stage. Hall, who had hired a carriage and a light wagon rather than travel by mail stage at night, found a foot bridge constructed of two series of logs supported by posts driven into the bottom; it was already submerged and in the center only one log remained. After helping the driver and his son unload the baggage from the carriage and wagon, Captain Hall, apparently sure of his sea legs after a distinguished naval career, took his sleeping infant, Eliza, in his arms and started across the foot bridge, while the horses struggled for footholds on the slippery corduroy road below. At the narrowest and most treacherous part of the bridge, his daughter awakened to the sounds of the rushing water and the driver cracking his long whip and "hallooing" his straining horses. At this point, "The child, who was in ecstasies at what she saw, clapped her hands, and jumped about in such a way, that I had the greatest difficulty in preserving my balance, the more so as I carried in one hand an umbrella, which I had unconsciously caught up to shelter the little thing's head from the rain, in the absence of her bonnet, mislaid in the confusion." After assisting Mrs. Hall and the child's nanny across, the men carried the baggage over, piece by piece. Only Eliza enjoyed the adventure, which her father labeled "the most formidable difficulty" that they encountered during their travels through Georgia. Given such obstacles, it is little wonder that Hall considered thirty to forty miles per day a good rate of travel.[33]

Accommodations are generally primitive in frontier regions, but they appear to have been particularly bad in the Georgia backcountry and improvements seldom seem to have followed the maturation of plantation society and town development. With the exception of Savannah and Augusta, which were not only older but maintained direct links with international commerce, towns failed to develop the infrastructure usually associated with capitalist urban development. In the absence of an extensive domestic commercial market and a large middle class, a deficiency critics drove home by making invidious comparisons with northern cities, there was little economic incentive to invest in building and maintaining fine public accommodations. Affluent planters who found reason to travel preferred to seek lodging whenever possible in private homes. In light of the rough clientele that frequented their establishments, the owners of public houses seldom concerned themselves about offending an occasional guest. Having survived the rigors of the road, weary travelers often found little relief when they sought places to dine during the day and lodging at night. With the notable exception of those times when they were received as guests in affluent plantation and town homes, travelers generally voiced the opinion that accommodations in Georgia were adequate at best and simply wretched most of the time. Actually, there were few true inns and taverns along the road in the backcountry; most were humble log homes where travelers could purchase a meal at a common table. The experience of the renowned British geologist, Sir Charles Lyell, was more typical than not:

> I had sometimes to put up with rough quarters in the pine barrens. It was cold, and none of my hosts grudged a good fire, for large logs of blazing pine-wood were freely heaped up on the hearth, but the windows and doors were kept wide open. One morning, I was at breakfast with a large family, at sunrise, when the frost was so hard, that every pool of water in the road was encrusted with ice. . . . They had placed me in a thorough draft, and, unable to bear the cold any longer, I asked leave to close the window. My hostess observed, that "I might do so, if I preferred sitting in the dark." On looking up, I discovered that there was no glass in the windows, and that they were furnished with large shutters only.[34]

Assessments of the food available for consumption at public houses varied but inclined toward the negative. While a few commentators echoed John Melish's satisfaction with the roadside cuisine, most failed to appreciate the standard fare of salt pork and corn bread and considered the culinary habits of backcountry Georgians too rudimentary for their liking. Wise travelers learned to carry provisions or simply did without such niceties as tea, sugar, and milk. Some travelers took in stride the absence of normal creature comforts along the road, although many apparently expected better than the revolting fare they received upon their arrival in Georgia towns. Even after it became the state capital, Milledgeville's hotels seem to have been especially dismal. European travelers in particular were rudely awakened upon their arrival in Georgia's inns and hotels, none more so than James Silk Buckingham.

Having earlier completed a study of the free states of America, Buckingham left New York for Charleston in January 1839 to begin a parallel investigation of the slave states. Traveling under the "distinguished patronage" of Prince Albert for the British and Foreign Anti-Slavery Society, Buckingham made it a rule not to stay in private homes, although he carried the requisite letters of introduction. Most travelers appreciated the value of such documents in a new country because they opened the doors to many of Georgia's finest homes, where hospitality was the order of the day. Persons of genteel birth were welcome for the quality of their company and because they brought welcome news of the outside world. Buckingham stated to his readers that he avoided staying in private residences because he wanted a more diverse view of southern society, although one wonders how welcome an avowed critic of slavery would have been in many private households. Whatever the case, his travels on both sides of the Mason-Dixon line convinced Buckingham that most Americans were simply unable to "distinguish between good fare and bad."[35]

Upon his arrival in Columbus one March evening after midnight, Buckingham secured lodging at the fairly new but already seedy Oglethorpe Hotel. Poor service by sleepy slaves, wretched outdoor toilet facilities in a region where water closets were an unheard of luxury, and a bed that literally fell to pieces finally exhausted his patience. In venting his wrath, Buckingham made clear to his readers the origin of his decidedly inhospitable reception:

> No bells are ever found in these hotels, though they are so large, and the servants are so far off and so stupid, that there is more need of bells here than in any other country; no curtains to the beds, broken washstands, basins without jugs, or jugs without basins, a dressing-glass shifted from room to room as required, no clothes' pins or pegs to hang a great coat, cloak, or any other garment on, and no closets or wardrobes to supply this deficiency—in short everything is so rude and imperfect as to excite one's astonishment that the keepers of such establishments should ever suffer them to remain so a single day, until it is remembered that the masters of American hotels, being generals, colonels, and majors, are too much the gentlemen to superintend anything except receiving the money; while their wives are still more disinclined to trouble themselves with household affairs; so that everything is left to the barkeeper or clerk, and the slaves under his direction; and these last, having no interest in the matter, neglect everything but what they are actually compelled to do; and therefore all things fall speedily into disorder.

Although Buckingham openly stated his opposition to slavery, such passages were undoubtedly damaging to the public image of the South because the presumption of veracity provided travel literature much of its popular appeal.[36]

Buckingham's opinion of the poor rural whites that he encountered during his travels was equally harsh. Citing a copy of Augustus Baldwin Longstreet's *Georgia Scenes* that he read in Macon which confirmed his own observations, he described the backcountry "crackers" as a "generally dissipated" group of vulgar barbarians. Significantly, in a region where planters, yeoman farmers, and slaves comprised the vast majority of the population, poor whites received a disproportionate share of attention in traveler accounts. As perhaps suggested by its longstanding importance in the southern literary tradition, the cracker stereotype played a central role in the formation of public perceptions of Georgia, although the precise etymology of the term is uncertain. Whether the word was derived from the sound of the long whips used by early herdsmen or stagecoach drivers or reflects the frontier practice of "cracking" corn into hominy, the term *cracker* began to carry negative connotations in popular discourse during the antebellum era. By the time Margaret Hall arrived in Georgia in 1828, a cracker was someone who squatted illegally on another man's land. That she hoped "to see some of them by and by" illustrates the nearly universal tendency among travelers to pass along secondhand information. When she finally left the comforts of the coast behind, Hall was horrified by the "disagreeable, gruff, and boring" manners of the "secondary classes," not to mention their tolerance for nasty fleas and bedbugs.[37]

In *Plain Folk of the Old South,* the historian Frank Lawrence Owsley criticized travelers for ignoring the large southern yeomanry or lumping small farmers together with the comparatively few poor whites who languished on the fringes of the southern agricultural economy, a falsehood perpetuated by the backwoods humorists and subsequent generations of southern authors. Although much of Owsley's interpretation of the old South is dated and clearly reveals his own ideological assumptions as a Nashville Agrarian, his reading of the antebellum traveler accounts was basically sound. Europeans made little effort to conceal their class assumptions when they visited the southern hinterlands, especially when their social prejudices were reinforced by conversations with members of the slaveholding elite. Coastal Georgia's leading planters were notably adept at shaping traveler perceptions about slavery, but they apparently saw no reason to conceal their contempt for poor whites, an attitude that southern humorists often adopted or parodied in their sketches and postbellum local color writers glossed over in the interest of white solidarity. Many travelers subsequently passed along such views to their readers by coloring their descriptions of the region's social arrangements with hearsay gathered around the dinner table, on the veranda, or at the receptions that the wealthy invariably orchestrated for distinguished guests.[38]

Compelled by the dictates of their chosen literary genre to seek veracity while voicing their own ideological conclusions, travelers often conveyed contradictory messages in their narratives. In one instance, for example, the use of offensive stereotypes while discussing the poor seems more the consequence of too literal acceptance of colloquial usage than obvious bad intent. Few if any antebellum travelers with antislavery principles worked harder to present the South in a positive light than the Swedish author Frederika Bremer. A stranger in a strange land, Bremer tended to parrot what she heard. When she recounted her visit with a family of "clay-eaters" in the forest near Augusta, she likened her hosts to the "sandhill people" in their ignorance, immorality, and lack of education, which she considered a direct consequence of being a free white minority in an area where slaves were in the majority. Not only did such folks suffer from the lack of public schools, they had "no feeling for the honour of labour and the power of activity." Had she gone no further, Bremer's description would have accorded well with the standard condemnations of the white poor voiced by her elitist contemporaries, European-born or otherwise. Yet when one reads beyond her initial repetition of local stereotypes, it becomes apparent that her clay-eater is a man of substance, a former overseer who had abandoned such work because he disliked flogging slaves. To be sure, the theme of self-redemption accorded well with the evangelical assumptions of the era and made it easier to judge the overseer the moral superior of his former employer. It also drove home the antislavery moral of her story. Still, Bremer's final comparison of the heroic clay-eater with the planter stands in marked contrast with her initial portrayal of poor-white Georgians. One trusts that her readers were edified to learn that "he, the freeman in the wild forest, with his pretty gentle wife, and his handsome children, was richer and happier" than the planter.[39]

Emily Burke was a New England Yankee who arrived in 1840 to teach at the Female Orphan Asylum in Savannah and subsequently counted teaching stints in "old field schools" among her diverse pedagogical experiences prior to returning north in 1849 after the death of her minister husband. The following year, Burke published an account of rural life in Georgia drawn from letters she had written during her stay in Georgia. Like Bremer, Burke blurred the distinction between poor whites and yeoman farmers but she was far less charitable in her conclusions, labeling Georgia a barbaric region that afforded "abundant room for missionary labors." As one might expect in light of her bourgeois social origins and evangelical outlook, Burke colored an otherwise astute analysis of the social origins of white poverty with numerous imperial observations that sometimes bordered on arrogance. Clearly, she considered poor Georgians the appropriate objects of direct remedial action.[40]

Burke wrote that clay-eaters, sand-hillers, and crackers were "instantly recognizable" by their sickly and sallow complexions and that their children looked old before reaching the age of ten or twelve, their countenances stupid, heavy, and "loathsome to the sight." As degraded and ignorant as slaves, she explained, poor whites had been driven to barren and sandy districts by the avarice of rich and powerful planters who monopolized the best soil. Most had no ambition and were reluctant to learn useful trades because of their antipathy to working alongside slaves in the shops, preferring instead a life of marginal farming supplemented by hunting and fishing. A rare young man with ambition might become an overseer, an occupation deemed quite honorable among the white poor, but slavery had rendered labor so disreputable that few sought gainful employment. By raising a little corn, garden truck, and cotton, poor-white families managed to meet their humble needs by exchanging small surpluses for luxuries like coffee, tea, and sugar, although seldom using anything not produced within their households. All too often, such families subsisted on black coffee, bacon, and corn bread. A woman Burke visited in the interior kept her small log house very neat, but "there was nothing belonging to it which the term comfortable could be applied." When the woman displayed a roll of cloth she had just completed after hours of hard work that began many days before with cleaning the seed from the cotton, Burke asked whether buying cloth would not have been cheaper. The woman replied that it would be "if her time was worth anything, but there was no labor she could perform that would bring her any money."[41]

From Burke's point of view there was nothing romantic or ennobling about this poor family's existence. The idea that yeoman households treasured a life of sturdy republican independence outside the pressures of the commercial market would have seemed absurd given her social values and obvious disinclination toward romanticism. No one in his right mind would freely choose to live in such primitive squalor, much less subject his family to such deprivation. Burke thought that the only hope for the future rested in the education of the young, which she deemed nearly impossible because of "the present feeling between the rich and the poor." Burke explained that when she gave two little girls from poor families free tuition while teaching in North Georgia, children from wealthy families made fun of their coarse, homespun dresses. She also recalled watching a planter's domestic servants "collect together in an adjoining room or on the piazza and indulge in a fit of laughter" over a poor-white woman's simple attire, leaving it to her readers to draw the implicit conclusion that the children and slaves simply had been expressing the attitudes of the master and mistress of the household. The tone of Burke's narrative also suggests her own heightened self-consciousness as an "other" from New England in a region that granted female teachers limited access to respectable social circles, yet simultaneously denied them genuine professional respect and recognition.[42]

Frederick Law Olmsted, the noteworthy landscape architect and seasoned traveler who first published his observations in the New York *Daily Times* under the pseudonym "Yeoman," was like Burke a thoughtful observer of Georgia's white common folk, although he also tended to stress the degeneracy and poverty of the yeomanry to promote his thesis that slavery had stunted the region's social development. Riding out of Savannah on a brisk winter morning in 1853, Olmsted met many vehicles on the road, including slave-driven wagons pulled by long teams of mules that were loaded with rice or cotton, a coach drawn by six horses, and a stylish carriage with "fashionably-clad gentlemen and ladies" attended by "primly-liveried negro-servants." Olmsted went on to explain that most of the traffic that he met that day consisted of small, one-horse carts steered by poor-white men and women, a contrast he drew to illustrate the negative impact of the slaveholding elite's life of luxury on the fortunes of free labor.[43]

Excluding their northern-made wheels, the one-horse carts looked to Olmsted as if they had been fashioned with simple tools such as axes and jack-knives. Made with little iron, the carts were "held together by wooden pins, and lashings of hide," with the driver characteristically perched on a "high peaked riding saddle." The carts mostly carried an assorted cargo of maize, sweet potatoes, poultry, wild game, hides, and forage for the horse, although some transported a bale of cotton as well. Intended as an indictment of the South's retarded industrial development, Olmsted's picturesque description also emphasized regional variations among the nation's small farmers. Revealing his own free labor assumptions, Olmsted described yeoman farmers in the North and the South as belonging to distinctive social classes because they lived in divergent social systems. Though many yeoman farmers in both regions still lived largely beyond the reach of the commercial agricultural market, a growing number of small farmers in the North had already abandoned their traditional Jeffersonian self-sufficiency and were successfully producing foodstuffs for expanding urban markets. An enterprising yeoman farmer in Georgia, on the other hand, would be more likely to concentrate his energies on acquiring the slaves associated with social mobility in a plantation economy. In light of the high market price that slaves commanded when Olmsted visited Georgia, the comparison was telling and delivered a powerful ideological message. Whereas the North's expanding domestic market provided substantial material rewards and illustrated the superiority of free labor in a progressive capitalist society, slavery restricted the southern yeomanry's prospects for social mobility by enabling wealthy planters to monopolize commercial production. Most small farmers in the South simply traded their tiny surpluses for useful goods that could not be produced within their own households. To further make his case, Olmsted also outlined the impact of seasonal irregularity on the variety, volume, and price of supplies, attributing the lack of development in Georgia towns to "the want of regular market-men."[44]

Olmsted also noted rigid class distinctions in town markets, describing the distance between the country folk and "the better class of planters and towns-people" as hardly different from that between the "wild Irish" and the English gentry. His various descriptions of poor Georgians as being coarse in "appetite and temper," riddled with "perverted, eccentric and intemperate spiritual impulses," ignorant of "the value of their own labor," and "almost imbecile for personal elevation" reflected the ideological assumptions of the North's evangelical culture and market society. Such statements may also be an indication that the rhetorical excesses of planter nabobs were finally coming home to roost; it was not much of a leap for northern readers to reach the conclusion that all Georgians were degenerate barbarians.[45]

Like Bremer, Olmsted did not consider poor Georgians beyond redemption when he visited the state in the early 1850s. A white woman he saw smoking a pipe and wearing a man's hat while returning home from market in a cart pulled by a small, black bull may well have been coarse, but his description of her also communicates a measure of respect for her resourcefulness. Moreover, Olmsted's republican sympathies are evident in his statement that while the "men with the carts were generally slight, with high cheekbones and sunken eyes" and "less than the usual stature of the Anglo-Saxon race," upon meeting him on the road they usually bowed "in a bold, but not uncourteous manner—showing themselves to be, at least, in one respect, better off than the majority of European peasants, whose educated servility of character rarely fails to manifest itself, when they meet a well-dressed stranger." White Georgians may have been crackers, but they were nevertheless Americans. Thus while Olmsted attributed the South's lack of development to slavery, he nonetheless took pride in the shared public rituals of republicanism that he observed even while traveling through rice country at the height of its aristocratic splendor.[46]

James Silk Buckingham, on the other hand, expected commoners to bend the knee to their social betters and described Georgians as sorely lacking in proper manners, especially in the yeoman districts of North Georgia. In light of his observations about public accommodations, it is not surprising that he described the "rudeness of manners among these dwellers in the woods" as unpleasant to "those accustomed to receive courtesy and respect from their attendants." Nor was he pleased when he learned that guests at an inn near Tallulah Falls shared the same table with servants and the driver, an egalitarian spirit reflected in the contempt that his host family expressed for low-country people and town dwellers alike.[47]

Moving south toward Toccoa Falls the next day, Buckingham and his family stopped at a large farm house and inn where he finally found the accommodations more to his liking. The next morning after breakfast he ventured outside to discuss crops with the farmers. Because the mountain climate was not suited for cotton, local farmers grew oats and maize and had planted a large wheat crop in response to its high market value the previous year. The resulting overproduction, however, had caused the value of wheat to plummet from two dollars to fifty cents a bushel. When an old farmer told Buckingham that he planned to emigrate to the Mississippi valley, the astonished Englishman asked what could induce him to embark upon such an adventure at his age. The disgruntled old man replied that "there was too much aristocracy here for him!" He defined the aristocracy as rich men who bought up land at extravagant prices running as high as ten dollars an acre, leaving none for poorer citizens. Moreover, the rent was high, "amounting to ten barrels of corn for a small farm of twenty acres." The primary source of the inflation in local land values was the attraction the area held for the wealthy because of the reputed therapeutic value of mountain springs. The affluent also flocked to the mountains during the summer season to escape the oppressive heat in the plantation districts. When Charles Lanman visited the area in 1848, he described Clarksville as a beautiful little village with two hotels and a mineral spring resort that served forty or fifty Georgia and South Carolina families every summer.[48]

At first glance it is difficult to account for the apparent anomaly of mountain farmers exhibiting market behavior in a region considered premodern by many historians. The development of a commercial economy in the mountain districts during the antebellum era, however, was typically restricted to specific locales and limited primarily to the tourist trade and the production of food crops in high demand in plantation districts. Buckingham's small vignette does little to resolve the historical debate regarding the social transformation of the Georgia upcountry, but it does suggest that even limited commercial development met with yeoman resistance in the late 1830s, a pattern that remained consistent throughout most of the remainder of the nineteenth century. Lured by the prospect of material reward, local farmers increased their wheat crop but suffered the consequences when the market turned downward, an experience that undoubtedly soured the outlook of many toward commercial production. Assuming that the farmer's attitude was not atypical, the local yeomanry realized that the expansion of market relations posed problems for small producers who believed land ownership was the foundation of republican independence. Even tenancy, a traditional means of acquiring freehold title to land in yeoman districts, showed signs as early as 1839 of becoming a dead end, a phenomenon that ultimately would spark farmer revolt in the closing decades of the century.[49]

In spite of the occasional insight one finds in the writings of such travelers as Bremer, Olmsted, and Buckingham, the limited and often distorted treatment of the white common people does little to remove the gaps in our knowledge of their lives beyond revealing the disdain shared by the better sort for their social inferiors. The primary focus of traveler descriptions of the rural poor was more ideological than objective. Such narratives helped to affix a negative stereotype to the southern white common folk that sometimes crossed the line between fact and fiction. The following description by Carlton H. Rogers of a "cracker" fresh from the pine barrens that he encountered on a train between La Grange and Atlanta in 1856 was inspired more by Longstreet's *Georgia Scenes* than actual observation: "In person he was tall, lean, and lantern-jawed, having what might be termed 'a vegetable countenance,' with *carroty* hair, *radish* cheeks, and a *turn-up* nose." Once Rogers applied the final touches of a huge chew of tobacco and a vociferous expectoration delivered with "the force of the deluge," the stereotype was complete.[50]

Nothing more offended the Victorian sensibilities of European visitors than the penchant many Georgians exhibited for tobacco, a highly favored target in traveler critiques of the manners and customs of plantation society. As one might expect, Buckingham led the pack in voicing his disgust, proclaiming that tobacco made men as "dissipated, reckless, violent, impatient, and sensual" as spirits and opium. Actually, Buckingham considered tobacco a habit that illustrated the vulgarity of Americans regardless of their sectional origins. He recommended that women refuse their lips to men who chewed because Americans would otherwise remain uncivilized. Tobacco "should be left to the savage tribes, with the tomahawk and the scalping-knife, the warwhoop and the rum-bottle, but be banished for ever from a people claiming to be polished and refined." Ironically, he observed, Indians never chewed tobacco and preferred instead to smoke the noxious weed. Only the most vile and vulgar classes in Europe chewed tobacco, the natural ally of beer and gin—an association that made it clear to polite readers where Buckingham placed Americans on the international social register.[51]

In Georgia, moreover, it was not only the common folk who liked a good chew. Shortly after his arrival in Athens in late June 1839, Buckingham attended a meeting of a debating society that conducted its meetings in a spacious room over the post office. Buckingham described those in attendance as mature adults and noted that most had military titles. Unfortunately, the newly planed pine floor was "spotted over like a leopard's skin" because there were no spittoons in the room. The combination of the heat, disagreeable odors, and the frequent pauses that speakers took to spit or rinse made it difficult for Buckingham to concentrate while they debated the question, "Ought the State to have the right to educate the children of its citizens?" Nor did he find any escape from "the sound of the labial ejection" in churches, at public meetings, or at many private parties. Like the portrayals of poor whites, such comic descriptions communicated an ideological message that presumably illustrated the negative impact of slavery on the South's social customs, a critical stance that often carried over into traveler descriptions of town society and development as well.[52]

Most travelers concurred with Buckingham's low opinion of Georgia towns. Established during the colonial era and made rich by the expansion of the plantation system into the interior, Savannah and Augusta were the generally acknowledged exceptions that supported a graceful social life and built environment that many travelers found appealing. To be sure, there were notable exceptions because opinions of town life reflected the individual backgrounds and tastes of specific travelers. William Gilmore Simms, for example, favored Savannah's classical lines over his native Charleston but was not impressed with Augusta, which he described as basically just a cotton depot. Tyrone Power was "exceedingly pleased" with Savannah's quiet, sandy streets and double rows of Pride-of-India trees and liked Augusta. Karl Bernhard avoided Savannah altogether because it "contained nothing worthy of observation." George William Featherstonhaugh found little reason to pause in any southern town:

> All these southern towns are very much alike: there is always one endless street filled with small linen-drapers' shops or stores, the owners of which call themselves merchants. In some of these stores ready-made clothes are sold, in others boots and shoes; a few of them contain the wares of iron-mongers, and perhaps one or two of them are small book stores. These, with at least one hundred dram-shops and dirty taverns, are what is to be seen in one of these long streets, crowded with men all upon a level in greediness and vulgarity; in short, there is nothing to detain a traveller who is in search of anything that is rare and interesting, but everything conspires to make him anxious to take to the roads again, be they ever so bad.

Still, it would be a mistake to dismiss lightly all traveler depictions of Georgia towns as the product of personal whim. Most visitors made some effort to render accurate descriptions of town landscapes, even if they laced their narratives with opinion and hearsay.[53]

Town life understandably became more primitive as travelers journeyed deeper into the frontier, although their cumulative observations provide an excellent overview of the process of town development in antebellum Georgia. When Basil and Margaret Hall arrived in Macon in late March 1828, some of the streets still had stumps and even trees in them, and many buildings were so recent that the wood smelled of the saw-mill. Newly painted signs marked the streets and various business establishments, where merchandise stood stacked in front as it might have been unloaded, while the bars in the numerous grocery stores were aglitter with new bottles and glasses and well stocked with barrels of Hollands, whiskey, and rum. Founded in 1823 yet still to appear on the maps, Macon was bustling with activity and seemed to be thriving, although many residents were troubled that its anticipated prosperity at the head of navigation on the Ocmulgee River had yet to materialize. Margaret Hall predicted Macon's prospects would begin to fade in a year or two because every town she had visited south of Philadelphia was in decay. In her opinion, the "slave system" was a curse to town development, although it was the flourishing cotton plantations that James Stuart observed in the surrounding countryside two years later that eventually made Macon prosperous. Two decades later, Frederika Bremer reveled in the beauty she saw there.[54]

Many travelers realized that both the prosperity and decay they saw in Georgia towns was rooted in plantation slavery, or that King Cotton was a creator and a destroyer. The same plantation economy that flooded Augusta's streets in winter with wagons from the country, loaded down its wharves, occasionally darkened its skies with dense black smoke from the steamboats, and supported a polite society that was informed, affable, literary, and hospitable, also contributed to the high level of violence, racial abuse, and fear of covert retaliation by disgruntled slaves in Georgia towns. In truth, there were relatively few cases of open revolt in the Old South, but rumors of slave insurrection were capable of bringing fear to a rapid boil in rural and urban communities alike.[55]

Actually, in a region where wood was a primary building material and open defiance resulted in brutal reprisals, white fears of slave arson were perhaps to be expected. The use of fire to vent dissatisfaction with landlords was a longstanding tradition among the rural poor in Europe, although the practice was typically associated with slaves in the southern United States. Several traveler accounts convey the impression that slaves suffered much abuse at the hands of hotel operators. Margaret Hall personally disliked the slave servants that she encountered in Georgia hotels, describing them as indolent, "nasty, black creatures," but she also condemned the brutality she witnessed. True to her aristocratic class assumptions, she attributed such abuse to the "comparatively small" number of gentlemen and ladies among a large lower-class population with "no feeling whatever for the unhappy wretches."[56]

One wonders how many acts of revenge by white incendiaries, accidents, or acts of nature were blamed on innocent blacks. Consider, for example, James Stuart's account of the great Augusta fire of 1829, which was still under investigation when he arrived nearly a year later. Another visitor reported later that 930 houses had burned in three hours. The initial arson investigation had resulted in the execution, dissection, and public exposure of a slave woman who died denying the crime. A pregnant slave woman was scheduled for execution in June when Stuart arrived in the city in March 1830, although she too professed her innocence. Stuart feared that both executions were on "very insufficient evidence."[57]

Fire stories undoubtedly made for entertaining reading, none more so than James Silk Buckingham's harrowing tale of his family's narrow escape when the Planter's Hotel in Augusta burned to the ground in June 1839. Owned by Judge Hale and favored by knowledgeable travelers as the last bastion of civilized hotel life before the frontier, the Planter's Hotel was one of Augusta's oldest and largest hotels, with four stories and 104 bedrooms. The wooden building was leveled within an hour of the sounding of the first alarm. Fortunately, Buckingham wrote, it was an isolated building because two fire engines arrived too late; one's hose would not reach the river, while the other was in poor mechanical condition. Only the heroism of Buckingham's man-servant, James Wright, prevented a total loss. Wright saved all of their trunks he could reach with ropes made from bed sheets, then jumped to safety onto mattresses twenty feet below. The investigation that followed pointed to Judge Hale's slaves. According to Buckingham's account, Hale was widely known as a kind and humane master, but resided elsewhere and had not been at the hotel recently because of illness. Hale's manager and assistants were also said to be very hard on slaves and excessive with the lash. Arson was a common form of slave revenge, "for by this means they often succeed in breaking up an establishment in such a manner as to lead to a sale of their own persons; and then they have a chance of release from existing tyranny, by being transferred to a new master, with a hope at least of better treatment." Readers were left to draw their own conclusions about the security of town life in Georgia.[58]

Assuming for the moment a hypothetical antebellum readership with an ongoing interest in such intellectual fare, one can reconstruct a fascinating linear account of the development of Columbus. Because of its relatively late emergence on the border of the Alabama territory, the city's birth and development were well documented by westward travelers. When Captain Basil Hall reached the Chattahoochee River at the end of March 1828, he took time out with his family to explore the future site of Columbus. As he later recalled, "We arrived, fortunately, just in the nick of time to see the curious phenomenon of an embryo town—a city as yet without a name, or any existence in law or fact, but crowded with inhabitants, ready to commence their municipal duties at the tap of an auctioneer's hammer." As Margaret Hall explained in a letter to her sister, "Basil says he has seen a town without inhabitants, but that he never saw inhabitants without a town." The Halls had arrived before lots could legally go on sale but already more than nine hundred people were present. Many of the houses were already built on wagonlike carriages in anticipation of securing title to specific lots. Enterprising carpenters had assembled piles of sawed lumber at strategic intervals, ready to build on speculation. Not only were carpenters and blacksmiths in great demand, grocery stores and bakeries were plentiful and a few attorneys had put out their shingles. Before departing for Alabama, Hall sketched the center of the unborn town with his camera lucida, an early type of opaque projector that relied on natural light and a series of lenses to cast an image onto a drawing surface where it could be traced with a pencil.[59]

Columbus's location at the fall-line rapids up the Chattahoochee River from the Gulf of Mexico contributed greatly to its rapid emergence as a magnet for the bumper cotton crops of Southwest Georgia and Alabama, making it an ideal location for mill development as well. In the words of one visitor in the spring of 1830, "Columbus is an extraordinary instance of the surprising celerity with which a town in a favourable situation, becomes a considerable place in this country." Laid off by commissioners in July 1828, within two years Columbus had a population of fifteen hundred, three churches, a post office, several brick buildings, and about 130 wood frame buildings, most painted and all on a regular plan. The hotel accommodations that later gave Buckingham nightmares were described by James Stuart as being quite nice.[60]

Still, Columbus remained an unsettled frontier town when Tyrone Power arrived four years later, largely because of the proximity of "Sodom" just across the river in Alabama territory. Outlaws, gamblers, and desperadoes, "all armed to the teeth," frequently rode into town for an evening's frolic before returning to their fallen women across the Chattahoochee, where "the sound of revelry proclaimed the orgies resumed." When the Irish actor took an afternoon walk in the rain, he saw parties of Creek and Choctaw roaming around drunk, each with a well-dressed slave to lord over his masters. He also strolled past well-supplied stores, warehouses filled with cotton, and planters busy selling their produce and making purchases for their families, as well as several mansions along the river and evidence of more under construction. Power concluded by saying that nowhere in the South had he visited a more promising place, yet one "more wanting in all that men usually consider most worth possessing," including "personal security, reasonable comfort, and well-executed law." He also reported that "affrays ending in blood are said to be frequent, apprehensions few, acquittal next to certain even in the event of a trial, and the execution of a white man a thing unknown."[61]

Curiously, in a region where druggists sold "Arkansas toothpicks," ardent spirits, and deadly poisons like hemlock and arsenic alongside sweetmeats and fruits, travelers seldom expressed fear of being robbed on the road. As we have seen, they had quite enough to worry about between the bad roads and the unpredictable weather. Small wonder that when Charles Lyell and his wife left Macon for Columbus by stagecoach in January 1846, for the first time their friends wished them a "*safe* journey, instead of a pleasant one." The Lyells arrived in Columbus a week after the final detachment of more than five hundred Indians had departed for Arkansas. The town had grown rapidly, but the geologist Lyell made note of the deep ravines and muddy rivers in the nearby countryside, evidence of the erosive impact of plantation development on Southwest Georgia's fragile landscape. Lyell also described the town's new cotton mills and the subsequent appearance of an anti-free trade party in Columbus, an indication of conflict between industrialists and planters who advocated unrestricted foreign commerce. Although they remained quiet in the presence of the planters, Lyell reported that northern-born residents complained freely to strangers about the difficulty of raising capital locally for mill development because the purchase of slaves was considered a better investment.[62]

The city's industrial expansion continued throughout the 1850s. After Frederick Law Olmsted spent several days in Columbus in 1853, he described it as the largest manufacturing town in the South other than Richmond, Virginia. Olmsted reported that power from the falls, if properly harnessed, could drive two hundred thousand spindles and a proportionate number of looms. Yet only between fifteen and twenty thousand spindles were running, operated mostly by "Cracker girls" from the country. In addition to the cotton factories, Columbus had a woolen mill, a paper mill, a foundry, a cotton gin factory, and a machine shop, among other industries, that all employed a large percentage of white laborers near destitution. Olmsted also reported that any work stoppage brought great hardship. Echoing Buckingham's earlier observations, Olmsted witnessed more gambling, intoxication, and cruel treatment of servants in Columbus than any other place he visited in the South. Unlike those of Macon and Montgomery, Alabama, which he liked, the hotel accommodations were so horrible that Olmsted advised invalids not to stop in Columbus. While it may simply be coincidence that Olmsted juxtaposed such a warning in his narrative with his description of the city's industrial capacity, the fact that he did nonetheless speaks strongly of the ideological construction of the South's urban and industrial development in the traveler accounts.[63]

For all the signs of industrial development that travelers observed in

Georgia, especially in towns located along the fall line, many leading planters and politicians felt uncomfortable enough with the factory system that an anti-industrial stance became a bulwark in the proslavery ideology. The use of slave labor in factories was clearly profitable, but many planters bristled at the tariff policies advocated by industrialists. As sectional conflict accelerated in the 1830s, the planter class increasingly came to see the factory system as a threat to its way of life. In the words of Robert S. Starobin, even leading southerners who accepted industrial growth "believed that industries had to be directed by slaveholding planters, not new slaveless entrepreneurs, so that the existing class relationships would remain unchanged." Ironically, the British antislavery activist Buckingham voiced an opinion that most large planters would have likely accepted as valid when he wrote that "the Factory system" was "detrimental to health, morals, and social happiness" under "the most favourable circumstances," much less "in its infant state" as in Georgia. Indeed, he concluded, "I do not wonder that the most humane members of the community deplore the introduction of factories in the South, and wish that the labours of the people should be confined to agriculture, leaving manufactures to Europe or to the States of the North."[64]

During his stay in Athens, Buckingham also observed that the country people voiced strong prejudices against townspeople. Believing themselves "the only people who rise early and work hard," planters and farmers were often contemptuous of townspeople and considered them "a class of mere idlers." Buckingham explained to his readers that the tension between town and country was reflected in the taxation policies of state and local government. Athens merchants complained that landowner legislators had contrived to shift the burden of taxation off landed property and slaves onto the towns. One historian has argued that the small town rather than the plantation was the center of the southern community and provided "a social anchor in a world that seemed always to be adrift." Emphasizing the central economic role of towns is logical if one defines the South as a bourgeois society. Yet in the absence of a mature market society and a capitalist city-system, such as existed in Europe and the North, Georgia towns primarily played an intermediary role in a plantation economy where real political and economic power was rooted in the countryside. As long as plantation slavery determined the rhythms of Georgia's economy, industrial development was confined largely to those areas that complemented the needs of large producers of staple crops. The industrial growth described by travelers was impressive but relatively miniscule in comparison with the industrial expansion underway in the North during the same period. Structured to meet the needs of local and regional markets dominated by large plantations, the industrial production of fall-line towns like Columbus did little to alleviate the state's dependence on outside marketing and credit facilities and manufactured goods. In the final analysis, the anchors of social stability in antebellum Georgia were its plantations and small farms. Their cultural attractions aside, interior towns are perhaps best understood as whistle stops where staple crops were prepared for export and imported foodstuffs and manufactured goods were warehoused for distribution. The value of Buckingham's observation is that it hints at the bonds of material and ideological interest that allied the white yeomanry with the planter elite that dominated state politics.[65]

Planters lent support to industrial development when it served their fundamental needs, such as the manufacture of inexpensive slave clothing, cotton gins, and basic farm tools, or railroad construction to reduce the cost of marketing their crops. Nor were they ignorant of the income potential of railroad stock. But whereas industrial capitalists in the North tended to invest their profits in qualitative improvements, such as new plants and equipment, southern planters redirected the bulk of their profits into slaves and land, a perfectly rational market choice that also reflected the ideological assumptions that governed their region. There is still much wisdom in Eugene Genovese's frequently quoted statement that "the South had a market economy; it did not have an essentially market society." Georgia's leading planter families all produced staple crops for the world capitalist system; although there were significant exceptions, most also remained premodern in their ideological commitment to paternalism, patriarchal values, and static class relationships based on aristocratic deference rather than democratic egalitarianism, an outlook that diverged significantly from the dominant free labor ideology of the North. Ironically, a primary purpose of the proslavery argument was to prevent the development of a market society in the South while preserving the planter elite's favored position in the international market economy. Until African Americans were free to sell their labor and the production of white yeoman households was redirected toward the commercial economy, a market society could not develop in the region. It would be well into the twentieth century before a genuine industrial revolution would finally come to Georgia.[66]

Long before the extreme ideological polarization of the 1850s, travelers were conscious of their participation in one of the great debates of modern history. Virtually all of the antebellum travelers gave some consideration to the importance of slavery in Georgia, and most placed the peculiar institution at the center of their narratives. Nevertheless, it is important to emphasize that slaveholders were not passive agents in the process. Well aware in a culture of honor of the importance of their public reputations, many leading slaveholders, particularly along the rice coast, worked diligently to shape the perceptions of their guests. Visitors such as Basil and Margaret Hall, Sir Charles Lyell, Frederika Bremer, and Amelia Matilda Murray, among numerous others, were all well received at Hopeton, the model rice plantation of James Hamilton Couper, where they were often "disarmed" by their host's gracious hospitality. Apparently, Couper enjoyed showcasing his paternalism and managerial expertise, possibly seeing himself as the South's first line of defense in an increasingly hostile world. As evidenced by a survey of the traveler accounts, Couper succeeded in tempering the antislavery attitudes of many visitors and even converted a few to the proslavery line. Even Fanny Kemble, who hated slavery, was impressed by his knowledge and the "extraordinary power" of his character. Perhaps Basil Hall said it best when he wrote, "Instead of seeing my way better as I went on, I found my ideas on the intricate and formidable subject of slavery, becoming rather less clear than I fancied they had been."[67]

Proslavery apologists argued that generations of experience with the "peculiar institution" had given southerners unique insight into African "nature," an assumption that several travelers parroted. Hall reported that newcomers from the North and England were much less patient in their dealings with slaves, an assertion Lyell reported hearing during his stay on the rice coast as well. Full of activity and eager to make a quick fortune in an unhealthy climate, northern slaveholders seldom made "allowance for the repugnance to continuous labor of the negro race, or the diminished motive for exertion of the slave." Both men also reported that the condition of slaves improved away from the coast, and not simply because of the healthier climate. Hall wrote of seeing whites and blacks working in the same field and seated in the same room. In Lyell's words, the "future progress" of coastal slaves was limited by less "familiar intercourse" with "individuals of a more advanced race" than enjoyed by slaves in the interior. In addition, Lyell asserted that Couper's slaves had it well compared with much of the peasantry of Europe, a standard proslavery argument that Hall rejected as pretentious. Another observer, however, saw nothing to applaud in the miserable life of slaves on rice plantations, an existence he contrasted unfavorably with that of criminals in state prisons.[68]

A military man who appreciated Couper's discipline, Hall informed his readers that he disliked slavery but insisted that slaveholders as a class deserved indulgence. In his global travels, he had seen greater scenes of revolting tyranny on war ships, in some army regiments, and in many homes and schools. Most planters, he explained, had inherited their way of life and were simply answering the call of duty to their families. Hall considered many of the planters he met good men who believed in using minimal force and acknowledged slavery's tyrannical effect on the character of their children. He also asserted that the end of the international slave trade and subsequent reliance on domestic reproduction of the slave population had resulted in better treatment. Yet however willing to admit that slavery was evil, few planters were ready to predict its demise in 1828. As a meliorist, Hall had little use for extremists in the debate over abolition, describing the issue as "one of the most profitless of all possible subjects of discussion." Because planters were practical "men of business," Hall stated that a more fruitful approach to reform would be to prove that better treatment resulted in less conflict, an elevation of slave character, and higher profits. Liberalization of slave treatment was hardly a step on the road to emancipation, although Hall's meliorist observations do convey well the intellectual climate just prior to the Nat Turner insurrection in 1831. As southern planters achieved greater class consciousness in the 1830s, they rapidly closed ideological ranks and abandoned the apologetics recorded by Hall. Slavery's defenders increasingly began to argue instead that rather than a necessary evil, it was the foundation of all superior civilizations. Meliorism is predicated on the belief that the world tends to get better and that man can aid in its betterment. The shift toward improving the material conditions of enslavement that Hall observed in the late 1820s undoubtedly encouraged the stabilization of slave families on southern plantations, which ironically made the institution more durable. In retrospect, amelioration posed little threat to plantation slavery beyond convincing abolitionist leaders of the futility of reform.[69]

As defined by the prevailing ethos of the planter class, an ideal estate was both patriarchal and paternal in its relations among a master, his family, and their slaves, a situation Lyell compared to "an hereditary regard" reminiscent of feudal Europe. Even Olmsted, who was hardly a friend to the plantation system, anticipated seeing slavery in its finest garb at the Bryan

County plantation of Richard James Arnold, who lived much of the year in New England but defined himself as a staunch paternalist. Some visitors, however, saw nothing that remotely resembled familial relations between masters and slaves on rice plantations. One of the first things that caught the eye of the Reverend George Lewis, a Presbyterian minister from Scotland who came to Georgia on church business in 1844, was a young man with an iron collar and bell fastened around his neck laboring in a field beside wretched-looking slaves who "moved, looked, and laboured, more like convicts than honest men."[70]

Ideological defenders of plantation life pointed to slave housing and care as further proof of the superiority of slavery to free labor. Guests sometimes accompanied their hosts on their daily rounds and dutifully recorded their impressions of plantation buildings and operations. The quality of slave housing varied greatly in Georgia, reflecting the wealth of individual planters, their personal regard for their "people," the desire to nurture an expensive investment, and the newness of the area. One of the more substantial slave settlements was described by Olmsted, a landscape architect whose eye for detail later found full expression in San Francisco's Golden Gate Park and New York's Central Park. Instead of the log cabins that Olmsted described as the norm, Richard James Arnold's largest slave quarter consisted of 42′ by 21′ frame buildings with shingled roofs. Bordering a wide street, the houses were subdivided into three rooms and a loft, and equipped with a brick fireplace, locked closets, rude furniture, locked outer doors, and shuttered windows. Each unit had a chicken coop and a half-acre garden plot. Olmsted thought the dirty and disordered interiors "a pleasant indication" of domestic lives with minimal interference, a lack of tidiness that profoundly disturbed Fanny Kemble during her stay on Butler Island. Most travelers described slave diet as simple and wholesome. Basil Hall also noticed that slaves preferred white cloth that they could dye purple "to suit their own fancy," an aside that illustrated how shared aesthetic values can survive and mitigate oppressive conditions. Identifying more with the social position of the planter class, even antislavery travelers tended to focus on the ways that slaveholders shaped the world in which the slaves lived, rather than the ways that slaves modified their circumstances to forge a separate cultural identity.[71]

Although they warned that power and passion often overruled the dictates of reason, travelers were in general agreement that providing adequate housing, diet, clothing, and health care was in a planter's self-interest.

When Lyell was at Hopeton, there were three separate hospital wards, one each for sick men and women, and one for lying-in women granted a month's rest after their confinement, "an advantage rarely enjoyed by hard-working English peasants." Curiously, he explained, slave women preferred their own houses to Couper's hospital, a common sentiment that baffled planters who failed to perceive their desire for autonomy. The planter's world view is also evident in Lyell's statement that because of the ignorance and indolence of slave mothers, the plantation mistress frequently sat up nights caring for sick slave children. Motivated by "a feeling of kindness, and a fear of losing the services of the slave," Lyell reported that such "attentions greatly attach the negroes to their owners."[72]

Travelers, including many who spoke out against slavery, often joined their planter hosts in the racist conclusion that paternalism had emerged in response to the African's presumedly childlike nature. Others denied a natural origin for plantation race relations, seeing the master's power as the bottom line, or the cruelty underlying his benevolence. In truth, paternalism was the "fragile bridge" that both white and black members of the plantation household used to keep the contradictions of a system based on racial, class, and sexual exploitation from exploding, a way for people who shared an isolated and intimate rural space to live and work together with a minimum of conflict. Because planters depended on the reproduction and productivity of African Americans, slaves seized the initiative to turn mutual obligations, duties, and responsibilities into rights. Still, the same reciprocity that brought implicit recognition of slave humanity from planters, reinforced the chains of bondage by linking slaves as individuals to their masters. Lyell's discussion of the attachment of slaves to their owners is best understood within this context. Yet as the most benevolent of masters learned to their dismay in the immediate aftermath of the Civil War, the bonds of paternalism were much weaker than they had traditionally believed.[73]

Reflecting shared Victorian assumptions, many travelers saw little of merit in slave marriages and religion, although both were powerful "weapons of defense" the slave community used to teach its members "to love and value each other, to take a critical view of their masters, and to reject the ideological rationales for their own enslavement." Planters also depended on the marriage ceremony and religion to enhance their authority among their slaves. Thus while slave marriage customs and religion offended the bourgeois mores of some travelers, others recognized both as part of the web of paternalism. Many travelers reported that planters encouraged slave marriages, although few expressed faith in slave commitment to the institution. Rules regarding marriages between slaves from different plantations varied greatly, although absentee or semi-resident planters like Arnold often disliked such unions because they created problems for overseers in their absence. Olmsted also observed that black preachers usually conducted the ceremony, while the master and mistress blessed the occasion with their presence. In the case of favorite servants, a white minister conducted the ceremony in the big house.[74]

Olmsted described slave preachers as men of vanity and self-confidence who had good memories and poetic talent, but he disliked what he labeled the crude religious practices of slaves and poor whites because they excited furious emotion. It is unclear whether he appreciated the centrality of Christianity in the paternalistic world view of planter spokesmen such as the Reverend Charles C. Jones and Bishop Stephen Elliott. The editors of Arnold's plantation journals conclude that the absence of Sunday entries suggests that "Sunday was the day set aside to worship the God who sanctioned slavery as a master-servant relationship, a day to be spent by both whites and blacks contemplating who was master and who was servant." Christmas thus played a cherished role in the proslavery ideology, just as it would in literary defenses of plantation life after emancipation. As recorded by Basil Hall, the slaves on Couper's sea island cotton plantation were granted three "holydays" at Christmas and furnished plenty of beef and whiskey, a type of "Saturnalia" in Lyell's words when no work was done and everyone celebrated.[75]

Couper's slaves were also free to sell eggs, poultry, and garden truck to buy molasses, tobacco, and other luxuries. Others sold fish and cypress canoes carved during their free time. Olmsted observed similar practices on Arnold's plantations, where the only restriction was against buying liquor, a prohibition Arnold found difficult to enforce because of grog shops that accepted stolen goods. According to Olmsted, "a swarm of Jews" had swept into southern towns in the last decade and had driven respected retailers out of business through their "unlawful trade with the simple negroes." Grog shops reduced the value of slave property, but the law against slave testimony in the courts worked against the "dominant power." Arnold's solution was to buy slave produce at high prices. With an established exchange rate of twelve for a dime, eggs were credited to slave accounts in his store, where he offered goods at wholesale prices. In Olmsted's opinion, such practices proved that slaves could be educated for freedom. Taught the value of labor in an open market, slaves should be allowed to purchase their freedom when their credits on balance equaled their fair market value.[76]

Some travelers argued that hiring out slaves amounted to practical training for freedom, although Charles Lanman reported that the brave steamboat pilot, Peter Parker, had refused his freedom many times. Parker piloted the *South Carolina* up the Chattahoochee River when Lanman was aboard in the winter of 1853–54. A strong swimmer, Parker had rescued many persons after boat accidents. According to Lanman, he split his salary of 150 dollars a month with his master. Moreover, black crewmen were accustomed to receiving "Sunday wages" beyond their regular pay. Upon their arrival at Columbus, passengers were invited to the upper deck, where the twenty crewmen were treated to a drink of whiskey by the mate and sang for the crowd. In Lanman's words, "Such facts as these need no comment from my pen, and ought to put to blush the ignorant fanatics of the North."[77]

Men like Peter Parker were exceptions that ideologues on both sides of the slavery debate used to argue their cases. To illustrate the superiority of free labor, Buckingham cited the example of Solomon Humphries of Macon, an intelligent yet illiterate former slave who became a successful merchant and purchased his family's freedom. As a rule, however, planters distrusted free blacks and disliked hiring slaves out for work off the farm. Although greater opportunities for slave autonomy existed in towns and cities, the division of labor on large plantations provided opportunities and rewards for individual initiative. Some travelers praised the skills displayed by slave mechanics and carpenters and the dignity and bearing of the slave drivers, who were in many instances de facto plantation managers.[78]

Olmsted was especially impressed with Arnold's watchman, Amos Morel. The steam machinery on Arnold's rice plantation made Morel's engineering training invaluable. At the time of Olmsted's visit, both his authority and wages were superior to those of the white overseer that Arnold employed because Georgia law required constant white supervision on plantations. As keeper of the keys, Morel was in charge of all plantation provisions, tools, materials, and produce, weighed and measured out rations, and supervised all the mechanics. His brother was the head servant in Arnold's mansion. Both men owned their own horses, dressed well, and had polished manners. Because Morel valued his position of authority on the plantation, he suited Arnold's purpose as a control over the overseer during his frequent absences. Such men were displayed with "fatherly" pride by planters to northern visitors "as proof that the slaves were well treated and could even thrive under the system."[79]

Even critical observers spoke well of the treatment of domestic servants on Georgia plantations. Buckingham wrote that their condition compared favorably with "servants in the middle ranks of life in England." In southern households, he continued, domestic slaves were adequately fed, well dressed, attentive, orderly, respectful, and easily governed, a far cry from his observations about Georgia hotels. Olmsted described Arnold's house servants as more intelligent and dutiful "than any I have seen before." Their labors were not only lighter than those of other slaves, Arnold provided his servants brick cabins with comfortable furnishings and gave more consideration to their health and happiness than free domestics received outside the South. Olmsted also claimed there was a marked preference for good-looking mulattos for "in-door occupations," explaining to his readers that whereas domestic slaves dreaded field work, field hands dreaded the big house.[80]

While they duly recorded the exceptional slave stories and passed along those portions of the proslavery argument that accorded with their individual beliefs and experiences, few travelers held illusions about the fate of the vast majority of slaves, which was a life of hard labor in the fields. Several wrote detailed accounts of cultivation practices and routines on rice and cotton plantations. True of their observations in general, their comments about the nature of field work marked the beginnings of later debates among historians. Whereas some considered the labor of slaves no more rigorous than rural work conditions elsewhere, others thought profit maximization the foremost purpose of staple crop production, even if it resulted in neglect and abuse. Visitors to coastal plantations generally agreed that the task system provided substantial benefits to industrious slaves that free laborers did not enjoy. In addition, Buckingham explained, any attempt by planters to alter established rhythms of work met with intense resistance, an indication of the ability of slaves to enforce customary work allocations.[81]

Travelers also described slaves as being adept at finding ways to resist the tyranny of overseers, especially along the coast where there were fewer resident planters. As reported by Olmsted, slaves left gates open against specific orders to the contrary, used fence rails for firewood, lamed mules, broke tools, set boats adrift, and did jobs poorly. Slavery not only resulted in misapplication of labor and excessive waste, "the proverbial stupidity and dogged prejudice of the negro," who had been "carefully poisoned with ignorance," made it exceedingly difficult for planters to introduce agricultural improvements. Yet with all the problems of plantation production, the South's wealth remained. If free labor was superior, why was the South prosperous and powerful? Olmsted's answer was that "certain circumstances" such as topography, soil, and climate, reinforced by a peculiar labor system that denied competition, had created monopoly conditions in southern staple crop production.[82]

Travelers also commented on the role that brutality played in the plantation system. Paternal kindness and occasional free time were inadequate solutions to slave resistance, despite Lyell's claim that whippings were infrequent because Negroes were a "mild and forgiving" people. Olmsted reported that some overseers abused slaves but most curried their favor to hide their own flaws. Arnold did not allow whips in the fields and drivers always administered the actual punishment. Olmsted wrote that sometimes two or three weeks passed without any punishment, but then it seemed "as if the devil had got into them all, and there is a good deal of it." The local nature of plantation authority gave the planter rather than the law the final word in the vast majority of cases, and men frequently disregarded the law for their own purposes. There was also a widespread problem along the coast with overseers who exercised uncontrolled tyranny during much of the year because of the large number of absentee planters.[83]

In light of his career in the Royal Navy, Captain Hall's comments about the lash and despotic authority are of interest. Dismissing the amusing tendency of planters to claim that conditions were worse in the next state, Hall believed that "men of sense and feeling" everywhere treated their slaves well, "not only because it is much more agreeable to be kind than cruel, but because the pecuniary advantages are always greater." Yet men often had no sense of command or control over their temper, so cruelty and injustice were inevitable, the more so in the United States where "the checks to the intemperate use of irresponsible power are merely nominal." In the South, where written laws could not be enforced and individual planter authority was uncontested, Hall argued that changes in the treatment of slaves must be gradual and in accord with the interests, prejudices, and customs of the planter class. While it was a mistake "to suppose that slaves labour sulkily, and under perpetual exercise of the lash," every planter "must be more or less a despot in spite of himself" to ensure obedience and subordination through fear in the absence of consistent motives to work. Although slaves usually performed their work with cheerfulness and could escape punishment by proper behavior, Hall wrote that it still seemed "indispensable to the working of this strange piece of moral machinery" that slaves be made "fully sensible" of the consequences of neglect or crime.[84]

Several travelers recorded discussions about the South's possible futures. Hall reported hearing speculation that Negroes would be "extirpated" as a race and that the climate would improve so whites could safely cultivate the land, or that blacks would either achieve dominance or be driven into the woods and mountains, "where they are to resume their natural habits, and live like wild beasts." Five years later, Charles Joseph Latrobe wrote that the black population would eventually "eat the white out of house and home" in a region "which appears as congenial to the habits and physical construction of the black as it is inimical to those of the white," or a mixed race would emerge "claiming an equality of rights and consideration." Frederika Bremer became convinced that colonization was the only solution. After training slaves in useful skills, which along with "the gift of Christianity" would be compensation for their suffering, the black population should be emancipated gradually and returned to convert the "heathen nations of Africa."[85]

The hopes of travelers such as Hall, Bremer, and Olmsted for peaceful amelioration of the slavery question became increasingly unrealistic. All three spoke out against slavery but tried to present both sides of the issue. In the 1850s partisans saw no reason to equivocate. A rare New Englander who took a proslavery stance was Nehemiah Adams, pastor of the Essex Street Congregational Church in Boston. Adams was an antislavery activist who came to Savannah for his health in 1854 and abandoned his abolitionist leanings. He expressed surprise at seeing slaves in good humor, concluding that everyday life in the South was a far cry from the pictures of slave auctions, separation of families, and fugitives hiding in dismal swamps so common in northern minds. "A better-looking, happier, more courteous set of people" he had never seen, making him wonder how their "unaffected politeness could have been learned under the lash."[86]

In addition, the Savannah fire department employed blacks, which Adams described as astonishing in light of the imagined "insurrectionary impulses of an oppressed people." Plus there was good order in the streets because of the 8:00 P.M. curfew, although Adams expressed his regret that white drinkers were not under similar restraint. Adams considered the strong religious instruction provided by whites impressive, and liked the way slaves dressed for the Sabbath and sang in church. There was no pauperism because every slave had "an inalienable claim in law upon his owner for support for the whole of life," which he contended illustrated that the idea of wages should be redefined to include other forms of compensation. Adams whitewashed over more offensive parts of slavery like whipping and slave sales, arguing that the abolitionists had forced the South from the road to emancipation. Under existing conditions, he concluded, abolition would result in the degradation of white women, race mixing would grow, and class and racial violence would explode. Nevertheless, talk about dissolving the Union was an "absurdity" because the Constitution and the Bible both sanctioned slavery, which Adams deemed an appropriate vehicle for bringing civilization to the African race.[87]

The British traveler Amelia Matilda Murray, who visited Savannah and Hopeton in February 1855, also voiced strong support for the South. Murray shared the opinion of the English housekeeper at the Pulaski House that blacks were childlike, devious, idle, dirty, and in need of "correction" now and then. The "Ethiopian character" of the "darkies" was of limited potential and at its best under the "good direction" of understanding whites. Negroes were a "light-hearted, merry, unreflecting race," excitable and impulsive but with a sense of justice. Good at mechanical employment, she continued, blacks also made honest, useful, and highly respectable servants if properly trained and managed, although they had probably reached their peak of social development. Unless England began to support the South against abolitionist "hot-headed zealots," the loss of islands in the West Indies was imminent. Nor was African colonization an acceptable policy because it amounted to "re-barbarizing the Christian world by giving fair fields" back to savages. In Africa, Murray wrote, black Christians would soon revert to "pagan habits." Her visit to Hopeton reinforced her opinion that blacks were incapable of self-government and would be miserable if free because God had created them "for labor under guidance."[88]

Possibly in direct response to Nehemiah Adams, the Maine physician and prohibitionist Charles Grandison Parsons wrote an abolitionist tract in 1855 entitled *Inside View of Slavery; or, A Tour among the Planters,* an account of his visit to the South in the winter of 1852–53. Significantly, Harriet Beecher Stowe wrote an introduction for his book, calling it a "simple, straight-forward narrative of an impartial witness" that was "candid and fair in its spirit." Most of his observations were based on his travels in Georgia, where Parsons had a number of relatives. Parsons challenged the happy picture of slavery in Savannah by contrasting the refinement and elegance found in the heart of the city with "the low, dingy, dirty, squalid, cheerless negro huts" in the suburbs, a painful reminder of "the fearful price paid by one class to support another." Explaining that slave life was easier in the city than elsewhere, Parsons reported that it was still no bed of roses. Slaves who worked in boarding houses and hotels like the Pulaski House, for example, were not even allowed to sleep in beds at the end of a hard day's work. Paradoxically, he continued, most slaves nevertheless said that they were content, fared well, and did not want freedom, which misled northerners who did not know they had been "educated to deceive in these matters."[89]

The gist of his argument was that slavery made the South inferior to the North in nearly every way. Unlike Olmsted, who also criticized the impact of slavery on the South's development, Parsons attacked the personal character of planters, portraying them as lazy drunkards, an opinion seconded by Carlton H. Rogers, who described "Southrons" as "constitutionally or climatically indolent" men fond of sitting in the shade, smoking, and drinking mint-juleps, while discussing the price of rice and cotton and the current value of their "niggers." His faith in the superiority of free labor also led Parsons to a rather remarkable conclusion:

> Slaveholders are beginning to see that the sons of poor white men in the South, who, by reverse of fortune, have been compelled to earn their own bread by the sweat of the face, are rising in the scale of intellect, and power, and would even now be ranked higher than their own sons, if personal merit were the only basis of honorable distinction. No honest, intelligent Southerner, who is thoroughly acquainted with the intelligence and business capacity of the different races in the South, will deny that the African is better qualified now to obtain a livelihood than the white man who rules over him, if both were left with only natural resources and the labor of their own hands to rely upon.

Parsons informed his readers that their inheritance from African mothers of a "good physical system" and a "good mental constitution" from Anglo-Saxon fathers made mulattos "the best specimens of manhood to be found in the South." Addicted to strong drink and gambling, he wrote, the slaveholding class fell easily into licentiousness and crime. The South's values were so perverted that professional gamblers were as highly regarded as doctors and lawyers.[90]

In addition, Parsons argued that the notion of superior slave treatment on large plantations was false. Not only was their diet and housing inadequate, slaves were subjected to barbaric instruments of torture, such as the thumb screw, the stocks, the bell, gags, paddles, and the notorious "Cotton planter's whip." "Nigger hunters" on the Flint River trained puppies with raw meat and blood drawn by slicing a slave boy's feet. Parsons also expressed outrage at what he had witnessed at a slave auction, especially the sale of a beautiful white "fancy girl." The "darkest feature" of slavery was that it hardened the hearts of "all who became familiar with it," slaveholders, nonslaveholders, and slaves alike. Among his graphic examples, Parsons included the story of a slave woman who had killed all thirteen of her children in infancy rather than have them grow up in slavery under an abusive master.[91]

"One of the strangest sights to a New England man" in the South was the widespread desecration of the Sabbath, which Parsons explained was a day many whites devoted to drinking and gambling. He dismissed the idea that slaves enjoyed a day of rest on Sunday because they were not given adequate time during the week to tend to such necessities as washing, sewing, cutting wood, and gardening. Even more shocking, the last Sunday before the statewide election in Georgia was known as "free liquor day," a political custom Parsons thought odd in a Christian land. Free liquor day, he informed his readers, was a time set aside by candidates for public office to invite their supporters to their headquarters "to partake of spirituous liquors" at their expense. Given such a loose moral environment, Parsons did not find it odd that church attendance was infrequent in plantation districts and in most Georgia cities. Only in Augusta did Parsons feel at home on the Sabbath. Slavery had corrupted the churches in the South, he wrote, and was "inherently in direct antagonism to Christianity."[92]

Only in the area of "prejudice of color" did the South fare better than the North, which Parsons concluded was the greatest obstacle still to be overcome by the antislavery cause in the free states. Because southern whites were accustomed to intimate if unequal associations with blacks, he believed that "if the slaves could be set at liberty to-day, there would be nothing of this kind to exclude them from genteel society." Although God had endowed each race with unique talents, he continued, the rights of man remained the same. That he was trying to pick a fight with easily angered men who considered themselves humane Christians is clear. And while his notion that the South was free of "prejudice of color" was absurd, his frank admission of the pervasive racism in the North is a reminder that an *Inside View of Slavery* was an ideologically charged polemic directed at northern audiences to further the abolitionist cause. Parsons thought that the popular belief that slavery was not the North's problem was helping to keep a great evil alive. His jeremiad called for the South to purge itself of the sin of slavery or gird up its loins for battle. The time for genteel travel was drawing rapidly to an end; the next generation of visitors to Georgia would be clad in blue and gray.[93]

The traveler accounts of antebellum Georgia were part of a larger pattern of critical exploration of southern society and culture. As early as the 1820s, rural Georgians found themselves at the center of a national and international debate over the place of plantation slavery in the world capitalist system. The literary historian Fred Hobson argues that "the southern rage to explain" dates to the emergence of a distinctive regional self-consciousness in the 1840s and 1850s. Under assault from without and "an indictment of every aspect of their civilization," literate Southerners first turned inward "to justify their past and their tradition." Although the precise moment of the ideological awakening of the antebellum South remains subject to debate, the traveler accounts reveal that the development of a distinctive regional identity encompassed a parallel rise in the class consciousness of the planter elite in Georgia. Stung by the criticisms leveled against their region, leading slaveholders worked assiduously to influence the portrayal of their way of life in traveler accounts. As evidenced by the pervasiveness of elements of the proslavery argument in the antebellum traveler accounts, Georgia planters succeeded to a remarkable degree in subverting the genre to their own purposes. The equally pervasive presence of abolitionist sentiments in the traveler accounts also revealed the inherent shortcomings of relying on transient observers to construct a literary defense of slavery. Driven by a compelling urge to "tell about the South," Georgia writers turned to poetry, novels, and especially backwoods humor sketches to fashion an indigenous ideological defense of plantation society.[94]

CHAPTER TWO

Tending the Rich Crop

The Georgia Humorists and the Literary Defense of Plantation Society

One of the most significant meanings communicated by the antebellum traveler accounts is literature's ability to create and subsequently redefine a new country. As we have seen, leading Georgians recognized the political importance of the "literature of place," especially the dangers inherent in allowing outsiders to shape popular perceptions of their region. Attempting to shape the ideological content of such narratives from behind the scenes was one way to attack the problem, but it hardly substituted for a strong indigenous literary defense. Accordingly, the defenders of plantation society began to seek their own voice in the 1830s by experimenting with a wide variety of literary genres, including novels, short stories, and poetry. In particular, Georgia writers displayed a talent for adapting the genre of humor writing to their own purposes.[1]

The ongoing effort to redefine the South's place in the nation resulted in a heightened ideological consciousness among writers who defined themselves in relation to a specific ordering of land and labor. The effort to reassert control over their own space in the social and political order from those who would redefine it in the eyes of the world by challenging the legitimacy of slavery culminated in a gradual movement toward consensus relative to the language of identity. Like their peers throughout the region, Georgia writers realized the significance of nomenclature. If outsiders succeeded in "renaming" the South within the world capitalist order, the subsequent debate would always be reactive rather than proactive, or reactionary in a political culture that took pride in its revolutionary antecedents. In response, the literary defense of plantation society that began to take shape in the 1830s had to define slavery and the southern way of life as moral or risk losing everything. The efforts of outsiders to affix a label of inferiority on the region also rubbed against the grain of many yeoman farmers who jealously guarded their autonomy and republican independence, which also played directly into the hands of the slaveholding elite by enabling them to present themselves as the defenders of the entire white community. In the words of historian Peter Kolchin, "The identification of slavery as central to the preservation of Southern 'liberty' marked the intellectual as well as political hegemony of slave owners throughout the antebellum South."[2]

The first fictional treatment of life in frontier Georgia to receive national recognition appeared in 1834 with the publication of *Guy Rivers: A Tale of Old Georgia,* the border romance that launched the literary career of William Gilmore Simms. Widely acknowledged for his keen eye for geographical and historical detail, Simms set his story in the North Georgia mountains to take advantage of popular interest in the discovery there of gold, which had sparked the first major gold rush in American history. Simms called *Guy Rivers* "a tale of Georgia—a tale of the miners—of a frontier and wild people." Widely regarded as a haven for embezzlers, runaway slaves, horse thieves, and cattle rustlers, the region around Auraria had acquired a well-deserved reputation for lawlessness. Moreover, Guy Rivers and his band of outlaws had a contemporary parallel in real life. The Sandtown community in modern Fulton County is on the eastern side of the Chattahoochee River and derives its name from the Sandtown Indians, who migrated there from the Alabama territory following the Creek War of 1813–14. According to John H. Goff, the premier student of Georgia placenames, Sandtown was a crossing point on the river for trails leading to gold diggings in the region, as well as a hangout for a band of marauders called the "Pony Club" or the "Pony Boys."[3]

As Simms admitted some twenty years later in the preface to a revised edition, *Guy Rivers* is not one of his stronger efforts. The novel not only reveals his youth and technical inexperience, it bears the mark of a hurried traveler. In *Auraria: The Story of a Georgia Gold-Mining Town,* the historian E. Merton Coulter correctly associated the historic town with the fictional village of Chestatee. Challenging the veracity of the setting of *Guy Rivers,* Coulter stated that Simms had never visited the gold region and had concocted his tale from information gathered from Charleston and Georgia newspapers and copies of the Auraria *Western Herald* that "he doubtless was seeing" in Carolina. This was pure conjecture because Simms had traveled through Georgia at least twice prior to the publication of *Guy Rivers.* And while newspapers were passed around extensively in the news-hungry countryside, the *Western Herald* was a frontier weekly of limited circulation that was not sent out of the state without advance payment. Moreover, the first issue of the *Western Herald* included an extract entitled "Indian Eloquence" from a larger unsigned piece by Simms called the "Children of the Sun," as well as a brief story entitled "The Robber's Wife" that appears to be a rough prototype for *Guy Rivers.* Even if Coulter's observation was correct, Simms's description of the landscape, the village of Chestatee, and a forest preaching spoke to the region, if not directly. Furthermore, his main characters reveal much about plantation society's social ideals, while his comic characters and scenes display a budding talent for humor writing that he drew upon later in his career.[4]

The story begins when a handsome young traveler is waylaid by the notorious outlaw Guy Rivers and the Pony Club while riding through the dark and dreary hills of Cherokee Georgia on his way to Tennessee. A fearless Carolinian of the "best blood of the English nobility" who is armed with pistols and a bowie knife, Ralph Colleton epitomizes the southern aristocrat, a man at home in polite society as well as on the rugged frontier. His late father, Colonel Ralph Colleton, had been a wealthy planter in South Carolina who had squandered his fortune on extravagant living before emigrating with his young son to Tennessee. The young hero had grown to manhood over the next fifteen years, although his father had never regained prosperity.[5]

In the meantime, Ralph's widowed uncle, Colonel William Colleton, had grown rich on several thousand acres on the Santee River in South Carolina where he lives with his beautiful daughter, Edith. Unlike Ralph's hapless father, who had married a poor woman for love, Colonel Colleton had married for position, loving only money and power. During their teens, Ralph and Edith had summered together at her father's retreat in Gwinnett County, touring the fashionable resorts in North Georgia. Sometime later, they pledge eternal love for one another, but the death of Ralph's father and his uncle's rejection of their marriage plans generates a romantic crisis. The young lovers part after Colonel Colleton tarnishes his nephew's memory of the mother he had lost in early childhood by belittling her as a "miserable peasant" and a nameless woman "from the inferior grade" who lacked refinement and education.[6]

Now twenty years old and driven to the point of recklessness by his lovesick melancholy, Ralph makes a daring escape, wounding Guy Rivers and suffering a wound himself in the process. Some miles down the road, a sturdy woodsman named Mark Forrester finds Ralph and takes him into Chestatee to the doctor. A rough and tumble village of thirty or forty mostly log dwellings, including a tavern, blacksmith shop, and courthouse that also serves as a jail, Chestatee is populated by gold-seekers and desperadoes. The village is illuminated at night by fires on raised platforms.[7]

A South Carolinian of sturdy yeoman stock, Mark Forrester plays a small but important part in the story. At the age of eighteen, Forrester had earned his spurs as a champion fighter at a militia muster. The woodsman describes himself in the backwoods brag tradition as having been six feet tall in his youth and able to "outrun, outjump, outwrestle, outfight, and outdo anyhow" any other lad in the district. Although his "small but inefficient patrimony" in Carolina still supported a younger sister, Forrester had never relished farming, his restless spirit more at home in the wild.

Colonel William Colleton symbolizes the corrupting power of greed on the aristocratic ideal and the social divisions that resulted in a republican society when the elite abandoned the chivalric code. The woodsman speaks to the distance created in the early 1830s between the southern gentry and the rest of the population by the unprincipled pursuit of wealth and power. Though he does not begrudge a deserving man the title of "squire," Forrester describes Carolina gentlemen as typically stiff, proud, and "pretty high in the collar." Forrester especially dislikes the title "mister" because it positions "people quite too far off from one another" and considers such formality appropriate only on those occasions when men are getting ready to fight.[8]

Simms also drew attention to the social distance between the egalitarian frontier and more settled regions through the character Lucy Munro. The niece of Wat Munro, the landlord of The Golden Egg tavern and one of the secret leaders of the Pony Club, Lucy is introduced as "belonging to a far more refined social organization than that in which we find her." Finely formed, slight and delicate, fair-skinned, and intelligent, Lucy has a maidenly reserve, ladylike dignity, and quiet serenity that is out of place in a backwoods tavern where the food is abundant but the company boorish and rude.[9]

Disguised to conceal the facial cut that he received during the unsuccessful ambush, Guy Rivers is present at the tavern when Ralph arrives. Mysterious, sinister, and in cahoots with Wat Munro, Rivers also has designs on Lucy, who wants nothing to do with him. Born Edward Creighton and formerly a lawyer in Gwinnett County, Rivers is wanted for the murder of a judge. Extremely intelligent but corrupted by his passions, Rivers hates young Colleton because he had fallen in love from afar with Edith Colleton back in Gwinnett County.

Two minor characters in *Guy Rivers* are of particular note because they reveal Simms's budding talent as a humorist. At the very moment that Mark Forrester arrives in Chestatee with Ralph, a crowd in the tavern is giving Jared Bunce a taste of frontier justice. A swindling Connecticut Yankee who cheats unsuspecting women, Bunce is a varmint of the worst sort. In the words of the woodsman, "He's a pedlar, you know, and that means a chap what can wheedle the eyes out of your head, the soul out of your body, the gould out of your pocket, and give you nothing but brass, and tin, and copper in the place of 'em." Speaking again through the character of Forrester, perhaps with the recent tariff fight in mind, Simms used Bunce to vent his own disdain for the North's unbridled acquisitiveness:

> They've got a jury setting on his vartues, and they'll hammer the soul out of him afore they let him git out from under the iron. I don't reckon they can cure him, for what's bred in the bone, you know, won't come out of the flesh; but they'll so bedevil bone and flesh, that I reckon he'll be the last Yankee that ever comes to practice again in this Chestatee country. Maybe, he ain't deserving of much worse than they kin do. Maybe, he ain't a scamp of the biggest wethers. His rascality ain't to be measured. Why, he kin walk through a man's pockets, jest as the devil goes through a crack or a keyhole, and the money will naterally stick to him, jest as ef he was made of gum turpentine.[10]

Because the courthouse and jail are largely symbolic rather than effective manifestations of law and order, the local regulators take action after Bunce saturates the village and countryside with shoddy merchandise. After tending to Colleton's wounds, Forrester goes to the tavern, where twenty well-oiled vigilantes have set up a mock trial presided over by Lawyer Pippin, a corpulent, vain, shady, money-loving blowhard with a gift for stirring up trouble to his advantage. Although he panders to the boisterous crowd by ridiculing the North as "a nation of pedlers," Pippin actually helps Bunce to escape, scheming to sue the regulators for property damages during the next court session. True to his nature, however, Bunce double-crosses his fellow conspirator and steals his fine horse, leaving a broken-down nag in exchange. Moreover, he sends a letter to the vigilantes that details the lawyer's role in his escape, leaving Pippin behind to wheedle his way out of a bad situation.[11]

Although the story line in the romance is of minor interest and proceeds in typical melodramatic fashion to a predictable climax, *Guy Rivers* contains several memorable scenes. The first is a Sabbath meeting in the forest. Praising Methodist circuit riders as society's moral champions, Simms drew a clear distinction between high church hypocrisy and the godliness of sectarian preachers like Parson Witter, a man of calm, heartfelt commitment who lives and preaches the simple doctrine of the good shepherd. The old parson is civilization's advance agent on the wild frontier, respected by all because of his impeccable character and egalitarian message. Although the crowd is sprinkled with religious hypocrites and an occasional "high stickler for church aristocracy," as well as many seeking only entertainment, the natural cathedral in the woods communicates the author's poetic view of nature as a visible sign of God's presence. Simms also understood that egalitarianism was not the only attraction of sectarian creeds on the frontier, where daily dangers beyond human control drove men to seek the protection of a higher presence. The Sabbath scene in the woods captures Methodism's sectarian appeal before the process of denominational maturation took over in the 1840s. Simms portrayed the itinerant preacher as a force for communal cohesion in the absence of more stable social institutions. In districts where circuit riders were later replaced by permanent churches with resident ministers, rural religion increasingly came to reflect the ideological concerns and social attitudes of plantation society.[12]

Simms also used a chance meeting between Ralph and Lucy on the road to the religious service in the forest to stage a discussion of the South's gender relations. Simms maintained that men were socially dominant, selfish, and prone to pursue the varied pleasures of the moment rather than matters of "real importance" such as love and religion. Deprived of much of their individuality by the merger of their identities with "the stronger sex," women had learned to content themselves with focusing their energies on matters of the heart. As Ralph explains to Lucy, the world was the natural habitat of men, whereas the existence of women was limited to the more narrow confines of the home. In reply, Lucy likens Ralph to "a moral Robin Hood" for restoring a small portion to women after robbing them of their "mental independence," but does not protest her dependent status within the South's patriarchal arrangements. In her words, "I complain not of the robbery—far from it; for, if we do lose the possession of a commodity so valuable, we are at least freed from the responsibility of keeping it."[13]

Near the benediction of the service in the forest, a torn and bloody boy rushes into the assembly. Immediately, all the men hurry off except Ralph, who as a gentleman waits "with praiseworthy decorum" until the preacher finishes. Upon learning that a rival group of ruffians has seized one of the richer gold claims of the Pony Club, Ralph mounts his noble steed and rides out to watch the excitement, still unaware of the identity of Guy Rivers. At the critical moment in the conflict that follows, a detachment of the "Georgia Guard" is seen approaching the camp along a distant ridgeline. Rather than give way to the authority of the state, the two groups of outlaws join forces. Whereas sectarian religion was a welcome intrusion on the gold frontier, the appearance of uniformed state militia was another matter. Both bands of bandetti know that the Georgia Guard had been created to break up illegal squatter settlements, protect the property of honest adventurers, and punish "frequent outlawries." In the narrator's words, the direct application of state power was necessary "in a country where the sheriff dared not often show himself."[14]

Although led by a manly captain and all fine-looking, well-formed, and intelligent men, the Georgians are no match for the evil Guy Rivers, who unleashes a rockslide upon their heads. Just as Rivers makes ready to polish off the captain, Ralph intervenes. In the ensuing scuffle, Ralph tears off the handkerchief disguising the outlaw's identity. When he makes public the failed ambush, Ralph discovers that the outlaws, now implicated in the murder of a large number of the Georgia Guard, are unwilling to act against their rival Rivers, though most detest the villain. Harried by their leaders into a succession of terrible crimes beyond their individual self-interest, the men are remorseful but remain silent. Simms observed that in the absence of rule and regulation, "the ignorant and uneducated man is quite too willing" to follow a leader "even though he be an ass." Deficient in education and birth and lacking in the habit of self-examination, such men readily divested themselves of "the difficulties and responsibilities of their own government," sacrificing their freedom in the process:

> To this they consent, taking care, in their great desire to be slaves, to be foremost themselves in tying on the bandage which keeps them in darkness and in chains for ever. Thus will they be content to live, however wronged, if not absolutely bruised and beaten; happy to escape from the cares of an

> independent mastery of their own conduct, if, in this way, they can also escape from the noble responsibilities of independence.[15]

The emphasis that Simms placed on the need for rule and regulation suggests that the ideal of the independent yet socially responsible man was hardly egalitarian given the condition of the "great mass" on the frontier. Significantly, only Ralph Colleton, the Carolina-born aristocrat, has the presence of mind needed to control his emotions at all times. Of noble blood and skilled in the ways of outdoor life, he is a natural leader, a trait Mark Forrester recognizes instinctively. When one of the ruffians attacks Colleton with a hatchet, for example, he calmly takes aim with aristocratic precision and shoots him in the head. Both are intelligent men but neither Wat Munro, the tavern landlord, nor Guy Rivers, the murderous lawyer, have the bloodlines to control their passions. Unlike Colleton, who had stood apart from the mob, Forrester had joined in the fight with the claim jumpers. Although stricken with guilt by the ambush of the Georgia Guard and not an outlaw himself, this act seals the woodsman's tragic fate. While making preparations to emigrate westward with his one true love later in the story, Forrester is murdered by the outlaws.[16]

From this point in the narrative, the romance progresses rapidly to its denouement. When the circuit court judge arrives, the outlaws arrange for Colleton to be convicted of Forrester's murder. The crisis brings his uncle to his senses and he rushes with Edith to Chestatee. Revealing his true identity to Edith, Guy Rivers offers to free Ralph for her hand in marriage. Edith rebukes the outlaw, vowing death before dishonor. To save his niece Lucy from the outlaw, Wat Munro reveals the true identity of Guy Rivers and exposes him as the murderer of Mark Forrester.

After the demise of Guy Rivers, Ralph and Edith convince Lucy to come and live as their "sister" in Carolina, conveniently resolving a potentially interesting love triangle. Although in love with Ralph and the romance's real heroine, Lucy Munro stands between the natural union of the Colleton cousins. By their marriage, Ralph and Edith cleanse the family name of her father's corrupting materialism, which restores the hero to his rightful place in society. Unattached, Lucy is left only with the platonic love of a spinster, perhaps as penance for her uncle's life of crime. Meanwhile, the peddler Jared Bunce and Lawyer Pippin, miraculously reformed, depart for a brighter future in the valley of the Mississippi River, leaving the Georgia Guard in sole possession of the gold frontier, the triumph of law and order complete.

The theme in *Guy Rivers* that society and human nature are in perpetual conflict also runs through the writings of the Georgia humorists, a group of writers whose exploration of the manners and customs of Middle Georgia helped to give form to an emerging literary genre. As Joel Chandler Harris later wrote, "By-the-by, if you will take a map of Georgia, pick out Putnam County, and then put your finger on the counties surrounding it—Morgan, Greene, Hancock, Baldwin, Jones and Jasper—you will have under your thumb the seat of Southern humor. Major Jones's Courtship belongs to Morgan County. Colonel Richard Malcolm Johnston's characters to Hancock. Unc' Remus was in Putnam. Simon Suggs was a native of Jasper. Polly Peablossom was from Baldwin." In retrospect, it seems somewhat incongruous that Harris elected to omit *Georgia Scenes* from his paean to Middle Georgia's literary genius because it was Augustus Baldwin Longstreet's classic that opened the national market to a rising generation of southern humorists.[17]

Historians of the American South have increasingly become aware that there were many *souths*. It would be a mistake, however, to allow variations in regional development through time to obscure the myriad of shared social, cultural, and historical experiences that contributed to the formation of a common political identity. Simply stated, from the perspective of Longstreet and his fellow humorists in antebellum Georgia, Middle Georgia was *the* South. The problem was that Middle Georgia, which in this context can be defined as the plantation zone that radiated outward along both sides of the fall line from Augusta to Columbus, was a region in flux in the early nineteenth century. One of the primary ideological functions of the South as a literary construct was to provide a shared sense of identity that helped to alleviate the potentially divisive impact of the tremendous changes unleashed by the westward expansion of plantation agriculture. Longstreet and William Tappan Thompson celebrated the virtues of rural life in the South, but they were troubled by the social turmoil that accompanied westward expansion. This concern spread to the works of lesser-known Georgia humorists as well. The desire to protect plantation society from further erosion is the distinguishing feature that separates the work of Georgia's antebellum humorists from that of later humorists who followed the southwestern expansion of the frontier. The literature of Georgia's antebellum humorists expressed more support for the cause of social stability than did the literature of humorists elsewhere in the South. Ironically, this conservative moral vision muted much of the comic potential in Georgia's antebellum humor tradition. The point is often masked by the understandable tendency of modern literary anthology editors to include Longstreet's hilarious sketches "The Fight," "The Gander Pulling," and "The Horse-Swap" rather than selections from the multitude of moralistic stories that more accurately characterize the overall literary output of Georgia authors from 1830 through the Civil War.[18]

That Georgia's humorists were ardent defenders of plantation society has often been obscured by the tendency of literary historians to portray the Old South as a bourgeois or middle-class society. The late Jay B. Hubbell, for example, described Middle Georgia as a region of small farms rather than big plantations where the long survival of "frontier characteristics" prevented the emergence of the aristocratic social arrangements that had evolved in Virginia and South Carolina. Such interpretations tend to freeze the region's historical development in the early nineteenth century when social relations between the planter class and the white yeomanry exhibited the fluidity characteristic of a frontier society. To be sure, Middle Georgia was home to many yeoman farmers, but it was also located in the heart of the Cotton Kingdom.[19]

Historian Eugene D. Genovese has illustrated convincingly how paternalism governed social relations within plantation households, but it remains less clear how leading slaveholders manipulated social relations within white society to their advantage beyond the obvious generalization that wealth translates into political power. Clearly, something more is needed to explain the slaveholding elite's dominance in white society. Ultimately, the issue boils down to explaining how leading planters came to accumulate such overwhelming power in a republican society with democratic traditions that the rest of the white population accepted their world view to the point of following their lead into a war to preserve slavery.[20]

Appropriately, most historians (including Genovese) now stress the proslavery ideology that coalesced in the 1830s as evidence of the slaveholding elite's efforts to consolidate its dominance in southern society at the expense of the egalitarianism inherent in the Jeffersonian and Jacksonian traditions. In antebellum Georgia, wealthy slaveholders were the foremost agents of ideological communication because of their tremendous local authority. Whereas a planter's personal authority was largely sufficient to maintain control on his own estate, however, the presence of a large population of independent yeoman farmers and an unstable poor-white underclass created an important, if limited, ideological role for town professionals in plantation society. Not surprisingly, it was this group that produced the largest number of authors, although many planters also cultivated literary ambitions. Although it is not possible to demonstrate the dominance of the slaveholding elite by exploring literary sources alone, a more-or-less unified world view reflecting the social development of the period and the cultural values, economic interests, and political concerns of the planter class is discernible in Georgia's humor tradition. To borrow a phrase, Georgia authors worked as "leavens of respectability and of gentility" with the planter elite "to lessen the crudeness and conquer the rudeness of the masses." And while the scenes, events, and dialects in the stories were authentic to Middle Georgia, contemporary readers understood that their authors were speaking of the South as well.[21]

A distinctively moralistic outlook in their writing is evidence that Georgia humorists accepted their ideological role as champions of plantation society. It is for this reason that their work provides useful insight into the ideal social relations the slaveholding elite desired in the white community. Planter patricians in Georgia were schooled from infancy in the proper social behavior needed to preserve the deference they expected from their social inferiors. But because virtually all white men had political voice and could express themselves in a variety of legal and extralegal ways, there were effective limits to the authority that could be exercised from above. For the slaveholding elite to maintain political and social control there was a need for compromise elsewhere, which the historian E. P. Thompson described in another context as toleration for a robust plebeian culture and "an inhibition upon the use of force against indiscipline and disturbance." Beyond the plantation, paternalism thus became more "theatre and gesture" than a personal relationship between white Georgians of different social classes, or "a studied technique of rule." Moreover, the distance between patrician and plebeian culture grew greater as plantation society matured and continued to expand into new areas, at least until the rising tide of abolitionist attacks forced a closing of class ranks in defense of slavery.[22]

By the mid-1830s, Georgia's leading slaveholders enjoyed tremendous social prestige and political power. Still, in a state where land *and* labor defined white male political identity, many nonslaveholding landowners were respected citizens in spite of the popular notion that the votes of common whites could be had for a few drinks. In truth, the support of the white yeomanry counted for a lot in Georgia, especially as long as leading slaveholders remained politically divided in spite of the broader social outlook they shared. Thus it is not surprising that the conflict between the Whigs and the Calhoun and Jackson factions within the Democratic Party influenced the work of the Georgia humorists. For example, humorists Longstreet and William Tappan Thompson were both politically active, although the former was a Calhoun Democrat and the latter a Clay Whig. Both men shared the belief that republican virtue was rooted in the land, mistrusted the Jacksonian masses, and decried the corruption of Georgia politics by those who pandered to uneducated commoners for votes. Only after sectional polarization over slavery destroyed the Whig Party and purged the Democratic Party of its Jacksonian commitment to national unity would Georgia authors begin to speak with a unified political voice.[23]

Committed as they were to the underlying ideological assumptions of plantation society, the Georgia humorists also joined in the broader debate regarding the South's future in American civilization. As were their literary peers, they were well aware of their role as spokesmen for the South in an increasingly hostile world. Equally important was their analysis of the changing manners, mores, and social relations of antebellum Georgia, a literary dialogue directed as much at southern readers as outsiders. This Janus-faced character, or the tendency of Georgia writers to address simultaneously two distinctive literary audiences, gave their work a creative cast that disappeared when the debate over slavery shattered the looking glass. The emphasis on internal reform that characterized the works of authors such as Longstreet and Thompson remained evident in the sketches composed by lesser-known Georgia authors in the 1850s. Yet, whereas slavery had played a secondary role at best in their early work, the next generation of authors introduced strident polemical defenses of plantation slavery to the genre in the decade leading up to the Civil War.[24]

Even when they elected to downplay the centrality of slavery in plantation society, the sketches penned by the Georgia humorists are best understood within the broader context of the proslavery defense. The "scenes" that they described to impart a more realistic picture of the South to their readers may or may not have been unique, but the content of their sketches often generated a significant ideological dilemma. As ideological defenders of plantation society, the humorists implicitly realized that they had to position the South as a superior civilization or risk being objectified, yet they saw much in Georgia that begged for intervention. Still, their sketches often worked at cross-purposes. By holding up the warts, flaws, and vices of their state to ridicule, humorists like Longstreet and Thompson hoped to make plantation society stronger by inspiring internal reforms, but unsympathetic readers could also seize upon such characteristics to stereotype the South as a blighted land.

All of this is not intended to communicate the impression that the Georgia humorists were a bunch of stuffed shirts, for much of what they wrote was truly funny. Nevertheless, they were committed citizens who took their political and social responsibilities seriously. The didactic tone of the writings of Longstreet and Thompson thus runs counter to the traditional argument that the humorists were not writing to civilize their neighbors, but simply to record a vanishing way of life. Acknowledging that literary expression served an ideological function, however, should not obscure the realistic flavor of the antebellum humor stories. To quote literary scholar James E. Kibler Jr., "Longstreet's is no idyllic rural realm, but a place of vices and virtues realistically considered." Standing at the point of transition between the frontier and civilization, the Georgia humorists realized that realistic settings, dialect, and laughter made it easier to deliver a moral message.[25]

Drawing their topics from the events of everyday life, such as hunts, fights, courtship and marriage, dances, horse races and other contests, militia drills, elections, the law and courts, religion, gambling, practical jokes, illness, drinking bouts, and the treatment of country bumpkins in the city, the Georgia humorists used the literary device of the frame to distance themselves and their readers from the harshness of life on the frontier. Longstreet, for example, created his narrative characters Abraham Baldwin and Lyman Hall to voice his disgust with poor public morality and uninhibited violence, naming them in honor of two Yale-educated forefathers who had provided Georgia with outstanding leadership in the more virtuous days of the early republic. As noted by two recent observers, Longstreet was also critical of "excesses in both town and rural living" and used "plain people who exemplify the best qualities as standards by which rude brawls or silly sophistications may be judged."[26]

The question that follows, of course, is to what purpose did Longstreet deliver his moral messages? A closer look at his personal and professional development and a critical reading of *Georgia Scenes* clearly reveals him more as a defender of plantation society than a champion of the common man. Born in Augusta in 1790, Longstreet's own maturation into adulthood coincided with the expansion of the Cotton Kingdom across Middle Georgia. Admitted to the Georgia bar in 1815, he began his law practice in the Middle Circuit. Two years later, he married Francis Eliza Parke of Greensboro, Georgia, and settled into a successful life as a lawyer-farmer. Elected to the state legislature from Greene County in 1821, he was named Judge of the Superior Court of the Ocmulgee District the following year. Longstreet stood for Congress in 1824, but the deaths of his eldest son and mother-in-law led him to abandon further efforts to win political office. After a long period of melancholy that culminated in a religious conversion, he returned to Augusta in 1827 and joined a prosperous legal practice. Drawing upon his experiences and conversations during his days of riding the circuit, Longstreet published several humor sketches in the Milledgeville *Southern Recorder.* He then purchased the *North American Gazette,* changed its name to the Augusta *State Rights Sentinel,* and began publishing additional sketches in 1834. The next year he published his collected sketches under the title of *Georgia Scenes;* the book made his literary reputation. Longstreet's subsequent literary efforts never came close to matching his achievement in *Georgia Scenes,* largely because the stifling concern for moral rectitude evident in his masterpiece runs rampant. The title of a collection of his later sketches published posthumously by his nephew, *Stories with a Moral: Humorous and Descriptive of Southern Life a Century Ago,* captured the essence of Longstreet's literary purpose.[27]

Longstreet was a state's rights conservative who praised the political virtue of the South's revolutionary forefathers; he also believed that agriculture was the foundation of republican society. Thus while he applauded the triumph of republican virtue as plantation society introduced order to the chaos of the frontier, he feared the potential for corruption inherent in town life. Although perhaps best remembered for the antics of his crackers and poor whites, nearly half of the sketches in *Georgia Scenes* deal with the upper crust of town society. As James B. Meriwether notes, his view of human nature underscored the savagery lurking beneath the thin veneer of civilization, a carnality often exposed at the crossroads between society and the frontier but equally evident in town society. Accordingly, he concluded that only the expansion of social controls such as education and religion under the leadership of a strong elite could overcome the primitive impulses unleashed by frontier expansion and further town development.[28]

In the words of a recent historian, Longstreet was "a man enchanted by the energy and exuberance" of the South, but "profoundly ill at ease with its values and its future." To be more specific, he hoped to restore republican values at a time when the South was entering an uncertain future, which promised to be a difficult task in light of the inherent flaws in human nature. Longstreet's pastoral remedy was for the South to return *to the gar-*

den by rejecting the false society of town life for a slaveholding republic of virtuous landowners. Looking back to a golden age when yeoman farmers and planters stood united because of their shared republican heritage, Longstreet sought simultaneously to control the savage impulses of human nature unleashed on the frontier and meet the growing threat posed by the urban North to the southern way of life. As Kibler notes, it is ultimately their shared values that unite the narrator Hall and the "simple" men into an organic community in Longstreet's sketch "The Shooting Match."[29]

Thus while the distinction is subtle, Longstreet is better understood as a student of the formative years of plantation society than a chronicler of life on the frontier. By contrasting the virtues of country life in the recent past with the dangers of contemporary town society, he communicated his moral and political concern for the South's future, a motive he later realized had been lost in the laughter inspired by some of his sketches:

> The design of the "Georgia Scenes" has been wholly misapprehended by the public. It has been invariably received as a mere collection of fancy sketches, with no higher object than the entertainment of the reader, whereas the aim of the author was to supply a chasm in history which has always been overlooked—the manners, customs, amusements, wit, dialect, as they appear in all grades of society to an ear and eye witness of them. . . . I have chosen the first fifty years of our republic in the course of which short space of time the society of the Southern States underwent almost an entire revolution, and at this date hardly a trace of the society of the first thirty years of the republic is to be found.

Longstreet's focus on the revolution in the republic holds the key to the ideological messages in *Georgia Scenes* and his less memorable later works. Writing at the moment of the Cotton Kingdom's triumph in Middle Georgia, he was searching for a safe passage for the South between the Scylla of Jacksonian democracy and the Charybdis of the North's expanding urban-industrial society.[30]

Georgia Scenes is a difficult work to analyze systematically. The sketches not only vary enormously in quality and tone, there is no apparent logic in their sequential arrangement. While some sketches are anchored in a specific point in time beginning in 1790 and running to the early 1830s, others are set in the indeterminate past. If one stretches the categories somewhat, sixteen of the sketches revolve around the evolution of southern recreations, while three others center upon marriage and the household. Underlying all of the sketches is the tension between town and country and the gradual emergence of social and moral controls over the violence and unrestrained behavior of the frontier. Law and order prevail, but it is a tenuous victory at best. The overall tone of the collection is set by Longstreet's anxiety over the decline of the republic, a mood conveyed strongly by the eroded landscape in "The Turn Out," which is ostensibly a humorous look at life in an old field school in 1790. Once rich and prosperous, the lands near where the school once stood had by 1832 become "barren, dreary and cheerless."[31]

Longstreet's comedic talents are most evident in his often-anthologized sketches "The Gander Pulling," "The Fight," and "The Horse-Swap." "The Gander Pulling," a satirical glance at the South's fascination with medieval forms of mock combat, is set in Augusta in 1798. When the narrator Lyman Hall, who is Longstreet's voice in sketches that deal primarily with men, comes across an "*advurtysement*" for a gander pulling, he decides to check out the fun the following Sunday. Unlike the chivalric Middle Ages, when a knight competed for his lady fair, the contestants each fork over twenty-five cents to a common pot, the prize going to the man who succeeds in snatching the head off a poor greased goose while riding past at a brisk canter. Because it is the Sabbath, there are only a few women present, and they are "from the lowest walks of life."[32]

Longstreet's critical opinion of women is also evident in "The Fight," although the sketch deals primarily with the theme of manly honor. Set in "the younger days of the Republic," the story revolves around a contest to determine the best man in the county. The narrator Hall observes in the introductory frame that in frontier times physical prowess rather than education, property, and moral rectitude had been the yardstick by which a man's fitness for leadership had been measured. The two best men in the county had risen to the top of their militia battalions because of their raw fighting ability rather than their command of military science. Naturally, everyone else in the county had long wondered which of the two was better in a fight. Yet because Billy and Bob seldom came in contact and were on friendly terms, the issue had remained unresolved, although "many a quart of old Jamaica" had been wagered on the question. Both men "were admirable specimens of human nature in its finest form."[33]

Standing 6′ 1″ and weighing a solid 180 pounds, Billy's reputation rested on the strength of his blows, while Bob was at his best after bringing his adversary to the ground. Although of slightly less height and weight, Bob had few equals at running and jumping, at wrestling none. In stark contrast to the manly ideals embodied in Billy and Bob, stands Longstreet's most famous literary character, Ransy Sniffle, a poor-white dirt-eater who had been frustrated repeatedly in his efforts to bring the two champions together in combat. Seldom has a character in fiction been equated so completely with an entire social class:

> Now there happened to reside in the county just alluded to a little fellow by the name of Ransy Sniffle: a sprout of Richmond, who, in his earlier days, had fed copiously upon red clay and blackberries. This diet had given to Ransy a complexion that a corpse would have disdained to own, and an abdominal rotundity that was quite unprepossessing. Long spells of the fever and ague, too, in Ransy's youth, had conspired with clay and blackberries to throw him quite out of the order of nature. His shoulders were fleshless and elevated; his head large and flat; his neck slim and translucent; and his arms, hands, fingers, and feet were lengthened out of all proportion to the rest of his frame. His joints were large and his limbs small; and as for flesh, he could not, with propriety, be said to have any. Those parts which nature usually supplies with the most of this article—the calves of the legs, for example,—presented in him the appearance of so many well-drawn blisters. His height was just five feet nothing; and his average weight in blackberry season, ninety-five.[34]

Unlike Billy and Bob, who as yeoman farmers were in harmony with Longstreet's agrarian order in spite of their lack of refinement, Ransy Sniffle is a monster lurking on the fringes of society, waiting to strike. For northern and European readers with antislavery leanings, Ransy became a literary symbol of the horrible impact of slavery on white society. Southern readers undoubtedly recognized the character as a caricature intended to provoke a good laugh, but there was no disguising Longstreet's warning of the danger to plantation society inherent in the poor-white population's lust for barbaric violence. Because evil lurked in the hearts of all men, all that was needed was a spark to bring it to the surface. In Longstreet's patriarchal universe, original sin had a female visage. As Hall explains, "It is said that a hundred game cocks will live in perfect harmony together, if you will not put a hen with them: and so it would have been with Billy and Bob had there been no women in the world."[35]

When both battalions meet at the courthouse for a regimental parade, the wives of the two men get into an argument while shopping at Zepheniah Atwater's store over who should be waited upon first. The fat hits the fire when Billy comes into the store to hurry up his wife, who announces loudly that "I'd o' been gone half an hour ago . . . if it had'nt o' been for that impudent huzzy." Not to be outdone, Mrs. Durham replies, "Who do you call an impudent huzzy? you nasty, good-for-nothing, snaggle-toothed gaub of fat, you." Rising to defend his wife's virtue, Billy calls Mrs. Durham a "sassy heifer" and threatens to "lick" her husband until he teaches her some manners, which sends Ransy off in a flash. When Bob confronts him over the incident, Billy realizes that a fight is unavoidable, the outcome of which is foreshadowed by his violation of the community's gender code. By interfering directly in the affairs of women, Billy had committed a fatal error. Had both wives gone home to tell their husbands about the incident, the subsequent fight would have been between equals. Thus while Longstreet considered the southern *code duello* an inappropriate way for Christian men to resolve conflict, he implicitly reinforces the code when Bob prevails in the fight that follows—an irony that he perhaps missed. Aristocratic notions of honor had permeated the lower ranks of society, but the common folk lapse into savagery when they try to emulate their social betters.[36]

Longstreet also emphasized the distance between Georgia's social classes by describing a "fair fight" as "catch as catch can, rough and tumble:—no man touch 'till one or the other hollos," a veiled condemnation of the popular recourse to violence among elites that implied a substantial danger to society when commoners acted likewise. Ignorant of the intricate rules of engagement that regulated combat between gentlemen, otherwise good men of common origin lapse into barbarism when trying to imitate the aristocracy. In the fight, Bob loses his left ear, a piece of his left cheek, and makes "a present" to Billy of his middle finger on his left hand, whereas Billy loses a piece of his nose and finally admits defeat when Bob brings him down and grinds dirt into his eyes.[37]

Both men take to their beds for several weeks to recover, implying perhaps a substantial hardship to their families because of the loss of their labor on the land. When they eventually meet two months later, Billy offers his hand to the man who had licked him in a fair fight, but claims to have been "sort o' cowed" by the knowledge that he had wronged Bob's wife and thus deserved to lose. A secure victor who understands a worthy opponent's need to preserve his manhood, and possibly realizes that the outcome could have just as easily gone the other way, Bob admits that only fear of his wife had prevented him from giving up. In other words, all the fight had settled was a minor transgression of the code of honor that united all white men within society. Had Bob not accepted Billy's explanation of defeat, his false pride would have made him the underdog in the contest that inevitably would have followed, a vicious cycle without end ultimately leading to complete chaos. Thus while honor had a rightful place within the affairs of gentlemen, religion, law, and education were a better means of controlling the dangers to plantation society still lurking in the expanding frontier. Lest his readers conclude that he approved of brawling, Longstreet tacked on a salute to morality in the final frame of the sketch:

> Thanks to the Christian religion, to schools, colleges, and benevolent associations, such scenes of barbarism and cruelty, as what I have just been describing, are now of rare occurrence: though they may still be occasionally met with in some of the new counties. Wherever they prevail, they are a disgrace to that community. The peace officers who countenance them, deserve a place in the penitentiary.[38]

Writing in the wise hero tradition of "slum naturalism," Longstreet positioned the narrator to make visible the hidden world of the white commoners to polite society. The ideological function of the gentleman narrator becomes evident when one realizes that he understands the significance but disapproves of the traditional rituals of manhood that characterize premodern societies, what Clifford Geertz describes as "deep play." Standing at a safe distance, the narrator serves as a cultural intermediary between polite society and the "rough boys" who still roamed the Georgia countryside in the mid-1830s. At first glance, the fact that the narrator condemns manly games such as fighting, horse racing, and gambling seems to suggest a bourgeois moral to the story but the social context is wrong. The defenders of plantation society were nonetheless aware by 1835 that their social order was being judged against the yardstick of Yankee capitalist culture. Trying to legitimate plantation society as a progressive force in the Atlantic community, Longstreet was feeling his way through an increasingly knotty situation by trying to police the traditional forms of male recreation.[39]

But as Geertz observes, the deeply rooted rituals of manhood in a premodern society are ironically a point of entry for the introduction of market behaviors. Rural merchants sponsor such events because betting gets more money into circulation, as does spending on peripheral activities like eating and drinking. Significantly, the fight actually begins in a store, an interior space open to women who have yet to assimilate the proper codes of public commercial conduct. They are not ladies and old Augusty definitely is not Boston; when the fight comes it is sure enough between two "cocks." Geertz also emphasizes Jeremy Bentham's rejection of deep play, or recreational activities that he considered irrational because of the high stakes involved. From the first blow, the narrator makes it clear that the contestants are way over their heads. Though the crowd takes great pleasure from the fight, both men take to their beds afterward to recover. Not surprisingly, Bentham concluded that deep play was immoral and should be outlawed.[40]

Like Bentham, Longstreet placed his bet on the social utility of moral authoritarianism. But real men, whether in Georgia or rural Bali, knew better. In deep games much more is at stake than money or material gain. Money matters, but honor matters more. Geertz makes the telling point that behavior that looks irrational from the perspective of an outsider is in fact very "meaning-full" to the participants. The true cockfighter does not play games for low stakes because the "brag" is not about money. Significantly, both men are also champions of their respective militia districts. The momentary chaos notwithstanding, the fight reaffirms the system of governance that provided social order in the backcountry. Bound together by seemingly primitive blood rituals, the men responsible for policing the rural countryside share a common ethos and are expected to rally to the man in the face of outside danger. Blood rites also reinforced the hierarchical relations that internally governed rural districts. Ransy Sniffle cannot be a champion because he is a genuine grotesque, but he nonetheless enjoys marginal membership in the patriarchal community of white men. From the perspective of polite society, however, the apparent lack of civility in blood sports was a formula for disaster.[41]

Longstreet's compulsion to sermonize, which was a trait unfortunately emulated by his fellow Georgia humorists throughout the antebellum era, works against the masculine humor in several of the sketches in *Georgia Scenes.* "The Horse-Swap," for example, is a delightfully ludicrous sketch that profits little from the narrator's lofty condemnation of cruelty to animals. Uncharacteristically, however, Longstreet elected not to frame the asocial behavior of Ned Brace in "The Character of a Native Georgian." An archetype for later pranksters in the southern humor tradition, Brace disrupts a church service and funeral and brings efforts to quell a fire to an abrupt halt when he pauses to drink from a bucket in the bucket line. Brace targets his practical jokes toward "the beau in the presence of his mistress, the fop, the pedant, the purse-proud, the over-fastidious, and sensitive." The narrator observes that he was such a skillful prankster, that it was generally impossible to bring him to account "without violating all the rules of decency, politeness, and chivalry at once." Through Brace, Longstreet made the point that hypocrisy and folly existed in all levels of society, a message he reiterated in "The Turf" by censuring the elite at play at the racetrack. As Hall and Baldwin note, many of the pleasure seekers buying their friends punch, drinking spirits, and making large bets had yet to pay honest debts.[42]

Longstreet reserved his most effective broadsides against the frivolous and immoral pursuits of town society for the sketches narrated by Baldwin that deal primarily with women. Because he believed that the rural household was the font of virtue in a slaveholding republic, Longstreet forcefully expressed his agrarian values in the distaff sketches. In "The Ball," for example, he denounces the preference in town society for European waltzes and gallopades over the old "jovial, heat-stirring, foot-stirring" dances of the early republic:

> Ye fair of my native land—ye daughters of a modest race, blush them away from the soil, which your mothers honored by their example, and consecrated with their ashes. Born to woman's loftiest destinies, it ill becomes you to stoop from your high estate, to ape the indecencies of Europe's slaves. It is yours to command—not to obey. Let vice approach you in what form she may—as the handmaid of wit and talents, the mistress of the courts, or the queen of fashion, fail not to meet her, with the frown of indignant virtue, and the flush of offended modesty.

Returning to the theme of a paradise lost, Longstreet casts a woman in the role of Eve. An attempt to imitate European aristocratic customs at a ball culminates in a duel in which one of the combatants shoots his opponent through the knees, a tragedy the narrator traces to a young lady's decision to delay her appearance an hour to make herself more conspicuous.[43]

In contrast, Longstreet celebrated the humble attire of simple country girls in "The Dance," while belittling the markedly ornate fashions popular in town society. When Baldwin visits a recently settled frontier county on business with a local magistrate, the squire invites him to stay for a "frolick" planned for the next morning at his one-room log house. Close on the heels of Billy Porter, a renowned black fiddler, Baldwin sees in the distance a group of "bouncing, ruddy-cheeked girls" in homespun dresses approaching the cabin, observing that the "refinements of the present day in female dress, had not even reached our republican *cities* at this time." The good times that follow bring back nostalgic memories, as well as bitter reflections on thirty years spent in search of fame and the heavy price paid. As a young man, Baldwin had abandoned the simple, wholesome pleasures of country life to seek his fortune but had found instead only disillusionment.[44]

Longstreet stated his agrarian values most forcefully in "The 'Charming Creature' As a Wife," a long sketch revolving around the narrator's nephew and his ruin through a bad marriage. The only son of a "plain, practical, sensible farmer, who, without the advantages of a liberal education, had enriched his mind by study and observation," George Baldwin was a talented, Princeton-educated lawyer who had begun his law practice in a city seventy miles from his father's plantation near LaGrange. Provided with a complete library by his father and very frugal, Baldwin had become successful enough by the age of twenty-one to seek a wife. Longstreet makes it evident early in the sketch that the young man's greatest mistake was choosing a merchant's daughter for his bride rather than a woman more at home on the land.[45]

Longstreet delineates his ideal of the southern lady in Baldwin's mother, a lovely, pious, practical, and suitably refined plantation mistress who was "perfectly versed" in "the statistics of domestic economy." Significantly, Baldwin's mother was skilled in the art of slave management. Although scolding and whipping her servants less than any mistress the narrator had ever seen, she made the most of their time through careful organization, firm rules, and personal supervision. "Without betraying any suspicions of their integrity," she made it clear that "she would have her biscuits uniformly of a size" and that theft would not go undetected, while exposing "her servants to as few temptations as possible." Not only were her slaves "well provided with every thing they needed" and indulged in their recreations, "no service was required of them on the Sabbath, further than to spread the table, and to attend it—a service which was lightened as much as possible, by having the provisions of that day very simple and prepared the day before."[46]

As a follower of John C. Calhoun, Longstreet had been deeply affected by the tariff fight in the late 1820s and early 1830s. George Baldwin's abandonment of the plantation and disastrous marriage to a "charming creature," the vain and hypocritical daughter of a wealthy but unlettered merchant with vulgar social pretensions, was a warning to the best sons of the South to divorce themselves from the evils of Yankee commercial dominance. The child of supercilious and morally bankrupt parents who had sent her to finishing school in Philadelphia to improve her marriage prospects, Baldwin's bride was a spoiled and excessively haughty beauty who had benefited little from her superior education. The essence of her character is communicated by her name, Evelina Caroline Smith. Again, Longstreet's message is clear—unless the South turned its back on the temptations of Eve, the loss of the garden was imminent. Striken by Evelina's feminine wiles and foolishly wanting to rescue her from the influence of her corrupt parents, George ignores his mother's counsel to find a woman with republican principles and Christian virtue. From the moment of his engagement, George's life goes downhill. Yet even Evelina's open flirtation with a young doctor and "unabated thirst for balls and parties of pleasure" are not sufficient to bring him to his senses. Not only does George let his legal practice decline, he allows his favorite horse to die from neglect, a terrible sin indeed for a southern gentleman! As his marriage date draws near, George finally realizes that he is betting "his earthly happiness on the forelorn hope of reforming Miss Smith's errors, after marriage; but his sense of honor was too refined, to permit him to harbor a thought of breaking the engagement." So enamored of Evelina "that any perils seemed preferable to giving her up forever," George is blind to the truth that his salvation lies in nullifying the marriage before it is too late.[47]

When the newlyweds go to visit his parents in LaGrange, Evelina spoils their homecoming because she is too snobbish to associate with the humble acquaintances of her husband's youth and rebuffs the attentions of his younger sisters. George's neighbors try to befriend his town wife in spite of "the natural disposition of plain, unlettered farmers" to shy away from "the quality," but Evelina shuns them. Unappreciative of their crude country humor but lacking a genuine lady's ability to move gracefully in any social milieu, Evelina repels everyone with her coldness. Moreover, her "irregular hours of retiring and rising, her dilatoriness in attending her meals, her continued complaints of indisposition, deranged all the regulations of the family, and begat such confusion in the household, that even the elder Mrs. Baldwin occasionally lost her equanimity." Everyone is overjoyed when Evelina decides to return to the city a week early.[48]

Settled at last in a comfortable house in the city, George's spirits revive in the hope that the responsibility of managing a household will reform Evelina, but it is a role that she rejects completely. Not only does she give her keys, the veritable symbol of matriarchal authority in a plantation household, to their shiftless cook, Evelina refuses to discipline Aunt Clary for fear of hurting the woman's feelings when a rash of wretched meals, idleness, insolence, and theft follows. Recalling her lack of respect for his family and old neighbors, George considers the "disgusting familiarity" she encourages from her servants especially galling.

Longstreet accepted slavery when it was regulated by plantation paternalism, but feared the consequences of unleashing the peculiar institution in an urban environment. When slaves were pampered and spoiled by arrogant parvenus like Evelina, the communal solidarity of white society gave way to open class divisions. Thus while the harmony that existed between planter families like the Baldwins and their more humble neighbors can be interpreted as a sign of Longstreet's commitment to middle-class, democratic principles, it is better understood as a reflection of traditional hierarchical arrangements in the southern countryside. When Evelina's father goes bankrupt after a bad cotton investment, the "charming creature" momentarily changes her ways, but her true nature soon prevails. When she relapses into her old habits, George drinks himself to death. The narrator blames George's death on his mother-in-law's improper upbringing of her daughter, a lightly veiled condemnation of the moral laxness Longstreet associated with the North's commercial society.

Longstreet addressed the domestic relations between masters and slaves in greater detail in "The Mother and Her Child," a sketch with a hard racist edge that communicates a measure of ambiguity in his paternalistic outlook. In the sketch, the narrator Baldwin goes to visit Mr. Slang, whose wife has a child that is around eight months old. When the baby, who is being tended in an adjoining room by a servant named Rose, begins to cry, Mrs. Slang tells her to "quiet that Child!" When the baby continues to fuss, Mrs. Slang threatens Rose, telling her to "fetch him to me, you good-for-nothing hussy you." Baldwin recalls that "as Rose delivered the child, she gave visible signs of dodging just as the child left her arms; and, that she might not be disappointed, Mrs. Slang gave her a box, in which there seemed to be no anger mixed at all, and which Rose received *as a matter of course,* without ever changing countenance under it."[49]

Pressing the child to her bosom and rocking it backward and forward, Mrs. Slang tries to comfort the child. Although her initial tone is less than friendly ("Muddins will whippy ole nassy Yosey. Ah! You old uggy Yosey!"), Mrs. Slang's behavior toward Rose takes a turn for the worse when a dose of paregoric fails to calm the distraught infant. When Rose repeatedly denies accusations of mistreatment, her mistress thunders, "You lie, you slut," and renders her "*a passing slap.*" Fortunately, the source of discomfort is discovered—a small feather lodged in the baby's right ear under his cap—before Mrs. Slang can do further bodily harm to her befuddled nursemaid. In the narrator's words, "The cause removed, the child soon changed its tears to smiles, greatly to the delight of all, and none more than to Rose." As a realist, Longstreet did not balk at revealing the troublesome relations of southern slaveholding households, but as a conservative one of his primary missions was to defend the peculiar institution.[50]

Although his sermons against gambling, drinking, and violence often work against the literary effect of his sketches, Longstreet's call for moral reform and rejection of the false society of towns and cities for the simple virtues of country life were part of a formula for preparing the South for the challenges that lay ahead. Restoration of the republican politics of deference that had existed prior to the advent of Jacksonian democracy was the second line in his defense against the threat growing in the North to the southern way of life. Calhoun Democrats and Whigs in Georgia parted company in their respective commitments to state's rights and national unity, but they shared a mutual animosity toward popular democracy and the presumed excesses of Jacksonian politics. In a story that first appeared in the Augusta *Mirror* in 1838, Longstreet revealed that he also distrusted the political scruples of the common man. In "Darby, the Politician," Longstreet tells the story of an unqualified blacksmith who gets elected to the legislature. Without openly identifying Old Hickory as the cause, the story clearly condemns the popular turmoil unleashed by Jacksonian democracy's challenge to the politics of deference in Georgia.[51]

Seeking an easier life for his large family, Darby Anvil decides to run for office. At a barbecue and shooting match, his fellow common men rally to his campaign against two lawyer-politicians. When the other candidates expose Darby as a scoundrel who earlier had fled Virginia in disgrace, the common men resent the attempt by their social betters to derail Darby's candidacy and elect him anyway. Reelected in the coming years, Darby nonetheless does nothing but drink grog during the recesses between legislative sessions. By voting in unison with his experienced counterpart in the legislature, Darby convinces the voters back home that he is doing a good job of looking out for their best interests. All the while, his lazy slaves, Sambo and Cuffy, are neglecting his property and his once-prosperous blacksmith shop falls into decline, which angers his wife and drives Darby deeper into his cups. Finally unseated, Darby is deserted by his friends and reduced to begging. The obvious lesson of the story is that government was better left in the hands of dedicated, knowledgeable, and independent men of property. Encouraged by Darby's success, worthless candidates had entered political life in every county in Georgia and subsequently passed many bad laws, the impact of which, according to the narrator, would be felt for generations. Longstreet closed the sketch with an appropriate moral, stating that "presumptuous ignorance should be reprimanded with a fearless tongue, its sins should be proclaimed abroad in warning to the people, and all good men should unite their efforts to redeem a State entirely from such influence."[52]

Following in Longstreet's footsteps, William Tappan Thompson also championed the cause of moral and political reform in his humor writings. Although his talent for comic exaggeration did not equal that of his mentor's, Thompson's command of the patois of Middle Georgia was excellent and his epistolary sketches and stories paint a realistic picture of rural life. Born in Ohio in 1812, Thompson went to work for the Philadelphia *Daily Chronicle* in his early teens, probably as a printer's devil. In 1830, he became the private secretary of James D. Westcott, Andrew Jackson's appointee as Secretary of the Florida Territory, and began to read law. Thompson moved to Augusta in 1834 or 1835 and renewed his legal studies while managing Longstreet's printing establishment. When the Seminole War erupted, Thompson enlisted in the Richmond Blues. His militia experiences inspired two sketches entitled "Recollections of the Florida Campaign of 1836" and "John's Alive, or the Bride of a Ghost; Being a True History of True Love." Thompson published both in his literary periodical, the Augusta *Mirror.*[53]

When the *Mirror* merged with a Macon periodical in 1842 to become the *Family Companion and Ladies' Mirror,* Thompson served briefly as co-editor before moving to Madison to edit a weekly entitled the *Southern Miscellany.* Within two years, Thompson had established his reputation as a humorist with his character Major Jones, a rustic farmer and homely philosopher through whom he commented on the customs and quirks of rural life in Middle Georgia. A collection of his Major Jones letters appeared in 1843, and an expanded edition was published the following year under the title *Major Jones's Courtship: Detailed, with Other Scenes, Incidents, and Adventures, in a Series of Letters, by Himself.* A revised edition in 1872 added two Major Jones letters and a series of sketches Thompson had published in periodicals in the late 1840s and early 1850s.[54]

Thompson discovered soon after his move to Madison in 1842 that the surrounding countryside was fertile ground for an aspiring humorist. According to Henry Prentice Miller, Thompson wrote the Major Jones letters to build the *Southern Miscellany*'s circulation, focusing on the "sober-minded middle-class farmers" to entertain his readers. Thompson also shared Longstreet's belief that the South was losing its republican virtue. Thompson's literary career blossomed in the 1840s—the same time that the older South's plantation economy was mired in a long economic depression caused by the rapid expansion into the fertile southwestern cotton frontier. Thus contemporary events seemed to confirm Longstreet's pessimism about the future. As critical as Longstreet of the shallowness of town society, Thompson was a stern moralist who celebrated the simple virtues of rural life. He also believed that individual liberty in the absence of civic responsibility led to licentiousness. Still, Thompson's crackers are a far cry from Longstreet's violent barbarians. In the preface to *Chronicles of Pineville,* he voiced his respect for "a class of good people" who were mostly "brave, generous, honest, and industrious, and withal, possessed of a sturdy patriotism," the vagabond and dissolute being rare exceptions. He seconded Longstreet's prediction that within a few generations education would improve the "happiness and usefulness" of the American backwoodsman, polishing away his peculiarities in the process. In many ways, Thompson was a more effective spokesman for plantation society because his main character symbolized the promise of social mobility through hard work and a good marriage. A rustic slaveholder who had not lost his common touch, Major Jones is no kin to Ransy Sniffle and "ring-tailed roarers" like Simon Suggs and Sut Lovingood in the southern humor tradition.[55]

Thompson published his first Major Jones letter in the *Family Companion and Ladies' Mirror* in 1842. The sketch centers on the return of Miss Mary Stallins to Pineville from the Female College in Macon and the Major's decision to pay her a call. Both live on adjacent plantations with their widowed mothers. The humor in the letter is derived from the town/country contrast between the Major's rustic manners and Miss Mary's ladylike demeanor. At one point, for example, the Major mistakenly interprets Mary's discussion of her course of study at the Female College as reference to her beaus, "Matthew Matix, Nat. Filosofy, Al. Geber, [and] Retric Stronomy." After nearly a year of finishing school, Mary is no longer the tomboy who used to go fishing and picking huckleberries with the boys. The evening's courtship comes to an abrupt end when the Major, who is a copious chewer of tobacco, extinguishes the fire with a voluminous expectoration of juice and beats a hasty retreat in the darkness. When Mary returns in the first of the *Southern Miscellany* letters, Major Jones has sworn off tobacco for literature. Exposed to the beneficial influence of domesticity, the rough-edged Major begins his gradual ascent in polite society.[56]

Jones's military title reflects his election to the command of a militia battalion, which is the subject of the third letter. When a battalion muster rolls around, the Major purchases a pair of high-legged boots, a "shaperdebraw" with red feathers, a blue regimental coat trimmed with gold, and a "pair of yeller britches of the finest kind" in preparation for the occasion. To keep his new uniform unsoiled during the ride from his plantation to Pineville, he decides not to try it on beforehand:

> Well, when I went to put 'em on, I couldn't help but cuss all the tailors and shoemakers in Georgia. In the first place, my britches like to busted and wouldn't reach more'n half way to my jacket, then it tuck two niggers and a pint of soap to git my boots on; and my coat had tail enuff for a bed-quilt, and stood rite strait out behind like a fan-tail pidgin—it wouldn't hang rite no how you could pull it.

Neither his horse nor the drunken country boys are much impressed with his fantastic regalia. When he finally gets his battalion marched out into a field, the arrival of candidates for the legislature politicking for votes results in a brawl in the ranks.[57]

In an era when a military title was a requisite for success in both national political parties, a satirical reading of the letter is tempting. Given his disdain for excessive display, one suspects that Thompson felt a bit uncomfortable when Whig candidates for high office applied Jacksonian symbols to their own purposes, although he undoubtedly recognized the value of martial images in American popular politics. Unfortunately, Thompson never returned to a military theme in the Major Jones series, although his earlier sketches in the Augusta *Mirror* had shown much promise in the area. It seems plausible that Thompson concluded that the topic did not appeal to female readers—the increasing frequency of domestic themes in his sketches suggests an awareness that women constituted a major portion of his audience and reflected the central ideological role assigned to the household in plantation society. Unlike Longstreet's tendency toward misogyny in his portrayal of women, Thompson's female characters are as a rule quite appealing. Sin is primarily the preserve of male dandies, phony Yankee adventurers, and drunkards. When Major Jones attends Mary's examinations at the Female College, he even concludes that the intellectual capabilities of women equal those of men. Indicative of the emerging role of the plantation lady in the South's ideological framework, Thompson saw women as the potential source of a great moral revolution. Like Longstreet, Thompson thought of the household as woman's rightful sphere, which is why he linked domesticity with social reform.

In characteristic Whiggish fashion, Major Jones also argues that education had little to offer many common men, concluding that "there's some men whose nateral smartness helps 'em along first rate, some what takes a mighty site of skoolin, and some that all the education in the world wouldn't do no manner of good—they'd be nateral fools any way you could fix it." Moreover, when Major Jones is called upon to deliver an oration at a celebration on the Fourth of July, he takes advantage of the occasion to contrast the virtue of the nation's Revolutionary forefathers with the widespread corruption of contemporary political affairs. The speech is a direct assault on Jacksonian democracy by an uncommon common man:

> Is we carryin out the great principles of our Ansisters? . . . Can any man look over our country, and see the pride, the meanery, the rascality, the corruption, the foppery, the monkeyism, the treachery, the dissipation, and the tetotal disregard for morality, religion, and virtuous principles, that characterizes the people of our day, and say Yes to these questions? No, feller citizens, he cannot. The truth can't be disguised . . . our boasted republicanism is fast fadin away—our free and glorious institutions is fast sinkin into contempt—our laws is set at defiance by bad men of every grade, and instead of givin evidence to the world of man's fitness for self-government, we is exhibitin the most melancholy proofs of his weakness, corruption, and perfidy.[58]

Continuing his jeremiad, Major Jones expresses his contempt for President Tyler, the spoils system, the "vulgarity and blackgardism" of the American Congress, the nation's worthless navy, the disgraceful conduct of the army during the Seminole War, the plundering of the treasury by thousands of defaulters in the preceding decade, and the reports every week in newspapers of murders, robberies, "and all manner of rascalities." Voicing a theme that runs throughout *Major Jones's Courtship,* the Major asks the crowd, "Do you think, if one of them plain old broad-brimmed, strait-collered, knee-buckled republicans was to come back, he could recognize his countrymen in the starched up, soap-locked, high-heeled, sickly-lookin dandys of the present day?"[59]

Major Jones concludes his speech by inviting the ladies to step forward and help to restore the nation's purity in the same way that the "Pineville Temperance Club" had driven liquor from public meetings, one of the few moral improvements that Thompson acknowledged over the past. By refusing to marry drunkards and avoiding the company of "squirts and dandies," the ladies would "bring every thing strate in no time." To massive cheers, Major Jones proclaims: "If *they* thinks more of a good character than they does of riches, who's gwine to sell his character for money? If they upholds virtue, who's gwine to dare to make game of religion? This is the proper field for the exercise of wimmin's influence."[60]

To be sure, most of the Major Jones letters are less blatantly polemical and deal with such themes as a coon hunt, a ride on a new railroad, the food at the Planter's Hotel in Madison, the trouble and confusion caused by the move into town from the plantation each winter, and the joys of hog-killing time, pulling "lasses" candy, and Christmas. In one respect, Thompson's humor sketches have more in common with postbellum local color writers than many antebellum humorists. Because he shunned the ribaldry, outrageous earthiness, wild exaggeration, and supernatural elements common in the southern humor genre, Thompson's letters and sketches are more likely to inspire genteel chuckles than raucous laughter. Like Longstreet, Thompson considered the humor sketch a vehicle for delivering moral lessons in a world detached from its moorings and feared the corrupting power of unrestrained materialism. Also like Longstreet, Thompson believed that maintaining the integrity of the rural household was essential if the South hoped to survive difficult times with its republican principles intact.[61]

Thompson expressed his views symbolically through the marriage of Major Jones and Mary Stallins. When both families move from their plantations to Pineville for the winter, Major Jones soon encounters competition from a slick northerner named Mr. Crotchett, a music teacher out to snare a rich, propertied wife. Under Crotchett's spell, many of the town girls had convinced their families to rush out and buy pianos, although Old

Miss Stallins rejects such extravagance during "these hard times." When a man posts notices offering a reward for his capture, Crotchett skips town when it is revealed that he is really a barber and a fugitive thief who had abandoned his family to avoid being sent to "Sing Song Penitentiary." To the Major's relief, Mary later confesses that she had been using Crotchett to test him, but her mother draws the appropriate lesson about training one's daughters for polite society. As the Major explains, "She ses she's gwine to keep a titer rein on her galls after this—and if given 'em complishments is gwine to make 'em take up with every dandy barber what comes bout town, they won't git no more college larnin—that they won't." The implicit message in the union that follows between the polished Mary Stallins and the rustic Major Jones is that the South's best hope of maintaining its integrity was through unity between planters, small slaveholders, and yeoman farmers, rather than risking marriage with the commercial North.[62]

Thompson made much the same point in "The Runaway Match; or, How the Schoolmaster Married a Fortune," a sketch that first appeared in the *Spirit of the Times* in 1848. In the story, an old Yankee schoolmaster arrives in Pineville in 1838 and starts courting "every gall in the settlement whose father had twenty niggers," but leaves town in a hurry when he is tricked instead into marrying "one of the blackest nigger wenches in Georgia." Slaves appear so infrequently in Thompson's early sketches that some readers might have found it difficult to draw conclusions about his views on slavery beyond his obvious acceptance of the institution as an integral part of southern life. Thompson and Longstreet apparently reached the conclusion that slavery was such an ideologically charged topic in the 1830s and the early 1840s that it was best to marginalize the topic rather than risk offending readers, although neither felt any qualms about peppering their humor with blatantly racist stereotypes. Always referred to as "niggers" in the parlance of Major Jones to show his rusticity, Thompson's slave characters never progress beyond minor roles for comic effect.[63]

The 1844 edition of *Major Jones's Courtship* ends with the birth to the proud couple of a son named Henry Clay, whose name expresses Thompson's Whiggish belief that wise statesmanship must be coupled with domestic harmony to preserve the South's identity in a changing world. Internal reform was the third leg in Thompson's literary platform for republican revitalization. He saw many things in antebellum Georgia that needed reform, including shiftless farmers, Sabbath-breakers, hypocrites and bullies, marriage for social gain rather than love, unscrupulous lawyers, Yankee scoundrels, and horse racing, to name but a few. Like Longstreet, however, his favorite target for reform was drunkenness.[64]

In *Georgia Scenes,* Longstreet had expressed his hope that drunkenness would soon "be unknown in our highly favored country" but admitted that "the monster still struggles, and stings, and poisons, with deadly effect, in many parts of our wide spread territory." It was Longstreet's desire that drunkenness would be "driven entirely, from the higher walks of life at least, if not from all grades of society" within ten years, a dream symbolically realized in Thompson's 1839 story "The Duel," a sketch in which an alcoholic planter is scared into sobriety in a fake duel. Thompson made it clear that demon alcohol recognized no class distinctions in "Man-with-the-Poker; or, How Sam Odum Come to Join the Temperance Society," a story he published in the *Spirit of the Times* in 1847. The first tailor in Pineville, Sam Odum was an industrious and fair-minded artisan, but one prone to long drunks. In fact, "Sometimes he would git so bad off that he would have to have the doctor to him for several days; and when he would git over his crazy spell, it would be a week before he could do any thing, and before he would look natural out of his eyes." Finally, a terrible night in the top of a sweetgum tree that nearly kills him makes Sam swear off drinking and join the local Temperance Society. Perhaps more than any other theme, Thompson's moral crusade against alcoholism reveals that literary reformers were still looking inward in the late 1840s in their search for ways to make plantation society more secure, while simultaneously moving toward a more spirited public defense of slavery.[65]

One literary character with roots in Georgia's antebellum humor tradition who escaped the moral outlook shared by Longstreet and Thompson was the nefarious Simon Suggs, a creation of the robust imagination of Johnson Jones Hooper. Hooper was the offspring of a distinguished North Carolina family of modest means. Joining his brother in Alabama in the mid-1830s, Hooper briefly tried his hand at a legal career before assuming the editorship of a country newspaper in 1842, employment that he found more suitable to his literary ambitions. He is justly remembered for his character Simon Suggs, a seemingly conscienceless confidence man, incorrigible scoundrel, and astute judge of human nature who lived by the motto "It is good to be shifty in a new country."[66]

What is sometimes overlooked is that Simon Suggs was a native of Middle Georgia, the son of a slaveholding farmer and hardshell Baptist preacher. First published by the humorist William T. Porter in his 1843 anthology, *The Big Bear of Arkansas, and Other Tales,* Hooper's story, "How Simon Suggs 'Raised Jack.' A Georgia story—By an Alabamian," speaks to the lure of the lawless frontier to young men on the make. Although the Reverend Jedidiah Suggs had tried to rear his sons "according to the strictest requisition of the moral law," Simon had contrived at an early age "to contract all the coarse vices incident to such a region," including fighting his mother's roosters at the local grocery, entering his father's plough horses in races, pitching dollars, and cheating at various games of chance.[67]

The story revolves around the seventeen-year-old Simon's skill with cards and his understanding of his father's true character as a hypocrite driven by false pride and greed. A rather simple-minded old man who thinks himself superior to his lesser-traveled neighbors because he but not they has been to Augusta, the elder Suggs proves an easy mark for his quick-witted son, who has no respect whatsoever for familial bonds when they interfere with his plans to escape the drudgery of the farm for more exciting places. One afternoon while his brother dutifully works in the field, Simon entertains himself by fleecing a young slave named Bill at cards. Upon seeing his father approaching some sixty yards in the distance, Simon quickly pockets the money over Bill's objections, wisely shifting his attention to finding a way out of the seemingly inevitable beating at hand. As he tells Bill, "May be daddy don't know, *right down sure,* what we've been doin'. Let's try him with a lie—twon't hurt no way—let's tell him we've been playin' mumble-peg."[68]

"Compelled to submit to this inequitable adjustment of his claim of a share of the stakes," Bill foolishly enlists in Simon's scheme to dodge the Reverend's wrath, who bellows loudly upon his arrival: "Soho! youngsters!—*you* in the fence-corner and the *crop* in the grass! What saith the Scriptur', Simon? 'Go to the ant, thou sluggard,' and so forth and so on. What in the round creation of the yearth have you and that nigger been a-doin?" Cool as a cucumber, Simon replies that they had only been wasting a little time playing mumble-peg, a game that consisted of bending over on one's knees and pulling a stick from the ground with one's teeth.[69]

When Bill haplessly lets Simon trick him into demonstrating the game, his "breeches and hide" are exposed to a merciless blow from his master's hickory stick, which knocks him into Simon and dislodges a well-concealed card. Though slow-witted, the Reverend realizes that the "oudacious little hellions" have been "throwing" cards and marches the lads off to "the Mulberry," the designated "scene of all formal punishment administered during work hours in the field." Simon watches with "painful interest" while his card partner is "strung up a-tiptoe to a limb" and flogged brutally.[70]

Reckoning that he is not strong enough to overpower both his father and brother, Simon decides shrewdly to risk it all on a game of chance, determined to turn certain defeat into a victorious escape in grand style to the Alabama frontier. When his turn comes for correction, Simon tells his father that giving him a beating would be a waste of time because he intended to make his living playing cards regardless. Underestimating his son's adroitness with a deck, the Reverend tries to shame Simon by calling him "a poor ignunt creetur" who would starve in a week if turned off his land.[71]

Simon's insight into his father's true character ultimately delivers him from the old preacher's patriarchal tyranny. He lures the Reverend into a game of cutting jack by wagering nearly eleven dollars in silver coin against a whipping and a pony. Simon's father takes the bet after making his son promise to tell everyone that he gave him the money if he lost, proclaiming that "it's agin nater, Simon; thar a'n't a man in Augusty, nor on top of the yearth, that kin do it!" True to his own nature, Simon takes quick advantage of the old hypocrite. The Reverend's clumsy efforts to stack the deck are to no avail, for Simon outcheats him and cuts the jack of hearts. Significantly, Simon realizes that flight is the only alternative to hypocrisy. To remain he would have to disguise his true roguish nature because plantation society was beginning to enforce more rigid standards of behavior in Middle Georgia by the mid-1830s. In contrast to Longstreet and Thompson, Hooper believed that the maturation of plantation society placed limitations upon the common man's freedom and social mobility. His story suggests that the window of opportunity for the next generation among the Georgia yeomanry was closing unless one took to the frontier.[72]

The link between the Georgia humor tradition and plantation society is illustrated by the literary career of John Basil Lamar. Born in Milledgeville in 1812, Lamar was a substantial planter with holdings in thirteen Georgia counties and Florida who made his primary residence near Macon. Brother-in-law to Howell Cobb, he served in the Georgia legislature from 1837 to 1838 and in the Seminole War in Florida in 1840. Elected as a Democrat to Congress in 1842, he soon resigned his seat because he disliked politics. Highly literate and well-traveled, Lamar supported secession, joined the Confederate army, and was killed in the Battle of Crampton's Gap in Maryland in September 1862. Lamar's known literary canon consists of six sketches. T. A. Burke was greatly impressed with Lamar's talent and included "The 'Experience' of the Blacksmith of the Mountain Pass" and the title sketch in his 1851 anthology of backwoods humor entitled *Polly Peablossom's Wedding.*[73]

"Polly Peablossom's Wedding" is a brief tale of a comic wedding that celebrates egalitarianism on the Georgia frontier. When Parson Gympsey fails to appear on time for the wedding of Miss Polly Peablossom and George Washington Hodgkins, the wedding party stalls for time by having the wedding dance first, seeing no reason to waste good fiddle music. Having sent his son out in search of the parson, Captain Peablossom regales the men with tales of his exploits in the Indian campaigns, the young boys amuse themselves by scuffling about, and the women preen and fuss. When the wedding party finally learns that the good Parson Gympsey had cut his leg to the bone while digging a new horse trough, the quick-thinking father-of-the-bride recalls that a newly elected magistrate, Squire Tompkins, can perform the service, although much to the dismay of the bride's mother, who insists that back in North Carolina the better sort always used a parson. His Georgia pride aroused, Captain Peablossom snorts: "Better sort of people, is it? *Quality,* eh! Who the devil's better than we are? An't we honest? An't we raised our children decent, and learned them how to read, write, and cipher? An't I *fou't* under Newnan and Floyd for the country? Why, darn it! we are the *very best* sort of people. Stuff! nonsense! The wedding shall go on."[74]

Like Longstreet and Thompson, Lamar was troubled by the decline of republican virtue on the fringes of plantation districts. The dilemma as defined by classically educated Christian men was how to maintain social harmony while striking the proper balance between moral rectitude, personal acquisitiveness, and civic responsibility. His often-repeated story "The 'Experience' of the Blacksmith of the Mountain Pass" recounts the religious conversion of a proud, free-thinking, mountain artisan at the hands of a sturdy Methodist circuit rider. Like Simms, Lamar viewed evangelical religion as the primary means of bringing order to the frontier. Moreover, evangelical religion added stability to plantation society by forging bonds of community between black belt planters and the yeomanry in the upcountry, wiregrass, and mountain regions. That Georgians had arrived at a transition point in history is hinted at by the story's locale in the "entrance to one of those gorges, or gaps, in the great Appalachian chain of mountains."[75]

Ned Forgeron, the blacksmith of the mountain pass, is no ordinary man.

Independent, handsome, and at the peak of his development, he possesses great strength and courage but has become something of a bully over the years. Having enjoyed "very few early advantages of elementary education," Ned nonetheless takes pride in being "a sort of political antiquary" and self-taught authority on Jefferson and Madison. As such, Folgeron is a man of some importance in county political affairs. More troublesome is his fondness for *radical* republican ideas in conflict with the more conservative republicanism of plantation society, an important indication of the limitations of the egalitarianism celebrated in "Polly Peablossom's Wedding." In the words of the narrator, "why he had treasured up an old and well thumbed copy of Paine's 'Age of Reason,' and affected skepticism as to the veracity of the story of Jonah and the whale, and Balaam and his ass, would be hard accounting for, unless it proceeded from the desire of a character for singularity and erudition."[76]

In addition, Folgeron had acquired a passionate aversion to preachers of the gospel, whom he considers hypocritical scoundrels. Upon learning that a preacher in Tennessee had ridiculed him in a sermon, he had vowed to "whip every Methodist preacher that passed the gap" to revenge the insult. That Ned is a man of his word is soon testified to by "the bruised features of many of John Wesley's disciples." Ultimately, however, Folgeron meets his match when the portly Reverend Mr. Stubbleworth is reassigned during the annual conference of the church from his circuit in the pine barrens to the mountain district.

When Stubbleworth finally arrives at the mountain pass, the blacksmith delivers an ultimatum to quit preaching, profess allegiance to Thomas Paine, and curse Methodism, or take a beating. To Folgeron's astonishment, it is he who takes a beating and is forced to quit molesting Methodist preachers. Thus vanquished, he agrees to come hear Stubbleworth preach at the Pumpkinvine Creek meeting house the next day and makes a "promise to seek religion, day and night." Moreover, the circuit rider commands Ned to "tear up Mr. Paine's *testament,* and turn your thoughts on high." The process of conversion thus initiated, the blacksmith undergoes a metamorphosis that culminates in his joyful rebirth at a camp meeting and testimony at a love feast. A happy man at last, he becomes a Methodist preacher himself.[77]

Read as a simple story of faith, Lamar's story has great appeal, which probably accounts for much of the tale's popularity among other authors. That Lamar portrays the pine barrens and mountains as beyond the borders of plantation society is significant, as was his conclusion that evangelical religion, the so-called true community, was the only force that could transform and bind the hinterlands to a higher order. A shared regional heritage and strong commitment to personal honor contributes to the free-thinking mountaineer's conversion and compels him to become an agent of Christian civilization when bested in combat. It is pivotal to remember, however, that slavery had shattered the unity of the Methodist Church several years before Lamar's story reached a national audience in 1851. Following the lead of evangelical ministers, many Georgia authors had already assumed a more active proslavery stance. While this trend is not evident in "The 'Experience' of the Blacksmith of the Mountain Pass," the denouement of Lamar's story does speak to the growing literary awareness in Georgia of the desirability of maintaining regional solidarity in response to the rising tide of antislavery criticism.

The ideological outlook found in Longstreet, Thompson, and Lamar is also evident in the work of lesser-known backwoods humorists. The lawlessness and debauchery of the frontier remained topics of interest, but with the maturation of plantation society, many Georgia authors followed Longstreet's example and affixed moral disclaimers to their tales. This literary appeasement of polite society is evident in several sketches in T. A. Burke's anthology *Polly Peablossom's Wedding,* including the editor's sketch, "A Losing Game of Poker; or, The Gambler Outwitted." In this sketch Burke captures the confusion and excitement of court week in rural Georgia villages, a time of celebration when folks of all ages, black and white, crowded the streets to enjoy a brief respite from work. As the author explains, court week was as much an occasion to violate as administer the law, generating as much gambling and drinking as justice because the officers of the law seldom enforced statutes to the contrary.[78]

The story revolves around a gambler's scheme to swindle a man out of the proceeds of a land sale. Because his intended mark is wary of playing poker with him, the gambler brings a lawyer into the scam. The gambler's plan is to get the rube drunk at the local grocery, lure him to the table, and have him witness the lawyer win a prearranged pot, a ruse that works like a charm. After the lawyer leaves the game, the mark sits down at the table and is promptly bilked out of a small fortune. But when the gambler later meets with his partner in crime to recoup his initial investment, the lawyer refuses to share his winnings, thus cheating the gambler at his own game.

There are several moral warnings delivered in Burke's brief tale, the strongest being that honest folk should not engage in sinful games of chance. While the lawyer's association with a dishonest gambler expresses the traditional rural disdain for town occupations, the narrator also makes it clear that gambling, excessive drinking, and disrespect for the law were no longer the social norm. In other words, fighting, gambling, drunken orgies, and playing pranks on the sheriff were still acceptable literary topics because the moral frame positions such behaviors in the past at a safe distance from contemporary polite society. Unfortunately, this compulsion toward moral didacticism tended to sanitize the sketches written by lesser-known authors as much as it did those written by Longstreet.[79]

Burke's anthology also includes an interesting sketch by a largely forgotten Augusta author by the name of T. W. Lane. Lane's tale "The Thimble Game" is a classic story of the country bumpkin in the city long before the arrival of the railroad and Augusta's growth into the refined "second city" of the state. Like Hooper's Reverend Jedidiah Suggs, the story's hero and his father both suffer from the flaw of excessive self-pride and learn a harsh lesson before returning to the country. Lane captured well the importance of the annual trip by wagon to the city to market the cotton "crap" and lay in a stock of winter necessities, explaining to his readers that to "the honest yeomanry of forty years ago, Augusta was looked upon as Paris and London are now viewed by us." Like the Reverend Suggs, many felt superior to their neighbors after a trip to the city, an experience Lane suggested was in truth more akin to partaking of forbidden fruit than drinking from the font of wisdom. As such, his story can be read as a tale of man's carnal nature after the fall, in this case the "Gimblet-man" playing the role of the snake:

> These annual trips were *the event* and *era* of the year, and the farmer returned to his home, big with importance and news. The dishonesty and shrewdness of "them Gimblit fellers," (CottonBuyers,) the extortions of hotel-keepers, the singular failures of warehouse steelyards to make cotton-bales weigh as much in Augusta as at home, the elegant apparel of the city belles and beaux, and the sights and scenes which greeted their astonished gaze, formed the year's staple of conversation and discussion.[80]

Named for his father, Peter Wilkins is the favorite of the settlement and a young man of experience who has been to Augusta sixteen times. After fleecing a Yankee in a horse-swap, he also has acquired the reputation of a sharp trader. Yet when he takes lightly his father's warning about the dangers of the city, Peter plays into the hands of the cotton buyer, who quickly cons him out of over four hundred dollars in a shell game. That knowledge alone is no protection in the sinful city becomes clear when Peter's father sets out for "Augusty" with another wagonload of cotton, determined to get his "munny" back from the "theavin' rascal" or have him jailed. Like his son, however, he cannot resist the temptation of the game. Lane then delivered the moral of the story, explaining, "Not only did Peter learn from his adventure in Augusta, the evils of betting, but ever since the time to which we have alluded, he always allows his factor to sell his cotton for him." Once again, plantation society triumphs over the wicked city.[81]

Although they admired the rugged independence and egalitarianism associated with life in the backcountry, Georgia's antebellum humorists were first and foremost spokesmen for a maturing plantation society that became increasingly oligarchic rather than democratic. Middle class only in the sense that most were town professionals who stood between wealthy planters and the yeoman majority in the social order, Georgia authors shared the ideological vision of the slaveholding elite. One need not posit conspiracy to see the process of ideological communication at work because men born and reared in a society dominated by plantation slavery after 1830 absorbed the ethos of their era, which emphasized law and order, correct moral behavior reinforced by evangelical religion, and elite leadership over popular democracy. Many Georgia humorists condemned aristocratic ostentation as socially divisive, but they understood the function of egalitarian rhetoric in a slaveholding republic. Thus while Major Jones speaks the dialect of the common folk of Middle Georgia, it was the patrician leadership of the late eighteenth century that captured the political imagination of William Tappan Thompson and Augustus Baldwin Longstreet.

When the war of empire with Mexico in 1846 reopened the prospect of adding vast new western territories to the public domain, Georgia authors rose to the challenge when the subsequent attacks on slavery reached a fever pitch. Previously, literary contempt for the North had been vented through stereotypical portrayals of Yankees as thieving scoundrels, while slaves had been assigned only minor roles in Georgia fiction. Indicative of the growing sectional crisis, slavery began to overshadow other literary themes. Having whetted his appetite for rhetorical combat during the earlier breakup of the Methodist Church over slavery, Augustus Baldwin Longstreet authored a defense of slavery under the pseudonym "Georgia" in a series of letters written in 1847 for *The Western Continent,* a Baltimore journal edited by William Tappan Thompson.[82]

Voicing his remarks directly to "sister" Massachusetts, Longstreet explained that Georgia had initially resisted slavery until South Carolina convinced her otherwise. "Indeed," he wrote, "the prevailing opinion of the whole family at that time was, that it was a mercy to the African race to bring them, even as slaves, from the miseries of their own country, to this." After Georgia's "reluctant" consent to allow slavery, "you and mother Britannia" had filled her ports, fields, and houses "with these unfortunate beings." "Kidnapped" by "man-stealers" in Africa, the first slaves carried "your blood and our mother's blood in their veins; but not a drop of mine." Speaking of the condition of the slaves upon their arrival, "Georgia" stated that "I have often seen my children weep over these wretched victims of Yankee avarice, while yours drove their trades, with all the same self-sufficiency, pertness, humor and disgusting suppleness, which marks the character of your Pedlars at the present day." Although the North must bear the blunt of the responsibility for introducing slavery to the United States, the burden of guilt did not rest on her shoulders alone: "That my children, in purchasing slaves from yours, delivered them from the most cruel bondage that man ever groaned under, is most true—that there was pity and compassion on the side of the producers, and none on the side of the vendors, is equally true; but for these things I give them no credit, because selfishness and not humanity urged them to the traffic."[83]

Positing paternalism as the only practical alternative to abolition in the absence of repatriation to Africa, Longstreet argued in a second letter that it would be sinful to set the old and helpless young adrift in a harsh world. In his third letter, Longstreet called for the extension of the geographical scope of slavery, which he stated would lessen the proportion of blacks to whites. Because each white man would own fewer slaves, "the better he will treat them—the certainly will he instruct them, and the more ready will he be to emancipate them." Returning to the meliorist arguments of the 1820s, Longstreet stated that extending the area of slavery and the number of slaveholders would lead to "closer intimacy," a warmer regard for slaves, and lessen the pecuniary sacrifice of educating and improving a slaveholder's dependents. Stating that "every body knows that the man who owns but three slaves, treats them better than does the man who owns fifty or a hundred," Longstreet argued that if the existing slave population could be redistributed at a ration of three to one slaveholder, "every man in the country" would free his slaves and "give them a start in the world." Each slaveholder was only awaiting "the moment that he could supply their places with white servants." "For verily, sister," he continued, "most of my children are just as sick of them as you are of their masters, and their masters are of you."[84]

The next year William Tappan Thompson brought Major Jones into the fray. Apparently, the antislavery tone of many traveler narratives had convinced Thompson that it was time to fight fire with fire. Speaking as Major Jones in the preface, Thompson extended an invitation to his audience:

> Readers, do you feel like gwine on a jurny to the north! If you do, jest take a seat with me, and I'll carry you from Pineville to Quebeck, and back agin in a little or no time. I don't know as I can offer quite sich inducements to travelers, as is offered by some of the pop'lar *writers* of the day; but if I can't promise you sich elegant style nor sich instructive and entertainin gossip by the way, I can carry you over the route as cheap as most of 'em, and with as little danger to your *morals.*

In a series of letters that follows, Major Jones recounts his adventures during a tour of the North in 1845, although for our purposes the most interesting letters are those written before he leaves Georgia.[85]

Major Jones informs his readers in his first letter from Pineville that because of the success of *Major Jones's Courtship,* he had decided to take Mary and little Henry Clay for a visit to the big cities of the North before cotton picking time. Although the crop was laid by and he had "a first-rate overseer to take care of the plantation," Major Jones explains that Old Miss Stallins thought the trip a waste of money and "wouldn't give a thrippence to see all the bominable Yankees in the world." He also remarks that they were planning to take Prissy to help care for the baby:

> I never did see sich a proud nigger before in all my life as she is 'bout gwine to the north. The galls has been makin some new frocks for her, and Mary ses she really does believe the creeter's head is turned; for she can't stand still long enuff to try 'em on. She don't think of nothing else but carryin her little massy Harry 'bout New York to look at the stores, and she's promised every nigger on the plantation to bring 'em sumthing from the north.[86]

The next letter begins with the major voicing his disappointment because his plans for taking Mary and the baby have fallen through. The previous night they had held a party to say goodbye to the neighbors. Unfortunately, old Mr. Mountgomery had warned Mary against taking Prissy along, telling the major "haint you got no better sense than to think of takin sich a valuable nigger as that with you, to have her fall into the hands of them infernal abolitionists?" Her eyes as big as "sassers," Prissy had asked in return, "Why Massa Gummery! . . . um wouldn't trouble me if I was long—a' Massa Joe, would dey?" To her dismay, Mr. Mountgomery had responded, "To be sure they would, nigger! . . . they'd take you whether you was willin or not, in spite of yer Massa Joe, or anybody else." Though Mary had remarked that "Prissy wouldn't leave us on no account—she knows as well as anybody when she's well treated," the damage had been done. Too scared to go, Prissy had exclaimed "den I aint gwine to no New York, for dem pison ole bobolitionists for cotch me."[87]

Next Old Miss Stallins had asked whether or not there was a law against stealing slaves, to which Mr. Mountgomery had exclaimed "Law! . . . bless you, no! They've sold all ther niggers long ago, and got the money for 'em—so the law don't care whose niggers they steal." At that point, Mary had refused to go on the trip without Prissy on hand to help care for the baby. When Mountgomery suggested in response that she could arrange for a servant in the North, Mary had exclaimed, "What! . . . trust my child with one of them good-for-nuthin free niggers?" When Mountgomery replied that he meant white servants, Old Miss Stallins had vetoed the notion, proclaiming "Goodness gracious! . . . white servants! Well, the Lord knows I wouldn't have none of 'em 'bout me." Mary had seconded her mother's view: "Nor me neither. . . . It may do well enuff for people what don't know the difference between niggers and white folks; but I could never bear to see a white gall toatin my child about, and waitin on me like a nigger. It would hurt my conscience to keep anybody 'bout me in that condition, who was as white and as good as me." Recalling the entire incident with anger, Major Jones informs his readers that "I never thought of them bominable abolitionists before, and I never was so oudaciously put out with 'em. It was enough to make a man what wasn't principled agin swearin, cus like a trooper."[88]

When Mountgomery explained further to Mary that the white servants had been "brung up to it," Mary had responded in classic *herrenvolk* fashion, "Well, . . . the more sin to them that brings 'em up to be servants. A servant, to be any account as a servant, is got to have a different kind of a spirit from other people; and anybody that would make a nigger of a white child, because it was pore, hain't got no Christian principle in 'em." Standing by principle, Mary had asserted that "niggers is niggers, and white folks is white folks, and I couldn't bear to see neither of 'em out of their proper place." Though disappointed to see his plans unravel, Major Jones had decided that it was too late to back out and elected to go north alone. In a significant afterthought, he addended the following to his letter to Mr. Thompson:

> Prissy's raised a perfect panick 'mong the niggers on the plantation 'bout the abolitionists. Pore creetur, her hart's almost broke cause she can't go to the north with her misses and little massa Harry; and I do blieve she's as fraid of the abolitionists as she is of the very old Nick himself. You ought to hear some of the niggers' descriptions of 'em. When Prissy told old Ned what Mr. Mountgomery sed—how they carried off all the niggers they could kotch, and put 'em in jail so they couldn't never go back to ther white folks, ses he to her—"Ki, gall, youna no tell dis nigger nuffin bout dem cattle; cus 'em, me hear old massa tell bout 'em fore you born. Aligator aint no suckemstance to 'em. 'Em got horns like billy-gote, and big red eyes like ball ob fire; and 'em got grate long forkit tail like sea-sarpent, and jes kotch up pore nigger, same like me hook 'em trout. Ugh, chile, dey wusser'n collerymorbus."[89]

Writing from "Augusty" in his third letter, the major describes the subsequent excitement generated by his preparations to leave the plantation for his trip northward. Naturally, Prissy warns "Massa Joe" not to "let none of dem bobolitionists kotch you." As he was making his final farewells to Mary, little Harry, Old Miss Stallins, and his slaves, the major recounts how "one of the little niggers" had rushed up to deliver a message from Aunt Moma telling him to "cum da!" As the major explains to his readers: "Pore old Moma was the fust nigger my father ever owned. She's more'n a hundred years old now, and her hed's as white as the cotton she use' to pick for us when she was a gall. She's been monstrous porely this winter, and hain't been able to go out of her little house in the yard, whar she's lived ever sense she was too old to do anything on the plantation." The faithful old servant scolds him for going away without saying good-bye to the woman "what use to nuss you, when you was leetle baby like leetle massa Harry." Predicting accurately that she would not survive her master's absence, she concludes by saying, "Pore ole Moma, lib too long—make trouble for white fokes; but Moma's time mose come." The emotional farewell to Moma is important because it establishes the major's paternalistic relationship with his slaves, a reference point from which Thompson expected readers to judge subsequent descriptions of conditions in the North.[90]

Parodying traveler descriptions of the city, Major Jones describes Augusta as "a monstrous pretty city" but informs his readers that "it ain't the place it used to was, not by a grate site." In particular, "the market-houses what a few years ago you couldn't hardly see for the wagons, looks more like pretty considerable large martin-boxes standin in the middle of the grate wide street, than places of bisness." Concluding his description of hard times with a warning, Major Jones observes that "the fact is, if the people of Georgia don't take to makin homespun and sich truck for themselves, and quit their everlastin fuss 'bout the tariff and free trade, the fust thing they'll know, the best part of their popilation will be gone to the new States, and what'll be left won't be able to raise cotton enuff to pay for what they'll have to buy from the North."[91]

In the Major Jones letters that follow from the North, Thompson relies upon the traditional pastoral device of the rube in the city to anchor the humor in his observations about northern society. Pretty much adhering to a standard proslavery line, Major Jones defends the South while denouncing abolitionist sentiment wherever he encounters it. Thompson was nonetheless Whiggish enough to admire "Yankee inventive ingenuity" and "the material progress of America." In the words of Herbert P. Shippey, "When he returns home to Georgia, the Major concludes his travel letters by praising Northerners for their patriotism and intelligence and criticizing them for not minding their own business." Glad to be home from his travels, Major Jones concludes by observing that "I've seed the northern people, in ther cities, in ther towns and in the country, and though I've got a good deal better opinion of 'em sense I've been among 'em a little, than I had afore, still I say, give me old Georgia yet."[92]

Thompson retained enough of his commitment to the Union to end his indictment of the meddling North on a positive note. That one Georgia writer had already begun contemplating separation from the North became evident when David L. Roath published a long allegorical poem entitled *Zara: A Romance* in 1851. Roath believed that the untrammeled avarice of northern bankers and speculators in an emerging machine age would despoil the rural South if left uncontested, although he found no fault in the honest pursuit of wealth. He dramatized the power of technology to accelerate movement through time to suggest a world no longer in harmony with nature, wondering if the inventor understood the forces he had unleashed:

Oh, Robert Fulton! mighty man of steam!
The power to Time unconquerable foe—
That levels mountains, roars above the stream,
And draws to light the riches hid below.
I'd like to ask you, did you ever dream
What you were bringing all the people to?[93]

In contrast stood the harmony of an agrarian life. Admitting that laziness often disgraced southern homesteads, Roath still saw great magic in the ability of careful husbandry to reap the bounties of nature:

The spacious barns were filled with ripened grain,
The ample recompense of daily toil;
The heart rejoiced as eye swept o'er the plain,
At growing product of the fertile soil;
The tasselled corn, the lofty waving cane,
Of our old mother earth the righteous spoil;
A sight would gladden any human creature,
Was that fair spot upon the face of nature.

Roath revealed in the next stanza that such riches were the product of slave labor:

And ever and anon the ploughman's song,
The greatest evidence of careless heart,
Was heard, as joyfully he passed along,
Performing truly his allotted part;
There entered in his mind no thought of wrong—
All unacquainted he with secret art,
Or any art at all, unless 'twas heeling,
When fearful of discovery in stealing.

Fields of grazing cattle and sheep and fowls of all description tended by "a respectable old nigger lady" complete his idyllic picture of the plantation, a charmed life of abundance, joy, and independence:

I like the farmer's life above all others—
The happiest since his round old Time began;
The feelings of his heart he never smothers—
He is your only independent man.[94]

The heroine of the romance is a beautiful, dark-eyed maiden who lives in a cottage on the Savannah River with her ancient mother. Named Zara Green but known as Sally, she is a good country girl of little formal education who is skilled in the household arts, so rich and appealing that men are driven to suicide when she ignores their advances. But Zara, who represents the South, is waiting for true love, knowing full well that her "two hundred niggers," two hundred thousand dollars in the bank, and miles of the choicest quality cotton land makes her an enormous prize on the marriage market. Driven not by the desire for material gain and viewing money only as giving "To life's dark picture the shade brighter side," Zara has unusual common sense, shuns "grin-provoking airs," gaudy dresses, and all pretense, and knows that none among the "ardent crowd" desire her for herself alone.[95]

The scene then shifts to Manhattan, "The First among the Cities of the Free!" Roark portrayed the city as a conglomeration of all the worst and best in life, a mighty "Babel of the West" where joy, luxury, and vice abound. Here lives Zara's corrupt older brother, Mr. Richard Green, who has made his living for the last thirty years as a ruthless moneylender. Mr. Green lives alone with his rum-soaked old housekeeper, who is nearly deaf and dumb and suffers from rheumatism, a lightly veiled comment on the North's treatment of servants. That he represents the North is also revealed by his lust for gold:

> His bride was money—'twas for that he strove
> With all the ardor that another knows,
> Who in prospective has the kiss of love,
> As to the rendezvous he gaily goes.
> Earth's concentrated beauty could not move
> One who like him his every effort throws
> Into that strife whose cares cannot be told—
> The soul-intoxicating, eager strife for gold.[96]

Together with a handsome young poseur named Count Mustache, an escaped felon of common birth, banker Green hatches a plot to defraud his sister of her riches and honor after he loses heavily in the crash of the "Humbug bank." His plan is to lure Zara to Manhattan, arrange for the charming Count Mustache to seduce her into a hasty marriage, and then divide her fortune between them. By promising to take her to see Niagara Falls and possibly Europe, he convinces his sister to accompany him to

New York. Zara and her mother prepare a huge feast to celebrate Green's return to Georgia. It has been twenty years since they were together, but Green quickly abandons his nearly blind mother, a possible allusion to the South's feeling of betrayal by the North. Although both regions shared the same cradle of liberty, the South stood in danger of being plundered and dishonored.[97]

Green repairs his cold, bleak mansion to set the stage properly, restoring some of the splendor lost during years of neglect while he ruthlessly pursued gold for gold's sake, rather than the good life that wealth should bring. He fires his drunken housekeeper, hires a new cook, and buys new carpets and mirrors, all to hide his financial distress from his unsophisticated sister. Of course, the romantic young country girl is initially dazzled:

> At everything she wonder'd in simplicity,
> That would have made a city lady laugh,
> Who ne'er had tasted of the true felicity,
> That Zara in the country used to quaff.[98]

Deeming Zara ripe for the picking, Green holds a great ball in her honor, the greatest ever seen in Manhattan. As planned, the Count stands out among her potential suitors because of his grace and gaudy gallantry. All the men flock to Zara, the true queen of the ball. Her natural radiance outshines the city's most beautiful women, all on glittering display in their finest jewels. Yet when Count Mustache tries to make Zara his love slave, she is not fooled:

> She knew that something was beneath a mask,
> She saw the knowing looks exchanged with Green.

Instead, Zara's attention is drawn to a handsome but somewhat seedily dressed young stranger named Charles Porcupine. This being a romance, it is love at first sight for both. The next morning over a late breakfast Green remembers back to a time long ago when unrequited love had closed his heart to all women. Still scheming, he confesses his troubles to Zara but she refuses to marry Count Mustache, determined to keep her virtue intact. Beyond all hope for redemption, Green and the Count attempt an abduction that fails and Zara and Charles live happily ever after.[99]

Too little is known about Roark to tease out all of the hidden meanings in his allegorical romance, but the underlying message seems simple enough. How much longer could the virtuous plantation South remain in familial union with a corrupt and avaricious kinsman without being plundered and dishonored? That Roark concluded his poem with a happy ending reflects standard romantic usage and quite possibly the momentary easing of sectional animosity in the aftermath of the Compromise of 1850. Nevertheless, the tension between the pastoral ideal of plantation society and decadent urban capitalism is the most memorable ideological message conveyed by *Zara.*

In 1853, Francis James Robinson published a collection of seven humor sketches entitled *Kups of Kauphy: A Georgia Book in Warp and Woof.* Little is known about Robinson except that he was a country doctor and newspaper writer who was born around 1820. Fiercely partisan toward the South before the Civil War, Robinson supported Rufus Bullock and the Republican Party during Reconstruction and apparently died in Oglethorpe County in 1870. Several of the sketches in *Kups of Kauphy* show the influence of Longstreet and Thompson in theme, setting, and dialect. Nor was Robinson above exploiting "darky" stereotypes for racist comic effect. Where Robinson broke with tradition was in making an eccentric black waiter the central character in a sketch.[100]

Although it is impossible to determine whether "'Old Jack' C——." was written in direct response to Harriet Beecher Stowe's *Uncle Tom's Cabin,* it is ironic that it had taken the escalation of ideological conflict over slavery to breathe life into an African American character in a Georgia humor sketch. Modeled on a real waiter who had become something of a local legend at a Madison hotel, Old Jack is an appealing character in spite of his obvious propaganda value as a symbol of the benevolence of slavery. Like his postbellum counterpart Uncle Remus, Old Jack is an archetype, or "one of a thousand" among a supposedly unexceptional slave population. Like Brer Rabbit, he is also a gifted trickster and a most remarkable natural man who is easily the match of whites foolish enough to test his native wit or provoke his wrath, although Robinson attributed his strength of character to the old man's ready acceptance of his assigned station in plantation society.[101]

Robinson also incorporated a lengthy proslavery argument into the frame of the sketch. Proclaiming it his duty as "a Southern man" to defend "patriarchal slavery" in the face of "the vilest slanders" being spread by abolitionist leaders, Robinson voiced his determination to bring the truth to the "nine-tenths of the foes of slavery" who had blindly joined their false crusade. Even if "Yankydom" would "not yield us the possession of higher and better motives," Robinson maintained that self-interest alone dictated proper attention to the care of slave property. Willing to "admit isolated cases of inhumanity," he nonetheless dismissed such acts as "reprehensible exceptions which no one views with greater detestation and abhorrence" than the slaveholders themselves. Beyond "pocket-nerve" considerations, there existed "a family tie created between master and slave, a bond which death does not even always dissolve!" Such bonds extended from generation to generation:

> We have often witnessed the exultation of an aged slave at the good fortune of "young massa," who in his infancy may have slept in her bosom and drawn the nourishment that sustained his infantile existence from the same fountain as did her own child, or again weep over the misfortunes of a young mistress, whose footsteps as she "toddled about" were directed by the same kind and faithful hand! Do these facts make slavery a curse? God forbid.

The South, Robinson informed his readers, stood willing to grant to the foes of slavery "the prejudices of education," but claimed as a constitutional guarantee the right "TO BE LET ALONE!" If granted her just rights, "the sunny South, in her characteristic generous spirit" would continue to "affiliate in kindly brotherhood with her Northern fellow-citizens," and thereby "perpetuate and preserve intact the glorious liberties we now enjoy." [102]

The publication in 1852 of Harriet Beecher Stowe's novel *Uncle Tom's Cabin* had an enormous impact on the southern literary imagination, inspiring spirited defenses of slavery well into the next century. One of the first ideological responses to Stowe in southern fiction came in 1854 when Caroline Lee Hentz published a domestic romance entitled *The Planter's Northern Bride.* A transplanted New Englander who spent many years roaming the South with her husband, Hentz was a prolific writer who remained widely popular until the turn of the century. Set in an unnamed Georgia town in a plantation district, the novel challenged Stowe's portrayal of slavery by contrasting the comfortable condition of slaves with the harsh life of northern laborers. Hostile northerners convert to the South's cause after seeing plantation paternalism firsthand. Though the next chapter includes a closer examination of the narrative, it will suffice for the present to note that her domestic romance works better as propaganda.[103]

Second perhaps only to *Uncle Tom's Cabin,* the fugitive slave narratives were among the most powerful weapons in the antislavery movement's literary arsenal. While not fiction per se, the fugitive slave narratives were undoubtedly dismissed as such by the majority of white southern readers. In particular, John Brown's *Slave Life in Georgia,* with its potent blend of sensational revelations of brutality and torture, accurate descriptions of farming practices, and free labor propaganda, delivered one of the most damning indictments of paternalism ever written, one that bluntly repudiates the benevolence outlined in *The Planter's Northern Bride.* Known as Fed or Benford in slavery prior to his escape and eventual migration to England, John Brown was an illiterate carpenter who dictated his memoirs to Louis Alexis Charmerovzow, Secretary of the British and Foreign Anti-Slavery Society. Published in London in 1855, *Slave Life in Georgia* shows Chamerovzow's strong influence, but it is the voice of a supposedly inarticulate man that gives the narrative its force and authenticity.[104]

Born in rural Virginia, Brown spent his early youth in North Carolina. When he was around ten years old, he was separated from his family and marched off to Middle Georgia with a gang of slaves, where he was purchased by a planter named Thomas Stevens whose plantation was near Milledgeville. As remembered by Brown, Stevens was "a poor jobbing carpenter" who had clawed his way into the ranks of the planter class by distilling stolen corn into whiskey. Unaccustomed to field work and heartsick for his mother, Brown endured many terrible beatings from his new master. Fortunately, an older slave who had once been free taught him the ropes and inspired his dreams of freedom.[105]

Brown's memories of his years of slavery in Georgia centered upon the endless suffering that he and his fellow slaves endured at the hands of cruel men. His is a tale of oppression and resistance that includes graphic descriptions of brutal beatings, sadistic punishments, and bizarre medical experiments. As if to counter the impression that parts of Brown's story were so incredible as to invite disbelief, a lengthy description of staple crop cultivation practices was included to lend credence to the rest of the narrative. In addition, Brown's narrative includes a relatively standard abolitionist critique of slave work, dress, housing, diet, and medical care. Of notable interest is Brown's justification of slave theft and the criminal underworld that existed in Middle Georgia. In retrospect, it is hardly surprising that such accounts enraged southern slaveholders.[106]

The last broadside fired by a Georgia humorist in response to attacks in the abolitionist press came in 1860 with the anonymous publication of *The Slaveholder Abroad; or, Billy Buck's Visit, with His Master to England. A Series of Letters from Dr. Pleasant Jones to Major Joseph Jones, of Georgia.* Once thought to have been authored by William Tappan Thompson, *The Slaveholder Abroad* was actually written by Ebenezer Starnes, who served as an associate justice on the Georgia Supreme Court from 1853 to 1856. In an introductory letter addressed to Thompson, Dr. Pleasant Jones explains that he had been in London with his most trusted servant, Buck, when *Uncle Tom's Cabin* appeared in 1852. In a series of letters presumably written during the next two years, he contrasts the suffering, destitution, crime, and abuse of servants in urban-industrial England with the advantages enjoyed by slaves in Georgia. In one of his more humorous scenes, Buck disrupts a meeting of the British and Foreign Anti-Slavery Society with a barrage of ludicrous wisecracks from the audience. Billy Buck is a far cry from Thompson's homespun cracker philosopher, although both share an earthy humor and rustic outlook. Nor does Starnes's literary creation come close to conveying the humanity of Old Jack, although both share a similar political function. The explosive debate over slavery had finally brought a new character to center stage in Georgia's humor tradition, a minstrel in black face whose sole purpose was to defend slavery by ridiculing its enemies.[107]

The final literary volley in the war of words that preceded the actual outbreak of hostilities was delivered by a slave named Harrison Berry, an Atlanta shoemaker whose attack against "fanatical abolitionists" appeared in the interlude between the election of Abraham Lincoln and secession. Modern observers differ widely in their assessments of the authenticity of Berry's *Slavery and Abolitionism, As Viewed by a Georgia Slave.* Most of the text is overtly academic and lacks the personal touch evident in John Brown's slave narrative. For the most part, Berry repeated the standard southern response to the abolitionist threat, emphasizing the biblical and constitutional foundations of slavery, the North's racism, and the hardships of urban-industrial life for the poor and elderly. Labeling abolition a "seven-headed, ten-horned beast" out to destroy the Union, Berry castigated antislavery agitators for bringing down planter anger upon the heads of hapless slaves who had been well treated when their owners felt secure in the possession of their property. He also warned the abolitionists to heed the lesson of Harper's Ferry before it was too late:

> You must recollect, fanatical sirs, that the slave children and their young masters and mistresses, are all raised up together. They suck together, play together, go a hunting together, go a fishing together, go in washing together,

> and, in a great many instances, eat together in the cotton-patch, sing, jump, wrestle, box, fight boy fights, and dance, together; and every other kind of amusement that is calculated to bolt their hearts together when grown up. You had better mind how you come here, and jump aboard of our masters; for I tell you, though we sometimes fight among ourselves, if another man jumps on either, we both pitch into him.[108]

The hard ideological shift in the humor writing of the 1850s reflected the overwhelming impact of the sectional crisis on the literary imagination of antebellum Georgians. In the 1830s and early 1840s, Augustus Baldwin Longstreet and William Tappan Thompson and their fellow humorists had hoped that internal reform and a restoration of the virtue of the early republic would preserve Middle Georgia's distinctive identity and institutions without sacrificing national unity. Ideological spokesmen for a social system that rejected the free labor assumptions of the urban-industrial North, Georgians with literary ambitions fashioned a pastoral defense of the South that revealed the regional and class consciousness of the slaveholding elite. The Georgia humorists initially defined the problem in terms of controlling the internal threat to plantation society symbolized by the frontier and isolating the countryside from the pernicious manners and mores of town society. The escalation of sectional conflict in the 1850s, however, made life more difficult for reformers in the South, especially after the antislavery movement in the North pushed aside or absorbed other reform causes such as temperance and women's rights. After 1850, the reform tradition had little chance of success in Middle Georgia; thereafter polarization ruled the day in the realm of King Cotton. Every agency of cultural expression was enrolled in the defense of plantation slavery as the secession crisis drew near.

CHAPTER THREE

Lay-By Time

Plantation Society and the Literature of Domesticity

One of the fundamental changes wrought by the market revolution that remade the United States from a colonial backwater into an emerging commercial power during the antebellum era was the transformation of domestic relations. Taking root first among the northern entrepreneurial classes, a new middle-class ideology began to take shape that stressed personal autonomy in the work place and every individual's responsibility as a free moral agent. Assuming the role of material provider in the new social order, middle-class fathers sought dominance in the public spheres of work and governance, assigning to their wives primary responsibility as caregivers and moral guardians within the private sphere of the household. Liberated from much of the time-consuming drudgery involved in maintaining a household by servants, whose labor signaled a family's entrance into polite society during the Victorian era, middle-class women in the North forged a distinctive cultural identity within their separate sphere. Infused with the evangelical fervor unleashed by the Second Great Awakening but denied access to the corridors of economic and political power, many woman dedicated their time and energy to the cause of social reform. Equally important for our purposes, women also assumed a major role as consumers and authors in the expanding literary marketplace that emerged during the first half of the nineteenth century.[1]

Yet as Elizabeth Fox-Genovese has shown, domesticity evolved differently in the antebellum South, primarily because the family remained central to the productive relations of plantation and yeoman households alike.

As in the North, the presence of servants in the household signaled a family's entrance into the lower ranks of polite society, but the fact that the domestic help were slaves indicates that the market revolution had committed the South to a fundamentally different road of social development. Their dedication to the cause of social stability and the concomitant necessity of defending the peculiar institution likewise limited the participation of southern women in social reform movements, although temperance provided an acceptable public outlet for evangelical energies. Not surprisingly, the literature of domesticity also acquired a distinctive sectional identity in the South.[2]

In its public identity, the literature of domesticity primarily took the form of the domestic novel. Revealing an "intensely political literary vision" aligned closely with the southern aristocracy, the authors of domestic fiction viewed the women of the slaveholding elite as a vehicle for social regeneration and waged "ideological warfare" in defense of plantation society. In the words of Elizabeth Moss, "the cultural agenda of the southern domestic novel reflected the fundamental conservatism of its readers and writers and their shared belief in the moral superiority of their region; embodying the unique concerns of the slave regime, it struggled to make that world and its values comprehensible to a national audience and, in so doing, brought the ideological underpinnings of the plantation South into sharp relief." The enormous popularity of the genre among American women assured a wide hearing for the proslavery argument.[3]

Writing in direct response to *Uncle Tom's Cabin,* Caroline Lee Hentz published *The Planter's Northern Bride* in 1854. Hentz was a transplanted New Englander who had emigrated with her husband to Cincinnati in 1832, where they both made a living as teachers. Hentz later made her home in Kentucky, North Carolina, Florida, Alabama, and Columbus, Georgia, where she resided when her husband's health failed. Her husband's bad health led Hentz to turn to literature for a livelihood. A prolific author, Hentz remained popular until the end of the century.[4]

In her preface to *The Planter's Northern Bride,* Hentz stated that her northern birth belied the notion that she was compelled by "hostility or prejudice" in her defense of the South from the forces of intolerance and fanaticism. Drawing her reader's attention to "the dark and horrible pictures drawn of slavery and exhibited to a gazing world," Hentz observed that "we have wondered if we were one of those favoured individuals to whom the fair side of life is ever turned, or whether we were created with a moral blindness, incapable of distinguishing its lights and shadows." During her residence in the South, she had "never *witnessed* one scene of cruelty or oppression, never beheld a chain or a manacle, or the infliction of a punishment more severe than parental authority would be justified in applying to filial disobedience or transgression." Instead, she had "been touched and gratified by the exhibition of affectionate kindness and care on one side, and loyal and devoted attachment on the other" and "the cheerfulness and contentment of the slaves, and their usually elastic and buoyant spirits." It was her "honest belief" that "the negroes of the South are the happiest *labouring class* on the face of the globe."[5]

The novel begins by introducing Mr. Russell Moreland, a southern planter who is traveling in New England because of business with one of Boston's "merchant princes." On a fine spring day, Moreland sets out to explore the surrounding countryside with his young mulatto servant Albert, who is handsome, well dressed, and speaks excellent English rather than dialect. The scene shifts to a village inn, where the landlord Mr. Grimby, "a hard repulsive looking man, with a dark, Indian face, and large iron-bound frame," invites Albert to join everyone dining around a common table. Somewhat offended, Moreland calmly instructs Albert to sit down at the table and departs the room. A northern gentleman follows him out and apologizes for the landlord's deliberate attempt at stirring up mischief, explaining that the village is "in the very hot-bed of fanaticism." In response to the gentleman's inquiry regarding the wisdom of bringing his servant into such environs, Moreland, a man of wealth and leisure, replies that he does not fear Albert's susceptibility to antislavery arguments: "If they can bribe him from me, let him go. I brought him far less to minister to my wants than to test his fidelity and affection." Nevertheless, he explains that if Albert fled "the pang would be as severe as if my own brother should lift his hand against me."[6]

Walking down the street, the pair comes upon Nancy Brown, a consumptive who had been turned out by Mr. Grimby when she became too ill to work. Positioned in the narrative to draw a contrast with Albert's robust health and security, Nancy must support her poor old mother but has not received wages for three weeks. Feeling pity, Moreland takes her heavy bundle upon his own shoulder. Addressing her readers directly as the omniscient narrator, Hentz interjected that Nancy had "probably been a faithful labourer" when healthy, but that a wage labor system severed any "claim to affection" that might otherwise exist between an employer and employee. Having paid her regularly for her services, her employer felt no obligation when she became ill and dismissed her to the care of the parish poorhouse, "without incurring the censure of unkindness or injustice." Shifting to Moreland's inner mind, Hentz contrasted the paternal care that sick slaves received under his roof: "It is true, the nominal bondage of the slave was wanting, but there was the bondage of poverty, whose iron chains are heard clanking in every region of God's earth, whose dark links are wrought in the forge of human suffering, eating slowly into the quivering flesh, till they reach and dry up the life-blood of the heart." By comparison, the slave enjoyed a much better life than the "thousand toiling operatives of the northern manufactories" and the free blacks "congregated in the suburbs of some of our modern Babylons." To illustrate further the superiority of personal charity to the public dole, Hentz has Moreland slip the doomed consumptive ten dollars.[7]

Upon returning to his room in the inn, Moreland asks Albert if he had relished his supper, to which Albert replies, "Please, Mars. Russell, don't do that again. I made 'em wait on me this time, but it don't seem right. Besides, I don't feel on an equality with 'em, no way. They are no gentlemen." Albert also relates how the men had called him "a show-boy" whose purpose was to disguise the true horrors of slavery. When his master interrupts the tale by saying that he needed time to think, Albert stretches out on the carpet and sinks immediately into a profound sleep. Stating that Moreland was unafraid to think deeply about the comparative conditions of the world's poor and subservient classes, the narrator observes:

> He did not seek to disguise to himself the evils which were inseparably connected with their condition, or that man too oft abused the power he owned; but in view of all this, in view of the great, commanding truth, that wherever civilized man exists, there is a dividing line of the high and the low, the rich and the poor, the thinking and the labouring, in view of the God-proclaimed fact that "all Creation toileth and groaneth together," and that labour and suffering are the solemn sacraments of life, he believed that the slaves of the South were blest beyond the pallid slaves of Europe, or the anxious, care-worn labourers of the North.[8]

The next morning, Moreland attends church with his new friend Mr. Brooks, an architect on hand in the village to build a bridge. Having sworn off romance after an ugly divorce back in Georgia, Moreland is nonetheless drawn irresistibly to an angelic voice emanating from the choir. The voice belongs to Eulalia Hastings, the universally loved "flower of the village." Unfortunately, Brooks explains, her father is the editor of an antislavery journal entitled the "Emancipator" and a visionary reformer who would not send a consumptive south if it would add ten years to a wife's or child's life. Brooks then relates how Hastings had taken a gigantic black runaway into his home and treated him like a guest, although the man's overbearing and insolent behavior had soon resulted in his eviction.

Shortly thereafter, Mr. Hastings engages Moreland in a public discussion of slavery. When asked if he justified slavery, Moreland replies not if one means the slave trade, which had been forced on the South by the British. Having accepted the responsibility for their unwanted charges, however, Moreland observes that it would be cruel to "cast thousands of helpless, ignorant, reckless beings" onto their own resources or to rely on "the tender mercies" of those who "rave of their injuries" but "hold out no hand to redress them." Rather it was the South's duty to render a slave's "life of servitude" as comfortable and enjoyable as possible. While admittedly reaping the benefits of their labor, masters nursed slaves in sickness, provided for them in old age, and sheltered them from want. Attributing the presence of a few hard masters to human nature and man's universal tendency to abuse power, Moreland argues that even the most degraded slave had it better in the South than Africa, where a worse form of slavery, superstition, blood sacrifices, and even cannibalism reigned. When Hastings responds by stating that such talk of Africa was surely exaggerated and that he would not presume to arraign the Almighty for placing the Negro there, Moreland vanquishes his adversary by trumping his argument with the race card:

> I am astonished that you do not question the justice and mercy of God, in creating this subservient and benighted race, with lineaments so devoid of beauty and grace, and swathing them in a skin, whose hue is the blackness of darkness, making a boundary line between us, as distinct, yea, more distinct than that which severs the noonday from midnight. The mulatto, in whose veins the blood of the white man is flowing and brightening their dusky tide, partakes of the beauty and intelligence of our race,—but take the native African, examine his lineaments, features, and peculiar characteristics, and say if he came from the hands of God in a state of equality with ourselves, endowed with equal physical and intellectual powers, intended for our bosom companions and familiar friends.[9]

To make a long story short, Hastings swallows his pride and eventually relents to the marriage of his daughter to Moreland when both become deathly ill after his initial refusal. Convinced that their love is real and drawn to the social advantages inherent in such a wedding, Hastings consoles himself by envisioning that Eulalia will "go forth as a missionary to bind up the bleeding wounds and smarting stripes of the poor slaves" and "teach their darkened minds the ways of salvation." The night before the wedding Hastings talks to Moreland about his daughter's antipathy toward blacks, recounting how she had been repulsed by the presence of the runaway in their home. Moreland explains that her instincts had been sound because he had discovered that the runaway was a liar who had robbed and tried to murder a kind master. Emotions rise when he also warns Hastings that he should abandon his abolitionist activities before they result in servile insurrection, but the minister intervenes to prevent postponement of the wedding.[10]

After an elegant but simple ceremony, the planter and his northern bride journey south, first by train and then by steamboat. During the course of their travels, Eulalia expresses her fear that she will "make a poor, inefficient mistress" and asks for her husband's guidance. Moreland replies that his slaves will adore her as a mistress because the "negro has an intense appreciation of beauty and grace, and feels the influence of mental superiority." The only thing that he fears as a slaveholder is her repugnance to the African race, which he says she must struggle to overcome. When the conversation turns to her repulsion toward the runaway who had been sheltered by her father, Moreland explains:

> My dear Eulalia, God never intended that you and I should live on *equal* terms with the African. He has created a barrier between his race and ours, which no one can pass over without incurring the ban of society. The white woman who marries a negro, makes herself an outcast, a scorn, a byword. The white man who marries a negress forfeits his position as a gentleman, and is excluded from the social privileges of his brethren. This is the result of an inherent principle of the human breast, entwined, like conscience, with our vitality, and inseparable from it. The most ultra Northern philanthropist dare not contradict this truth. He may advocate amalgamation with his lips, but in his heart, he recoils from it in horror. He would sooner see a son or daughter perish beneath the stroke of the assassin than wedded to an African, whom he professes to look upon as his equal and his friend. Nature has

> marked a dividing line, as distinct as that which separates the beasts of the field, the birds of the air, and the fishes of the sea. And why should any one wish to violate this great law of nature,—this principle of homogeneousness? The negro feels the attraction of his kind, and forms, like ourselves, congenial ties.[11]

When Eulalia asks her husband about the violence inherent in slavery, he replies that "it is an evil which has never yet approached my plantation or household, and never shall, unless necessity lays its iron hand upon me." Rather than explore the obvious opening, Hentz adroitly sidesteps the problem of necessity by having Eulalia proclaim, "Ah! If all masters were like you, slavery would be robbed of its terrors and its gloom." Moreland replies that he is no better than the majority, "perhaps not as good." Although there were bad masters and mistresses, public opinion considered their character "as unnatural and execrable as the cruel and tyrannical parent of the North. There is no such thing as irresponsible power at the South. We are made responsible to man as well as to God, as our tribunals of justice can prove by abundant facts."[12]

At long last the young lovers arrive at his town residence in Georgia, which is located about two day's journey from his plantation. Hentz's description of the house and grounds establishes the pastoral grandeur of plantation society in the mind's eye of the reader:

> It was a large and handsome building, stuccoed and painted in imitation of marble, surrounded by a piazza, supported by massy pillars, which were covered with the same artificial porphyry. A wide passage ran through the centre of the house, opening into the garden through doors of green lattice-work, and making a channel through which waves of fresh air were constantly flowing. The yard in front was laid out in terraces, and semicircular hedges of roses and cape jessamines enclosed two airy and vine-mantled summer-houses, on either side of the avenue. Two lofty oaks, whose gray trunks were twined with dark green ivy, stood as sentinels over these domes of flowers, and gave an air of dignity to the tasteful elegance of the scene. A hedge of cedars, shaven on the top into a kind of table-land, on which the gossamer spread its silvery web, margined the yard, and relieved by its deep, rich verdure, the white paling that surrounded it.

The narrator rounds out the picture by introducing the household, which includes Moreland's sister Ildegerte, a spirited woman with shining black hair and black eyes; her husband Richard Laurens, a pale northern physician who is the victim of hereditary consumption; Moreland's three-year-old daughter Effie, a spoiled elfin "child of indulgence"; Effie's nurse Aunt Kizzie, an exceedingly rotund mammy archetype who has authority over the other servants; and Netty, "a nice, trim-looking mulatto girl."[13]

The next day, Richard, Ildegerte, and her personal servant Crissy depart for Cincinnati in the hopes that Dr. Darley, the physician under whom he had trained, can effect a cure for his consumption. When Moreland elects to ride on horseback alongside his sister's carriage during the first day of the journey, Eulalia is somewhat embarrassed to find that she and Effie are the only whites among the black members of the household. She is also somewhat amazed at the amount of work involved in managing her new household. The narrator proceeds to outline all of the household staff's jobs and responsibilities, which include cooking, picking up wood, toting water from the spring, scrubbing floors, and washing and ironing clothes. In addition to being nurse, Aunt Kizzie is the "plain seamstress" who cuts and makes the slave clothing; Netty is the chambermaid and fine seamstress who makes her master's shirts and Effie's wardrobe; Albert is the valet de chambre and gentleman at large; and Kizzie's Jim is a handyman who does "a little of everything and not much of anything," the implication being that his main job is to keep happy the woman around whom the entire household revolves.[14]

Next the narrator introduces Kizzie's mother, an infirm old woman who lives in her own little cabin. A "kind of *elect lady,* to whom all paid respect and reverence," Aunt Dicey is "a simple-hearted, pious old soul, who had been favoured with marvellous revelations from the other world, and thus acquired the influence of a prophetess among her people." The narrator interjects that there was an Aunt Dicey in almost every large household in the South, observing that the old family nurse who had "devoted the vigour of her youth and the energies of her womanhood to her master's interests" looked upon his children "with worshipping tenderness, and dreams that the babes of Paradise are cradled in her dusky arms." Hentz also informed her readers that only a cruel master or mistress imposed a hard task on aged slaves or exposed them to neglect and suffering, bringing melodramatic closure to the scene by observing that "we have seen a whole family drowned in tears by the death-bed of a slave: the head of the strong man bowed on his breast in wordless sorrow, while woman's softer soul *in woe dissolved aloud.*"[15]

The scene shifts to Ohio, the home of Harriet Beecher Stowe, and the hotel where Richard and Ildegerte take lodging for the duration of his treatment by Dr. Darley. Whereas her master and mistress dine in their room because of Richard's illness, Crissy takes her meals in the kitchen with the other servants. Although Crissy resists the antislavery arguments of the kitchen help, whom she considers beneath her station, she cannot resist the free labor arguments of the ultra white Softlys. As Richard sinks closer toward death, Ildegerte is too distracted to recognize Crissy's anxiety and distress over the pending escape that the Softlys have arranged. Having primed her readers by stating in her preface that Crissy's abduction was based on a true incident, Hentz explains that the plan was to send her out on a boat on the Ohio River until the furor over her escape died down, then bring her back into the city. Guilt-ridden about letting down her mistress, Crissy has second thoughts and tries to back out at the last minute but is not strong enough to resist the Softlys and soon finds herself on the river in the cold night air, without wrap or shawl.

Exhausted, Ildegerte falls asleep but is awakened around midnight by the terrible sound of her husband gurgling in his own blood. She calls frantically for Crissy but to no avail; Richard is dying but she is alone. Because the wire to the bell in her room is broken, she must leave him to go get help and rushes into the room of Mrs. Softly. In wild despair, Ildegerte drags Mrs. Softly to Richard's side, who is lying there "all ghastly in his blood." Ildegerte faints when her husband dies, only to awaken in the bed of Mrs. Softly, who denies knowing anything about Crissy's whereabouts. When Ildegerte realizes that Mr. Softly is not around at such an unseemly hour, she puts two and two together, faints again, and takes to her sick bed for weeks. The meddling of the Softlys in another American family's private domestic affairs had caused unmentionable agony for a woman at her hour of greatest need. Exploiting the high melodrama for maximum propaganda effect, Hentz undoubtedly hoped that her readers would blame the abolitionists for making it impossible for southerners to travel through the North, even for medical emergencies. Although it is impossible to assess the full ideological impact of such sentimentalism, there was no mistaking the intentional parallels between her literary technique and that of Harriet Beecher Stowe. By combining such intense melodrama with a fervent plea for Union, Hentz delivered an impassioned ideological rebuttal to Stowe's antislavery message.[16]

The scene shifts back to the Moreland household a few days after Richard and Ildegerte's departure for Cincinnati. Moreland asks Eulalia to go with him to the plantation, where it is cotton-picking time. As they are making their preparations to depart, Russell explains that he had implemented the task system on his plantation because of the African's unique attitudes toward work:

> There is one trait in the negro character of which you may not be conscious. You cannot make them work habitually beyond their strength. You can get a certain amount of labour out of them, and beyond that they will not go. Masters and overseers, having learned this fact from experience, seldom attempt to push them over this boundary. If they do, they meet with an obstinate resistance which coercion never can overcome. This peculiarity is one of the negro's greatest safeguards from the requirements of selfish power. The self-interest of his employer is enlisted on his side, and we all know what a powerful principle it is.

Moreland also informs his northern bride that he had studied the Negro physiologically as well as mentally and morally, and discovered some remarkable characteristics that made him especially suited for labor in a tropical climate: "In the first place, his skull has a hardness and thickness far greater than our own, which defy the arrowy sunbeams of the South. Then his skin, upon minute examination, is very different from ours, in other respects as well as colour. It secretes a far greater quantity of moisture, which, like dew, throws back the heat absorbed by us."[17]

Hentz uses the journey to the plantation to speak directly to traveler accounts of the Georgia backwoods. After Kizzie prepares a feast for their two-day journey to the plantation, and Moreland graciously yields to Eulalia's desire to take Effie and Kizzie along, the happy family bid adieu to the household servants. To increase the comfort of his wife, his sprightly daughter, and the gargantuan Kizzie, Moreland decides to ride on horseback alongside their carriage. To her astonishment, as Eulalia boards the carriage she finds two nice pillows inside and asks Kizzie to remove them. Kizzie explains, "Wait a little, missus, while I tells you the raal reason. When we stops at night, you won't find a pillow-slip fir to scrape your feet on, let alone your honey-sweet face. There ain't no quality folks at the stopping-places, and the piney-woods people have mighty curious ways of doing things, I tell you missus." Because his wife is "not familiar with the phases of backwoods life," Moreland recommends that she defer to Kizzie's judgment about such matters.[18]

Eulalia marvels at the glorious scenery that engulfs her when they enter the forest. By conflating scenes and images gathered during her extensive travels throughout the Southeast into a composite Arcadian landscape, Hentz hoped to counter the dreary descriptions of the backwoods characteristic of the traveler accounts. In a scene more suggestive of the garden of Eden than a primitive wilderness, the enchanted travelers pause to dine at a beautiful spring gushing right out of a rock. Back on the sandy road, their euphoric mood is soon shattered when they encounter a carriage carrying Claudia, whose eyes flash with fiery scorn when they fix upon her former husband. An abrupt change in Claudia's demeanor occurs, however, when she hears Effie and her arms open toward her daughter as the carriages move past one another. Utilizing sentimentalism to drive home a powerful ideological message by discreetly linking the loss of the garden with the possible breakup of the Union, Hentz inserted the scene in her narrative to alert readers to the pain and agony of divorce, a powerful metaphor in an age wedded to the use of familial symbols in all forms of public and private discourse. Enraptured just moments before, Eulalia can only wonder, "Why had this woman come in her dark, splendid, terrible beauty, between her and her happiness?" [19]

That night the weary travelers stop at a log cabin. In a scene reminiscent of Charles Lyell's account of his visit to the Georgia backcountry, Eulalia notices that the cabin's windows have wooden shutters rather than glass. Though the evening is warm, the only source of light is a bright lightwood fire burning in a tumble-down chimney. With the traveler accounts clearly in mind, the narrator describes the master of this small world and his dependents:

> A man, hard-favoured and sun-browned, who had evidently been at work in the field, sat in his shirt-sleeves, smoking a long pipe, in the back door. A woman, nearly as brown as himself, dressed in the coarsest homespun, stood looking out of the front window, while two girls, one about twelve, the other fifteen, with short, thick, coarse brown hair hanging in masses over their eyes, while dark calico sunbonets covered their heads, were peeping over her shoulders. They all appeared very clean and tidy, though rough and uncouth. Their frocks were of a dark indigo colour, and they all wore dark-blue woollen mitts. Why they were so careful of these members, which were of the hue of mahogany, was a mystery, especially the two girls, whose feet were bare as Eve's were in Paradise.[20]

After Kizzie puts Effie to bed in one of the big room's four beds, the scene shifts to the evening's humble repast. The narrator explains that "tumblers and goblets were unknown luxuries to this family of primitive habits. A large dish of bacon and greens, flanked by tremendous hoe-cakes, was the crowning glory of the table. A remnant of a cold sweet-potato pie, and some gingerbread cakes, as large as cheeses, were extra flourishes of gentility, introduced in honour of the guests." Thankful for Kizzie's "home dainties," Eulalia accepts only a cup of milk. When their host comments on the lady's lack of appetite for "such coarse vittles" and recommends that she spend some time in the woods with his girls to improve her appetite, Moreland responds in such a way as not to offend his dignity, observing that while he sometimes envied "the labouring man his keen appetite and sound sleep," they had indulged in a late lunch.[21]

"Well, squire, it's the truth," the farmer responds, proclaiming that he "wouldn't change places with nobody." His formula for happiness and health was hard work and simple living. He and his wife "hain't had a day's sickness, to speak of, since we was married, and the gals are as tough and healthy as all out doors." When Moreland asks about chills and fevers, the farmer replies, "Pho! What's that? We don't call that sickness. Shake a little one day, up and smart as a pipestem the next." The only thing he lacked and wanted was an education for his girls, whom he planned to send to school that year if his crop was good. The farmer observes in good Major Jones fashion that "eddication is a beautiful thing in a woman; it don't matter so much in a man, 'cause he's more natteral smartness; but it does set a woman off mightifully." Eulalia warms to her hosts, particularly "their homely good sense, contentment, and appreciation of each other," but cannot help but notice the girls' advanced age and think of the advantages that would accrue to them in New England, "where the blessings of education are as diffusive as the sunbeams of heaven, gilding the poor and lowly as well as the rich." At this point in the narrative, Hentz makes good use of a major technical advantage the genre of domestic fiction enjoyed over travel literature. Though stereotyped, her backwoods characters effectively neutralize the wooden characterizations of the white common folk found in traveler accounts because the realistic dialogue conveys a stronger sense of their humanity.[22]

"Knowing the early habits of this class of people," Moreland takes Eulalia for a walk to save her the unspeakable embarrassment of intruding upon their bedtime preparations. Hentz uses the walk to make known to her readers a southern version of the road to social mobility. When Eulalia observes that the isolated life in the wilderness must be terribly lonely, her husband replies:

> And so it is; and yet, you see, this life has its own peculiar enjoyments. You must recollect that it is comparatively but a few years since the red man was lord of these woods and plains, and the wild beast made its lair in their shades. This man, energetic and intelligent, is breaking in, as they say, a new portion of the country, and by and by the wild places will show the beauty of cultivation. He has already made money enough to purchase some negroes, who assist him in the field, he being chief workman, as well as overseer. His children, I doubt not, will be rich, and be associated with the magnates of the land. Our social system is like the tree bending over you Eulalia,—its roots, without grace or beauty, are hidden in the earth, from which they derive strength and support; its hardy trunk rises, without ornament, brown and substantial; then the branches extend, green with foliage, and the birds of the air make their nests among the leaflets.[23]

Departing the next morning, the travelers arrive at the plantation just before sunset. "And now for the first time," Eulalia realizes that she is "the wife of a Southern planter." Hentz presents a sweeping panorama of the scene for her readers: "All around, far as the eye could reach, rich, rolling fields of cotton, bearing the downy wealth of the South, stretched out a boundless ocean of green, spotted with white, like the foam of the wave. Long rows of white-washed cabins, extending back of the central building, whose superior style of architecture distinguished it as the master's mansion, exhibited some black sign at every door, to show the colour of the occupants." So Eulalia can "witness a true plantation scene before the duskiness of twilight," Moreland orders the bugle blast to call the workers in early from the fields: "Soon, returning in grand march from the fields, came the negroes, poising on their heads immense baskets, brimming with the light and flaky cotton. Little children, looking very much like walking semi-colons, toddled along, balancing their baskets also, with an air of self-importance and pride." After they deposit their burdens at the gin house, the slaves gather around Moreland. Dismissing the stories about insurrections that cause Eulalia to fear momentarily for her husband's safety, the narrator exclaims, "Safe! Napoleon, in the noonday of his glory, surrounded by the national guard, was not more safe—more honoured or adored."[24]

"More like a father welcomed by his children than a king greeted by his subjects," Moreland stands at the center of "the sable ring," which makes his northern bride feel enormously proud. As Hentz explains to her readers, "An impression of his power, gently used, but still manifest, produced in her that feeling of awe, softened by tenderness, so delicious to the loving trusting heart of woman." Eulalia also realizes that she must assist her husband with the responsibilities of the master, rather than "sit idly in a bower and do nothing for those who were toiling for her." Next they visit the quarter, where Eulalia meets the slaves, including the matriarch of the quarters. Overjoyed that her beloved master has found an appropriate mate, Aunt Dilsy announces to Eulalia: "I've been praying my Hebenly Massa to send him a good wife, good crishen wife, to be his 'zilary in 'nevolence and piety. Now poor Dilsy willing to lay down and neber wake up no more."[25]

Assuming the narrative voice, Hentz returns to the theme of slavery as a blissful life compared to that of northern and European free laborers, much less Russia's forty million slaves. She asks her readers to consider who is really free:

> Are you free? Are we? No! There is a long chain, winding round the whole human race, and though its links be sometimes made of silver and gold, nay, even twined with flowers, it is still chain, and if the spirit struggle for liberation, it will feel the galling and the laceration, as much as if the fetters were of brass or iron. For six thousand years the cry of *freedom* has been going up from the goaded heart of humanity—freedom from the bondage and mystery and necessity of life—and still it rends the heavens and echoes over the earth. And the answer has been, and now is, and ever will be—"Be still, and know that I am God."[26]

In the mysterious great chain of being that linked all of humanity, the closest thing to heaven on earth is the plantation. As she gradually becomes more adept on horseback, Eulalia joins her husband on his rounds around the plantation, which is a paragon of self-sufficiency and progressive management. In addition to a saw-mill and a grist-mill "built on the margin of a roaring stream," there is a blacksmith's shop, a carpenter's shop where furniture for the slaves is constructed, and weaving and spinning rooms where cotton and wool are manufactured into slave clothing. Each slave cabin has its own garden, poultry yard, and melon patch. Moreland is portrayed as a merciful patriarch who sits in judgment of all transgressions reported by the overseer. In addition to paying the slaves for all labor beyond their appointed tasks, he purchases the cotton and corn that they produce for themselves. All have ample spending money, "not being obliged to use one cent of it for the necessities of life." [27]

"It was with reluctance that Eulalia left the plantation," her repugnance and fears toward Africans having been replaced with "the sincerest attachment and the deepest interest." Unfortunately, news from Dr. Darley of Richard's death awaits when they return to town. Moreland's grief turns to anger; he expresses only pity for Crissy but vents his wrath toward cowards who work in stealth to bring harm to his family rather than confront him face to face:

> Great God! What will the end of these things be! What will be the end of unprovoked attack, injustice, and aggression on one side, and exasperated feeling, wounded honour, and disregarded brotherhood on the other! Oh! my wife! my dear wife! If it were not for thee, I would rather rend asunder, with one mighty effort, the ties which bind the South and the North, than live with this burning under-current accumulating strength from a thousand sources, and undermining our institutions, our prosperity and happiness! Perish the body, if the spirit be wanting there! Madness to talk of union, with bitterness and rancor and every evil passion rankling in the heart's core! [28]

Shortly thereafter, a new character enters the story to reinforce Hentz's argument that abolitionism was the snake in the American garden. Posing as a northern minister, Mr. Brainard arrives on the scene, wins the family's confidence and gains access to the Moreland plantation. Hiding behind the cloak of religion, Brainard is treated like a savior by the childlike slaves. When Uncle Paul, the slave preacher, is mesmerized by his portrayal of Africa as a great country rather than a blighted land, the abolitionist works late into the night to win over his new disciple. Not one to unveil all of his designs at once, "He had been strewing a gunpowder train the length and breadth of his journey, and waited the favourable moment to apply the kindling spark and let the blazing track be seen,—a fiery serpent winding through the land!" [29]

Soon Vulcan the blacksmith and others join the conspiracy and the fires of insurrection "began to roar." Less than a fortnight after his arrival on the plantation, Brainard has Vulcan working secretly at night forging crude weapons. The "Satanic Prince" also begins planting the seeds of rebellion at a plantation eight miles away where he preaches on alternate Sundays.

The plot is uncovered at the last minute when two blacks are arrested during a bank robbery orchestrated by Brainard. Accompanied by his family, Moreland rushes to the plantation to save his "poor deluded people." Uncle Paul comes to his senses and intervenes in the nick of time when Vulcan seizes his master in his gigantic arms, although both the blacksmith and Brainard later make good their escape to the North. Order restored, Moreland presents his infant son to his slaves as their new master to restore the paternalistic bonds between his white and black families for generations to come. Rather incredulously given the course of recent events, Hentz explains that "the admiration, love, and devotion which the negro feels for the children of a beloved master, is one of the strongest, most unselfish passions the human heart is capable of cherishing."[30]

Having restored tranquility to his domestic establishment, Moreland takes his family to Massachusetts for a joyful family reunion. To emphasize the point that it was the North's responsibility to silence the voices of fanaticism, Hentz stages a lecture at the Lyceum hall, where Dr. Darley, the wise spokesman for the West, arranges the downfall of the abolitionist Brainard. Exposed by Darley, the villain appeals for help to Mr. Hastings, who still hates slavery but sides with justice and the South. Moreland forgives a repentant Vulcan but refuses to take him back; the penalty for his transgressions is freedom. Hentz draws closure to her long narrative by stating, "We know there are some who will throw aside these pages, with the impression that they give false and exaggerated views of Southern Life; but, with a conviction that a God of truth beholds the lines traced by the hand which He has formed, we give them to the world." Her last word is a warning that the North and the South are "branches of the same parent tree, and the lightning bolt that shivers the one, must scorch and wither the other."[31]

In spite of her desire to eradicate sectional prejudice, Caroline Hentz was a propagandist who ironically accelerated ideological polarization in spite of herself by "politicizing the domestic sphere" in her fiction. Given the centrality of domestic production to the South's economy, she could hardly have done otherwise. Like Augustus Baldwin Longstreet and William Tappan Thompson, Hentz recognized the fundamental importance of defending the moral virtue of plantation society, a concern that also radiates through the private forms of domestic literary expression. Whereas the force of Hentz's narrative was directed outward, the letters and diaries of the planters reveal the inner workings of their lives. Yet in the words of historian Steven M. Stowe, what planters said in private "reappeared in the public rituals that proclaimed their social power."[32]

Unlike other forms of contemporary writing, the literature of intimacy was largely a private concern, although many men and women recognized the public value of their diaries and letters during the bitter postbellum ideological struggle to redefine the South's identity. Most never intended for their private thoughts to be read outside their family circles. Quite often, women kept journals and collected family letters simply to leave a record of their lives for their children and grandchildren, a common way to achieve a measure of immortality in the nineteenth century that also imparted a degree of ideological unity across generations. Though it is unlikely that many were aware of the contributions they were making to the future study of southern culture by describing their family life, work, and religious practices, among other things, journals and letters provide valuable insight into the private and public lives of literate Georgians in the nineteenth century. In particular, the literature of intimacy illuminates what families considered important in their daily lives and how they responded to events at home and abroad that touched their local affairs.[33]

Many women in Georgia also used their journals as tools for self-examination and reflection in their personal search for identity in a patriarchal world. Some treasured the opportunity to speak their minds without worrying about the restrictions polite society imposed on a woman's public discourse, but most accepted and wrote within the formal guidelines of what was considered proper for a lady. In Elizabeth Fox-Genovese's words, the journals kept by southern women "testify to the variety of personalities but invariably betray a sense of self as the product of specific personal and social relations." In antebellum Georgia, literate women were most concerned with their standing before God, their families, and society, although not necessarily in that order. Journals, and to a lesser extent letters, gave individual women a means of measuring their progress against the gender conventions and religious ideals of plantation society and helped them to judge their successes and failures at living according to the dictates of their station in life. It is precisely this pervasive self-concern for the author's place in society that often accounts for the curious lack of intimacy in what is perhaps the most intimate form of literary expression. Husbands and wives were not only reserved in their conduct toward one another in public, most apparently observed formal rules of behavior in private as well, a cultural norm that Hentz captured by having Eulalia address her husband as Moreland rather than Russell.[34]

Women thus held much in reserve in their journals, as if someone were reading over their shoulders. Clearly, a woman's journal was seldom meant to be completely private, although it is uncertain how many husbands read what their wives wrote. Journal writing also functioned as a female rite of passage wherein daughters learned under the guidance of their mothers "to fashion identities in conformity with the expectations of their near kin." For the children of the planter elite, writing letters was considered part of one's social education. Parents well understood the importance of style and proper manners in a hierarchical society and criticized the letters written by their sons and daughters accordingly, while delivering moral and social lessons in letters addressed to their children. Private literary expression thus reinforced the class consciousness of the leading planter families.[35]

Life for the women of the slaveholding elite was shaped by the household concerns associated with plantation production, such as the work rhythms of the seasons and slave management. That they were at the top of the social hierarchy is also evident from their reflections about their educational experiences and marriages, two of the pillars of polite society. In addition, they shared many of the interests, responsibilities, and worries of rural women in general, including religion, sickness and death, and the well-being of their families. Fox-Genovese argues persuasively that the persistence of the household at the center of productive life in the rural South illustrates the pervasive impact of plantation slavery in an age when urban capitalism in the North was redefining the home as a female sphere apart from the "real" world of work. To be sure, farm women throughout the United States were no strangers to hard work during the antebellum period and beyond. Leisure was a by-product of affluence, but few rural women were strangers to the world of work after they came of age. Yet long after the consolidation of industrial, commercial, and financial power in the urbanizing North, slavery and household production continued to delay the South's capitalist development by reinforcing plantation paternalism and isolating yeoman farmers from the transforming power of the commercial market. Contrary to the romantic myth of the idle plantation mistress, the wives of Georgia planters played a vital role in the production of wealth. As Catherine Clinton has observed, in a paternalistic world "many southern women felt a powerful identification with the land." Not surprisingly, the view from the big house looms large in Georgia's literary record.[36]

In spite of the power of the big house as an ideological symbol, it is somewhat difficult to make generalizations about the dwellings of Georgia planters beyond the obvious statement that the vast majority were the central structures in a community of buildings many observers likened to a small village. Many were in a constant stage of development that reflected the growth of families and their rising or falling fortunes. In her old age after the Civil War, Cornelia Jones Pond wrote the following description of her childhood home in Liberty County for her grandchildren:

> My earliest recollection of our plantation home is a house of two stories. Two large rooms were below and two above with lower and upper halls between with two "shedrooms" opening on the back piazza. There was a wide front piazza fronting on a pretty flower garden in the form of a semi-circle. The house was situated in a large grove filled with beautiful trees of native growth: live oaks, red oaks, hickory nuts, cedars, holly, pecans, and persimmons. Upon many the wild jessamine grew and formed beautiful festoons of yellow flowers in the early spring. The gray moss also hung in festoons from the live oaks. Two beautiful large magnolia grandiflora trees were to the right of the house on the side as you drove up.

In the mid-1840s her father built an addition of four large rooms, two above and two below, added four brick pillars to the front porch, and painted the house white and the blinds green.[37]

The planter residence on the coastal plantation where the Yankee schoolteacher Emily Burke was employed in the early 1840s was less substantial, consisting of a tall, one-story house set upon four posts about five feet off the ground, with four rooms below and two in the roof, and two broad porches. In addition to the main residence, which housed the planter and the women of the family, there was a separate house occupied by the steward where the boys also slept, separate houses for the cook, washer-woman, and milk-maid, as well as a kitchen, storehouse, stable, hen-coop, hound kennel, corn-house, and shed for the corn mill. All of the buildings were enclosed by a fence, with the big house situated in the center. Some distance away but within sight of the planter's "watchful and jealous eye" stood the slave quarter and gardens.[38]

One of the most faithful chroniclers of plantation life in the Georgia cotton belt was Dolly Lunt Burge, who was born in Bowdoinham, Maine, in 1817 and was married at the age of twenty-one to Dr. Samuel H. B. Lewis. After she experienced a difficult childbirth in 1841, the family was advised to move to a warmer climate and decided upon Georgia the next year because her younger sister was married to a doctor in Zebulon who accepted her husband as his partner. When a second child died soon after birth in 1843, Dolly began teaching school because of the family's poor financial condition. Her husband then shifted his practice to Madison but died of fever in September of that year; his death was followed six months later by that of their daughter. Finding herself alone in Georgia, Dolly took a job teaching elementary school in Madison. In 1850, she married a widower named Burge who had five children. After a miscarriage, she gave birth to a daughter she nicknamed "Little Sadai," her only child to survive infancy. When Burge died of tuberculosis in 1858, he left his widow a nine-hundred-acre plantation near Covington. Surviving the war and Sherman, the widow Burge married the Reverend William J. Parks for companionship in 1866, moving to his home in Oxford, where he served on the Board of Trustees of Emory College. When Parks died in 1873, she was forced to sell his home in town and returned to the Burge plantation, where she was joined two years later by her widowed daughter and her five children. Outliving her daughter by several years, Dolly finally died of consumption in 1891, having survived three husbands, her children, and several grandchildren. Her diary spans twenty-seven years.[39]

Few sources communicate the distinctive rhythms of the seasons in rural Georgia as effectively as Burge's diary. Prior to the cataclysm of war, there is a sense of timelessness in her journal beyond the seasonal variations in plantation routines. It is easy to lose track of the year while reading her descriptions of the events in her daily life. Seemingly insignificant details only reveal their full importance when viewed within the context of antebellum rural time. Take for example her simple entry for 25 April 1848, "new potatoes for the first time this year," or "Green apple pie, the first this year," written four days later. Both were welcome reminders of the refreshing variety of spring and summer after the often dreary and monotonous country fare in late winter and as such were worthy of recording.[40]

By combining Burge's seasonal diary entries over the years, it is possible to reconstruct the feel of working life on a Georgia cotton plantation. The weather permitting, winters were spent finishing the picking, ginning, and marketing of the cotton crop, killing and processing hogs, cutting wood and splitting fence rails, making necessary repairs, clearing new ground and spreading manure, sewing mattresses and clothing for the household, and settling accounts with servants and merchants. Spring meant plowing the corn and cotton fields, planting a large vegetable garden, sowing corn and cotton, replanting where needed, cultivating the fields, and taking wheat to the mill, as throughout the year. Summer brought more "chopping," or weeding in the cotton fields, and thinning the crop to a stand, then additional cultivation until the crop was "laid by," or tall enough that it no longer needed to be weeded. The reduction of field work released slaves for more plantation repairs, clearing new ground and ditches, building fences, pulling fodder, and cleaning the gin house for the beginning of the harvest in late summer. For the mistress of the plantation summer also brought more sewing, preserving vegetables and fruit, and spiritual and social renewal during revival time. The work of autumn centered around the all-important cotton harvest, bulk buying of supplies such as coffee, sugar, and salt from Augusta for the coming winter, digging potatoes, gathering peas, shucking corn, sowing wheat, and deciding whether to renew the overseer's contract for the next year. The Burges liked to have the year's business completed by Christmas so the plantation household could relax and enjoy the holiday before beginning the cycle anew in January.[41]

Over five decades ago the Georgia-born historian Ulrich B. Phillips began his study *Life and Labor in the Old South* by discussing the weather. Borrowing an old fixture from the proslavery argument and following in the tradition of geographical determinism adhered to by Frederick Jackson Turner, Phillips wrote that the weather had been "the chief agency in making the South distinctive" by fostering the cultivation of staple crops under a system of plantation slavery, a chain of causation that had in turn resulted in a "regional rivalry for power" and ultimately a bold "stroke for independence" by the South. A later generation of historians led by Kenneth M. Stampp challenged his theory of the natural origins of the plantation system as a poorly veiled defense of his native region's racial institutions that denied individual human agency, yet few Georgians in the nineteenth century would have voiced disagreement with the emphasis Phillips placed on the weather. Most rural folks, however, would have seen divine rather than natural forces at work.[42]

Whether they scratched out a living on a hardscrabble farm or enjoyed a relative life of luxury on a thousand rich acres, rural Georgians paid close attention to the weather. Too much or too little rain at the wrong time, a sudden storm, lightning fires, and drastic changes in the temperature could all spell instant disaster. The same day in early April 1851 that her husband began planting his cotton crop, for example, Dolly Burge witnessed a storm such as had "not been known for years," writing in her diary afterward that "it continued during the night, one thunder cloud after another passing over & discharging its watery burden. O such a night." Two months later she wrote that it had not rained in four weeks and the crops were "very much parched." On still another occasion she described a storm that had blown down hundreds of trees and done great damage to the corn and cotton crops. When another tremendous storm interrupted a less than satisfactory sermon by a church elder, Burge worried that the thunder that shook the meeting house was a sign "that our Heavenly father was angry with us."[43]

Perhaps the most memorable account of an antebellum storm was recorded in a pair of letters written by the Reverend Charles C. Jones and his wife Mary to their eldest son describing the impact of a massive hurricane that ravaged coastal Georgia in early September 1854. Unable to take flight like a poor kingfisher he watched struggling valiantly against the wind, the Reverend Jones had little choice but to gather his household together to weather the storm:

> The wind veers northwest. It blows a hurricane! There goes another tree! The top of the grand hickory is off! I was upstairs fastening the windows. A loud jar and explosion below! "What's that?" I rushed down, and a perfect upstir. Both shutters of the two large windows opening into the front piazza, although fastened back, suddenly and at the same moment blown to with a loud report, shivering many panes of glass in each. Your Aunt Abby for a moment much frightened. Servants picking up the glass in both rooms. Rain driving through the broken panes. Waiters, sheets, etc., crammed in and water shut out. All the pride-of-India trees in the front yard down but two. Two of the poplars snapped off. Three locust trees torn up. There goes the old cedar on the lawn! Poor old fellow, riven from top to bottom, split in two. How the wind roars![44]

Nearly every plantation in Liberty County experienced great storm damage, but in the words of Mary Jones, Savannah "suffered beyond description." An epidemic of yellow fever was already "raging with fearful and awful results" when the hurricane hit, blocking the streets with uprooted trees, leveling houses, and casting the city into a "horror of darkness" that lasted several nights. She then lamented, "Only think of the poor sufferers under such circumstances—the sick, the dying, the dead, all shrouded in darkness; not a ray of light with which to administer medicine or to catch the farewell look of affection or perform the last sad offices!" The Jones family felt lucky only to have lost their beloved trees, causeway bridge, and assorted plantation buildings and crops. To the Reverend Jones, the hurricane was both a sign of God's mercy and a rebuke against worshipping temporal possessions, whereas his wife thought it a test of faith, praying, "Oh, that my spiritual house may be founded upon the Everlasting Rock, which neither rain nor storms can beat upon or destroy!"[45]

Reading the vagaries of the weather for signs of the workings of Providence was a natural response among a religious people who lived close to nature, a means of coming to terms with forces beyond their ability to control. Riding out terrible storms together also strengthened plantation households by reinforcing the bonds of mutual obligation. Rural Georgians stood in awe of nature's power to alter their fate at any moment, accepting stoically the problems generated by the weather as part of every farmer's existence. The day-to-day problems of slavery were another matter. Many planter families saw themselves as part of a new covenant, a chosen few singled out by the Almighty to tame the wilderness and bear a unique burden, although it is surprising that more did not sympathize with pharaoh's struggle to tame Moses. The surviving journals and letters of the period hint strongly that discussing the problems of slavery among themselves contributed much to the development of class consciousness within the planter class. Fostering awareness of common problems was the first step to concerted political action by the leading planter families in Georgia. The ties of kinship and culture were strong, but it was slave ownership that defined the identity of the planter class. In many ways their shared experiences trying to control their troublesome property presented an even greater test than storms and floods. The problems of slavery were always present, often quite intimate, and understood as the by-product of a relentless power struggle that always stood ready to disrupt the harmony of every planter household.

Among the seemingly endless problems planter families discussed in their personal correspondence were the impact of slave resistance on productivity, damage resulting from accident, carelessness, or willful intent, slave theft, and abusive overseers, to name but a few. For absentee owners such as Charles Manigault and his son, Louis, slavery was first and foremost a business, at least on their Georgia plantations. Slave resistance, punishment, and overseer behavior were factors inevitably associated with plantation production. It was the elder Manigault's opinion that a planter's profits and reputation hinged more upon careful management than anything else. For resident planters with strong commitments to Christian paternalism and their local communities, slave discipline presented more thorny problems because many took pride in the humane and just treatment of their "people." Dolly Burge, a converted Yankee who developed a close attachment to the slaves on her husband's plantation and considered punishment an unpleasant but necessary duty, faithfully observed the biblical injunction against working on the Sabbath, including cooking. On one occasion, after some of her slaves ruined her enjoyment of the day by pilfering her Sunday dinner, she wrote, "These little cares & perplexities, how they annoy & perplex me." Ella Clanton Thomas, who lived just out of Augusta and was the daughter of one of the state's richest planters, sent her slave, Isabella, to her husband's plantation in Burke County because she could not break her of stealing, writing afterward in her journal, "I have had so many trials with her that with my consent I don't think I shall ever have her for a house servant." Yet because Isabella had been her son's nurse, Thomas was troubled by the disciplinary action she had taken, confessing "that to this girl I have a feeling amounting nearer to attachment than to any servant I ever met with in my life." Her attachment, however, did not prevent Isabella's eventual sale.[46]

For hard-nosed businessmen like Charles Manigault, the sale of a slave was simply the final instrument of labor control. Manigault felt no compulsion against selling a slave who failed to measure up to his expectations in the rice fields or dared to present discipline problems. When a neighboring planter with whom he shared an overseer had problems with high numbers of runaways, Manigault wrote from Paris in 1847 that he never experienced such difficulties because the first sign of trouble on his estate led to an immediate sale. In his words, "I always made it a rule to sell every runaway—and they are fully aware of this, Several having been sent to New Orleans."[47]

Although the ultimate solution remained the same, planters who valued the sanctity of the slave family, such as the Reverend Charles C. Jones, agonized over the moral dilemma presented by separating slave families. After repeated difficulties with a slave named Jane, who had been captured after running away to Savannah and hiring herself out for wages, Jones and his wife decided to sell her whole family. Ironically, their commitment to the integrity of the slave family later resulted in a greater tragedy than had they simply sold Jane. Leaving behind what must be one of the most detailed records of a single slave sale, Jones worked diligently with his son to negotiate the sale to a planter who promised to keep her family intact. A few months later when he sold a mare belonging to Jane's father and settled his plantation account, Jones sent a check for $84.75 to his son to forward from Savannah, with careful instructions to register the letter first. Unexpectedly, his honesty led to a disturbing revelation. Not only had Jane died, the rest of her family was in the hands of a slavetrader in New Orleans. Perhaps needless to say, Jones told his son to hold the check.[48]

The Jones family members expressed outrage at the unexpected outcome of a long and difficult ordeal, but the sale of Jane and her family illustrates that their Christian ideals and the slave system could never be reconciled completely, even though their puritan outlook made it difficult to brook compromises. To be sure, the churches were among the most ardent defenders of the status quo antebellum and most Georgia planters probably suffered less agony in reconciling their religious beliefs and slavery. Yet the Jones family could no more guarantee the sanctity of a single family than they could bring Christianity to the slaves without first muting its fundamental promise of liberation. It is even possible that the Reverend Charles C. Jones's long struggle with a periodically disabling nervous disorder was psychosomatic, the consequence of his inner realization that it was impossible to serve two masters. Such a reading of the evidence would give new meaning to his admonition to his eldest son not to mix his law career with the "management of Negro property."[49]

As Jones learned firsthand, the demands of plantation management taxed the resources of all the adults in the family, including the master's spouse. A plantation mistress was not only expected to oversee the operations of the household, she often acted as her husband's surrogate in his absence, training that ultimately proved invaluable to wives and widows during the Civil War. This is not to glorify the women of the planter elite, for compared to yeoman and slave women they lived in the lap of luxury. Rather it is simply to acknowledge the distance between the myth of the idle plantation mistress and reality, as well as between the elite of fundamentally different social systems. Plantation romancers often drew glowing comparisons between the upper crust in a young slaveholding republic and the aristocracy of Europe that elevated the southern lady to fantastic heights. Yet well-born Europeans would likely have found the notion of a working landed elite more unusual than the mistress of a Georgia plantation. In a letter to her sister, Margaret Hall even expressed her annoyance at "how much time morning visits occupy in this country owing to the bad habit the ladies have of never being ready to receive company."[50]

Unaccustomed to the burden of Victorian fashion codes in the subtropical Georgia climate, Hall also failed to appreciate that even the most affluent plantation mistresses normally had many responsibilities to fulfill before they were ready to receive polite calls from European travelers. Few women in Georgia, for example, stood in higher esteem in society than Mary Jones. In the words of one historian, "No planting community could boast deeper religious convictions, higher intellectual cultivation, gentler social refinement, or greater material wealth" than Liberty County. Together the Reverend Charles C. and Mary Jones owned three plantations totaling more than thirty-five hundred acres and well over one hundred slaves. Known widely as the "Apostle to the Blacks" for his missionary activities among the slaves, the Reverend Jones was also active in the regional and national affairs of the Presbyterian Church. In a letter written in May 1854 to his oldest son, Charles C. Jones Jr., who was studying law at Harvard, the Reverend Jones sketched his wife's daily routine. Rising between half-past five and six o'clock in the morning, Mary Jones began her day by bathing, reading, and preparing for family worship at seven. After breakfasting, overseeing the clean-up of the dining room, and ordering dinner, she put on her sunbonnet and large working gloves and spent nearly two hours in the flower and vegetable gardens keeping a crew of slave boys "as busy as bees" sweeping, watering, weeding, planting, and pruning. Next she took "a walk of observation and superintendence" around the kitchen yard, orchard, and lawn, sometimes accompanied by visiting friends or relations.[51]

Around ten o'clock she came inside and freshened up before making sure that the house was in "perfect order." Jones then set her seamstresses about their appointed tasks, superintending the planning, cutting out, fitting, and sewing necessary to keep the plantation household supplied with clothing, towels, and linens. By the time the yards had been swept, the walks sanded, the family pets fed, and the cook had "her culinary world all in neat order," she was ready to receive guests, or to spend an hour or two reading, writing, or dozing before dinner. After dinner she retired awhile, probably to escape the heat and humidity, reappearing in the middle of the afternoon dressed for the evening, ready to entertain during the social hours. Family worship and quiet time for reading, writing, or conversation brought her day to a close.

The amount of time reserved by Mary Jones in her daily routine for personal enrichment reflected her affluence and possibly the fact that her three children were grown. More typically, plantation mistresses bemoaned in their journals and letters the loss after marriage of the leisure taken for granted during childhood. Overseeing the operations of the household, childcare and instruction, nursing the sick, and tending to one's social obligations were time-consuming responsibilities. Beyond the normal routines of farm life, each season also brought specific tasks that demanded special attention. The postponement of weddings, barbecues, and religious revivals to summer was a concession rural Georgians made to the accelerated work pace of the spring. Yet most farm households learned that the best way to complete important jobs quickly was to blend work with play. Syrup-boilings and candy-pullings, corn-shucking parties, hog-killing feasts, and the Christmas holiday all provided additional incentives to work harder at the precise moment when failure to do so might bring disaster. Such times also placed additional burdens on plantation matriarchs, who seldom neglected their responsibilities. Even when they were making a tour of mineral spring resorts for her husband's health, Mary Jones included detailed instructions in her letters to her daughter at home about managing the household in her absence.[52]

Such training was an integral part of the education of the daughters of the slaveholding elite, just as sons were groomed to fill the shoes of their fathers. With the exception of individuals with rare natural ability, the sons and daughters of the yeomanry received little if any formal education outside the home. For the most part, the limited opportunities available in the professions were monopolized by planters and their sons. Although to a lesser extent than in the North, education did provide a measure of social mobility. But the simple truth was that the plantation system had less need for an educated middle class than the expanding urban industrial North. Mobility existed, but in the South's relatively static society it was considered enough that the sons and daughters of common white farmers follow the vocation of their parents, their labor much too precious to sacrifice to years of schooling. Appalled by the seemingly cavalier attitudes toward education they saw among Georgia planters, Yankee schoolteachers who came South to practice their profession soon found that their bourgeois assumptions about public education were sorely out of place. With the exception of those who married Georgians and modified their beliefs accordingly, most could not comprehend the educational practices of plantation society. Emily Burke, for example, condemned the lack of a system of public education as one of "the many evils that arise from the peculiar institutions of the South," and speculated that planters feared that if all whites were educated, slaves would learn by mimicry and begin making plans for freedom.[53]

Burke also observed that the so-called "free schools" in Georgia were associated in the popular mind with poverty. Rather than submit themselves to public ridicule, many common whites preferred that their children remain uneducated. Whereas in the past only families rich enough to afford private tutors had educated their children, Burke reported that planters in some areas had pooled their resources to fund select schools and academies that often provided an excellent education. In general, however, Burke thought that children in the South were not as advanced educationally as those in the North because they did not start school as early. The only areas where southern children were as strong were the sciences and Bible study. Amelia Akehurst Lines, another teacher from the North who struggled to make a living in Georgia, concluded that "people here can not prize education very highly or they would not take their children from school to put them in the cotton field." Neither was Lines pleased when she found a hickory stick in her schoolroom one morning with its implicit hint "that some of my wild flock needed the benefit of it." Only after she met her future husband while she was teaching at the Southern Masonic Female College in Covington did Lines begin to feel better about her decision to come to Georgia.[54]

In contrast to the critical impressions recorded by northern schoolteachers, the authors of postbellum memoirs looked back with fondness on their early educational experiences. Although his work will be considered in a later chapter, the local color writer Richard Malcolm Johnston's better stories include those which explore his antebellum career as a teacher and schoolmaster. Undoubtedly, the watershed of the Civil War and Reconstruction and the worries and responsibilities of adulthood often made childhood on the old plantation seem a golden age of innocence in retrospect. Unlike letters and journals, however, which enjoy the advantage of immediacy, memoirs are subject to the various distortions that accompany the aging process, such as memory loss and selectivity designed to preserve or enhance the author's reputation. By definition memoirs are also public rather than private documents and are thus more susceptible to direct political influences and uses, especially during times of intense ideological conflict such as occurred in Georgia in the closing decades of the nineteenth century. The efforts of the planter class to reconsolidate its hegemony against the alternatives offered by New South and Populist ideologues made a strong impact on the postbellum literary imagination. By glorifying the old plantation system, postbellum authors were creating an archetype for a new society, even when they saw themselves as simply waxing nostalgic for a lost age.

Bearing all this in mind, postbellum memories of education before the war provide a useful counterbalance to the journals written by Yankee schoolmarms. Cornelia Jones Pond, who was born in Liberty County in 1834, recalled beginning her education at the Jonesville Academy at the age of five. Located four miles from her father's plantation in a village in the pine barrens where her family spent the summers to escape the unhealthy swamp, the Jonesville Academy was a large, one-room school with a chimney at each end, which Pond recalled as being the responsibility of the boys. Her teacher was Samuel McWhir Varnedoe, a successful local planter and graduate of Franklin College in Athens who later served two terms in the state legislature and founded the Valdosta Institute in 1866. Pond remembered Varnedoe as a good teacher but one who relied extensively on the rod to maintain order. The Jones children walked to school from their home a mile away, carrying their lunch in a tin bucket. After her brother enrolled in Franklin College in 1843 and her sister left for a private school in Macon two years later, her mother began sending the son of their cook along to carry her lunch and to "keep the cows off" because Cornelia was afraid of runaway slaves. Always an avid reader and speller, Pond remembered studying algebra, geometry, and Latin when she was eleven, and trigonometry the following year. When she was fifteen, her father enrolled her in the Montpelier Female Institute in Macon, a school operated by Bishop Stephen Elliott, and later transferred her to the Methodist Female College in Madison.[55]

Rebecca Latimer Felton, who grew up on a plantation near the Covington-Decatur Road, also attended the Madison Female College, where she boarded with the school's president and shared first honors when she graduated in the summer of 1852. Felton had begun her formal education in a field school built by her father, Charles Latimer, before transferring to a school operated by a woman in Oxford, Georgia. Later her family had moved into Decatur so she could continue her education at Dr. John S. Wilson's academy. Felton recalled that it had taken her a year and a half to complete the full course at the Madison Female College, which included French, music, and drawing. She met her future husband, Dr. William Felton, when he delivered the commencement address to her graduating class, which consisted of twelve girls.[56]

Like Cornelia Jones Pond, the renowned scientist Joseph LeConte grew up in Liberty County and lived in Jonesville in the summer months. In his autobiography LeConte recalled being influenced by two teachers during his childhood. The first was his father, Louis LeConte, who encouraged his sons to study science and kept a large botanical garden on his plantation on the swampy border of McIntosh County. Joseph attended the nearby country school for nine years and was taught by nine different teachers. The only one he remembered with regard was Alexander H. Stephens, the future vice president of the Confederacy, describing him as a strong moral teacher who enjoyed playing ball with the boys. LeConte also recalled that the bigger boys were allowed to study outdoors unsupervised on nice days and described the schoolhouse as "a mere rough board shanty." In addition to the "three R's," he recalled studying an "extremely simple" curriculum consisting of "Greek, through Xenophon; Latin through Livy; and mathematics, through algebra and geometry." Also like Pond, the LeConte children walked to school and took a cold dinner in a bucket, which was carried by one of the five or six slave boys "whose business it was to cut up wood for the house and the kitchen and to wait on the cook," although the LeContes were the only students favored by such service. LeConte recalled that the yard boys "considered it a great honor to be selected" because the job was easy and they joined in the sports and games during the lunch hour. When he was fifteen LeConte enrolled in Franklin College, where he graduated in 1841.[57]

Together antebellum journals and letters and postbellum memoirs confirm that formal education was largely the preserve of the wealthy. Some careers in commerce or the professions were open to men of humble birth with talent, ambition, and energy as long as they accepted the dominant ethos of plantation society. Because Georgia's commercial life revolved around plantation production and planters monopolized leading positions in the professions, young men on the rise seldom forgot who buttered their bread. In a social system where power and prestige were rooted in ownership of land and slaves, wise fathers directed their sons with professional ambitions into the law and politics, although some considered careers in academia, medicine, and commerce acceptable alternatives. Still, even among the most affluent families the most important institution of learning in antebellum Georgia was the plantation itself. Joseph LeConte wrote that during their childhood he and his brothers had watched all of the operations of his father's plantation with "intensest interest." A planter's sons began their lessons in slave management early by emulating their father and observing his authority in day-to-day action. Their education in the various rituals of deference associated with paternalistic social relations set them apart from other men, making it almost impossible for anyone to misjudge their station in life. Even young men who completed their formal education outside the South and sought their primary livelihood in the towns and cities maintained close ties with the land. After he began his legal career in Savannah, for example, Charles C. Jones Jr. lessened his family's dependence on a factor by acting as its unofficial purchasing agent, a practice he continued during his tenure as mayor of the city, throughout his service with the home guard during the war, and after his law firm relocated in New York City during Reconstruction.[58]

The primary purpose behind the formal education of the women of the planter elite was to refine the skills necessary for easy movement in polite society. Professional careers for women in Georgia's patriarchal society simply did not exist beyond teaching, which was commonly considered beneath the dignity of well-born women before the war. Similar to the relationship between their brothers and fathers, young women learned the fundamentals of household management from their mothers, as well as the art of dressing and behaving like a lady. Letters between mothers and their daughters or between sisters were typically laced with talk of religion, fashion, budding courtships, parties, society gossip, and the latest activities of family, servants, and friends. Planters sent their daughters away to school to finish preparing them for their debut in polite society, which essentially amounted to making one's formal announcement of entry into the marriage market. In the words of Catherine Clinton, "Female academies and seminaries fitted women strictly for their preordained role in plantation culture: that of a well-read elite serving as wives and mothers to the master class."[59]

Outside the planter elite, few women in rural Georgia would have been able to identify with the Augusta childhood of Ella Gertrude Clanton. As described by Nell Irvin Painter, Ella spent her girlhood sleeping late, reading voraciously, visiting friends, dressing prettily, and writing letters. Her father, Turner Clanton, was one of the richest men in the state, his estate valued in 1864 at $2.5 million in Confederate money. Writing in her journal in 1855, the twenty-one-year-old wife and mother described her life following her graduation from Wesleyan Female College in Macon at seventeen. After visiting two resort springs during the summer after her graduation, she had made her debut in society that winter, although there had been no dancing because she was Methodist. Next had come "the great moment in the life of the belle," her courtship by James Jefferson Thomas, a Princeton graduate from a leading Burke County planter family, and their engagement and marriage, which they had celebrated with a summer trip to the North.[60]

Marriage completely reordered the lives of the daughters of the planter elite. Indeed, it is difficult to overemphasize the importance of marriage in plantation society. Marriages were more than the most important social events of the season. Families could be made or broken by a single vow in a system where kinship played a major role in defining one's rank in society. It was not without insight that postbellum writers built many of their stories around the theme of a good or bad marriage. Thus while a marriage was a time of celebration that brought together family and friends from afar, it was also a time of great tension. Young men and women had much more to fear than the loss of the carefree days of their youth because a false step at the altar could result in a total fall from society and even ostracism by one's family. In a hierarchical society based on male property rights, marriage was both a personal and a political act, a contractual union that verified or denied the legitimacy of entire kinship networks and political alliances. Yet historians who stress kinship over class identity in the antebellum South may be overlooking the social barriers that existed within as well as between kinship networks. In both cases marriage served to delineate rank in the social pecking order. The willingness of families to ostracize their young rather than endure public disgrace illustrates the limitations of kinship as a force that transcended class concerns in antebellum society.[61]

Despite the efforts of their mothers to prepare them for the change, matrimony presented new challenges for the daughters of the planter elite. Assisting one's mother or acting as her surrogate now and then was a far cry from assuming complete control of the management of a new household. Mary S. Mallard, the daughter of the Reverend Charles C. and Mary Jones, wrote to a friend in Maryland describing what it was like to be "a novice in the housekeeping art," asking her to "imagine me standing, receipt book in hand, giving direction to one of the colored society, who says she has never cooked for 'white folks' and knows nothing about it!" Although her father had provided her with a fine home and servants, Ella Clanton Thomas had difficulty adjusting to a life of reduced circumstances. Nearly three years into her marriage, she wrote of hiring out most of her sewing because it was a job she disliked, although her mother had to foot the bill because her husband's short crop the year before was forcing them to practice an economy that was "hardly consonant with my nature." Late in life, Rebecca Latimer Felton recalled that after her marriage her "entire life was soon absorbed in home service and home making and the care of my babies and the duties that fell upon the women of my class and kind in caring for a considerable number of slaves and in keeping up the requirements of a plantation home in the country."[62]

Life in a country household could also be a lonely experience for young women accustomed to a more lively social milieu, especially when inclement weather virtually engulfed them in isolation for days at a time. In December 1852, Harriet Alexander wrote to her mother in Washington, Georgia, that "it is a relief to a solitary female, to write trash, when I haven't anybody to talk it to. I write so many letters, that they furnish a safety-valve for all my notions, thoughts and ideas." Some women turned to their journals to vent their creative urges. From her country home located six miles from Augusta, Ella Clanton Thomas wrote in 1855 that "it does indeed seem like one of the quiet joys of memory to again have thee to confide in for with their thoughts filled with busy care, men are not always ready to enter into all those silver threads of feeling, which make up the poetry of life."[63]

Women also turned to their journals in times of hardship. Disease and death were mysterious forces lurking in the shadows that shaped one's perceptions of life from childhood onward. Because both were universal experiences, they brought families and communities together. Neighbors tended to one another's crops and children in times of sickness and came together to bury their dead. The death of a child was an especially grievous experience that few mothers were spared. Margaret Mitchell understood her history well when she placed childbearing at the center of southern female identity in *Gone with the Wind.* The high rate of infantile mortality was also a hard test of a woman's faith in God's benevolence. When her newborn son, Joseph, died less than three weeks after birth, Ella Clanton Thomas wrote the following passage in her journal:

> Now I do indeed begin to know what are the trials of life—Within a few weeks I have become a mother, and last night about half past ten oclock the little treasure which had been loaned me for so short a time, winged its flight to the God who gave it. "The Lord giveth and the Lord taketh away, Blessed be the name of the Lord." But oh it is hard. Nature rebels and turns shudderingly away from the thought that tonight my poor little darling will sleep its first sleep in its grave.[64]

Two years later Thomas was heartbroken again when her six-month-old daughter, Anna Lou, succumbed to a lengthy illness. Four years after the death of her daughter, Susan, Dolly Lunt Lewis remembered the bitterness of that night and expressed her inability to reconcile herself to her loss, asking God's forgiveness for her "selfish feelings" and voicing her desire to join the child in heaven. A year later when she witnessed the death of a neighbor's child from whooping cough and measles, she wrote:

> I spent the night as promised. Child very sick. Called again to-day to it & witnessed its departure to the Land of Spirits. Innocent Lamb, by the merits of Christ ye are prepared for the joys of Heaven. We should not wish to call them back to the sins & strife of life. Better that they were folded in the fold of Christ and secure from every danger. But I know well how to sympathize with the distressed & bereaved parents.[65]

Nor were children spared the agonies of dealing with the death of a loved one or neighbor. A child's first funeral could be a traumatic affair even when it occurred outside the family. Rebecca Latimer Felton recalled in her eighties that the sight of neighbors preparing the coffin of a woman had filled her "with an awful dread that my mother might die, too." Felton remembered vividly how the thought of the woman's orphaned children had brought her to the brink of hysteria in the graveyard when the first clods of dirt fell on the coffin. Small wonder that well into his adulthood, the death of a servant triggered severe anxiety in the Reverend Charles C. Jones, or that reports of illness and death even outside the family left Jones and his wife profoundly concerned for the spiritual readiness of their eldest son. A year without sickness or death in the family was perceived as a remarkable blessing and a sign "of mercies undeserved." Much more than the weather, the intimacy and universality of sickness and death made the power and presence of God real to rural Georgians. Yet as tragic as was the death of a loved one or neighbor, life on the land continued. Death and illness were hard but accepted parts of the natural flow of rural existence. People grieved and the memories of lost loved ones lingered but the demands of the land remained.[66]

This is not to suggest that work overrode all other considerations in the Georgia countryside or that people only turned to God in hard times. Still, plantation and yeoman households were large and the margin of error in the annual cycle of work small. Undoubtedly, some individuals succumbed to their grief but most remained mindful of their responsibilities in the networks of dependency that characterized rural life because to do otherwise brought more suffering to others. Georgians turned to God to sustain them through times of sorrow, but they also celebrated their Christianity in their daily lives and on special occasions. People interpret the world with the forms of symbolic expression that have acquired legitimacy in their particular social environments. For the majority of literate Georgians in plantation society, Christianity provided the primary language of identity. Religious values and beliefs permeated the politics, social relations, and forms of cultural expression in plantation society.

The grounding of religion in material reality is evident in the impact the abolitionist movement made on plantation society. By defining slavery as antithetical to Christianity, abolitionists struck at the moral center of southern identity, turning the language of communion to conflict when both sides turned to the Bible to justify their positions. That the churches were among the first institutions to polarize along sectional lines is direct evidence of the power of material concerns to foster ideological division among people who share the same religious heritage. Yet delineating the precise relations between religion and power within the plantation system is more difficult. Clearly, religion acted as an agent of accommodation and resistance in master-slave relations. It is less clear how evangelical Christianity created communal bonds that transcended class divisions in a hierarchical society, or how the egalitarianism of evangelical religion resulted in deeply rooted guilt feelings among slaveholders alleviated only by the catharsis of war, as some historians have argued. Unfortunately, the vast majority of Georgia's antebellum population remains silent within the historical record.[67]

The historian of camp-meeting religion in the antebellum South, Dickson D. Bruce Jr. argues that religion often serves a social role by providing a way for individuals to resolve the contradictions of an unstable life into a meaningful world view. Camp-meeting religion helped people to deal with the difficulties and uncertainties of frontier life by offering a coherent explanation for their place in the universe, which in turn served the interest of society by creating order from chaos. In the early nineteenth century, the search for order took the form of a war with hedonism because the majority of the South's population remained unchurched. Although he leans more toward seeing attacks on dress, whiskey, gambling, dancing, and the theater as expressions of support for social cohesion and stability, Bruce also suggests that at least early in the century such sectarian attacks might have been an expression of "a protest morality of the disinherited" against the licentiousness of the planter class. The danger of social protest during outdoor religious revivals lessened over time. In the 1840s, camp meetings rapidly disappeared with the rise of stable Methodist and Baptist congregations led by slaveholders, a process of denominational maturation that signaled planter dominance within southern society.[68]

One finds numerous indications of the expanding influence of plantation society in the detailed account written by Emily Burke of her visit to a camp meeting in North Georgia sometime in the 1840s. While camp meetings may have been on the decline elsewhere, country people in North Georgia still considered the annual religious celebration the most important social occasion of the year and dated other events in their lives against the last meeting. Yet it is precisely the social character of the camp meeting described by Burke that reveals just how much outdoor revivals had changed. As recorded by Burke, the main topics of conversation among the young were the cost and elegance of the latest fashions on display and who would be crowned the new "belle" that season, a rage for fancy dress that filtered down to the kitchen and field workers and made revival time very prosperous for merchants and milliners. Roughly analogous with the celebration of Thanksgiving in the North, she continued, camp-meeting time also coincided with the removal of planter families to their winter residences because "the hospitable and generous planter of the South on occasions such as I am now describing not only made provision for the entertainment of his own family and numerous relations but also for a large company of strangers." Because entertaining on such a grand scale was a major undertaking, planter families brought along all their "goods and chattels" from their summer retreats, departing for their winter homes from the campgrounds.[69]

In contrast to the spontaneity one associates with camp meetings on the southern frontier, the permanence of the campground visited by Burke is striking. Consisting of a square lot of about one and a half acres of land laid out amid a shady grove of gigantic oaks, the campground had an old church in one corner for regular Sabbath services and a large, open tabernacle designed to provide minimum shelter for large assemblies in the opposite corner. Resembling a "city market" more than a church, the tabernacle consisted simply of a tremendous roof supported by pillars:

> On every side of the square, all fronting the center, the fathers of the principal families constituting these assemblies have each their own family residence. These little habitations are built of logs, having a piazza in front, and their number is sufficient to enclose the entire square, while in the background are arranged all the outhouses belonging to each, such as the kitchens, stables for the horses, and also pens for the swine and folds for the herds and flocks and coops for the chickens, all of which have been previously stalled for the coming slaughter. And I ought not forget to mention in this connection the kennels for the hounds and watch dogs, which are needed even more at such places than on the plantations and which in many parts of Georgia and South Carolina constitute the only police of the place.[70]

In front of every log house there was a platform of four to five square feet raised six feet from the ground and covered a foot deep with dirt to serve as the foundation for illumination fires. Together the fires cast a light bright enough to read by with ease and emitted millions of sparks and "wreaths of curling smoke" into the overhanging trees. At night the family elders congregated near the fire to watch over the playing children, while during the day hundreds of "richly and gaily dressed" young people made their rounds or gathered in small groups during the intervals between worship services. Each day at sunrise several blasts from a hunting trumpet called everyone to morning prayers and songs of praise filled the air. Four sermons followed during the day at regular intervals, two in the morning and two in the afternoon. Although many slaves preferred worshipping alongside their owners, separate services were provided out-of-hearing by the white ministers for those who wanted "that freedom in speaking, singing, shouting and praying they could not enjoy in the presence of their masters." That the only signs recorded by Burke of the religious enthusiasm formerly characteristic of outdoor revivals were among the separate services for the slaves may have been an oversight, but more likely reflects the maturation of plantation society. As for the sinners among the crowd, Burke wrote that a large framed saloon had been erected just beyond the church square where they were free "to drink whiskey, smoke cigars, play cards and steal horses," their "curses and blasphemies" ringing out in stark disharmony with "the fervent and incessant prayers of the righteous" that "ascended on high like holy incense from within the camp." Simon Suggs would have felt right at home.

Because religion was the one area where Yankee schoolmarms and plantation mistresses stood on common ground as long as they skirted the issue of slavery, their journals and letters are rich with references to the beliefs and practices of the time. Upon one occasion Burke attended Sabbath services in a barn-like meeting house where whites were seated up front and blacks in the rear. Because of slave illiteracy, the minister read aloud two lines of a hymn at a time, which the congregation then sang back. Dinner on the grounds, socializing, and mail delivery followed before everyone returned to the church for more preaching in the afternoon. For many women in rural Georgia, such "Love feasts" were peak experiences that merited careful reflection later in their journals. While the intensity of their individual commitment varied, plantation mistresses took their religious responsibilities seriously. Many became involved in the religious education of their slaves or attended black spiritual gatherings when white church services were unavailable. While some went to listen to the slave spirituals or to reaffirm their own feelings of intellectual superiority, others expressed admiration for the emotional intensity they witnessed during slave religious ceremonies as evidence of deep spiritual commitment.[71]

Nevertheless, few plantation mistresses developed a genuine appreciation of slave humanity, however much the punishment or sale of individual slaves might trouble them. A sexual double standard in the South that winked at miscegenation was another matter. Ella Clanton Thomas recorded in her journal her belief that all southern women were abolitionists at heart, perhaps hoping that her husband would read the passage and take the hint. More likely, her statement reveals her frustration at the moment rather than a true commitment to emancipation. When the end of slavery came and her family's world collapsed, her racial attitudes hardened quickly in response to black challenges to the deference she expected. Like their husbands, plantation mistresses had everything to lose and little to gain from the abolition of slavery. Historians who see plantation mistresses as prisoners in disguise are forcing modern aspirations onto the past. Plantation mistresses were willing accomplices in a system of racial and class exploitation that supported their privileged universe. When challenges to plantation slavery came, they were among the system's most ardent defenders. After the deprivations and heartaches of a long war brought nagging doubts to the surface that they dutifully recorded in their journals and letters, most still remained true to the cause until the bitter end. While many came to accept the destruction of slavery as an inevitable and just consequence of an ungodly war, the same women in their old age rallied repeatedly to the Confederate flag to defend plantation society, past and present.[72]

Whereas the antebellum traveler accounts show the influence of outside pressures on the development of regional and class consciousness among the planter elite in Georgia, the literature of intimacy clearly reveals that paternalism was the primary force that shaped the social and cultural attitudes of the planter class. Simply stated, it was their shared experiences with slavery more than the hated abolitionists that united Georgia's leading planter families. The increasingly strident attacks on slavery, however, compelled an inner search for an ideological justification for their way of life. In a society where "legitimacy and dominance made up the knot that the planters had to keep tight if they were to survive," the pervasiveness of the proslavery ideology in the literature of domesticity reveals a desire to dominate by persuasion rather than force. However, one author with intimate ties with the South turned her private reflections about slavery into a public ideological broadside against plantation society after the Civil War began.[73]

According to an old tradition, the celebrated English actress Frances Anne Kemble became so fearful that her government was intent on intervening in the American Civil War on behalf of the South that she decided to rush into publication an exposé of plantation slavery that she had written over two decades before. Although friends and foes alike once credited her book with influencing England's decision to remain neutral, this seems unlikely because President Lincoln issued the Emancipation Proclamation months before the release of the English edition of Kemble's *Journal of a Residence on a Georgian Plantation in 1838–1839* in May 1863, while the American edition did not appear until after Gettysburg and Vicksburg. A popular polemic largely forgotten soon after the war, Kemble's *Journal* is recognized today as a valuable if minor literary achievement, a highly readable and still powerful record of a remarkable woman's personal struggle against slavery.[74]

Born into a distinguished family of actors in 1809, "Fanny" Kemble had already achieved fame as an actress by the age of twenty. In 1832 she began a two-year tour of the American stage with her father with the intent of restoring the family's fortune. In the summer of 1834, however, she abandoned her acting career to marry Pierce Mease Butler of Philadelphia. Butler and his brother were the heirs to their grandfather's large estate in Georgia, which included a rice plantation on Butler Island, a sea-island cotton plantation on St. Simon's Island, and some seven hundred slaves. When Roswell King Jr. resigned as manager of the plantations, Pierce Butler brought his wife, two young daughters, and their Irish nursemaid to Georgia, arriving late in December 1838. During the next three and a half months, Kemble kept a detailed journal of her life on the Butler family's plantations, devoting special attention to slave treatment and culture. In mid-April 1839 the family returned to Philadelphia, where Kemble spent the next year polishing her account. Marital problems throughout the next decade that culminated in a bitter divorce in 1849, and her misgivings about bringing the personal affairs of the Butler family before public scrutiny, caused Kemble to set aside plans to publish her journal, possibly because her husband had received custody of their daughters. The war forced her to reorder her priorities.

Like the majority of the antebellum travelers, Kemble placed slavery at the center of southern existence. In many ways the Butler family's plantations were ideally suited to an antislavery propagandist's cause. Unlike James Hamilton Couper and Richard James Arnold, whose commitment to paternalism was strong, the Butlers managed their plantations with strict military discipline. A recent biographer of the family describes the Butler estate as a "self-contained world" isolated from the network of community relationships developed by slaves who lived on other coastal Georgia plantations. The conditions Kemble witnessed during her stay in Georgia reflected decades of absentee ownership and control by overseers given a free hand as long as they delivered a good income to their employers.[75]

Moreover, Kemble's supporting role as mistress on a pair of large plantations provided her an unusual vantage point for an antislavery propagandist. A passionate woman who made no effort to conceal her conflict with her husband over slavery, Kemble tried to paint an accurate picture of her physical surroundings. Her descriptions of the coastal flora and fauna, the planter residence and its furnishings, and the rice mills, cook shops, and blacksmith shops evidence a good eye for significant detail, as do her less objective descriptions of conditions in the slave settlements such as diet and clothing. To be sure, Kemble shared many of the biases common among outside observers of plantation life, describing for example the field hands as "stupid and brutish" compared to the skilled mechanics and artisans. Yet her self-awareness as a woman in a patriarchal relationship and consciousness of her new responsibilities as mistress to slaves who immediately tested her benevolence and willingness to remedy their plight infuse her journal with a unique appeal. Despite her Victorian assumptions about marriage, family, personal cleanliness, religion, and work, which led her to make many condescending and racist judgments, Kemble recognized the humanity, individuality, and cultural distinctiveness of the Butler slaves and their communities. In addition, she was one of the few visitors to a Georgia plantation before the Civil War who gave careful consideration to the world of slave women.[76]

During her husband's first visit to his plantations, he had observed that men and women were required to perform the same tasks in the field without the traditional adjustments for sex, age, and strength, "a noble admission of female equality" in Kemble's mocking words. Butler subsequently instituted changes in the task system that reduced the work load of women relative to men, but Kemble reported that inequities remained. Women who had borne from five to ten children were rated the same as young women in the "prime of their strength," while "stout, hale, hearty girls and boys" did nothing but tend to younger children in the absence of their mothers. In Kemble's opinion the real problem was field work, which she believed left slave women totally degraded. Treating a woman like "a human hoeing machine" and separating mothers from their children most of the day had dissolved the bonds holding slave families together, leaving filth, ignorance, and moral neglect behind.[77]

On both plantations Kemble received frequent visits from slave women in the afternoons after they completed their daily tasks. Some petitioned for sugar, rice, and baby clothes, but the requests that she recalled most forcefully were those for extensions of the three-week period allotted after childbirth before mothers were forced to return to the fields:

> One poor woman, named Molly, came to beg that I would, if possible, get an extension of their exemption from work after childbearing. The close of her argument was concise and forcible. "Missis, we hab um pickanniny—tree weeks in de ospital, and den right out upon the hoe again—can we strong

> dat way, missis? No!" And truly I do not see that they can. This poor creature has had eight children and two miscarriages. All her children were dead but one.

Kemble observed that the conflict between a slave woman's productive and reproductive value tended to be resolved toward the former on the Butler plantations, although more thoughtful masters kept closer tabs on their long-term investments and ready capital and allowed a longer period of confinement before and after childbirth.[78]

Kemble reported that slave women on the Butler estate were compensated for their fecundity with lighter work loads and larger food and clothing allowances. One woman expressed succinctly her awareness of the value of her children to her master's family when she proclaimed, "Look, missis; plenty little niggers for you and massa; plenty little niggers for you and little missis!" Yet in contrast to the findings of recent historians who argue that the family was central to slave survival, Kemble maintained that slave family bonds were as weak as "the short-lived connection between the animal and its young," although the urgent request by a woman named Psyche that she intervene to prevent the dissolution of her family suggested otherwise. Kemble's intervention prevented the breakup of Psyche's family, but she concluded that there were few bonds between children and their fathers and that the bond between mother and child was broken early because mothers felt no need to support and educate their children. The slaves on St. Simon's Island described the senior Roswell King as a cruel manager who resolved disagreements between husbands and wives immediately by remarrying both to other parties. One slave told Kemble that slave men often had wives on more than one plantation without objection from masters and overseers, while a woman named Sophy related how drivers exploited their authority over female slaves. She had borne a son to one of the drivers after he forced her to accommodate his sexual desires, explaining to Kemble that "we do anything to get our poor flesh some rest from de whip; when he made me follow him into de bush, what use me tell him no? He have strength to make me."[79]

Another factor that Kemble considered evidence of the instability of slave families was the presence of several mulattos on the sea-island cotton plantation, a difference her husband attributed to the openness of St. Simon's Island compared to Butler Island. When she noticed a child who resembled Bran the driver, and Bran's strong resemblance to Roswell King

Jr., Butler acknowledged that the two men were probably brothers. Kemble reported that the higher standing of the overseer's illicit children within the plantation division of labor did not go unnoticed by the other slaves. A mulatto woman named Sally requested more than once that she be released from field work because of her color and that she be allowed to learn a trade. From Kemble's point of view, Sally's color awareness was the ultimate sign of her degradation because she had "accepted the contempt" of her master as a sign of her own race's inferiority.[80]

No antislavery treatise would be complete without a discussion of whipping and Kemble's was no exception. She dismissed the theory that self-interest mediated against excessive use of the lash, arguing that angry men succumbed quickly to passion and readily sacrificed "not only their eternal, but their evident, palpable, positive worldly interest" as well. In particular, the stories she heard from slave women brought home the immediacy of the tragedy. A woman named Louisa told Kemble of fleeing into the swamp when a driver refused to believe she was ill and threatened to bind and flog her when she failed to complete her assigned task two days running. From her study of interviews conducted with female ex-slaves by the Works Projects Administration during the New Deal, Deborah Gray White concluded that "playing the lady," or feigning illness from mysterious female complaints, was a strategy of personal resistance that often proved effective because "getting the maximum amount of work from women of childbearing age while remaining confident that no damage was done to their reproductive organs was a guessing game that few white slave owners wanted to play or could afford to lose." Apparently, such was not the case on the Butler estate. A woman named Die, who came to Kemble asking for meat and flannel, related how she had lost fourteen of her sixteen children and had suffered four miscarriages, one after being drawn up by her arms and lashed. Kemble expressed her shame that she was powerless to prevent such "villainy" even though she was the master's wife. Her husband grew so annoyed with her endless supplications in behalf of his slaves that he asked Fanny not to bother him with further complaints.[81]

Not one to give up easily, Kemble sought ways to circumvent her husband's request by using her legitimate authority as mistress to reform slave conditions on his plantations, although she soon learned the limitations of her influence. When her passion for cleanliness finally began to show some results in the slave settlements, she was saddened by the realization that she could not promise much-needed repairs. As a good Victorian mother with two young daughters, Kemble struggled to teach slave mothers what she considered proper childcare practices, but the time she spent making baby clothes and her small gifts of food were more appreciated by the slaves than her campaign for personal hygiene. Kemble discovered after her arrival that nursing was one of the traditional duties of the plantation mistress. Contrary to the prevalent assumptions of her time, she wrote that slaves were actually less disease resistant than whites. Above all else, the filthy infirmaries, rampant sickness, high infantile mortality, and the fatalism of slave parents reaffirmed her conviction that slavery was evil.[82]

Religious instruction among the slaves was another common responsibility among plantation mistresses in Georgia that Kemble undertook after receiving permission from her husband. Although deeming it "zeal without understanding," Kemble recalled being impressed by the "immensely strong devotional feeling" among the slaves on Butler Island, who were allowed to go into Darien to church once a month and met on intermediate Sundays in the house of the head cooper. Yet only the abolitionist movement and northern public opinion, she wrote, had prevented the total neglect of the spiritual needs of the slaves in the South. Though many planters had learned that limited religious instruction enhanced their control over the slave population, others recognized the contradictions inherent in the Christian tradition and the potential for religion to serve as a force for liberation as well as oppression. The story of Sinda, who had once brought the plantation to a standstill with her millenarian prophecy, and the hopes of a woman named Mary that there would be no slavery in heaven both illuminated the slaveholder's dilemma. Kemble aptly described the process of bringing the message of Christianity to the slaves as "very ticklish" because it was difficult to determine "how much they may learn to become better slaves, and how much they may not learn, lest they cease to be slaves at all." In prophetic prose she foretold the coming apocalypse: "As it is, they are putting their own throats and their own souls in jeopardy by their very endeavor to serve God and Mammon. The light that they are letting in between their fingers will presently strike them blind, and the mighty flood of truth which they are straining through a sieve to the thirsty lips of their slaves, sweep them away from their cautious moorings, and overwhelm them in its great deeps, to the waters of which man may in nowise say, thus far shall ye come and no farther."[83]

PART TWO

The Interregnum

CHAPTER FOUR

A Harvest of Fire

Plantation Society at War

Writing to his sister Clifford in Washington, Georgia, from his post in the Washington Territory in November 1860, Edward Porter Alexander pledged his support to the South's pending secession from the Union: "We suppose from the latest news we have that Lincoln is elected, and if so I hope and expect to be called in to help secede. If he is once inaugurated, it will be too late to oppose him, as the purse and the sword will be in his hands and the Army and Navy are sworn to obey his commands. If he is elected I believe the interests of humanity, civilization, and self-preservation call on the South to secede, and I'll go my arm, leg, or death on it." That this son of a prominent slaveholding family joined his peers among the elite of plantation society in linking secession with the interests of humanity was indeed portentous. Resigning his commission in the United States Army, Alexander returned east and accepted a captaincy in the new Confederacy, rising to the rank of brigadier general during four years of wartime service. The long-awaited moment of truth had arrived.[1]

Basking in the optimism captured by the South Carolinian poet Henry Timrod in "Ethnogenesis" in 1861, the majority of white Georgians joined Alexander in welcoming secession with their heads held high in proud defiance, although a sizeable minority accepted the inevitable with some hesitation. War fever was running so high by early spring that the firing upon Fort Sumter was greeted with wild enthusiasm. Appropriately labeled the "national jester of the Confederacy" by a modern biographer, Charles Henry Smith's Bill Arp wrote to "Mr. Linkhorn" in April that the citizens of Rome, Georgia, were so hot "they fairly siz when you poor water on them." Eager to teach the meddlesome Yankees a lesson, men from all walks of life began to organize military companies, confident of swift victory.[2]

As the literary historian Jay B. Hubbell once observed, the immediate effect of the outbreak of the Civil War on southern writers was to reaffirm their belief that the South must have a distinctive literature. Free at last from the North's literary dominance, patriotic southerners longed for a great cultural awakening. Yet as Hubbell and others have observed, the anticipated renaissance largely failed to materialize, especially in Georgia. With the exception of "Little Giffen," Francis Orray Ticknor's ballad honoring the valor of the Confederate soldier, Sidney Lanier's war novel *Tiger-Lilies,* which was not published until 1867, and Kittrell J. Warren's comic exploits of a roguish deserter, *Life and Public Services of an Army Straggler,* Georgia writers produced no traditional literature during the war worthy of mention other than the acid-tongued satire of Charles Henry Smith.[3]

Elisabeth Muhlenfeld contends that the reason the literature of the Civil War era is "the perennial poor relation" in a rich literary tradition can be found in the extraordinary circumstances of the time. Simply stated, the Civil War evolved rapidly into a social revolution, or a war to abolish slavery. As Muhlenfeld correctly observes, "The people of the Confederacy viewed their cause as nothing less than a revolution," an interpretation confirmed by the letters and diaries written by Georgians during the war. From the perspective of the Georgia homefront, fighting a revolution left little time or energy for traditional literary pursuits, especially in a region that lacked adequate publishing capabilities. This is not to say, however, that Georgians were too busy to set aside time for private literary reflection.[4]

The war infused the literature of intimacy with a public political voice that grew more clamorous after Sherman brought the conflict directly to Georgia households. Those who kept journals became increasingly aware that they were speaking to a wider audience than their families and kin, an awareness also evident in many of the letters written during the war. Hardened by suffering, deprivation, and the loss of beloved sons, husbands, fathers, and brothers, angry that their way of life was perishing before their eyes, and motivated by the desire to tell the truth as they saw it, those who remained behind on Georgia plantations sharpened their pens into swords. When defeat on the battlefield sealed the Confederacy's fate, the surviving sons and daughters of the plantation South carried the fight into the pages of history. Although most accepted the war's outcome as willed by God, many Georgia authors turned to literary guerrilla warfare in the decades that followed, often drawing upon stores of ammunition preserved in their private records.[5]

Reflecting in July 1861 upon the rush of events that had followed the attack on Fort Sumter, Ella Clanton Thomas wrote in her journal that she had never been more proud of her native state. The city of Augusta had already sent ten companies of troops off to war, while her husband had been named first lieutenant in the Richmond Hussars. Although she would soon sing a different tune, Thomas wrote that she had no desire for him to remain at home "in the lap of inglorious ease" when duty and honor called. Wanting nothing but "*to be let alone*" by "a people like ourselves whose republican independence was won by a rebellion, [and] whose liberty was achieved by a secession," Thomas angrily condemned the North's attempt to coerce the South as "preposterous." Lincoln's call for men, money, and a blockade of southern ports also brought the realization that "indeed we are now in the midst of what all of us have read of—thought of—and dreamed of before, but never realized—A revolution—There are very many I very much fear who do not realize it now."[6]

Just prior to Lincoln's election, the Reverend Charles C. Jones had written to his son that he did "not apprehend any very serious disturbance" in the event of secession because war would not benefit "the substantial interests of the free states." Moreover, he argued, the Constitution provided for withdrawal of states from the original compact to avoid injury or ruin. Secession was simply an extension of the right of self-government, and as such "the cornerstone of the republic." Jones expressed his hope that separation could be avoided because the consequences might later prove disastrous, but believed that unity without liberty was meaningless. In his words, the primary goal remained "Union if possible—but with it we must have *life, liberty, and equality.*" In the aftermath of the November election, however, he realized that the South stood on the edge of a new frontier: "The times are remarkable; the questions before the people momentous. The final issues are with Him who rules among the nations. A nation to be born in a day, without a struggle, would be a wonder on earth."[7]

Convinced by early January that the dissolution of the Union had become necessary for the South's survival, Mary Jones looked forward to the new year "with the sad foreboding that it may be only one of trial and suffering," then freed her sons from a childhood vow to support and defend the Union pledged to her during a visit to Independence Hall in Philadelphia. Meanwhile, life in rural Georgia went on pretty much as usual as the day of withdrawal from the Union drew near. In a letter to her mother dated 25 January 1861, Mary S. Mallard began by discussing a favorite servant's pending wedding celebration, then told of her husband's visit to his ailing father. Wedged in between tales of her young daughters' capers, however, one also finds the following: "How do you feel now, dear Mother, that we are in a foreign land? Did you illuminate when you heard of Georgia's secession? Savannah does not seem to have made as great a demonstration as when Carolina seceded. What is to be done with those Georgians who unfurled the Stars and Stripes when the news reached them?"[8]

Her brother, Charles C. Jones Jr., traced the current crisis back to the Missouri Compromise. The South would have been better off, he wrote, had it ignored Henry Clay's calls for compromise over the issue of slavery in 1820 and 1850. Blaming the abolitionists for the dissolution of the Union, he wrote that "had we manfully resisted the first aggression, we might have stifled the serpent in its den, and not now have been suffering from the poisonous brood which with hissing tongue and noxious breath are crawling everywhere and polluting the otherwise wholesome air of this once pure and happy country." Though it was "a sad sight to see our national flag lowered," he expressed his belief that "two races" had arisen in the United States, which while "claiming a common parentage, have been so entirely separated by climate, by morals, by religion, and by estimates so totally opposite of all that constitutes honor, truth, and manliness, that they cannot longer coexist under the same government."[9]

After he completed his term as mayor of Savannah, Jones accepted a commission as senior first lieutenant with the Chatham Artillery, a home guard unit assigned the defense of the city. Fearful of Savannah's precarious position, Jones vowed that he would "most cheerfully give my life in defense of our common beloved home, and in support of honor, nationality, and principles for which we are contending." Unlike many southerners, his father thought the prospect of European intervention in the Confederacy's behalf unlikely, citing the distaste of despotic and aristocratic governments for American republican ideals and hesitancy to aid "revolutionists" for fear of setting a dangerous precedent at home. Jones believed that interest alone dictated relations with European powers. "A kind of Providence" had arranged "the provisions for man's necessity" so that loss of any product, such as cotton or tobacco, was but a "temporary inconvenience." As he explained in a letter to his son, a people's economic interests changed over time and came second to more fundamental concerns such as life and liberty.[10]

It would be a mistake, however, to take such statements too literally without first recognizing them as originating in a world view grounded firmly in the political economy of slavery. Individual citizens and governments alike justify their entrance into war with lofty ideals. Once hostilities begin and unexpected consequences follow, events have a way of stripping away the patriotic veneer that hides fundamental material concerns. As did planters elsewhere in Georgia, the Reverend Jones realized that the failure of the Confederacy would result in the failure of "everything of value in property." Planters were practical men who understood the source of their favored position in society. Like Jones, many took whatever steps available to protect their investment in plantation slavery, even when such actions resulted in direct conflict with the policies and needs of the Confederate government.[11]

As often proves the case, revolution was a harsh mistress who failed to redeem all of the pledges made in her honor in the early days of the war. For the second time in American history, southern planters risked everything on a calculated gamble to expand their political and economic liberties, looking back on their revolutionary heritage with great pride. Aware that their interests as slaveholders were on a collision course with the free labor ideology of a capitalist society entering an industrial revolution, Georgia planters had arrived at the uneasy consensus that secession was their only hope for survival. Yet when Lincoln publicly raised the stakes by putting slavery on the table beside the preservation of the Union, the South's so-called revolution turned an ominous corner.

Writing to his father in September 1862, Lieutenant Jones called Lincoln's pending emancipation proclamation a black and diabolical bid to incite insurrection among the slave population, although he predicted correctly that the move would have no effect "under the present circumstances." Uncomfortably aware that the "Age of Gold" had given way to the "Age of Iron," or that the North had the power to change "present circumstances" in the near future, he warned his father of perilous days ahead. The "infamous" Lincoln was out to "subvert our entire social system, desolate our homes, and convert the quiet, ignorant, dependent black son of toil into a savage incendiary and brutal murderer." With one deft turn of the cards, the "great emancipator" had brought the revolution home to the revolutionaries. Lt. Jones angrily denounced the North as "an example of refined barbarity, moral degeneracy, religious impiety, soulless honor, and absolute degradation almost beyond belief." Nearly two years later, his uncle still found the recent course of events difficult to contemplate. As he wrote in a letter to his niece, "Are we not living in a peculiar age?"[12]

In the words of historian James L. Roark, "The Civil War was the critical moment in the planters' history, and their responses to events provide valuable insight into the mind and character of the South's antebellum aristocracy." In his study of the impact of the Civil War and Reconstruction on the fundamental beliefs and behaviors of the planter class, Roark makes the convincing argument that extreme situations like wars and revolutions force the clarification of ideological commitments that often operate below the surface in more peaceful times. Like Eugene D. Genovese, Roark views planters in the antebellum South as a hegemonic class with a distinctive world view rooted in their position as slaveholders in a hostile world. He also contends that the South's nonslaveholding white majority ordinarily deferred to planter political leadership and accepted slavery because of white supremacy, white democracy, and "the promise of white equality," or social mobility. Thus when the Civil War began, Georgians stood fairly united in a common cause, although the deprivations of war rapidly brought class divisions and ideological disagreements to the surface.[13]

Georgia planters soon realized that their expectations for a rapid resolution of the conflict were ill-founded. As the Reverend Jones wrote in February 1862, the Federal forces remained resolute in spite of their early setbacks, the North's resources were enormous, and the South could not rely on foreign intervention in the "long and desperate war" that lay ahead. Under such conditions, he believed that the proper military course for the South was to pursue a Fabian policy, develop its agricultural and manufacturing resources fully, and prepare to "live as independent of the world as we can" until the North realized the futility of trying to conquer and subjugate over eight hundred thousand square miles of territory. Because the former United States had become "one workshop of war," it was unlikely that the war would end quickly. The war gave the masses their daily bread and thousands were rolling up huge fortunes. Ultimately, he concluded, the credit and existence of the Confederacy depended on its people. The immediate task was to secure the reenlistment of troops for the duration of the war.[14]

Success in a modern total war against a powerful and determined adversary called for a degree of unification that would have been difficult under the best of conditions for a nation founded upon the principle of decentralization. Even if factors outside the South's ability to control fell into place, a successful defensive war depended on strong military and political leadership from the planter elite, loyal military service for the duration by common whites, massive expansion of the South's industrial capacity, and a fundamental reordering of farm production. In addition to increasing the already extensive demands on planter and yeoman women, the combined burden of simultaneously supplying the Confederate armies and the civilian population placed a severe strain on the Georgia countryside.

In the mythical aftermath of defeat, the legend arose that southern gentlemen had rallied to the man to defend their homes and way of life from the Yankee invader, while their wives and mothers had labored valiantly alongside their loyal slaves back on the plantations. That the Confederacy survived as long as it did lends substantial credence to this legend. Yet as their letters and journals make clear, the planter elite carried enough class baggage that the story is somewhat more complicated. For men accustomed to the local prerogatives of rank, adjusting to the centralized structure of authority in military life sometimes proved difficult. Many believed that their rank in the military should reflect their rank in society, an ambition more easily realized in the home guard than in the regular army. Not only did armchair generals abound, criticizing the policies and decisions of the Confederate and state governments became a favorite pastime. To be sure, many planters were simply struggling to balance their commitment to the defense of their homes and families and the Confederacy's need for troops elsewhere, especially along the coast where the threat of invasion remained constant. Nonetheless, the fact remains that a significant number of Georgia planters used their wealth and social connections to evade military service or to secure more advantageous positions in the home guard, many in response to pressure from their wives.[15]

In nineteenth-century Georgia fiction, the women of the master class were often portrayed as staunch defenders of social distinctions, a tradition that remained unchanged in real life during the war. The historian George C. Rable argues that "rather than burying class distinctions beneath a spirit of general sacrifice, the Confederacy's economic woes widened the social and political distance between the haves and have-nots." Although there is some evidence to the contrary in the literature of intimacy, especially in the aftermath of Sherman's invasion of Georgia, the war did indeed stretch "the conservative vision of an organic society to the breaking point." Ella Clanton Thomas, for example, expressed outrage in her journal toward criticism of her father's offer to sell meal at half its market value of two dollars to families of volunteers from Richmond and Columbia counties in the spring of 1862. When an editorial signed "A poor soldiers wife" in the Augusta *Constitutionalist* pointed out that meal at ten cents a bushel would be expensive without transportation, Thomas voiced her disgust with the "ungrateful wretches." Ironically, a few months earlier she had concluded that the postage rate of ten cents per letter was a serious hardship for the families of poor soldiers, writing that it would deprive their children of bread. During a visit to Atlanta, Thomas paid a socially correct call to a hospital but confessed later that "conventionalism" kept her from expressing her gratitude and sympathy to a wounded gentleman. Repulsed by the death and discomfort she witnessed, Thomas wrote that it must be difficult for "a man of refinement and education" to endure common association with "men essentially different from him."[16]

Such class attitudes were so ingrained among the slaveholding elite that Thomas felt no hesitancy about expressing them in her journal. Neither did planter families see anything wrong with using their governmental connections to further their private interests. When the Jones family, for example, was finalizing the purchase of a plantation in Burke County as a safe haven for their investment in slaves, Charles C. Jones Jr. worked assiduously to arrange the best possible deal with Confederate commissary agents in Savannah for his family's surplus grain and livestock. Writing from Maryland in the aftermath of Gettysburg to his wife Sallie at their plantation in Hancock County, Edgeworth Bird spoke of the local men and boys who had been wounded or killed, expressed his desire for the return of his personal servant, and gave her advice regarding plantation and slave management. Reflecting upon their hard world, Bird also recommended that she pay off all their debts because Confederate money was at a great discount below gold. Dr. George W. Peddy of Heard County, who was the Fifty-Sixth Georgia Volunteer Regiment's surgeon, speculated in surgical instruments, mules, and horses to reduce his family's debts. Peddy also advised his wife to kill and dry their beef before it was impressed by the army.[17]

Still, one risks imposing the standards of modern nationalism on the past by reading a lack of patriotism into such actions, even if Edgeworth Bird called "grab" the game of nations and individuals. In the long run, few Georgia families emerged from the Civil War unscathed. The number of choices available in the face of hardship, however, was directly proportionate to one's station in life. Wealthy planters and highly educated professionals were more likely to be aware of conflicting ideological commitments, but their ability to negotiate favorable compromises was vastly superior to that of the yeoman farmers and poor whites who filled the ranks of the Confederate armies. Such actions, however, reflect the efforts of families to juggle conflicting personal and social commitments more than a lack of patriotism.

One of the most vocal critics of the war's disproportionately severe impact on common whites was Charles Henry Smith. A dedicated patriot who feared the central power of the Confederate government but had even less use for Governor Joseph E. Brown, Smith directed his strongest attacks against self-serving behavior on the homefront. While critical of the suspension of habeas corpus and the Confederate government's taxation and inflationary currency policies, Smith reluctantly accepted such actions as legitimate wartime measures. What worried him the most was the detrimental effect of a divided and rapacious government on the citizenry's commitment to the cause. Though critical of draft dodgers from all walks of life, Smith warned through Bill Arp that conscription laws that favored the rich, a home guard that sheltered extortionists and false patriots, and excessive levels of taxation by all levels of government worked to erode public confidence in the war effort.[18]

As Smith foresaw correctly, widespread deprivation on the southern homefront undermined popular support for the war. In light of the widespread illiteracy among rural Georgians and the limited availability of literary evidence, it is not surprising that our understanding of the war's impact on the yeoman homefront remains sketchy. But because men from specific locales generally served together, some lines of communication between illiterate soldiers and their relatives were kept open by their literate comrades in arms. One can also draw logical inferences from the letters and journals written by plantation mistresses and their relatives. Signs of deprivation among leading planter families, for example, suggest deeper levels of suffering among the rest of the population. The yeomanry's early enthusiasm for the war soon gave way to disaffection within the Confederate ranks in response to the suffering and hardships endured by loved ones at home. Without slaves to hold down the fort, small farms bore a heavy share of the war's burden. Taxes-in-kind and impressment proved especially onerous once tiny surpluses were exhausted. The historian Stephen

Hahn links the desertion rate in the Confederate army directly to letters from loved ones describing the deterioration of conditions at home. One woman wrote to her son, William Asbell, "I want to know if you can speair me sum lether to make us sum shoes for we can not get shoes heair and we will go bair foot." A reluctant soldier who nonetheless had answered the call to duty, Asbell did his best to guide his family through troubled times by including practical advice in his letters.[19]

With the exception of emancipation, nothing generated more turmoil in rural Georgia than the impoverishment of the yeomanry, a tragic consequence of the war that continued to reverberate through the countryside for decades. Historians remain divided in opinion as to why the nonslaveholding majority was willing to fight to preserve the interests of the slaveholding minority, although the notion that life and liberty were rooted in land and slave ownership coincided nicely with the planter argument that the North was out to destroy the South's whole way of life. As the growing number of desertions in the Confederate ranks reveals, however, many common soldiers drew a clear distinction between defending their homes and fighting to preserve plantation slavery and understood that nothing would be gained from the South's independence if their families perished in the process. Nor were the leading planter families immune from the temptation to close class ranks in response to the hardships of war, even when they sympathized with the suffering of the less fortunate. To borrow another statement from Rable, "Even widespread suffering could not overcome traditional social distinctions; pride of birth and class survived despite the wreckage of so many families."[20]

As one might expect, the war quickly became the dominant topic of conversation in the literature of intimacy, although many of the concerns traditionally addressed in the private correspondence of planter families remained unchanged. Local news, visiting relatives, crops and climate, and illness were common topics addressed in letters to fathers, husbands, and sons in camp. In their letters home, men described their life in camp, passed along news about soldiers from the community, circulated the latest political and military rumors, and included explicit instructions about managing the land in their absence. Edgeworth Bird of Hancock County also remained mindful of his daughter's social education, reminding her to write well and neatly because he shared her letters with many gentlemen, and to tend to her duties faithfully and honestly, say her prayers, and lead a virtuous life. His wife maintained the family tradition after she joined him in Virginia in the spring of 1862.[21]

The letters between Dr. George W. Peddy and his wife, Kate Featherston Peddy, are of interest because they communicate the hopes and anxieties of an ambitious young doctor trying in spite of the war to do well by his wife, who was the daughter of a prominent planter. The Peddy letters also reveal the loneliness and insecurity caused by wartime separations, as seen for example in the following passage from a letter she penned in October 1862: "How can I stand it much longer, not to hear from you? My darling, where are you oh! Where can you be this stormy nigh[t] while the wind moans and howls arou[n]d the house and through the tree? I do feel desolate and broken hearted—nothing to live for. Honey, have you forgot your pour babie or have you ceased to love her?"[22]

Dr. Peddy was also uncharacteristically frank in the way he expressed his longing for his wife, at least until she properly chastised him for his indiscreet prose. Apparently rumors about camp life also made their way home because she feared that he would fall prey to the "inebriating bowl" or even worse temptations. A passionate woman, Kate also wrote of being jealous after he mentioned making the acquaintance of a beautiful woman. Having overcome his initial fear that revealing his innermost feelings was unmanly, the young doctor confessed in a letter written from Dalton, Georgia, in January 1864, "I love you with an ardor that's rarely felt and known by others of my sex."[23]

Kate Peddy's insecurity was more than a reflection of her loneliness for her husband. Although men like George W. Peddy and Edgeworth Bird tried to reassure their loved ones at home, the war forced women into unaccustomed roles beyond their traditional household responsibilities. In their letters and journals, the women of the planter elite wrote of organizing and attending relief fund musicals and balls, getting together to write letters and make care packages for soldiers, and attending to benevolent work in hospitals, all while waiting anxiously for news from the front. Lacking the factories necessary to keep a modern army adequately clothed, the Confederate government encouraged southern women to pick up the slack through domestic production, albeit with limited success. Responding to requests from their husbands and sons for clothing and provisions to supplement their meager military fare, those who were able forwarded trunks to their men at the front, often under the care of trusted slaves. After fighting began in North Georgia in 1864, some soldiers even sent their laundry home by train and arranged brief visits with loved ones.[24]

Warm, durable winter clothing was an especially valued possession at the front, although securing safe storage during the summer months, when winter gear was a burden on rapid marches, was apparently quite a problem because of widespread theft in the camps. In her postwar memoir *Life in Dixie during the War,* the Lost Cause patriot, Woman's Christian Temperance Union activist, and sometime poet and novelist Mary A. H. Gay recalled receiving a letter from her brother in the spring of 1864 asking her to assume what might well prove "a perilous trust" should the winds of war shift rapidly. Deeming it their patriotic duty, Gay and her mother agreed to store nine large dry goods boxes of winter gear for a group of young officers, fully aware of the possible consequences should Federal troops discover the contraband in their home. Hiring a two-horse wagon and driver to transport the goods from the train depot to their home in Decatur, Gay converted their company dining room into a Confederate storeroom. In a variant of the endless silver-in-the-well stories that appeared after the war, they knocked a hole in the ceiling to hide the clothing when the Yankees drew near in July. Later during General Sherman's ten-day armistice to evacuate Atlanta, Gay smuggled out the clothing under the nose of the enemy.[25]

Though less dramatic than Mary Gay's bold resistance to the Yankee invaders, uncounted numbers of Georgia women served the Confederate cause more effectively simply by staying at home and maintaining production on their family lands, a job that became increasingly difficult as the war dragged on year after year. Having already managed a plantation by herself for nearly three years, the widow Dolly Lunt Burge was better prepared than most for the difficult task that lay ahead in 1861. But by the end of the year the war had already begun to impact her plantation near Covington:

> Battle after battle has been fought & it still goes on. The enemy has blockaded our coasts so that we can neither export our produce or import our needfuls. Some of the best blood of the country has been spilled. O the horrors of war. The privations, the hardships to which our soldiers are exposed. Every thing is very high: Coffee, 75 cents & not to be had at that. Salt, 18 & 20 dollars a sack & every thing in like proportion; bagging, 30 cents a yard & rope, 25 a pound while cotton is unsalable.[26]

Like farmers throughout the South, Burge developed ways to cope with wartime shortages and inflation, while chronicling her seasonal plantation routines pretty much as she had always done. The biggest dilemma she faced in the spring of 1862 was whether or not to plant cotton, writing on

26 March that "everybody says we must plant little or no cotton." Like many planters, Burge was torn between doing her duty by planting more provision crops and her fear that the war would soon end and leave her without a marketable crop. That same month, the Reverend Charles C. Jones cut back on the amount of cotton at his inland plantation, Arcadia, concluding that there was not "the faintest prospect in the world now apparent for a peace." Burge also shifted part of her cotton land to corn, although she confessed in her diary that she disliked doing it. Meanwhile, she wrote, the fall of New Orleans in late April further aggravated the problem of shortages, raising the price of molasses to $1.25 a gallon. On 1 May, Burge confided in her diary that "the poor must suffer for everything is so high."[27]

By that summer even the affluent in Georgia were finding it increasingly difficult to spend their money. In Burge's words, "I have hundreds of dollars in my pocket book & yet I cannot buy a yard of calico to make my Sadai a sunbonnet." Mary Jones wrote to her daughter in August that she was contemplating ripping up a mattress for wool to make winter clothing for the slaves. Women accustomed to buying rolls of cloth for their household needs began a desperate search for spinning wheels, cotton cards, and yarn, bemoaning the loss of distaff skills once universal in rural households. Although she knitted socks for her husband throughout the war, Cornelia Jones Pond later recalled how difficult it had been to learn to operate a loom that her father purchased to make slave clothing. Pond also remembered learning how to make plaited hats from palmetto leaves, dyes from the bark of trees and bushes, candles from myrtle berries, tallow, and lard, and coffee from sweet potatoes and parched okra seeds. In addition, the Pond family extracted opium from a single poppy in their garden for medicinal purposes.[28]

Finding themselves even more alone after the conscription law was implemented in 1862, plantation mistresses and yeoman women struggled to pay inflated war taxes. As one would expect, the planter class was in a better position to meet its obligations. In March 1864, Burge sold three bales of cotton at seventy-five cents per pound to pay her taxes. For once inflation had worked to her advantage. Direct military requisition of farm produce was another matter. On 30 October 1864, she wrote that three Confederate soldiers had breakfasted at her plantation, afterward impressing three barrels of corn, nine hundred pounds of fodder, and nine bushels of wheat. Disturbed by her unexpected losses, Burge bemoaned her loss in her diary:

"Oh, what a wretched thing is war! Truely no man can call anything his own." Still mindful of her civic duty, she nonetheless rode into Covington two weeks later to pay her Confederate tax, although the tax commissioners were not to be found. Writing in October 1863 from Chickamauga Station, Edgeworth Bird warned his wife in Hancock County to expect the impressment of her horse but to "bear it cheerfully."[29]

Although disease and death were hardly strangers in rural Georgia households, the war magnified both to frightening new dimensions. The Jones family found itself battling an epidemic of measles at Montevideo compounded by a mysterious illness acquired by a group of slave men who had been impressed into service on Savannah's fortifications. In March of the following year, the Reverend Jones passed away. Two months later Mary Jones expressed her grief and isolation in a letter to her son by bemoaning, "*I am all alone.*" Dolly Lunt Burge linked the death of her nineteen-year-old stepdaughter from consumption directly to being separated from the young man she had been intent on marrying, who had been "among the first to leave." Tortured by the uncertainty caused by irregular mail, she continued, the young woman's constitution had finally broken. Whereas in the past a death in the family had drawn communities together, the sheer volume of destruction wrought by the war forced increasing numbers of Georgians to mourn their losses in isolation.[30]

Almost as difficult to endure was the anguish over the uncertain fate of husbands, brothers, and sons far away from home. Writing from Richmond in April 1862, Sallie Bird told her daughter to pray earnestly for her father in his moment of "great peril" during the Peninsula campaign. Wounded later that year at Second Manassas, Edgeworth Bird was still in Georgia recuperating at Christmas but returned to see action at Gettysburg and the battle of Chickamauga. Ella Clanton Thomas expressed her great relief when her husband emerged unscathed from the fighting around Richmond amid horrible rumors to the contrary. Writing in her eighties during World War I, Rebecca Latimer Felton still had vivid memories of her mother's fears for her only son when he marched joyfully off to war in 1861, feelings shared by Josephine Clay Habersham for her son as well. During the day on 1 July 1863, Habersham read a great deal, sewed, listened to her younger children recite their lessons, and enjoyed "a nice dinner of fish" caught by her husband, while the Confederacy entered what was arguably the most significant week of the entire war. She also received a short letter that day from her son which kept her "in an agony of tears" throughout the night. Praying that God spare her "poor heart the misery which burdens so many hearts at this time," she did not sleep until daylight. Though her prayers were answered that night, her sons Joseph Clay and Willie both perished the following year in the Battle of Atlanta.[31]

In late 1862, Wylie Jarrett McClatchey sold his farm in McMinn County, Tennessee, and moved his wife and three sons to a farm he had purchased near Marietta. A slaveholder and ardent secessionist, McClatchey left Tennessee because his land was in a strong Unionist area, deciding upon the Marietta area because of the Georgia Military Institute for the education of his sons. Too lame for military service, McClatchey took his slaves and the family silver south when Sherman entered Georgia, although his wife, Minerva Leah, elected to stay behind on their plantation with one of their sons and a niece. Her diary, which runs from January 1864 to September 1865, contains a remarkable account of life under Yankee occupation during the summer of 1864. As her world crumbled around her, she turned to her diary for comfort. On 5 August, she also recorded a strange dream:

> I was half asleep, half awake this morning—and thought I was up, and out on the porch—giving the men drinks of buttremilk, as I often did, there was a crowd around, each waiting his turn, when my son John came up from the gate—he looked as pale as death and emaciated till no one but his mother would have known him. I thought I was awake and it was really my dear boy I saw. The surprise awoke me—and it was only a dream—but oh what a sad one. It fills me with fear and anxiety. What does it portend?[32]

In mid-October, McClatchey learned that her son had been wounded in Virginia in June and had died the following month. Like countless parents, she grieved terribly yet tried to accept her loss with Christian stoicism, writing that "the Lord has been good to me, I must not question his doings." Yet it especially pained her to think that her son had suffered alone. Even the trees and birds, she wrote, seemed "to droop and weep with me in my sorrow." On 1 December she recalled that a visit by her youngest son, who was en route to join his Confederate comrades in Tennessee, had filled her eyes with tears with thoughts of his brother. She hoped only to join all of her family some day in heaven, where there would be no wars, separations, or troubles. When Mary Gay learned in early 1865 that her half-brother had been killed in Tennessee, she found it more difficult to accept his death as God's will. Although a woman of deep faith, Gay felt personally responsible because she was a passionate secessionist who had applauded when he answered the call to war.[33]

The rising tide of death and deprivation gradually began to take its toll.

An army of veiled women in black became reluctant to sacrifice their remaining men to the war, while their men in uniform found it increasingly difficult to remain apart from their suffering families. Meanwhile, the North grew stronger every day in spite of its early reversals on the battlefield. The sweet oil that Bill Arp mockingly advised "Mr. Abe Linkhorn" to put on his factories in January 1862 to prevent rust for want of southern cotton provided more than ample lubrication for the North's powerful industrial machine. The legendary ingenuity of its women and the impressive gains achieved in Georgia's industrial production aside, it was the South that soon found itself unable to clothe its armies of soldiers and slaves. Indicative of the localized mindset that prevailed across the South, propertied Georgians found it harder and harder to reconcile their own interests with those of the Confederate nation. Such disaffection on the homefront undoubtedly contributed to the Confederacy's downfall. In Rable's words, "Private jitters soon led to doubts about the cause itself."[34]

There was nonetheless a world of difference between having doubts and abandoning the cause altogether. Although popular support for the war had weakened, many among those with the most to lose remained loyal to the war effort until the bitter end. As long as the ragged Confederate armies continued to hold their own on the field of battle and the fighting remained for the most part on distant soil, most white Georgians maintained the belief that the South would prevail. Having grown tired of a defensive war that demanded many sacrifices from a civilian population living in constant fear of invasion, they cheered when General Lee took the war into "Yankeedoodledom" in the summer of 1863, although the long lists of battle casualties that filled the newspapers afterward convinced many that the end was drawing near. Though reluctant to admit defeat, others began to place their faith in divine intervention, hoping against tremendous odds for a last-minute miracle. Reflecting their evangelical belief in a punishing yet forgiving God, some simply could not imagine that the South's suffering would go unrewarded. If all else failed, perhaps the presidential election in the fall of 1864 would bring the war-weary North to its senses. A red-bearded general from Ohio soon laid such notions to rest.[35]

Prior to the arrival of Sherman in the state of her birth, Augusta Jane Evans attempted to boost morale on the Confederate homefront by publishing *Macaria; or, Altars of Sacrifice,* a novel that most observers consider the most important piece of fiction produced in the South during the Civil War. Mirroring its impact on domestic relations within plantation households, the war legitimized a new role for the women of the slaveholding elite in domestic fiction. Expected to be passive to aggressive men in times of peace, the archetype of the southern lady was transformed by war into a spartan woman willing to sacrifice her traditional prerogatives to the cause of Confederate nationalism. Traditionally, war stories had played a key role in the play of boys by helping to define male gender roles. As the Confederacy moved toward total war, Evans recognized that such stories might play an equally important role by helping to legitimize new roles for elite women in plantation society.[36]

The degree to which the war had transformed the genre of domestic fiction becomes evident when comparing *Macaria* to *The Planter's Northern Bride,* which Caroline Lee Hentz had published a decade earlier. Whereas the earlier novel is little more than a proslavery tract, secession had muted the necessity of defending the peculiar institution as long as the Confederate nation survived, an ideological message that Evans delivered implicitly by omitting any reference to slavery on her dedication page:

> To the
> Army of the Southern Confederacy
> who delivered the South from despotism, and who have won for
> generations yet unborn the precious guerdon of
> constitutional republican liberty:
> to this vast legion of honor
> whether limping on crutches through
> the land they have saved and immortalized,
> or surviving uninjured to share the blessings their
> unexampled heroism bought, or sleeping dreamlessly in nameless
> martyr-graves on hallowed battle-fields whose
> historic memory shall perish only with
> the remnants of our language,
> these pages are
> gratefully and reverently dedicated
> by one who, although debarred from the
> dangers and deathless glory of the "tented field,"
> would fain offer a woman's inadequate tribute to the noble
> patriotism and sublime self-abnegation of her
> dear and devoted countrymen.

As Evans revealed in the closing stanzas of her paean to Confederate manhood, utilitarian concerns loomed large in her ideological agenda for the elite women of plantation society. In classical Athens, Macaria had saved the city from invasion by giving herself in sacrifice to the gods, a gesture that the paired heroines of the story ultimately emulate by sacrificing their hopes for domestic happiness on the altar of Confederate nationhood. With nearly half of the South's white male population dead or wounded by 1864, the possibility of domestic bliss which had been the planter's northern bride's reward for accepting slavery was becoming increasingly rare. To paraphrase Drew Gilpin Faust, necessity had legitimized fictional invention.[37]

Possibly reflecting the difficulties she encountered redirecting the well-established gender norms of domestic fiction to new ideological purposes, or perchance merely to satiate the thirst of war-weary readers for romantic escapism before turning to more serious matters, Evans devoted nearly three-fourths of her book to setting the stage for the Civil War. For the purposes of this narrative, the characters and story line of her tale of sublimated romance are of less importance than the ideological concerns that transform the final quarter of the narrative into a political novel. According to Jay B. Hubbell, Evans wrote *Macaria* between June 1862 and March 1863. Hence, the aspirations, hopes, and fears voiced in the novel exemplify the ideological high tide of the Confederacy.[38]

Evans began by taking her readers back to the momentous sequence of events that had transpired in the immediate aftermath of Abraham Lincoln's election in 1861. Although the South had warned that the election of a sectional president would signal separation, the North had "sneered at the threat" and the die had been cast:

> The 6th of November dawned upon a vast populous empire, rich in every resource, capable of the acme of human greatness and prosperity, claiming to be the guardian of peaceful liberty. It set upon a nation rent in twain, between whose sections yawned a bottomless, bridgeless gulf, where the shining pillars of the temple of Concord had stood for eighty years; and a grating sound of horror shuddered through the land as the brazen, blood-clotted doors of Janus flung themselves suddenly wide apart. Lincoln was elected. Abolitionism, so long adroitly cloaked, was triumphantly clad in robes of state—shameless now, and hideous; and while the North looked upon the loathsome face of its political Mokanna, the South prepared for resistance.

As recalled by Evans, the news had been received with "a stern calm gloom" that was "appropriate in men who realized that they had a revolution on their hands."[39]

After seven states led by South Carolina, "ever the *avant courier* in the march of freedom," had seceded in response to Lincoln's election, many had deluded themselves in the hopes that the dissolution of the Union would be peaceful. Russell Aubrey, the hero of the story who had risen from childhood disgrace to political prominence in the South, had stated his conviction "that no bloodless revolution of equal magnitude had yet been effected, and that we must prepare to pay the invariable sacrificial dues which liberty inexorably demands." Accordingly, he had begun applying his prodigious energies to the study of military tactics well before the attack on Fort Sumter "crushed the last vestiges of 'Unionism,' and welded the entire Confederacy in one huge homogeneous mass of stubborn resistance to despotism."[40]

When the story line shifts to the tyrannical aristocrat Leonard Huntingdon, who abandons his initial resistance to secession and accepts a commission in the Confederate artillery, he and his estranged daughter Irene are at long last reconciled. In the flush of frustrated patriotic enthusiasm, Irene proclaims, "Oh, father! If I were only a man, that I might go with you—stand by you under all circumstances. Couldn't you take me anyhow? Surely a daughter may follow her father, even on the battle-field?" Huntingdon laughs off his daughter's outburst but admires her dauntless courage. Days later as Major Huntingdon prepares to depart, she reiterates her lifelong quest for utility in a man's world: "I think that every man in the Confederacy who can leave his family should be in our army; but a stern sense of duty does not prevent people from suffering at separation and thought of danger. I should be unworthy of my country if I were selfish enough to want to keep you from its defence; and yet I were unworthy of my father if I could see you leave home, under such circumstances, without great grief. Oh! if I could only go with you! But to have to stay here, useless and inactive!"[41]

Assuming the narrative voice at the beginning of the next chapter, Evans rallied her readers to the Confederate flag by describing the immediate transformation wrought by the war in the fictive town on the Georgia fall line where much of the novel takes place:

> W—— presented the appearance of a military camp, rather than the peaceful manufacturing town of yore. Every vacant lot was converted into a parade-ground—and the dash of cavalry, the low, sullen rumbling of artillery, and the slow, steady tread of infantry, echoed through its wide, handsome streets.

> Flag-staffs were erected from public buildings, private residences, and at the most frequented corners, and from these floated banners of all sizes, tossing proudly to the balmy breeze the new-born ensign of freedom—around which clustered the hopes of a people who felt that upon them, and them only, now devolved the sacred duty of proving to the world the capacity of a nation for self-government.

"Loathing and detestation," she continued, had "succeeded the old affection for the Federal government" and the word *Union* had become "everywhere the synonyme of political duplicity, despotism, and utter abrogation of all that had once constituted American freedom, and rendered the republic, in earlier years, the civil Pharos of Christendom."[42]

Future historians would have to coin another adjective than spartan to describe the "stern resolution and self-abnegation" displayed by southern women as they rose in defense of their newborn nation: "Mothers closed their lips firmly to repress a wail of sorrow as they buckled on the swords of their first-born, and sent them forth with a 'God-speed!' to battle for the right; fond wives silently packed their husbands knapsacks, with hands that knew no faltering; and sisters, with tearless eyes, bent by the light of midnight lamps over canteens which their thoughtful care covered for brothers who were to start to the scene of action on the morrow." Evans drove home the moral of the story by observing that "a nation of laboring, nimble-fingered, prayerful-hearted, brave-spirited women, and chivalric, high-souled, heroic men" had "never learned that Americans could live and not be free." Lest her readers forget the goal for which they still labored, the narrator offered the following prayer: "Grant us our reward, oh God! The independence of the land we hold so dear."[43]

Having kept her star-crossed lovers at bay for most of the novel, Evans was obligated by the conventions of domestic fiction to resolve the romantic tension between Russell Aubrey and Irene Huntingdon. According to the standard formula, the hero and the heroine invariably overcame all obstacles and settled down into domestic bliss. Symbolic of her creator's lofty ambitions for all of southern womanhood, Irene elects instead to wed herself to the Confederacy and insists that he do the same. Foreshadowing his eventual albeit heroic doom on the field of battle, Irene proclaims, "Oh, Russell! I can be brave, and strong, and patient; I can bear to see your dear face no more in this world; I can give you up to our country, and not murmur that you died defending her liberties—if I have the conviction that, in noble death, you found the gate of heaven—that I shall meet you again when my God calls me home." Struggling for composure as his lifelong true love throws ice water on his sensual desires, which can only be fulfilled in marriage according to the dictates of polite society, poor Russell must console himself with patriotism, evangelical religion, and a kiss.[44]

Drawing extensively from personal correspondence with General Pierre G. T. Beauregard, Evans also incorporated a detailed account of the first battle of Manassas that undoubtedly quickened the pulses of many readers. Resplendent in his black plumed hat, Colonel Aubrey comes upon his old adversary Major Huntingdon, who has fallen on the field of battle. Their "lifelong hatred and jealousy" are forgotten in their shared commitment to a noble cause and animosity toward a common foe. Mortally wounded, Huntingdon encourages the young hero to give the bayonet to the advancing enemy. Though wounded in the process, Aubrey rallies his regiment and joins the final charge that routs the Federal troops. After pursuing the fleeing Yankees for a mile, Aubrey rides back to the battlefield to find Huntingdon:

> Hideous was the spectacle presented—dead and dying, friend and foe, huddled in indiscriminate ruin, weltering in blood, and shivering in the agonies of dissolution; blackened headless trunks and fragments of limbs—ghastly sights and sounds of woe, filling the scene of combat. Such were the first fruits of the bigotry and fanatical hate of new England, aided by the unprincipled demagogism of the West; such were the wages of Abolitionism, guided by Lincoln and Seward—the latter-day Sejanus; such the results of "higher-law," canting, puritanical hypocrisy.[45]

Joined back in Georgia by her paired heroine Electra Grey, who shares her love for Aubrey but also commits her future to the Confederacy, Irene occupies her time by making bandages. When Electra announces that she is going to Richmond to engage in "true womanly work" in the crowded hospitals, Irene pledges to join her lifelong friend after visiting the family plantation to put her affairs in order. When Electra observes that "a long dark vista stretches before the Confederacy," Irene replies, "Yes—a vista lined with the bloody graves of her best sons; but beyond glimmers Freedom—Independence." Speaking directly through a mournful Irene to a female readership struggling with the emotional trauma of lost and wounded loved ones, Evans proclaimed: "Could I have foreseen the spirit which actuates the North—the diabolical hate and fiendishness which its people have manifested—and had I known that resistance would have cost the lives of all in the Confederacy, I should have urged Secession as the only door of escape from political bondage. Rather would I have men, women, and children fill one wide, common grave, than live in subjection to, or connection with, a people so depraved, unscrupulous, and Godless." Presaging the long and turbulent commitment to state's rights that continued to reverberate through the South's political culture after the destruction of the Confederacy, Irene informs Electra that the "ultimate result can never affect the question of the right and propriety of Secession," stating that she looked to a just God to avenge "the countless graves of our dear and gallant dead."[46]

Evans then redirected the ideological focus of the narrative to the necessity of maintaining virtue in a slaveholding republic, reminding her readers of the dangers of faction and demagoguery. Fortunately, the Confederacy was "a thoroughly homogenous people, with no antagonistic systems of labor" to necessitate conflicting commercial interests. "Purified from all connection with the North, and with no vestige of the mischievous element of New England Puritanism, which like other poisonous Mycelium, springs up pertinaciously where even a shred is permitted," the Confederacy would prosper if it stood vigilant as Lycurgus against the corrupting temptations of great wealth. Another potential danger had also occurred to Irene:

> Unless our planters everywhere become good agricultural chemists, and by a moderate outlay renew their lands every year, the planting interest will gradually drift westward, in pursuit of fresh fertile fields, and thus leave such of the more eastern states to possess great advantages in the water line to engage in manufactures of various kinds. That negro labor is by no means so profitable in factory as field, seems well established; and if this condition of affairs is allowed and encouraged, contrariety of interests will soon show itself, and demagogues will climb into place by clamoring for "protection."

Irene instructs Electra that the solution was free trade with all of the markets of the world "except Lincolndom." Although there was no love lost between Europe and the Confederacy, "the rigid laws of political economy" would "forge links of amity." "If our existence as a Republic depends upon the perpetuity of the institution of slavery," she continued, the aim of Confederate legislators "should be to render us *par excellence* an agricultural people—and, with the exception of great national arsenals and workshops, to discourage home manufactories."[47]

Ultimately, the responsibility for protecting the Confederate republic against the dangers of faction "and the dastardly maxims of luxury and effeminacy" would fall to its mothers, wives, and sisters. Anticipating a retreat into domesticity after victory removed the necessity for the exercise of agency in the public sphere, Irene explains to Electra that southern women had "no desire to usurp legislative reins." Instead, their appropriate work consisted of molding "the manners and morals of the nation; in checking the wild excesses of fashionable life, and the dangerous spirit of extravagance; of reckless expenditure in dress, furniture, and equipage" that had "threatened ruinous results before the declaration of hostilities." Married belles and beaux should not be tolerated in good society, and women "who so far forgot their duties to their homes and husbands, and the respect due to public opinion, as to habitually seek for happiness in the mad whirl of so-called fashionable life, ignoring household obligations, should be driven from well-bred, refined circles, to hide their degradation at the firesides they have disgraced."[48]

Upon their arrival in Richmond, Electra and Irene immerse themselves in the arduous but necessary task of tending to the Confederate wounded. Speaking directly to her readers through the narrative voice, Evans delivers what is the most important moral of the story: "Thus, by different, by devious thorny paths, two sorrowing women emerged upon the broad highway of Duty, and clasping hands pressed forward to the divinely-appointed goal—Womanly Usefulness!" Week after week, the pair of Confederate heroines walk "the painful round from patient to patient, administering food and medicine to diseased bodies, and words of hope and encouragement to souls, who shrank not from the glare, and roar, and carnage of battle—but shivered and cowered before the darling images which deathless memory called from the peaceful, happy Past."[49]

To bring a long story to a close, Irene rushes to Colonel Aubrey's side when he is mortally wounded in the Seven Days conflict while defending Richmond. Whereas Russell is overjoyed to die in his one true love's arms, Irene finds solace in his final acceptance of Jesus. Shifting the scene back to Georgia, Evans brings *Macaria* to an end with Irene looking over Electra's shoulder toward the cemetery at a tall marble shaft marking the final resting place of her fallen hero:

> Sands of Time were drifting stealthily around the crumbling idols of the morning of life, levelling and tenderly shrouding the Past, but sorrow left its

> softening shadow on the orphan's countenance, and laid its chastening finger about the lips which meekly murmured: "Thy will be done." The rays of the setting sun gilded her mourning-dress, gleamed in the white roses that breathed their perfume in her rippling hair, and lingered like a benediction on the placid, pure face of the lonely woman who had survived every earthly hope; and who, calmly fronting her Altars of Sacrifice, here dedicated herself anew to the hallowed work of promoting the happiness and gladdening the paths of all who journeyed with her down the chequered aisles of Time.[50]

That Evans had struck a chord among the women of the slaveholding elite is evidenced by the widespread discussion of *Macaria* in the literature of intimacy. The public reception to her experimentation with the gender norms of the domestic novel likewise reveals that she had touched a raw nerve in plantation society by glorifying the movement of Confederate women into the public arena. Equally striking in retrospect is her decision to downplay the proslavery argument in her narrative. Particularly telling is her failure to explore the problems that plantation mistresses were encountering with slave management on the homefront. The idea of rushing to the aid of the sick and wounded undoubtedly appealed to many readers, but maintaining plantation production was more essential to the Confederate war effort. By 1864 it was also clear that slave agency would play as important a role in determining the future of plantation society as the quest for womanly usefulness among Confederate women.[51]

Georgia planters had realized early in the war that the security of their property in slaves was directly related to the proximity of Union troops. Indeed, the war brought a profound moment of truth to men and women who had taken the loyalty of their slaves for granted. In the words of Leon F. Litwack, "The Civil War threatened to undermine traditional relationships and dissolve long-held assumptions and illusions." Although accustomed to the trials and tribulations of domestic management, many plantation mistresses nonetheless found it difficult to assume full command while their men were away. But as long as rural Georgia remained largely isolated from the major theaters of combat, plantation production continued in spite of the hardships of war. In later years, plantation romancers would elevate the myth of the lady and slave fidelity to new heights while trying to restore ideological coherence to the postwar South. Wartime letters and diaries, however, present a more complex picture of slave accommodation and resistance. Many slaves remained faithful to their masters, but others struck boldly for their freedom. The majority continued to work much as before while struggling to keep their families intact. Masters at testing the parameters of their bondage, even those who remained on the plantation understood that change was in the wind.[52]

The first major indication that the balance between white oppression and black liberty had shifted came with President Lincoln's announcement after Antietam of his plan to free the slaves in the rebelling states, although most Georgia slaveholders realized that such a move would have little immediate effect. As Bill Arp jested, "Mr. Lincoln, sir, I am afraid you are taking in more ground than you can tend." In other words, real emancipation would only follow conquest. Though "mighty near naked" and on half rations, fighting southerners had sworn "by the ghost of Calhoun" to "eat roots and drink branch-water" forever rather than accept Lincoln's "abolition dynasty." Arp joked that "every free negro will get in the cotton-patch now, sure; for the tarnal rebels do every thing by contraries." In a related letter written by Charles Henry Smith in early December 1862, Arp mockingly proclaimed that the glorious day was nearing "when Niggerdom is to feel the power of your proclamation, when Uncle Tom is to change his base and evacuate his cabin, when all the emblems of darkness are to rush frantically forth into the arms of their deliverers, and with perfumed and scented gratitude embrace your Excellancy and Madam Harriet Beecher Stowe!"[53]

But as many coastal planters discovered to their dismay early in the war, black Georgians became increasingly aware of the opportunities for liberty at hand. More than thirty-five hundred black Georgians served in the Union army or navy before the war's end. In addition, the North's early conquest of the sea islands had a strong impact on the local slave population, which made great strides toward autonomy after the planters fled to safety on the mainland. In the meantime, the disruption in the traditional lines of patriarchal authority caused by the war created a tide of resistance and runaways that plantation mistresses throughout the state found alarming. In late March 1862, Kate Peddy wrote to her husband that there had been seven runaways in Troup County in the past week and that one of her father's slaves had told his overseer that "he was not afraid of no white man." Her father planned to sell the man rather than tolerate his insolence. Late in the summer of the following year, Edgeworth Bird instructed his wife in Hancock County to do the same with a troublesome slave named Peter: "I do not wish you annoyed, and I am very certain there should be no such negro on a place *in such times.* I am gratified and very thankful that the balance of our people behave so well." Nevertheless, a number of Bird's slaves participated in an aborted rebellion in Hancock County the following October that resulted in eighteen arrests and four convictions for insurrection.[54]

Operations on large coastal plantations were disrupted the most by the war, at least prior to Sherman's apocalyptic arrival in North Georgia. Louis Manigault wrote in his plantation journal in June 1862 that the "unrighteous and diabolical War" was causing great distress, especially among the house servants. Manigault observed further that such resistance made him "more than ever convinced that the only suitable occupation for the Negro is to be a laborer of the Earth, and to work as a field hand upon a well disciplined plantation." When a half-starved slave carpenter returned to the plantation in August 1863 after hiding out with a group of runaways in the swamp for over a year, Manigault promptly sold him the next month for eighteen hundred dollars to a man from Columbus, making good on his father's earlier recommendation to a neighbor in a similar situation.[55]

The response of leading paternalists like Charles C. Jones to slave resistance and flight was a clear indication of the depth of the crisis along the coast. In July 1862, the Reverend Jones wrote that no slave could be relied upon to resist the temptation of gaining freedom by going over to the enemy. Especially shocking was his sister's loss of a family favorite named Joefinny. Feelings of betrayal were common among paternalistic masters who prided themselves on being loving and benevolent. For the moment, he believed that the "safest plan" was to secure all boats and guard the rivers. Fifty-one slaves had already fled Liberty County. What worried the Reverend Jones was the fact that the slaves knew every road, swamp, creek, and plantation in Liberty County and could easily "pilot an enemy into your *bedchamber!*" Later that month he attended a public meeting in Hinesville to adopt measures to stop the exodus of slaves in Liberty County. The planters who attended the meeting saw no impropriety in requesting that a company of state troops be removed from the coastal defenses and reassigned to protect their property.[56]

After giving the matter some thought, Lieutenant Jones recommended to his father that planters take the law into their own hands if the military and civilian authorities refused to act:

> Terrible corporal punishment, accompanied with close and protracted confinement in the county jail, or public punishment followed by banishment

> from the county and sale in some distant part of the country, seem to me to be proper in cases where the offenders are apprehended under circumstances indicating a purpose on their part to desert to the enemy. . . . No mercy should be shown. . . . If insensible to every other consideration, terror must be made to operate upon their minds, and fear prevent what curiosity and desire for utopian pleasures induce them to attempt. If allowed to desert, our entire social system will be upset if the supremacy of the law of servitude and the ownership of such property be not vigorously asserted in cases where recaptures occur.

Such passages reveal how the war had torn asunder the mask of paternalism to expose the ugly visage of oppression underneath. Eventually, the Jones family attempted to solve the problem by relocating a large number of slaves to an inland plantation that they purchased in Burke County explicitly for that purpose.[57]

As aptly phrased by James L. Roark, the war "plunged planters back to earth." The idealistic discussions that followed in the wake of secession were pushed aside by the practical problems of survival. The loss of revenue from cotton and related shortages, government intrusion through conscription, high taxes, trade restrictions, and inflationary monetary policies, conflict with white nonslaveholders, war damages, the burden of unaccustomed responsibilities on slaveholding and yeoman women, and the disintegration of slavery all worked to erode the South's social unity, yet the planters somehow remained ideologically united as a class in spite of the tensions that were dissolving the harmony of their individual households. Roark argues that the primary goal of the planter class was preservation of plantation slavery, which increasingly created conflict with a government committed to political independence at all costs. Indeed, an independent nation without plantation slavery would have been a pyrrhic victory to the landed elite. Significantly, the struggle to define the nature of social relations in rural Georgia did not end with military defeat and emancipation. After the war the remnants of the proslavery ideology that had been subsumed into the ideology of Confederate nationalism were resurrected in the Lost Cause ideology during Reconstruction.[58]

For the most part, rural Georgia was spared the destruction of combat until the Battle of Chickamauga in late September 1863. Although the Confederate army had succeeded in driving the Union forces back into Chattanooga, the arrival of Ulysses S. Grant and William Tecumseh Sherman in the city boded ill for Confederate Georgia. The long-awaited arrival of the invader was at hand. After suffering defeats at Lookout Mountain and Missionary Ridge, the vastly outnumbered Rebel army fell back into defensive positions in Northwest Georgia. Grant's reassignment to Virginia left Sherman in command of an army of one hundred thousand men ready to march southward the following spring.[59]

Of all the reasons that white Georgians cited for supporting secession, defense of their homes was perhaps the only item in the Confederate lexicon of war that applied universally. To repeat George C. Rable's telling statement, "In Confederate rhetoric, brave men would protect defenseless women and children, but now the supposedly defenseless had to fend for themselves." Rable argues that what made Sherman unique was his blunt determination to bring the war directly to the southern homefront, a new tactic that afterward became standard in modern war. By striking at "the heart of the home," Sherman hoped to destroy the public morale needed to sustain a large army in a difficult war. Left alone to face "the true prince of darkness" and his legions, Confederate women were forced to choose between making a stand or taking flight from the terrible storm gathering in the distance.[60]

Whether they elected to remain in their homes or to seek refuge elsewhere, many Georgians turned to journals and letters to vent traumatized emotions or capture the historical moment for subsequent generations. Such documents communicate the intense anxiety and anger felt by those who were still uncertain as to which direction Sherman's forces would take. Initially, there was the problem of sifting through the wild rumors that preceded the movement of Union troops. Although uncertain whether Sherman's army would enter Heard County should Atlanta fall, for example, Dr. Peddy thought it unlikely and reassured his wife that she need not be "uneasy about the enemy getting to our home." Anticipating that the Union forces would advance along the railroad for logistical reasons, Peddy concluded in September that his wife would be safer at home because their house was located a considerable distance away. Less than a week later in anticipation of the Confederate army's retreat toward Atlanta, he advised that she prepare to move south at once, but flight simply was not an option for Kate Peddy because of the pending birth of their son. Indeed, one wonders in retrospect how much solace she took in his instructions to maintain her "unsullied dignity as a lady" should ten thousand "Yankee cowards" appear at her door.[61]

For those families who lived along the Western and Atlantic Railroad between Chattanooga and Atlanta, the major concern was when not whether the Union army would arrive. In May 1864, Minerva Leah Rowles McClatchey wrote in her diary at her home near Marietta that "everything is in confusion, no one knows what to do with our negroes and stock, nor our ownselves—almost everybody is moving off in hope of securing something." Unlike McClatchey, who decided to stay put, Mary E. Robarts and her sister Louisa eventually fled Marietta with their widowed mother, although such a decision for older women who defined their self-image in terms of the household was extremely difficult. As Robarts wrote on 21 May 1864 to her cousin, Mary Jones, "But oh, those horrid Yankees! How can I see them enter this place and live? I am so afraid of them!" The movement of Union troops into Georgia also resulted in an exodus of slaves from neighboring plantations and accelerated yeoman disaffection with the war. While refugeeing in Atlanta, Charles Henry Smith wrote in "Bill Arp the Roman Refugee" of his regret "that some of our households of the African scent" had fled to the enemy to increase "the stock of *odour d' Afrique* in Northern society." Upon his return to Rome, Arp met his friend "Big John," a reluctant "meelish" home for good after a brief adventure in the military. Having barely escaped Yankee fire, Big John was done with the war, proclaiming, "I'm agin all wars and fightins. I am opposed to all rows, and rumpusses, and riots. I don't keer nigh as much about a dog fight as I used to."[62]

Alone on her farm with one of her sons and a niece, Minerva McClatchey found herself in the middle of the Confederate army as it prepared for the advancing Union forces. Although she could hear cannon booming and pickets firing, McClatchey felt relatively secure because General Hood's headquarters were within sight of her house. On 1 July she wrote in her diary that her house was full of officers and gentlemen, all "courteous and kind" but unwilling or unable to tell her of their pending retreat, which was signaled the following evening by the kindling of small fires to illuminate the road for night marching. The next morning the sound of bullets whizzing near her house announced the arrival of the Yankees, in hot pursuit of the Confederate cavalry. Later that morning, General Hooker and his staff arrived. Pleased to make the acquaintance of a citizen who had not fled her home in fear of Yankee cruelty, Hooker assigned a detachment of guards to protect the premises, although the men left shortly thereafter. McClatchey wrote that the officers who passed through during the day behaved very well but did nothing to prevent the complete looting of her storeroom and kitchen, as well as the total destruction of her crops and chickens. During the next several days, only a series of guards detached at her request by General Thomas prevented her house from being ransacked. Meanwhile, the shrieks and groans of the wounded subjected to the rough transport of ambulances and wagons on the nearby road kept her in constant thought of her "own poor boys who are in similar dangers—and liable to like suffering."[63]

McClatchey recorded sporadic instances of abuse from the "strange rough men" who passed her house during the coming months, but admitted in her diary that her family survived largely through the unexpected courtesies of Union troops. A cavalry major from Ohio who lodged in one of her upstairs rooms, for example, left her a good supply of provisions when the Federal forces pulled out in early November. The next group of soldiers to arrive treated her badly, however, scavenging what little wood remained on her property and confiscating her only cow and calf. The light of burning houses in the night finally convinced McClatchey that the rumors of "a grand march to Savannah" were true. Ordered to rid themselves of their excess baggage, the soldiers who had befriended McClatchey replenished her larder with confiscated goods and provisions. When the Union troops departed on the morning of 14 November, she could not repress her tears over the thought of having benefited from the benevolence of men marching south "to bring tears and suffering to those I love." That evening she watched in terror as Marietta, Kennesaw Mountain, and the railroad burned.[64]

After the fall of Atlanta in September, Sherman became convinced that it would be extremely difficult to defend the Western and Atlantic Railroad. Rather than risk depleting his forces protecting his line of supply, Sherman telegraphed a request to General Grant in early October to cut loose his army and march against Savannah. What was strikingly modern about Sherman's plan was his intent to "make Georgia Howl!" Initially hesitant, Grant came around to the idea when Hood took his army into Alabama. After dispatching a contingent of troops to keep Hood occupied, Sherman and his army of 62,000 men set out from Atlanta on 16 November. As he rode out of the city early in the morning, Sherman paused for one last look: "Behind us lay Atlanta, smouldering and in ruins, the black smoke rising high in air and hanging like a pall over the ruined city. . . . Some band, by accident, struck up the anthem of 'John Brown's soul goes marching on';

the men caught up the strain, and never before or since have I heard the chorus of 'Glory, glory, Hallelujah!' done with more spirit, or in better harmony of time and place."[65]

After camping in sight of Stone Mountain near Lithonia, Sherman's troops passed through Covington. Although he considered the hordes of slaves that flocked to his army a major military encumbrance and resisted the utilization of black soldiers in the Union forces, Sherman wrote that the slaves were "frantic with joy" at his arrival. Without question, the slaves saw Sherman as a liberator rather than the devil: "Whenever they heard my name, they clustered about my horse, shouted and prayed in their particular style, which had a natural eloquence that would have moved a stone. I have witnessed hundreds, if not thousands of such scenes; and can now see a poor girl, in the very ecstasy of the Methodist 'shout,' hugging the banner of one of the regiments, and jumping to the 'Feet of Jesus.'" That night at a plantation house where he made camp, Sherman later recalled meeting an old, gray-haired man "of as fine a head as I ever saw." When asked whether he understood about the war, the old man replied that he had been waiting for an "angel of the Lord" since childhood. Though the North claimed to be fighting for the Union, the old man explained, slavery was the cause of the war and the North's success meant his freedom, a truth that all the slaves understood.[66]

In Sherman's mind Georgia was free for the taking. Sherman acknowledged later that some plundering had occurred but remained sensitive to the scores of tales of his army's brutality that appeared in the press after the war. In his memoirs, he stated that he "never heard of any cases of murder or rape." In the words of a recent biographer, "rape and murder were practically nonexistent," although another historian suggests that in "all likelihood black women served as the unfortunate sexual spoils when Union soldiers asserted their traditional right of military conquest." Sherman's appearance in their state as a liberator of the slaves was hard enough for white Georgians to bear. What Sherman failed to perceive was that his army's rape of mother earth was experienced vicariously as something akin to rape by women who derived their social identity from the land. The dictates of polite society muted the use of such language in one's intimate correspondence, but the journals and letters of many Georgia women reveal that rape is an appropriate metaphor to describe their experience of Sherman's march to the sea. In particular, the violation of the sanctity of their sleeping quarters left plantation mistresses aghast. Years later, the mere mention of Sherman's name brought instantly to mind one of the most terrible experiences of their lives.[67]

The various accounts of Sherman's march written by Georgia women exhibit a fairly consistent pattern. First came the rumors that Yankee troops had been sighted, followed by their sudden appearance, brief pillaging, and rapid departure. Occasionally, a lucky plantation was spared, such as Edgeworth Bird's estate in Hancock County. The wealth of stories relating how the Yankees had been outwitted that circulated after the war aside, frantic efforts to hide precious valuables and livestock were rarely successful, although the proximity of swamp and forest land, the fidelity of servants, the rate of the Union advance, and luck all played a part in those instances where provisions and possessions were saved. What made the experience terrifying for women was the fact that new groups of soldiers continued to arrive over a period of days or weeks, often several times in one day. The feeling of helplessness and the constant fear of being ravaged was a nerve-racking ordeal for women accustomed to deference from their social inferiors and respect from their equals. Moreover, the gallantry observed by Minerva McClatchey during Sherman's long occupation of Marietta apparently diminished as his army moved into the heart of the plantation belt. In any event, an occasional kindness did little to calm emotions subjected to a torrent of abuse, real or imagined.[68]

The detailed journal accounts left by Mary S. Mallard and her mother, Mary Jones, are in many ways representative of the experience of mistresses and their households on large plantations in Georgia. Anticipating childbirth and fearful of remaining in Atlanta, Mallard had joined her mother at Montevideo in Liberty County, ironically concluding that the plantation was a safer haven from Sherman's advancing army. Mary Jones was returning from another of her plantations in her carriage on 13 December 1864 when she encountered a Union soldier on horseback who advised her to turn back or risk losing her horses. Making their way along a rough, obscure road through the woods, she and her driver finally arrived safely at Montevideo well after dark. Fearing the imminent arrival of a raiding party, her daughter had some trunks of clothing and valuables taken into the woods, along with their carts, horses, and oxen. That evening her husband, the Reverend Robert Q. Mallard, arrived for a quick visit before riding out on a mule to join the Confederate forces.[69]

The next afternoon Mallard received the news that her husband had been captured by Hugh Judson Kilpatrick's cavalry. On the morning of 15 December, Union troops finally appeared at Montevideo, demanding horses, mules, and whiskey. The men searched the house, ordering Mrs. Mallard to turn over the keys to all her trunks and bureaus. As the preeminent symbol of matriarchal authority in slaveholding households, the loss of the keys was indeed significant as yet another indication of the failure of plantation society to fulfill its patriarchal obligation to defend the integrity of a lady's domicile. To Mallard's mortification, the men handled everything in sight. Shortly before dinner, the process was repeated by five more Union troops dressed as marines. The following afternoon, forty or fifty men ransacked their pantry, "ripping open the safe with their swords and breaking open the crockery cupboards." During their frenzied search for valuables, the soldiers broke open her mother's worktable. Angry at not finding treasure, "they took the sweet little locks of golden hair" that her mother kept as mementos and trampled them on the floor. At the same time, more men cleaned out the sideboard and her grandfather's old liquor case. During this "horrible nightmare," she wrote, "It was vain to utter a word, for we were completely paralyzed by the fury of these ruffians." Reflecting upon the day's hellish events, Mallard vented her anger: "It is impossible to imagine the horrible uproar and stampede through the house, every room of which was occupied by them, all yelling, cursing, quarreling, and running from one room to another in wild confusion. Such was their blasphemous language, their horrible countenances and appearance, that we realized what must be the association of the lost in the world of eternal woe. Their throats were open sepulchres, their mouths filled with cursing and bitterness and lies."[70]

The Jones family's nightmare was just beginning. Around four o'clock in the morning they were awakened by soldiers who were apparently looking for young women. In the words of the widow Jones, "The agony of that awful hour no language can describe!" Alone, friendless, and in total terror, the women huddled around the bed with the children and prayed through the night for deliverance. Afterward they learned that a soldier had voluntarily guarded the house, which they interpreted more as a sign of divine intervention in direct response to their prayers than an indication of individual Yankee chivalry. Women who had endured such a night would never again look upon the North without mistrust and apprehension, feelings that they undoubtedly transmitted to the next generation.[71]

In the coming days the number of visits lessened in number but not in intensity. A day without Yankees was a blessing spent in fearful anticipation of their return. Although many of her slaves abandoned Montevideo in search of freedom, Mallard reported that many who remained were subjected to repeated outrages by Union troops. In other cases, the slave men remained at their houses to protect their wives "from the hands of these infamous creatures." When one of their slave women ran into the house to escape being assaulted by a Union soldier, Mary Jones confessed to her journal that "my heart palpitates with such violence against my side that with pain I bear the pressure of my dress." Only her faith in God and dreams of Confederate independence sustained the widow Jones through her ordeal. On 3 January, she wondered to herself, "Where will all this perfidy, insult, and injury to the helpless, the fatherless, and the widow end?"[72]

Completely cut off from the outside world, the Jones women had become prisoners in their own home, afraid even to open their doors and windows. Mention of Yankees was enough to send their children scurrying for cover into the house "like a bevy of frightened partridges." The widow Jones thought that such suffering was surely a sign of God's terrible judgment upon the sins of her people, although she did not draw the logical association with slavery. Even the widespread desertion of her servants did not shatter her belief in the sanctity of the peculiar institution, although she admitted that "radical reforms" would be needed if the Confederacy gained its independence. She saw little hope for the future of the "African race" should a liberator filled with racial hatred and contempt emerge victorious. On 11 January, she wrote that "with their emancipation must come their extermination." Ten days later in response to the increasing levels of slave rebellion and flight to Federal lines or vacant plantations in Bryan County, she lamented that "we dare not predict the end of all this, if the Lord in mercy does not restrain the hearts and wills of this deluded people." The fate of her sons unknown and her world in tatters, she looked toward an uncertain future yet remained defiant, proclaiming that "every development of the enemy but confirms my desire for a separate and distinct nationality."[73]

While the world was collapsing around Mary Jones, Joseph LeConte was trying desperately to reach Liberty County to rescue his daughter, nieces, and widowed sister on her plantation. Professor of chemistry and geology at South Carolina College in Columbia since 1857, LeConte operated a chemical laboratory for the Confederate army during the war. After a long detour through Southwest Georgia, he finally reached his sister's plantation on 2 January 1865. An adventurous optimist who apparently seldom lost his sense of humor, LeConte had begun to doubt the success of the Confederate cause just days before, although deeming such thoughts a wicked sacrilege. At considerable personal risk and with the help of loyal slaves, LeConte escorted a group of Liberty County women and several trunks filled with their most treasured possessions to safety in Southwest Georgia before returning to his family in South Carolina. Braving storms, rising water, hazardous water crossings, and the bitter cold in true pioneer fashion, LeConte's party eventually reached Albany near the end of the month.[74]

To his pleasant surprise, LeConte came upon several old friends and neighbors as his party neared Albany. Whereas the LeConte and Jones families of Liberty County only became refugees to escape the desolation that settled over the land in Sherman's wake, many Southerners had taken to the road at the first hint of conflict, some to protect their investment in slaves, others to protect their loved ones. It has been estimated that at least two hundred fifty thousand Southerners fled their homes during the war, more often than not to towns and cities. While the poor came in search of jobs and food, the wealthy often came to revel in a final frenzy of "social madness." For those to the manor born like Ella Clanton Thomas of Augusta, performance at social functions remained the ultimate test of a person's class origins. Thomas also thought the explosion of parties and sociables a welcome release for minds no longer able to endure the constant pressure yet grown accustomed to the long war.[75]

For wealthy young belles like Eliza Frances Andrews and her sister Metta, refugeeing in Southwest Georgia was a glorious adventure. Although Sherman had bypassed the little town of Washington en route to Savannah, it remained unclear in December 1864 whether he would strike next at Augusta or Charleston. Rather than take any chances, Judge Garnett Andrews sent his daughters to join their older sister and her two children on their plantation near Albany, where they remained until April 1865. Over forty years later, Eliza Frances Andrews published an annotated copy of her youthful wartime journal. During her long and productive life, Andrews achieved recognition as a minor novelist, amateur botanist, and teacher. Born in 1840 to a self-described life of aristocratic privilege, "Fanny" was an ardent Confederate patriot who only came to appreciate her father's Unionism later in life. Her wartime journal deserves recognition as a minor literary classic.[76]

During their four-day trip from Washington to Macon, the Andrews sisters traveled through the "Burnt Country" near Sparta. Riding in a rough wagon with an escort of Confederate officers, they slowly made their way through the ravaged countryside along a road lined with the carcasses of horses, hogs, and cattle. In some places the stench became so terrible that they held their noses or used cologne to mask the odor. Every plantation showed signs of pillage, while "Sherman's Sentinels" were all that remained of many homes. So many hungry soldiers crowded the road that Andrews likened it to "traveling through the streets of a populous town all day."[77]

Safe at last in clean, comfortable lodgings at the Lanier House in Macon and exhausted by her rugged travel, Andrews turned her mind to fashion, possibly to forget the terrible images of the desolate landscape through which she had just passed. Frizzing her hair and donning a headdress of black velvet ribbon and gold braid, Andrews dressed for dinner: "I put on my pretty flowered merino that had been freshened up with black silk ruchings that completely hid the worn places, and the waist made over with Elizabethan sleeves, so that it looked almost like a new dress, besides being very becoming, as the big sleeves helped out my figure by their fullness." Reflecting back upon carrying on "the common business of life" amid war and destruction and the willingness of the young "to laugh and dance and be merry in spite of the crumbling of the social fabric" around them, Andrews wrote in her old age that youth would always have its innings and that "never was social life in the old South more full of charm than when tottering to its fall."[78]

Relatively secure and abundant in agricultural riches, Southwest Georgia became a favorite haven for wealthy refugees from Georgia and the Upper South. Determined to follow the expected routine of a belle, Andrews spent her days making social calls, playing cards and backgammon, walking in the piney woods already in their spring bloom of yellow jessamine and forget-me-nots, listening to the slave spirituals at the praise house, and visiting the "cracker people" in the neighborhood in search of young recruits for a Sunday school. On 2 February, she spent the evening at a neighboring plantation "rehearsing for tableaux and theatricals" and delighted in a splendid supper topped off with ice cream, sherbet, and cake made with real white sugar. Though homesick for her family home in Washington, Andrews wrote several days later that one good thing the war had done among its many evils was to bring her "into contact with so many pleasant people we should never have known otherwise." On 16 February she wrote that she did not get home from a party in Albany until well past four o'clock in the morning. Clearly, war was not hell for everyone in Georgia.[79]

Yet true to Sherman's original intent, those parts of the state that he attacked found little cause for celebration after his departure. One of the first things that Dolly Lunt Burge did after the Yankees left was to visit her graveyard, which she happily found undisturbed. Lucky enough to salvage a mule and a little wagon, Burge shared her good fortune with her neighbors by hauling wheat to the mill, a most unusual activity for a widow. As she explained in her diary, "Never did I think I would have to go to mill. Such are the changes of life." As it had done since the initial outbreak of hostilities in 1861, the war continued to redefine traditional gender roles in the South, albeit in ways that suggested that the collapse of plantation society was at hand.[80]

Like many Georgia families throughout the war, Mary Gay and her mother had invested heavily in Confederate bonds, which later left them "as poor as the poorest, and as hungry too" when their value collapsed. Yet like Burge, Gay turned her attention to helping the less fortunate. Impressing a nearly worn-out horse abandoned by the Union army into service pulling a jerry-rigged wagon, she transported supplies through war-stricken country from Social Circle to Decatur, walking the entire way to rest the poor animal. When she learned of a provision store in Atlanta where war hardware could be bartered for necessities, Gay began collecting minié balls. On a cold, windy day in late November, she discovered the spot where retreating Confederate troops had exploded a magazine, a bonanza that fed many poor people through the winter. While digging lead with dull case-knives, the women and children would sing "When This Cruel War Is Over," then have a good cry. Minerva McClatchey and her son collected scrap lumber from abandoned Federal camps and scavenged nails from burnt buildings, "glad to make any shift to live." Traditionally a time of celebration and renewal of paternalistic bonds on Georgia plantations, Christmas was a sad time for those who remained on the land in 1864. Cornelia Jones Pond later recalled that "the little children thought that the Yankees would not let Santa Claus come." Little Sadai Burge retreated to her bed in tears after finding her stocking empty. She was soon joined by her mother when the slave children came in calling "Christmas gift mistress."[81]

Their faith in "the hand of Providence" intact, Georgians went about the grim business of rebuilding shattered lives amid the turmoil of the new year. As they had for generations, farm families turned to the land to see them through hard times, burying themselves in the normal routines of life to dispel thoughts of all that had been lost. The collapse of law and order in many areas, however, indicated that the end was drawing near. Small groups of refugees began drifting back to homes ravaged by Sherman's bummers or opportunistic scavengers. As Minerva McClatchey wrote in January, "Many citizens are almost as bad as the Yankees, one waggon after another goes by, loaded with plunder of various kinds, gathered from camps or empty houses." The reality of defeat finally dawned on Eliza Frances Andrews while she raced Union troops that were advancing eastward from Columbus in April. Momentarily trapped in Macon's wild confusion, she finally admitted, "We are whipped, there is no doubt about it."[82]

All the while, rural blacks had begun flocking to the nearest town or city to celebrate their pending freedom. In Athens a noisy crowd danced around a liberty pole in the center of town, although local whites cut it down during the night. As observed by Leon F. Litwack, whites and blacks alike would retain "emotionally charged memories of this critical moment in their lives." During the closing months of the war, the women of the slaveholding elite struggled to come to terms with the collapse of the "natural order." Some turned their thoughts to good and evil, others to ways to reform the institution of slavery short of manumission. Ella Clanton Thomas fantasized that southern women would be avenged when Yankee soldiers consorted with mulatto women. Angry and confused by feelings of betrayal and loss, women who well understood that class privilege and slavery were inexorably intertwined experienced a profound emotional crisis during the breakdown of the paternalistic system they had always taken for granted. The widow Burge expressed a common dilemma facing Georgia planters at the end of the war. Upon learning near the end of May that many planters were "allowing" former slaves to remain on the land if they remained obedient, she wrote in her diary: "What I shall do with mine is a question that troubles day & night. It is my last thought at night & the first in the morning. I told them several days ago they were free to do as they liked. But it is my duty to make some provision for them. I thank God that they are freed & yet what can I do without them?"[83]

Although it is impossible to determine how many Georgia planters shared Burge's feelings about the end of slavery, many accepted defeat with Christian stoicism. Minerva McClatchey's reaction to Lee's surrender was typical: "Can it be so? It is painful—humiliating—but we must submit. It is God's will, and whatever The Will is for the best." As the Charles C. Jones family's letters poignantly reveal, it is simply impossible to untangle religion, slavery, and republican notions of property and liberty within the ideology of Confederate nationalism. In much the same way that they accepted disease, death, and the vagaries of the weather, rural Georgians saw the hand of God in every event in the war. Each success was interpreted as a sign of divine favor and justification for the Confederate cause, each defeat as righteous punishment and a call for national and individual critical evaluation. As Mrs. George J. Kollock wrote to her son in September 1863: "If the Nation would only seek the Lord and give Him the praise that is due unto his name, cry to him & pray with fervant hearts, then would he spare our land & defend our people; but No! Individuals there are who earnestly seek His face; but as a people, we do not love God, nor obey his commands, therefore we need to be disciplined, and the godly must suffer heavily with the wicked, for the national sins."[84]

Not surprisingly, a wave of revivals swept through the Confederate army in northern Georgia late in the war, a tragic prayer for deliverance by desperate men who realized that the end was drawing near. But the simple truth was that impassioned appeals for divine intervention were no protection from an enemy equally convinced in the righteousness of his cause and materially equipped to finish the job at hand. In the final analysis, Lincoln had seized the Cromwellian moment in 1862 when he wedded the preservation of the Union to emancipation. Although some Georgians considered Lincoln's assassination righteous retribution, a "sweet drop among so much that is painful," others deemed it "a piece of unnecessary barbarity" fraught with dire political consequences.[85]

There was also a world of difference between accepting defeat and reconciliation with a hated foe. As Eliza Frances Andrews confided to her diary in early 1865, "If all the words of hatred in every language under heaven were lumped together into one huge epithet of detestation, they could not tell how I hate Yankees." In April she admitted to being "crushed and bowed down" in sorrow but not in shame, angrily proclaiming, "No! I am more of a rebel to-day than ever I was when things looked brightest for the Confederacy." The Georgia countryside and towns were filled with unreconstructed rebels who echoed Bill Arp's defiant blast, "Who's sorry? Who's repenting?" When Confederate soldiers rioted in Augusta in May, a fearful Ella Clanton Thomas nonetheless refused to label the disturbance a rebellion because "rebel" had become "a sacred word now, worthy to be ranked with such words as Home, Heart & Heaven." The corpse of the Confederacy buried in the scorched earth, Georgia planters turned their thoughts to reclaiming the land, trusting in the sun's redemptive warmth and hoping that peaceful weather would last through the season. Deeply rooted and nourished by the rich soil of hatred and defiance, plantation society was entering yet another winter of discontent. Whether King Cotton would be restored to his throne remained open to question.[86]

What, then, can we conclude from the record of life in Georgia during the Civil War preserved in the literature of domesticity? Although fiction for the most part took a back seat to more pressing concerns, Augusta Jane Evans outlined an ideal of female patriotism in *Macaria; or, Altars of Sacrifice* that spoke dramatically to the ideological foundations of Confederate nationalism. The impact of the war on Georgia households, however, exposed the fundamental contradictions in the political arrangements and social relations of plantation society. Moreover, by entering their perceptions of the war into the historical record, the authors of journals and letters were stockpiling ammunition for the bitter ideological struggles that plagued Georgia in the closing decades of the nineteenth century. Whether published or not, the literature of intimacy was a bloody shirt that contributed to the eventual triumph of the Lost Cause ideology.

CHAPTER FIVE

Reclaiming the Scorched Earth

Reconstruction and the Literary Response

Safely home in Macon after his long trek from Virginia but sick in body and spirit, Sidney Lanier expressed poetically in "The Wedding" the despair felt by many Georgians at the South's forced reunion with the North:

> O Marriage-Bells, your clamor tells
> Two weddings in one breath.
> *She* marries whom her love compels:
> —And I wed Goodman Death!
> My brain is blank, my tears are red;
> Listen, O God:—"I will," he said:—
> And I would that I were dead.
> Come groomsman Grief and bridesmaid Pain
> Come and stand with a ghastly twain.
> My Bridegroom Death is come o'er the meres
> To wed a bride with bloody tears.
> Ring, ring, O bells, full merrily:
> Life-bells to her, death bells to-me:
> O Death, I am true wife to thee!

Inspired by talk of independence and liberty, and eager to defend their homes and the southern way of life, the white nonslaveholding majority had followed the planter elite's lead into a political revolution. Those who survived the fall of the Confederacy soon found themselves amid a social revolution of unanticipated magnitude, one that failed to achieve many of its primary objectives but nonetheless transformed the lives of most rural Georgians. In the words of Eric Foner, "Like a massive earthquake, the Civil War and the destruction of slavery permanently altered the landscape of Southern life, exposing and widening fault lines that had lain barely visible just beneath the surface."[1]

Looking into the postwar abyss in 1865 in a companion piece entitled "Wedding-Hymn," Lanier prayed for guidance to smooth "the life-road of this man and wife" united in bloody matrimony, but warned in "Timeo Danaos! A Voice of the Night" that the freedmen should beware of Greeks bearing the "gift" of emancipation. Writing in Negro dialect to the "white man what prints de papah," Lanier chided the supposedly foolish and childlike reaction of blacks on a Bibb County plantation to their initial taste of freedom. In his unpublished and little remembered story, freedman Jim Steveson describes a recent public meeting "ob de niggahs" to consider what to do with the seven million white people "now beggin' at our dores" and otherwise dependent on the "charities" of their former slaves.[2]

Like many white Georgians, Lanier channeled his hatred of the North toward the freedmen, taking a perverse delight in his offensive racist language and stereotypes. The meeting begins in Aunt Keziah's kitchen but soon moves outdoors to escape the heat and "de unpleazunt oder." Considered by the crowd a "distinguished gemplum f'om abroad" because he lives on a plantation four miles away, Steveson recalls that when he stepped forward to make an address, "all de niggahs hollered an' stawmped an' clapped deir hands, an' dat same unpleazunt oder filled de air, but I sorter liked it dis time."[3]

Lanier's bitter experiment in "darky" humor also ridiculed the leadership abilities of plantation preachers. Steveson relates how he brought the "congregation" to tears with his story of "how de niggah cum to be black an' how his nose cum to be flat," a mocking reference to the biblical tale of Shem and Ham that had long been a favorite among the defenders of slavery. Like many white Georgians in 1865, Lanier equated emancipation with the loss of racial purity, although miscegenation actually declined after the war. As Steveson explains: "Niggahs, sez I, de nose is done cum straight, an' de skin is gittin' whiter ebery day, by de use ob a new skin-powdah, which dey call Missegennit. De niggah was once trod wery heavy flat in de dus': he is now wery powuful. You kin git what you want. What does you all want? sez I."[4]

In response, one man had shouted that he wanted "a waggin-load o' water millions an' some papah collahs," while another had expressed his longing for all the preserves he could eat and a pair of boots. A woman had proclaimed her desire for a white satin head-handkerchief, a piano, and marriage to "Mister Butlah." All that old Aunt Charity had wanted was for "little Dick" to be "eadickated for de gawspel" so he could "preech unto de people eben as de Ass preeched unto Balaum!" As is often the case in Georgia's literary tradition, Lanier's angry diatribe reveals an unintended truth. While his intent was to reveal the supposedly childlike freedman's lack of readiness for life without his master's guidance, Lanier also communicates the strong desire among former slaves for independence, dignity, and a taste of the good life long denied them on the plantation. Significantly, the determination of the freedmen to acquire land was almost as disturbing to Lanier as racial intermarriage. Steveson explains to the editor that the meeting had erupted into violence: "I wants dis plantation, sez one big niggah whoze acquaintance I had not de honor: no, sah, I wants dat sez big Isaac: no sah, sez Unc' Fisher, I'm gwine to take dat: an' so in a few minnits dey all begin to fite about de plantation."[5]

A few days later when Steveson went to town, his delusions of grandeur were shattered by what he found there. Unfortunately, his Yankee redeemer's understanding of freedom for the black man was quite different from what he had expected: "I seed, in town, a free niggah, a-workin'!!!! I seed a large buck niggah, with a chain upon his free Angle-Saxwhen legs, an' a big bawl hitched to it, a-sweepin' up de street!!!!! I seed a niggah what wuz too lazy to swing his arms: an' de marshal (golly, I thought marshals wuz dead,—hung by Mr. Linkum) tied his hands up to a jice, to save him de trouble, so he sed!" To his dismay Steveson was told that he must support his present wife, "dough which ob de seben I is to support, de Lord knows!" Moreover, when he became hungry and grabbed a ham, a soldier in blue struck him down and threw him in the guardhouse. To his amazement, upon his release the guard ordered Steveson to go home and get to work, to which he replied, "Me sah, go to work!!!!! Does you call dis freedom? I calls it free-*dam!* I wants suf'fen to eat."[6]

As do all fairy tales, Lanier's story had a moral, although as befitted the times, the ending was uncertain. Having learned that the North's notions of freedom are hardly his own, Jim Steveson comes to his senses and realizes that his life in slavery had been better. Hungry, alone, and friendless, he tells the "white man what prints de papah!" that he would be very happy "to lib wid you de res' ob his life" and do any sort of work for "vittles an' your ole close," closing with "I is sorry dat I has to sign myself, No longer yours."[7]

Not surprisingly, the dark undercurrent of white hostility that underlies the black minstrelsy tradition in Georgia literature surfaced during times of social and ideological disarray alongside wistful memories of a golden era when blacks supposedly had known and accepted their place in plantation society. One can only speculate why Lanier decided against publishing "Timeo Danaos! A Voice of the Night." The scarcity of publishing opportunities for southern authors in the immediate postwar years possibly gave his artistic judgment time to calm his overheated emotions. A son of the urban South who later came to reject the plantation economy as a stifling manifestation of commercial exploitation, Lanier was a gentle man who may have had second thoughts about the story's hard edge. More memorable as social commentary than art, the story also captures a unique historical moment in Georgia. Badly shaken but anything but gone with the wind, the planter elite faced two enormous obstacles in its struggle to redeem its dominance in state and local affairs and reestablish control over black labor. Their influence in national political life destroyed, southern planters realized that the desire of Radical Republicans for fundamental reconstruction of the South and the determination of the freedmen to shape their own destiny stood in their path. Concerned primarily for the moment with the difficult task of restoring life to their impoverished lands, Georgia's yeoman farmers were a wild card waiting in the wings.

From the perspective of a proud, bloodied, and angry North, the problem was how to bring a still defiant if vanquished foe back into the Union without sacrificing the political changes engineered during the war. In their literary campaign to win back a measure of what had been lost, or at least stop the postwar hemorrhaging in the plantation economy, former Confederates like Charles Henry Smith argued that a suitably humbled South stood hat-in-hand and ready to rejoin the Union, asking only for understanding and the fair treatment worthy a former adversary who had acquitted himself honorably on the field of battle. Writing as Bill Arp in September 1865, he explained to Artemus Ward, the pseudonym of the Yankee humorist Charles Farrar Browne, that he was trying to harmonize, soften his feelings, and "subjugate myself to the level of surroundin circumstances, *so-called*," but was tired of the stream of abuse being directed against the South by northern editors:

> But talkin the way I see it, a big feller and a little feller *so-called,* got into a fite, and they fout a long time, and everybody all round kept hollerin, "hands off," but helpin the big feller, until finally the little feller caved in and hollered enuf. He made a bully fite, I tell you, Selah. Well, what did the big feller do? Take him by the hand and help him up, and brush the dirt off his clothes? Nary time! No sur! But he kicked him arter he was down, and throwed mud on him, and drugged him about and rubbed sand in his eyes, and now he's gwine about huntin up his poor little property. Wants to confiscate it, *so-called.* Blame my jacket if it ain't enuf to make your head swim.[8]

An unreconstructed rebel to the core, Arp had taken his oath of loyalty and meant to keep it, but stood unashamed and unrepentant. "Poor but proud," Arp was doing his "durndest to harmonize" but had to admit that the sight of "a black-guard goin around the streets with a gun on his shoulder" made him "hate the whole Yankee nation." "The whole of Africa" had come to town and was refusing to work on the plantations, "livin on rosting ears and freedom, with nary idee that the winter will come agin, or that castor-oil and salts cost money." As Arp concluded, "Harmonize the devil! Ain't we human beings? Ain't we got eyes and ears and feelin and thinkin?"[9]

In another essay on Reconstruction entitled "Bill Arp on the State of the Country," Smith continued his attack on "newspaper scribblers" who slipped "down to the edge of Dixey every twenty-four hours" to "peep over at us on tip-toe," then "run back a-puffin and blowin with a straight coat tail" hollering for everyone to look out because the South was not dead. Eager to feed a news-hungry public, northern newspapers and magazines gladly sponsored a few brave souls who dared to venture below the Mason-Dixon line. The war correspondent Whitelaw Reid jumped at the chance to join a party of federal officials who undertook a voyage of inspection and observation through the conquered states. Named managing editor of the New York *Tribune* by Horace Greeley in 1868, Reid later served as minister to France from 1889 to 1892 and ambassador to England from 1905 until his death. Reid explained in the preface to his 1866 publication, *After the War: A Southern Tour,* that he had spent most of the year beginning in May 1865 traveling in "the late Rebel States." Recalling the South's "frenzied joy at the prospect of bloodshed" in 1861 with the depressed mood of the countryside after the war, Reid could not help but gloat a bit in the aftermath of the "Rebellion." Together with the travel accounts of Sidney Andrews, John Richard Dennett, and Edward King, Reid's observations provide a useful counterbalance to the perceptions of early Reconstruction contained in the literature of intimacy and fiction written by contemporary Georgians. Whereas the main themes in the writings of former Confederates were loss and resistance, the primary concern of northern travelers was finding a way to reap the economic spoils of war without rending further the political fabric of the nation.[10]

Led by Chief Justice Salmon P. Chase, the expedition departed on the first of May on the *Northerner,* an ocean-going revenue cutter. After arriving in Savannah, where the sea islands were still under freedman control and work was in progress clearing the river of obstacles intended to prevent the passage of Union ironclads during the war, Reid's group toured Fort Pulaski and caught sight of Jefferson Davis, who had recently been captured in "semi-female disguise." Reid's description of Savannah accords well with Smith's observation about the hostile northern press. Led to believe that Savannah, Charleston, Wilmington, and Richmond were fine cities, he cautioned northern readers to exercise caution before accepting pretentious southerners at their own valuation. In truth, Savannah was simply "a scattered, tolerably well-built town of twenty thousand inhabitants," not a city on the order of Cincinnati or Chicago, much less New York or Boston.[11]

Reid described the people of Savannah as polite but sullen, observing, "It was evident that they felt conquered" and were ready to submit "in whatever policy the Government should adopt," which he considered a "golden opportunity" for a statesman to step in and "shape and mold" southern institutions. Unlike Charleston, which had been deserted by whites, Savannah "had been taken, inhabitants and all" and business was progressing much as usual. Except for outdated fashions, Reid saw no signs of suffering: "Save that the schools were filled with negroes, and the rebel newspapers had been succeeded by loyal ones, and guards in blue, instead of gray, stood here and there, it was the rebel Savannah unchanged." Although not recognized as such by Reid, all three were in fact major changes that a southern "city" could not endure quietly for long.[12]

As northern travelers frequently had done before the war, Reid breakfasted at the Pulaski Hotel. Describing the fare as very poor, he dined at a common table with a dozen former Confederate officers. Shabby furniture, broken dishes, and the absence of forks evidenced four hard years of war, although there were plenty of polite black waiters to go around and the bar was doing a thriving business "in bumpers of liquors altogether too strong for the climate." He recalled overhearing local residents comment as they freely spent hoarded greenbacks to treat their returning heroes, "Well, Colonel, you don't come back victorious, but I'm d——d glad to see you, any way. Your old friends are proud of you. Come and have a drink," and "Sorry about that ugly wound, Captain. A hand is a bad thing to lose, but it wont hurt you among the ladies of Savannah. There are plenty that you can persuade to give you one. What'll you drink?"[13]

While in Savannah, Chief Justice Chase received a delegation led by an articulate mulatto preacher who inquired into the federal government's plans and asked what the freedmen needed to do to secure unjustly deprived rights and the franchise. Reid reported that Chief Justice Chase expressed the fear common in the North that the former slaves in the interior, who lacked the culture of the Savannah group, might be tricked into voting for tickets designed by their old masters, thus casting their influence to "the side of bad morals and bad politics." A "coal-black" man assured Chase that his people could distinguish between friends and enemies and that their leaders would be able to control the votes of the field hands on the plantations. One man maintained that blacks knew the difference between Union and Rebel politics better than northerners because "some of our people stand behind these men at the table, and hear 'em talk; we see 'em in the house and by the wayside; and we *know* 'em from skin to core, better than you do or can do, till you live among 'em as long, and see as much of 'em as we have." The threat of such a political alliance soon sparked a hostile reaction among white Georgians.[14]

When Chase also voiced apprehension about the negative power of uneducated voters, the delegation's leader reminded the Chief Justice that one in ten white Georgians was illiterate and claimed that given the opportunity to educate their young, eighty percent of the black population would be literate in three years, so deep was the desire to learn. The preacher also argued that federal assistance was good, practical politics, basically offering the black vote in return. Another delegation of less cultivated and more coarsely dressed blacks reported numerous atrocities at the hands of old masters, including whippings and ear croppings. While some freedmen were bearing such oppression patiently, Reid reported, others were angry and "full of revengeful thoughts." Reid thought a slave insurrection improbable, but warned that any man on the levees of the Mississippi River could "loose the floods of half a continent." Such press played into the hands of Radical Republicans in the North and large southern landowners by helping both to mobilize public opinion for action.[15]

Wherever Reid went the unsettled condition of labor was the dominant topic of conversation. Few whites spoke of making wage arrangements with the freedmen and those that existed resembled "mexican peonage" in that debt was already being used to reinstitute slavery. Still, Reid met no freedmen who favored colonization. Most simply wanted for whites to be "removed from what they consider their own country." Whereas most blacks wanted land, it was the want of labor that troubled white landowners. Many whites envisioned an apprenticeship system or similar means to legally bind black labor to the land. Reid "found no Georgian who, now that his slaves can no longer be made to work for him, expects to work for himself. . . . Work is for 'niggers'—not for white men."[16]

Neither did planters acknowledge the wisdom of selling off part of their lands to finance their survival on their remaining acres, believing it dishonorable to their fathers or doubting that buyers could be found. One planter stated the dilemma of his class quite succinctly. If he sold his land, how would he make his livelihood, for he had no other trade or profession? As he told Reid, "I own these lands, and, if the niggers can be made to work, they'll support me; but there's nothing else that I know anything about, except managing a plantation." An indication of how little the planter outlook had changed was his conviction that making the freedmen work was the key to his survival. Reid argued that necessity eventually would transform southern social relations unless the planters succeeded in cheating the federal government and making a sham of emancipation, a remarkably accurate prediction by a free labor optimist. He also maintained that when planters finally put their lands on the market "rather than honestly attempt to work them with free labor," northern entrepreneurs would enjoy "such an opening as rarely coffers twice in one capitalist's lifetime." Yet as C. C. Jones Jr. and his mother discovered to their dismay, land values had collapsed but the market for Georgia plantations in the North was severely limited.[17]

Reid's account of his discussions with "Rebel" visitors in Savannah suggests that what the landed elite in Georgia considered fair treatment boiled down to exchanging their loyalty to the Union for unrestricted control over black labor, an accommodation they deemed perfectly reasonable between honorable white men. To his astonishment, Reid's white visitors failed completely to grasp his argument that they had sacrificed their constitutional rights through armed rebellion against the nation. The only thing they were willing to surrender was slavery. In his words, "They stand ready to claim everything, if permitted, and to accept anything, if required," which was a direct call for the federal government to take charge of a dangerous situation.[18]

Only in Atlanta were Georgians adjusting with rapidity "to the new order of things." Unlike Richmond, Atlanta was rebuilding quickly, a boomer spirit also observed by Andrews, Dennett, and King. According to Reid, no fewer than four thousand mechanics were at work and an equal number could have been employed had materials been available. Nearly two hundred stores had reopened and the streets were crowded with drays and wagons. Trade was a third greater than it had ever been. Still, "the faces one saw on the streets or behind the counters were not the faces of men with whom you would choose to do business." He concluded that "the traces of the bad passions and disregard of moral obligations which the war has taught, are written almost as plainly on the faces as are Sherman's marks on the houses of Atlanta."[19]

Reid also reported widespread suffering among Union men in North Georgia as a consequence of the restoration to political power of old secessionists. Moreover, southern gentlemen liked Andrew Johnson "because he is conservative on the nigger" and few took their oaths of allegiance seriously. The final argument in Reid's case for federal intervention in the South was the widespread squalor, misery, and demoralization of the population. Amid "the hustle and whirl of Atlanta" he recalled seeing "a poor, half starved, half naked white woman, gathering her little children about her, and cowering in the gray dawn over the dull embers by which, in dull wretchedness, she had watched through the weary night."[20]

Surrounded by the "sad destruction" of the war, planters refused to buy into Reid's argument that wage labor was the solution to all of their ills, the first step on the road to recovery and reunion. The "handsome tigers" who had led the South through the war demanded total control or total exclusion of black labor via colonization, seeing no middle ground for compromise. When Reid suggested that the former slaves were just intoxicated by their first taste of freedom and would soon settle down to work if paid fair wages, a young Alabamian replied, "I tell you, niggers are niggers. You're talking about a different class of laborers altogether." Reid considered it manifestly obvious, however, that the freedmen had no faith in their old masters.[21]

Although neither was as closely connected with the Republican Party as Whitelaw Reid, the journalists Sidney Andrews and John Richard Dennett also made strong cases for more extensive federal intervention in their reports of their experiences while traveling in Georgia in 1865. Andrews was a correspondent with the Boston *Advertiser* and the Chicago *Tribune* who traveled through the Carolinas and Georgia between September and November, whereas Dennett had been dispatched by *The Nation* and wrote thirty-six articles relating to a nine-month tour from July 1865 to March 1866. Trained as a journalist at Harvard, Dennett had served as superintendent of plantations with the Port Royal experiment during the war. One of the central concerns of his sponsors at *The Nation,* who included the magazine's editor E. L. Godkin and Frederick Law Olmsted, was the role to be played by the South in the newly reunited nation.[22]

Andrews arrived in Milledgeville just as the Georgia state convention was beginning a thirteen-day-long session. While his account of the proceedings is largely beyond the scope of this study, the mood of the convention as reported by Andrews undoubtedly made a strong impression on northern public opinion. His statement that "it would be a mockery to say that this was a Convention of loyal men" communicates the overall tone of his reports. Not only was the "States-rights heresy" dominant, the call for federal compensation for the loss of slaves was "scarcely less than an insult," while the convention's legislative actions made it obvious that the intention was to make the freedmen slaves again in all but name.[23]

The spirit of defiance Andrews witnessed in Milledgeville was even stronger in Albany, which he described as a "dirty, slovenly, and shiftless" little town of twenty-five hundred persons that had been an important Confederate storehouse during the war. Andrews quoted one man as saying, "I have my pardon in my pocket, and have taken the oath three times . . . but I'll be d——d if I ain't as big a Rebel as I ever was!" More disturbing was the widespread immorality and lawlessness Andrews observed during his visit to "the House of Judge Lynch." When he tried to intervene in a racial quarrel, Andrews sparked the drunken wrath of a former Confederate major. He reported that when the old black man involved in the incident returned with five Union soldiers to arrest the fierce major, they encountered his gang in front of the hotel. With only thirty troops under his command, the post commandant stood by helplessly while the major horsewhipped the old man, who Andrews explained had always been a free man. That evening a mob gathered in front of the hotel. The landlord, a former Confederate captain, advised Andrews to remain in his room unless he was prepared to kill or be killed. Later from a safe distance, Andrews asked his northern readers, "Wasn't this a pretty dish to set before a little Yankee whose only weapons were a pen and inkstand!"[24]

Deeming it the only honorable course of action, the hotel landlord and his clerk, who was also a Confederate veteran, slipped Andrews out the back to safety at a house on the edge of town, where he wisely boarded a freight train at 5:30 in the morning rather than wait for the mail train two hours later. While the mob in Albany undoubtedly had enjoyed a good laugh at his expense, the "little Yankee's" pen was in fact a potent weapon. By reporting that many of the town's leading citizens had been involved in the incident, Andrews reinforced the negative impressions he had seen in Milledgeville. Although it is impossible to determine whether such reports impacted the federal government's Reconstruction policies, they undoubtedly prepared the northern public for further intervention by portraying Georgia's leaders as drunken, unrepentant, and lawless traitors. A few days later Andrews reported from Columbus that the statewide elections had returned former Confederates to office, which he labeled an intentional test of the North's will.[25]

The hostile political climate also affected the prospects for investment in Georgia. Both Andrews and Dennett recorded widespread evidence of the return of northern capital throughout Georgia, although popular resistance to trading with Yankees remained strong. A young New Yorker with reputed Wall Street connections told Dennett that northern investors had reopened credit lines with older firms, hoping to collect longstanding debts. Dennett argued, however, that entrepreneurs could avoid messy associations with local whites by employing freedmen in agriculture, lumbering, and "similar branches of business" linked with the foreign market, a bias that reflected his experience with the Port Royal experiment. The underlying issue was the relation between land, labor, and the market for staple crops.[26]

In early January 1866, Dennett wrote from Macon that deference to southern "social and political theories and opinions" would not ensure a safe climate for northern investment in many parts of Georgia. In Stewart County, a landowner had asked two Union officers from Ohio to cancel a three-year lease on two plantations. Planning to plant cotton, they had purchased the necessary supplies, tools, and mules, and contracted the labor of forty freedmen. The landowner's neighbors, however, told him "that no Yankee should be suffered to live in that country" and that his tenants would be killed and his house "burned over his head" if he followed through with the arrangement. Another northern investor had decided to sell his share of a business to his southern partner rather than risk personal violence or bankruptcy, concluding that "this country won't be any place for Yankees or niggers when the troops are mustered out." [27]

The willingness of Georgia planters to use legal and extralegal force to restore their control over black labor often created conflict with the Freedmen's Bureau, although as the historian Lewis Nicholas Wynne has written, "Despite the frequent abuse heaped upon it by whites, the agency greatly aided the reestablishment of planter control over the Southern economy." Essentially, the federal government's failure to institute a program of land redistribution set the stage for the revival of the plantation system. By interpreting the aversion of blacks to labor for white planters as a sign of "indolence," the agents of the Freedmen's Bureau often played directly into the hands of the landed elite. Although no longer laborlords in control of a large slave population, Georgia's cotton belt planters remained a force to be reckoned with as long as their property in land remained intact. Only along the rice coast would the old planter families fail to restore long-term productive control over the land. There is significant literary evidence of the failure of individual planter families to hold onto their lands after the Civil War, but the plantation system survived and spread into the upcountry and wiregrass regions in the ensuing decades. None of this was apparent in 1865 and 1866. As pointed out by Foner, the all-absorbing question that dominated conversation among southern planters was "will the Negro work?" [28]

Andrews maintained that "fair treatment" rather than compulsion was the key to restoring plantation productivity. He applauded the experiment with sharecropping instituted by a paternalistic former Confederate colonel in Lee County, who treated his former slaves with dignity. Still, as the testimony of a freedman on another plantation who was seeking assistance from the Freedmen's Bureau reveals, the potential for conflict within share arrangements remained strong:

> Ole mass'r had 'greed to give we one tird de craps, an' we dun got 'em all up,—got de corn shucked, an' de tatees digged, and de rice trashed; an' ole mass'r he dun gone sold all de craps, an' he bringed we all up yere yes'erday, an' gif we seven dollar fur de man an' he wife to buy de cloth wid to make we clofes, an' he say may be he gif we some shoes; an' he dun gif we'n none o' de tatees, on'y de seven dollar fur de man an' he wife; an' den he tell we ter

come on de plantation no mo'; an' he say we all bof mus' make livin' on we'ns freedom; an' we got not'ing fur all de work on'y de seven dollar fur de man an' he wife, an' we got no corn nor not'ing for de winter.[29]

Premodern in his understanding of the nature of work, the freedman had no desire to market the product of his labors. Yet for all their other differences, the agents of the Freedmen's Bureau and Georgia planters shared common ground in their understanding of the commercial value of cash crops, a consideration that began almost immediately to militate against the freedmen's desire for autonomy. On Christmas morning in 1865, John Dennett chanced upon a speech being delivered from the door of City Hall by Colonel Curkendall of the Atlanta Freedmen's Bureau to a crowd of about two hundred blacks and a few whites. That work was the primary concern of the Freedmen's Bureau quickly became clear to Dennett. Curkendall told the freedmen that they could expect no land and that insurrection would not be tolerated, but if "they would behave like men" their recently acquired civil rights would probably be expanded to include the suffrage. Justice would be given to all regardless of race. Education of their children and the restoration of productive relations with the "many good men in Georgia who would be their friends if they were industrious and well-behaved" were the surest ways to acquire the ballot more quickly. While the cost of supporting a large indigent population undoubtedly influenced federal Reconstruction policy, the Freedmen's Bureau's actions also reflected the Republican party's ideological faith in the moral economy of free labor and the sanctity of private property in an age when laissez-faire principles dictated against direct welfare support. In addition, many federal officials apparently shared the assumption held by many southern planters that the freedmen were incapable of productive labor except under direct white supervision.[30]

As Curkendall later admitted openly to Dennett in his office, the actual operation of his agency was not in line with the hopeful optimism of his speech. Racial violence was a daily occurrence on Atlanta's streets, while his garrison was too small to police the countryside. In January 1866, Dennett wrote that the Freedmen's Bureau was actually quite popular in the thirty-four county districts around Macon because of its efforts to arrange work contracts between planters and freedmen, revealing to the northern public that local citizens even served as bureau agents on the local level. The major dilemma facing federal officials was finding a way to get the freedmen back into the fields as rapidly as possible while protecting them from the mounting tide of white violence. Dennett reported that all blacks in the Macon subdistrict who had not found employment by the first of February were to be arrested and treated as vagrants. On the other hand, planters were angry because the Freedmen's Bureau's required wage standard of twelve dollars a month with food and medical care was two dollars above the prevalent local rate. Nevertheless, Dennett estimated that a planter in the Macon area still stood to make a profit of forty percent per laborer per year. The implicit message to northern readers was clear. Resistance to a free market economy was not only irrational, it indicated that southerners were not sufficiently reconstructed to assume full equality within the Union. Rebel leaders were patiently biding their time until the removal of troops left the freedmen defenseless.[31]

The publication in 1871 of yet another traveler account entitled *The Southern States since the War* by an Englishman named Robert Somers revealed that England also had a stake in the restoration of the plantation system. Somers spent two weeks in Georgia in late 1870 during a tour across the South to study the region's postwar progress and prospects for development. According to Somers, a great revolution in agricultural practices was taking place in Georgia that included improved methods of land preparation and plantation management, better varieties of cotton seed, more widespread use of fertilizers, and the propagation of practical knowledge through agricultural societies, conventions, fairs, and periodicals. Of particular interest to Somers was the large volume of cotton produced in Middle Georgia and South Carolina on small farms by white labor. He also noticed small patches of cotton being grown near towns and villages, "where fruits and vegetables cannot be so well preserved from depredation by vagrant or destitute negroes as in former times." Somers stated that these new areas of cotton production had caused speculators to underestimate the South's annual output of the fiber. He also explained that the large plantations were still in transition. Because they no longer commanded the necessary capital and labor, planters were cultivating fewer acres, selling out, or renting sections on shares. Somers did not draw the implied association with the loss of labor control, but explained that the planters were impatient for the removal of outside political agitators as well.[32]

Somers observed that while its farmers had a long way to go before they would match Europe's superior agricultural practices, Georgia's proximity to the world's great cotton markets, mania for railroad expansion, and untapped timber reserves made it ideally situated for further development, although the national tariff system hindered direct foreign trade. An indication of the shift of the colonial nexus from the Liverpool-London connection to New York was the return of empty trains to the interior after they deposited their cotton in Savannah. The great American staple producers were forced to sell in the cheapest market and buy necessities such as meat and coffee in the dearest, an old complaint that reflected the South's postwar decline. In effect, what Somers was describing was the postwar reintegration of the South into the nation's economy as the United States moved closer toward core status in the world capitalist system, a development that he as a loyal British imperialist looked upon with a mixture of admiration and dismay.[33]

Still another northern traveler who came south during Reconstruction was Edward King, who toured the South during the whole of 1873 and the first half of 1874. As King explained in the preface to *The Great South,* a revealing title that publicly proclaimed a rising spirit of economic reconciliation in the North, his journey was undertaken "at the instance of the publishers of *Scribner's Monthly,* who desired to present to the public, through the medium of their popular periodical, an account of the material resources, and the present social and political condition, of the people of the Southern States." King stated further that he and the artists associated with him had been "every where kindly and generously received by the Southern people" and had "endeavored, by pen and pencil, to give the reading public a truthful picture of life in a section which has, since the close of a devastating war, been overwhelmed by a variety of misfortunes, but upon which the dawn of a better day is breaking."[34]

King observed that the development of manufacturing in the region between Aiken, South Carolina, and Augusta illustrated "what may be done by judicious enterprise in the South." "Filled with the newest and finest machinery," the Augusta cotton factory had a capital stock of six hundred thousand dollars and delivered a quarterly dividend of five percent. Thousands of spindles and hundreds of looms were busy along the banks of the "noble" Augusta canal, where fine flour mills and tobacco factories were also located. King also observed that Augusta exhibited "a life and energy worthy of the brightest of Northern cities of its size." He was particularly impressed by the Cotton Exchange that had been founded in 1872, informing his readers that cotton culture throughout the entire section had "greatly increased since the war," largely because planters had finally realized the wisdom of utilizing fertilizers to increase their yields. Unfortunately, the planters in the surrounding countryside paid insufficient attention to crop diversity, which left them dependent on the outside world for their supplies and brought financial distress when the cotton crop failed. "According to universal testimony," the freedmen worked well if paid well. Moreover, small farms seemed to be increasing in Middle Georgia and much of the cotton brought into Augusta was "raised exclusively by white labor."[35]

Shifting the attention of his readers to politics in the next chapter, King stated that Reconstruction had been a failure in Georgia. The focus of his narrative on the remarkable volume of entrepreneurial activity in the state capital also communicated the implicit message that the time for political experimentation was past. Contrasting Atlanta with Savannah, King observed that there was "but little that is distinctively Southern in Atlanta," which he described as "eminently modern and unromantic." After tracing the history of Reconstruction in Georgia, King explained that "no fair-minded man" could deny that there had been glaring injustices practiced on both sides. Significantly, black political participation had been reduced two-thirds from a high of ninety thousand voters. "To judge from the testimony of native Georgians who are Republicans," the Ku Klux Klan had driven black voters from the polls, which was "naturally to be expected after the occurrences in Louisiana, South Carolina, and Alabama." King cautioned that "the revulsion from tyrannical ignorance and carpet-baggery" might "prove as baneful in its results as has its degraded and disreputable opposite," although his subsequent remarks revealed that his primary concern was protecting investment rather than the civil rights of the freedmen.[36]

Moving by railroad toward Savannah, King remarked that the "transition from the brisk air and reddish uplands of Northern Georgia to the sluggish atmosphere and sombre voluptuousness of the lowlands of the coast" was startling. Charmed by "the odorous tropical" appeal of "the forest city," King waxed poetic in his pastoral description of the environs around Savannah, but what impressed him most was the bustle of activity along the picturesque levee of Savannah: "Looking down from the bluff, along whose summit 'the Bay,' the principal commercial avenue, runs, one sees a forest of masts; a mass of warehouses, not unhandsomely grouped; cotton-presses, surrounded by active, chattering toilers; long processions of mule-teams, crowds of sailors talking in every known language, rice-mills, high mysterious stairways, and wondrous effects of light and shade on their broad steps, winding walls, and railroad wharves."[37]

Arriving in Savannah in late autumn, King and his party were "amazed at the masses of cotton bales piled everywhere." Lining the commercial avenues for "hundreds and hundreds of rods," the cotton was eventually transported by seemingly endless processions of drays to the riverside to be "swallowed" by huge black ships. Reminiscent of antebellum traveler accounts, King informed his readers that talk of cotton dominated the conversation everywhere he went: "At the great stone Custom-House the talk was of cotton; at the quaint old 'Exchange,' in front of which Sherman reviewed his army in 1865, cotton was the theme; and in all the offices from end to end of long level Bay street, we encountered none save busy buyers and factors, worshiping the creamy staple, and gossiping rapturously of 'middlings' low, and profits possible."[38]

Likewise remarkable had been the statewide recovery and expansion of an integrated railroad system. Devastated during Sherman's march to the sea, the railroad interest stood second only to agriculture but the enormous disparity between the volume of exports and imports revealed a deficiency in Georgia's economic recovery. As noted by King, most of the vessels that entered the port of Savannah were "compelled to go there in ballast." Indeed, "If cotton were taken away from the town, there would be little vivacity left." Still, King painted a picture of remarkable progress, although he advised against the intrusion of sectional politics into the workings of the market by repudiating the state debt. As he explained to his northern readers, "in spite of all the drawbacks and failures of an imperfect and vexatious labor system," it would be "hardly wise to threaten the State's credit with destruction, because of the irregularities which the government inaugurated by reconstruction brought into existence."[39]

King nonetheless acknowledged that hardships had resulted from Georgia's colonial relationship with the North. To convey the magnitude of the problem to northern readers, King quoted the bitter assessment of the situation by an unnamed journalist:

> A Georgia farmer uses a Northern aze-helve and axe to cut up the hickory growing within sight of his door; ploughs his fields with a Northern plough; chops out his cotton with a New England hoe; gins his cotton upon a Boston gin; hoops it with Pennsylvania iron; hauls it to market with a Concord wagon, while the little grain that he raises is cut and prepared for sale with

> Yankee implements. We find the Georgia housewife cooking with an Albany stove; and even the food, especially the luxuries, are imported from the North. Georgia's fair daughters are clothed in Yankee muslins and decked in Massachusetts ribbons and Rhode Island jewelry.

Like Henry Grady, King believed that diversified industry "would make of Georgia, in twenty years, a second New York," but concluded that agriculture would remain "the main stay of the commonwealth" for the foreseeable future notwithstanding the impressive progress of numerous manufacturing centers.[40]

Most impressive of all was Columbus, which King described as "a lively, thriving town" that one day would rival Lowell or Manchester because of its "exceptionally fine" water power. Situated right in the center of the cotton belt and "pierced by six important railways," Columbus received about 130,000 bales of cotton yearly. Although the Chattahoochee River's potential had only begun to be realized, the city's textile mills employed hundreds of women and children. In stark contrast with antebellum traveler accounts, King described the streets as "wide and cheery," the shops and stores as "quite fine," the "residences pretty," and found "charming" the little town built by the mill proprietors across the river for their operatives. "True, there were hosts of idle negroes roosting in shady places about the squares," he continued, but they were "found everywhere in the South." When he asked a superintendent why the managers of the cotton mills refused to employ black workers, the man smiled quaintly and replied: "Put a negro in one of those rooms with a hundred looms, and the noise would put him to sleep."[41]

Though the progress in agricultural production was impressive, King thought it might be doubled were it not for the proliferation of shiftless blacks and poor whites throughout much of the countryside. African Americans were acquiring an increasing number of small farms but "recklessly" devoting their exclusive attention to cotton. King also described black farmers as being "fond of the same pleasures which their late masters gave themselves so freely—hunting, fishing, and lounging," a gentle critique of the resistance of rural Georgians to the Yankee work ethic. The white inhabitants of the piney woods and swamps located in the southern part of the state were likewise "indolent, uneducated, complaining and shiftless." As depicted by King: "They are all of the same stamp as the old woman who explained to a hungry and thirsty traveler that they could n't give him any milk, 'because the dog was dead!' Applying his perceptive powers to this singular remark, he discovered that the defunct dog had been wont to drive up the cows to be milked at eventide, and that since his death it had not occurred to any of the family to go themselves in search of the kine."[42]

Possessed of "a kind of subdued thirst for negro gore," the "rural Caucasian" was excessively prone to violence. Once initiated, quarrels among the white lower classes in the South's sparsely settled agricultural sections also grew into feuds "cherished for years, until some day, at the cross-roads, or the country tavern, a pistol or a knife puts a bloody and often fatal end to the difficulty." Considering the character that the revolution had assumed in Georgia since the fall of the reconstruction government, however, King thought it "astonishing that the two races get on so well together as they do." His portrayal of the rural poor differed little from that of the antebellum traveler accounts in that the Georgia cracker still remained beyond the pale of civilized society.[43]

King described polite society in Savannah and most of the towns as "good and cultured" but was present on occasions when latent animosity toward the North surfaced. During his travels, Sidney Andrews observed that men who had actually participated in combat were more likely to accept the war's outcome than shirkers or those who had served in the home guard. Andrews also reported witnessing "some unusual exhibitions" of "feminine bitterness" in Georgia, an observation seconded by King. The stoic relief expressed by the women of the slaveholding elite at the end of the war soon gave way to rancor under the combined weight of bitter memories of their losses and the tensions created within their households by emancipation. Historian Nell Irvin Painter has written that whereas Reconstruction was experienced as a political and farm upheaval for white men, it brought about a more intimate crisis for women of privilege like Ella Clanton Thomas. Managing household slaves had never been easy before the war, but labor had been relatively reliable and experienced. Imbued with a paternalistic ideology that defined slaves as childlike dependents of their owners, plantation mistresses felt betrayed and resentful when self-interested free labor entered "the private world of house and yard." Moreover, with the exception of apprenticeship laws, there were no legal constraints on household employment. Not only did the women of plantation society resent negotiating the domestic services of servants once taken for granted, they found themselves in competition with nouveau-riche northerners who often hired away the best workers.[44]

The so-called "servant problem" would continue to loom large in Georgia's literary imagination well into the next century, a legacy of African American resistance and unfulfilled white expectations frequently overlooked by historians until recently. In particular, the loss of deference expected by plantation mistresses was difficult to accept. Every white household that could afford to employ black servants was transformed into an intimate battleground. Not surprisingly, the racial attitudes of formerly paternalistic matriarchs hardened as their households deteriorated. Their entire identity once centered upon their unquestioned authority within presumably harmonious and stable domestic arrangements, such women had a difficult time adjusting to the postwar order and clung tenaciously to the racial etiquette of the past. As C. Vann Woodward has written, "Slavery had been vastly more than a labor system, and the gap that its removal left in manners, mores, and rituals of behavior could not be filled overnight." The defiant pride that Eliza Frances Andrews had expressed in her journal the month before gave way to despair in early May 1865: "The props that held society up are broken. Everything is in a state of disorganization and tumult. We have no currency, no law save the primitive code that might makes right. We are in a transition state from war to subjugation, and it is far worse than was the transition from peace to war. The suspense and anxiety in which we live are terrible."[45]

Women who had accepted emancipation as divinely ordained realized that a difficult transition lay ahead. When Dolly Lunt Burge learned in mid-May that the United States government had freed all the slaves, she wrote in her diary that "the Disposer of All knows best & will do right." On 21 May she observed, "I had a long conversation with my man Elbert to-day about freedom & told him I was perfectly willing but wanted direction." Because she believed that bondage was in accord with Christianity, the end of slavery left Ella Clanton Thomas "bewildered" and her faith momentarily wavered. Initially, Thomas felt "the kindest possible feeling" for the freedmen after the war, but it was not long before domestic problems wrought a change in her attitude. Having owned more than ninety slaves before the war, Thomas was totally unaccustomed to housework. Like her mother, she blamed the Yankees for sowing dissention among "a well contented, happy race of people." The sight of former slaves enjoying their freedom on the streets of Augusta was especially hard to take when so much work was left undone on white estates. On 29 May, Thomas wrote that the day before she had seen a group of black women "promenading up the streets with black lace veil shading them from the embrowning rays of a sun under whose influence they had worked all their life." Two weeks later she confessed to her journal "that I do most heartily despise Yankees, Negroes and everything connected with them."[46]

During the darkest days of the war, the women of Georgia's slaveholding elite could still take comfort in their social position, a by-product of birth and wealth reinforced by the Old South's elaborate racial and sexual etiquette. With the exception of the arrival of black troops in the village of Washington, nothing infuriated Eliza Frances Andrews more than the refusal of her "new masters" to render to her the deference she expected as a lady. Writing in her diary on 14 May 1865, Andrews recalled an incident that had occurred that day on her way to church. When she came upon a group of former Confederates, they all took off their hats and cleared a pathway. Yet when she encountered a group of Yankees and freedmen soon after, she had to give up the sidewalk and "flank them by going out into the dusty road." So enraged that she carried her anger into church, Andrews wrote later that "it is the first time in my life that I have ever had to give up the sidewalk to a man, much less to negroes!" As in Georgia's larger towns and cities, Washington was soon overcrowded with so many freedmen and Yankees "that ladies scarcely ever venture out," even to church. Andrews cited as further evidence of the crudeness of the Yankees their willingness to be seen walking around town with black women and their boisterous participation in two "negro balls."[47]

As one might expect from "upstarts who are not used to having servants of their own," she wrote, the Yankees were "very capricious in their treatment of negroes," even resorting to whippings, a practice observed by the Reverend John Jones in Southwest Georgia as well. Although many of her father's former slaves had abandoned Haywood, a large enough number remained faithful to enable the Andrews household "to keep up appearances and set a respectable table." A carpenter named "Uncle Osborne" even hired himself out for provisions such as sugar and coffee for her family. Like Ella Clanton Thomas, Andrews blamed the Yankees for spoiling the "poor darkeys" with "false notions of freedom," writing that she had "heard several well-authenticated instances of women throwing away their babies in their mad haste to run away from their homes and follow the Northern deliverers." In direct contrast stood her father, who "would never let any of his negroes suffer," though she admitted that the freedmen had been treated less kindly by others.[48]

The fact that Haywood was a gathering place for the surviving elite of the Confederacy is significant because Andrews mulled over in her diary what had been discussed that day at the dining table, whether it had been fantasies of military revenge, predictions of a pending race war, or the evils inherent in federal intervention in the South's internal affairs. Anticipating their disappointment that freedom had brought starvation and misery rather than wealth, she predicted that the former slaves would undoubtedly rise up against the white race. Yankee schemes "to 'elevate the negro' by putting into his ignorant, savage head notions it is impossible to gratify" were to blame:

> They are sowing the wind, but they will leave us to reap the whirlwind. No power on earth can raise an inferior, savage race above their civilized masters and keep them there. No matter what laws they make in his favor, nor how high a prop they build under him, the negro is obliged, sooner or later, to find his level, but we shall be ruined in the process. Eventually the negro race will be either exterminated or reduced to some system of apprenticeship embodying the best features of slavery, but this generation will not live to see it. . . . The higher above his natural capacity they force the negro in their rash experiments to justify themselves for his emancipation, the greater must be his fall in the end, and the more bitter our sufferings in the meantime.[49]

Later in the summer of 1865, the Andrews family reluctantly cut back from twenty-five to five house servants at Haywood, dwindling resources finally overcoming their paternalistic qualms. Although she took some pleasure in domestic labor, Andrews wrote in her journal on 22 August that "it does seem to me a waste of time for people who are capable of doing something better to spend their time sweeping and dusting while scores of lazy negroes that are fit for nothing else are lying idle." Overwhelmed by the heat and fatigue, she realized that housework was not the "joke" she had imagined it, especially when one was also expected to entertain guests. Reflecting on her inability to buy the latest New York fashions, Andrews wrote that she intended "always to dress as well as my means will allow," but would "attempt nothing in the way of finery so long as I have to sweep floors and make up beds." She also voiced her determination to bear poverty with true Lost Cause pride because nothing was "more contemptible than broken-down gentility trying to ape rich vulgarity—not even rich vulgarity trying to ape its betters."[50]

For women steeped in the proslavery ideology, negotiating free labor household arrangements was a frustrating business, yet one that paled in significance to the drama that unfolded each year during Reconstruction after the harvest. In the words of historian Leon F. Litwack, the "tenuous peace" that existed on the land during the year evaporated under the tensions generated by settling wages, dividing crops, and negotiating new work contracts for the coming year. Whereas plantation labor was undesirable to blacks who wanted complete independence from their old masters, most white landowners longed for the rigid controls of slavery. Ironically assisted by the hated Freedmen's Bureau, Georgia planters had succeeded for the most part in getting black labor back into the fields by 1866, although the wage system favored by northern travelers never really had a chance because of the chronic shortage of capital. In response to the initial agency of blacks who considered working for a share of the crop a step toward eventual land ownership, a sharecropping system regulated by the Freedmen's Bureau gradually began to take shape in Georgia.[51]

By subjecting such arrangements to a variety of legal and extralegal sanctions, the planter class began to restore its control over black labor in the cotton belt. Thus while emancipation and federal political and economic intervention posed major problems for Georgia planters, the restoration of the production of staple crops for the world capitalist market revived the plantation system in Georgia. Only along the rice coast did the planter elite fail to reassert its dominance. Led by men like Tunis Campbell, coastal blacks resisted the restoration of white political control as long as the Republican Party remained influential in Georgia. Although some white planters managed to restore production on their old estates, bumper crops in Louisiana eventually depressed the rice market, while the expansion of the timber industry centered in Darien lured black workers away from the fields.[52]

In addition, General Sherman's Special Field Order 15 in January 1865 had raised African American hopes for land ownership by setting aside coastal lands from Charleston to northern Florida for the settlement of freedmen on small farms. Although white planters successfully lobbied the federal government to disallow their claims after the war, the so-called "Sherman titles" gave enough blacks a taste of land ownership to complicate the efforts of white planters like Pierce Butler to resume production on their old lands. In March 1866, Butler and his twenty-eight-year-old daughter, Frances, returned to Georgia from Philadelphia. Unlike her famous mother, Frances Anne Kemble, Frances Butler was an ardent pro-southerner who defended plantation slavery. Although she never mentioned her mother's journal in the text, her 1883 publication *Ten Years on a Georgia Plantation since the War* was a direct rebuttal of Kemble's abolitionist arguments. When her father died in 1867, she continued to manage the Butler family's estate in Georgia, fleeing to her house in Philadelphia during the malaria season. In 1871, she married the Reverend James Wentworth Leigh, a Cambridge-educated clergyman who joined her in Georgia and took over the management of the Butler plantations. When the Reverend Leigh took a ministerial position in England in 1876, the Butler heirs left the estate under the management of an agent in Savannah. By the 1890s most of the land was back in a natural state.[53]

Written in England after her departure from Georgia, Leigh's book consists of extracts from letters written during the decade after the war that she connected later with narrative. Like her mother's antebellum journal, *Ten Years on a Georgia Plantation since the War* is highly polemical, a spirited attack upon "Northern adventurers" who had "encouraged the negroes in all their foolish and extravagant ideas of freedom, set them against their old masters, filled their minds with false hopes, and pandered to their worst passions, in order to secure for themselves some political office which they hoped to obtain through the negro vote." In direct contradiction to her mother's portrayal of Pierce Butler as an emotionally detached absentee landlord, Leigh described her father as a caring paternalist, so beloved by "our people" that they refused to work for anyone else. In fact, she wrote, several of the slaves he had sold to settle his debts had returned to the Butler Island plantation after emancipation. Perhaps unable to imagine the existence of familial or spatial bonds within the black community, Leigh interpreted this as one of many signs of their loyalty to her father. Although it was too late to plant a full rice crop, Butler quickly arranged for the freedmen to work on half-shares. With the help of her German maid, his daughter set out to restore order to the household after hanging a picture of General Lee over the mantelpiece.[54]

The initial honeymoon period, however, soon floundered over the issue of work. Leigh wrote that the freedmen "talked a great deal about their desire and intention to work for us, but their idea of work, unaided by the stern law of necessity is very vague, some of them working only half a day and some even less." Conditions were even more unsettled on the plantation on St. Simon's Island, where the freedmen "had tasted of the tree of knowledge" and resented turning the land back over to their former master. Leaving his daughter and her maid on St. Simon's, Butler returned to his rice plantation. Like many of her peers, she soon grew tired of her limited diet and trying to manage a household with "raw field hands." Upon one occasion, her German maid apprehended a woman brushing her teeth with her employer's tooth brush after dipping it in used bath water, which Leigh considered the childish deed of an inferior little removed from savagery rather than a possible act of mocking defiance.[55]

When they returned from Philadelphia the following spring, Butler resumed management of the Butler Island rice plantation and rented out his cotton lands on St. Simon's on shares. With everyone working in the fields, his daughter wrote that she once again found herself shorthanded in the house. Moreover, she found it impossible to make the freedmen do odd jobs, such as cleaning up the grounds near the big house or making a garden. Even having butter churned required constant attention. Although "perfectly good-tempered," the freedmen refused to accept her expected work pace and routine. In exasperation she wrote that she "generally found that if I wanted a thing done I first had to tell the negroes to do it, then show them how, and finally do it myself." Whereas she considered her father's sharecropping arrangements as applying to plantation work in general, the freedmen saw them as applying only to field work. In addition, because her father allowed the freedmen to draw food, clothing, and money on account, she feared "trouble when the day of settlement comes."[56]

Moving to block the reinstitution of a modified form of slavery in the South and the resurgence of southern political power on the national level made possible by President Johnson's relatively lenient plan for Reconstruction, the Radical Republicans pushed through a new program in the spring of 1867 that demanded political and civil rights for blacks. As Numan V. Bartley has aptly summed up the situation, "In the short term black enfranchisement would produce Republican congressmen and dam the flood of southern Democrats to Congress; in the long term it promised to encourage a free-labor capitalism that would make the South more like the North and promote a Republican version of national harmony." Correctly reading the program as an assault on Georgia's traditional labor relations and social structure, Bill Arp hinted that the Radical attempt to force "nigger ekwality" would result in white resistance throughout the South, a prediction borne out by the tide of Ku Klux Klan violence that swept his home state.[57]

Writing to her sister in late June, Frances Butler expressed her fear of "terrible trouble by-and-by with the negroes" because of the federal government's division of the South into military districts in response to exaggerated reports of white violence. She predicted that the effort of "the most despotic Government on earth" to gain political control by disfranchising white males and mass voting of blacks would only "goad the people into acts of rebellion and resistance." Promises of full social equality in exchange for their votes were "exciting the negroes to every kind of insolent lawlessness." Butler argued further that the efforts of the "abolitionists" to institute social equality went against "hard ethnological facts."[58]

When her father died that August, she returned to Georgia in November with her brother-in-law "to carry on his work and look after the negroes." After hiring an overseer and a financial agent for the coming year, she undertook the task of settling her father's accounts with his African American labor force. Working many nights with his large plantation ledger, which contained a careful recording of "the work each man had, or had not, done every day for nearly two years," she carefully weighed the credits and debits of over three hundred accounts. As Leigh tersely observed in 1883, "I might have saved myself the trouble." In spite of her scrupulous efforts to be fair, everyone felt cheated, "most of them thinking that each man was entitled to half the crops." In the coming decades Georgia planters and merchants learned how to exploit the furnishing system's credit mechanisms to expand their control of the rural labor force, black and white. In the words of C. Vann Woodward, the crop lien system became the "financial bailing wire" that held the South's postwar agricultural machinery together and ensured the uninterrupted outward flow of colonial tribute to "the ultimate lords of credit."[59]

Viewed in retrospect the crop lien system and sharecropping are best understood as transitional arrangements between plantation slavery and mature capitalist agriculture, which utilized free labor and mechanization. As events on the Butler estate revealed, conflicting notions of work and time made the transition from slave to free labor difficult at best. Their memories of slavery intact, the freedmen did not consider provisioning and medical care as items to be taken into account when dividing the products of their labor. To be sure, many former slaves along the coast had some experience with market relations because the task system had rewarded individual initiative. Yet for an essentially premodern work force accustomed to seasonal time and measuring its productivity by the completion of specific tasks, the transition to clock time was hard. As Leigh later recalled, every man on the plantation insisted that he had not missed a single day's work in two years. Deference to her deceased father's authority precluded open challenges to his accounts. She wrote that the men did not "seem to think I wished to cheat them, but that I was powerless to help matters, one man saying to me one day, 'You see, missus, a woman ain't much 'count.' "[60]

Although she soon grew tired of explaining to each freedman why he was not going to receive half of his crop, Frances Butler was astute enough to realize that the underlying issues were "independence and dignity." Many claimed that her father had given them land for long and faithful service. Overall, she paid out over six thousand dollars, several men receiving two or three hundred dollars apiece. So many freedmen immediately invested in land she wrote that "it seemed doubtful if I should have hands at all left to work." Unfortunately, she observed, those who bought land in Darien failed to secure titles and soon lost their property. Others bought land in the pine barrens, which was "so poor they could not raise a peck of corn to the acre," an ideologically charged statement undoubtedly intended to convince readers of the wisdom of remanding to white southerners sole custody of the so-called "Negro problem."[61]

As interpreted at the time by Frances Butler, her experiences as a resident landlord illustrated the superiority of slavery to free labor. What she feared most after assuming control of her father's estate was the transformation of local labor negotiations into a political struggle with wider implications. Like many of her white contemporaries, she resented the intrusion of the Freedmen's Bureau into the negotiation and enforcement of labor contracts, although the agency often ruled in favor of local planters. Essentially conservative in its refusal to tackle the problem of land redistribution and instinctively biased toward employers in contractual disputes, the Freedmen's Bureau's efforts to restore the productivity of the plantation economy undermined the federal government's efforts to transform southern society by expanding black political and civil rights.

Unusual because of her access to outside capital, Frances Butler responded to Reconstruction by trying to preserve the trappings of paternalism through a series of reforms on her plantations, including a plan to divide the old hospital building made famous in her mother's journal into a school, church, home for old women, and birthing center. Sharing her mother's Victorian notions of confinement, she considered home birth "wretched and improper" and was appalled by the resistance of the old and young alike to her plan. Neither were her white maid's efforts to reform the household staff successful. The underlying problem was deference, however, not health care or the quality of domestic service. During slavery Georgia planters had willingly accepted irregular service in exchange for complete deference within the plantation household. Now Butler's household servants not only refused to follow her white maid's instructions, they resisted their employer's efforts to compel standards of dress and behavior linked to slavery, such as her requirement that women wear head handkerchiefs. No longer willing to address their former owners with the customary titles of deference, the freedmen also refused to remove or touch their hats in polite acknowledgment upon passing.[62]

It was perhaps inevitable in such a climate of mistrust and fear that efforts to expand the suffrage resulted in widespread conflict. The rise of so-called northern adventurers like Tunis Campbell to political power translated directly into a loss of labor control, a change that few white landlords were willing to abide for long. In relentless pursuit of the Democratic Party's interrelated goals of white supremacy and home rule, the planter elite unleashed a wave of terror and economic coercion in 1868. Little wonder that both Frances Butler and Ella Clanton Thomas wrote that they began sleeping with loaded guns nearby. By 1870 the Republican Party was near collapse in Georgia. With the Democratic Party and Ku Klux Klan in control of the countryside, the Reconstruction experiment in Georgia was drawing rapidly to an end. As Bartley has observed, southern planters no longer represented a significant hindrance to the expansion of northern capitalism. The threat of the national political resurgence of the planter class removed, the northern Republicans sacrificed black rights for social stability and easier economic access to the South.[63]

One literary indication of the changing national racial climate was the inclusion of an essay entitled "Bill Arp on Nigger Equality" in Charles Henry Smith's *Bill Arp's Peace Papers,* which was published in New York by G. W. Carleton and Company in 1873. Reflecting upon the racial situation after President Grant's reelection, a still-defiant Arp asked how much longer it would be before the Radical Republicans finally gave up and allowed the freedman to "relaps into his nativ obskurity." Arguing that mixing races was "agin natur" and in conflict with fundamental hierarchical principles, Arp foresaw only one future for blacks in the South: "The nigger wasent made to keep a post offis nor set on a jewry. He wasent made for intelektual persoots. He was made to dig, and ditch, and grub, and hoe, and plow a mule, and tote things about for white foaks, and nothin else don't soot him, and that don't soot him as well as doin nothin."[64]

Arp maintained further that efforts to improve the Negro race in the absence of white control would be fruitless. Turned loose on an island, the Negro would "quit wearin close and go to beatin tin pans and eat lizzards before you git out of site." Arp claimed to like the black man but only in his proper place, which was "kontrolled by white folks, and taken care of, jest like we control our childern." Because they were nothing but lifelong ignorant children, it was "God's blessin to em to hav to liv under sumbody's dominyun." The reestablishment of white dominance over black labor advocated by Charles Henry Smith was part of a larger pattern of dependency emerging in rural Georgia. Although the movement of white farmers in the upcountry and wiregrass regions into the plantation economy varied in speed depending on factors such as railroad expansion, the spread of the crop lien system and cotton production unleashed a commercial revolution that undermined the traditional independence of the white yeomanry at the same time that it undermined the dream of yeoman self-sufficiency among rural blacks. As Eric Foner has written, "Thus began the forging of a new class structure to replace the shattered world of slavery—an economic transformation that would culminate, long after the end of Reconstruction, in the consolidation of a rural proletariat composed of the descendants of former slaves and white yeomen, and a new owning class of planters and merchants, itself subordinate to Northern financiers and industrialists."[65]

Yet as Foner correctly observes, linearity in historical change only becomes clear in retrospect. Rural Georgia continued to be a shifting landscape in which it was difficult enough to deal with the conflicts of the moment, much less imagine the shape of the future. Moreover, the level of traditional literary output remained severely depressed, although a few Georgia writers found publishers for their work and a New South literary revival centered around the Atlanta *Constitution* loomed on the horizon. Still, by focusing on the past and the Yankee invader, the Old South's literary defenders during Reconstruction were sowing the seeds of the Lost Cause ideology in the rich soil of memory. At the same time, however, a literary challenge to the plantation system appeared in the poetry of Sidney Lanier that foreshadowed the explosion of farmer unrest later in the century.

The first literary champion of plantation life to step forward in Georgia after the war was Mary Louise Cook, the wife of a wealthy planter in Columbus who published *Ante Bellum. Southern Life As It Was* under the pseudonym Mary Lennox in 1868. A work of little literary value patterned loosely on *St. Elmo* by Augusta Jane Evans, *Ante Bellum* is a poorly conceived romance that takes the reader through a tortured maze in the process of weeding out the villains and arranging the appropriate marriages of the heroines and heroes. The novel's real value lies in what it reveals about the conflation of the proslavery and Confederate ideologies into the Lost Cause ideology after the war. Dedicating her book to the "Friends of the South" in the hopes of taking their minds off "the dull monotony of the present gloomy state of our country" through "delightful memories of the happy past," Cook stated that if her sentiments offended anyone, "it must be remembered that they only indicate in a slight degree that feeling which helped to bring about the long and bloody war."[66]

Set in the early 1850s, the story begins when a handsome boy of fifteen walking along the banks of the Chattahoochee River comes upon a beautiful, blue-eyed girl singing a tearful song. A ten-year-old orphan of noble Charlestonian origin, "Lula" has fallen under the dominance of a mean widow named Mrs. Grant who lives in a brick mansion in town. Young Charlie Herbert is ecstatic when he learns that the girl's full name is Louise Graham because his mother is her deceased mother's adopted sister. Yet when Mrs. Herbert and Charlie arrive at the mansion to take Lula home, they are turned away by Mrs. Grant, who has no love for the child but depends on her hard work around the household. Determined to protect her investment in Lula, Mrs. Grant decides to fight the Herbert family's claim of guardianship in court.

The patriarchal Mr. Herbert arrives that night and takes command of the situation. Consumed by grief, Lula has fallen deathly ill. Bravely assisted by a household servant whose love for the child overcomes her fear of her mistress, the Herberts bring in a young doctor before Mrs. Grant returns. Eventually, the Herberts overcome the widow's resistance by taking advantage of her greed. At this point in the story the reader learns that Mrs. Grant had come south as a teacher many years before. Taking advantage of his grief-stricken desire to restore domestic happiness in his life, she had snared a rich, upcountry widower. Subsequently, she had established "a New form of government" in his household, one "exactly the reverse of the mild and gentle discipline of her predecessor."[67]

In addition, while she had come south an inveterate abolitionist and had lost an early teaching position for clandestinely teaching her employer's household slaves to read, Mrs. Grant had become a feared and disliked mistress after acquiring her own slaves. Dr. Clinton delivers the expected ideological judgment of the North when he informs Mr. Herbert that her misguided efforts had made "the hitherto contented and faithful servants . . . suddenly morose, disobedient, and unhappy." Of course, Mr. Herbert agrees and observes that northerners were always harsh masters because they did not understand "the naturally indolent negro" and soon became frustrated when their accustomed standards of efficiency were not met. On the surface a nostalgic rendering of the old proslavery defense, Cook's use of the name Grant for the story's major villain also suggests that her critique served a contemporary purpose. Mr. Herbert speaks to the postwar labor problem as much as the past when he states that slaves were seldom overtasked by native southerners, although "discord generally ensues, where two natures, so diametrically opposite as those of the Yankee and negro are brought in contact."[68]

By no coincidence the next villain to appear in *Ante Bellum* is George Raymond, another former schoolteacher from the North who had used his oratorical talents to weasel his way into the Virginia aristocracy by marrying Kate Sunderland, the last survivor of a noble F.F.V. family. Shortly thereafter, Raymond had revealed his true character by gambling away the Sunderland family fortune and driving his wife insane by taking away her only child. Significantly, only the loyal and beloved Sunderland house servants read his character correctly from the beginning. After Raymond injures a slave for not opening a gate quickly enough to suit him, a slave woman remarks that her poor mistress had "done sacrificed herself and her niggers to that white man's hansum face and glib tongue." An old black patriarch delivers the final judgment when he laments that "our white folks are r'al gentlemen and ladies, and is satisfied with nigger's work, cause it sure if 'tis slow, but dem thar Yankees always kills the goose to get the golden egg."[69]

When Cook finished writing her novel in mid-1867, it was difficult to imagine sectional reconciliation, especially after the hard shift in federal Reconstruction policy that spring. Too much the lady to take the gloves off completely, her tone is nonetheless decidedly unreconstructed and her sentiments regarding black labor accord perfectly with the proslavery defense one encounters in the diaries and letters of her social peers. Cook also attacked northern finishing schools for staining the virtue of good southern girls and delivered a broadside against Yankee dietary habits which reveals that the forms of cultural resistance are varied indeed. After Lula recovers from her illness, she is taken to live at Belvoir, the Herbert estate that overlooks the Chattahoochee River. When December rolls around, Lula is naturally drawn to the kitchen, where Uncle Joe and Aunt Betty are involved in the culinary preparations for the annual Christmas celebration. Whereas Aunt Betty is enamored of fashionable new Yankee recipes, Uncle Joe has no use whatsoever for excessive planning or Yankee frugality in the kitchen, describing such fare as ox-tail soup, stuffed calf ears, and stewed sheep-trotters as fit for neither man nor beast:

> Why bless your heart, honey, there aint a nigger nor a dog on this plantation that would eat a calf's ear or a sheep foot. 'Twas jes' t'other day I flung one of dem same trotters to Tasso, but he 'tended like he warn't hungry and turned up his nose and walked off, like he was insulted. Presently a plantation dog came 'long, I 'vited him to lunch, he smelt it, then turned his head away. After while he takes it up, and runs a little ways off and buried it in the ground, where he let it stay,—dat's all de use *he* got for Yankee sweetmeats.[70]

Cook's attack on Yankee culinary frugality is somewhat incredulous given the lean times, but it sets the stage for her argument that the South's Christian paternalism was vastly superior to the North's untrammeled materialism. Appropriately, the scene shifts to the first gray light of dawn on Christmas morning, where "dusky forms were seen stealthily gliding through the house at Belvoir, depositing in some conspicuous place humble tokens of affection for the beloved master and mistress, as well as for the children of the family," and where cheerful cries of "Christmas gift!" are soon heard ringing throughout the big house. Perhaps no other literary image communicates the ideal of paternalistic reciprocity within a racial hierarchy as well. Cook's memories of Christmas on the old plantation stood in stark contrast with her description of racial conditions after the war:

> But where, oh! where are those humble friends now? Unbidden tears spring to the eyes in answer to this query. Dissension and discord were sown between the two races, and the faithful and once happy domestics became suspicious of their former friends, and are now idle and miserable wanderers, without home or country. Many of them have perished from want and exposure, and the few who have returned to beg shelter and protection of their former owners, are glad to eat of the "crumbs that fall from their master's table."[71]

Late in her novel, Cook returned to the theme of Christian benevolence by praising the role that plantation mistresses presumably had played in bringing the benefits of civilization to their barbarian charges. Cook also argued that the responsibilities of a Georgia plantation mistress had left her precious little time for the pursuit of leisure. In addition, she depicted the plantation mistress as the vital force that had held plantation society together and the final barrier against "constant turmoil and confusion," a likely reflection of a self-confidence born during the long war. Though "necessarily the companion and friend of the negroes," the mistress had been a bulwark of plantation production and had inspired respect and obedience from her servants. Speaking directly to her readers, Cook stated that those who do not "understand the peculiarities of the negro character," such as a childlike willingness to serve one's betters with "implicit obedience" in exchange for kindness and protection, simply "have much to learn, in order to comprehend his nature and the influences that are brought to bear on him." Simply stated, Cook posited the restoration of paternalism as the only solution to postwar racial discord in Georgia.[72]

Cook concluded *Ante Bellum* with her reflections upon the war's impact on "the happy condition of affairs in our favored land." She acknowledged that the Confederate cause had been lost in spite of the hardships endured by the southern people and the "brilliant victories won by our gallant troops against overwhelming numbers," but remained reluctant to let go of the past. Ready to commit the "delightful associations" of plantation life to the mythical world of history, poetry, and song, never to be revived except in "holy remembrance," she nevertheless cautioned southerners against forsaking the inheritance of their fathers. Though at its nadir and "bound like Ixion to the wheel, and condemned like Sisyphus to roll a stone to the mountain top," with God's help Dixie would once again "rear its head proudly above the other powers of the earth." Such statements lend credence to the interpretation of the Lost Cause ideology as a cultural revitalization movement when viewed in conjunction with the concrete actions that planters took in 1868 to restore their preeminence in rural Georgia.[73]

The ideological trajectory of Sidney Lanier's development as an artist during Reconstruction, on the other hand, reveals that not every Georgia author remained as fixated as Mary Louise Cook on the sacred memory of the Old South. Upon first glance there was little in Lanier's childhood beyond his love of nature that foreshadowed his emergence in 1869 as a spokesman for a New South of sturdy, independent yeoman farmers. The son of a Macon lawyer and staunchly Presbyterian mother who taught her children to love music and literature, Lanier was pursuing an academic career at Oglethorpe College near Milledgeville when the Civil War began. Enlisting in Virginia as a private in the Macon Volunteers, Second Georgia Battalion, Lanier refused three offers of promotion during the war to remain near his brother Clifford. Transferred to duty upon a blockade runner in 1864, he was captured and imprisoned at Point Lookout, where he contracted the lung disease that eventually caused his early death in 1881. His health broken, Lanier had great difficulty finding a secure livelihood after the war. After working as a hotel clerk and teacher in Alabama, he returned to Macon in late 1868 to clerk and read law in his father's office. Finally in 1873, Lanier began a seven-year tenure as a flutist with the Peabody Symphony in Baltimore, where he also began lecturing in literature at Johns Hopkins University in 1879 and composed some of his most widely acclaimed poetry.[74]

Lanier's ideological evolution paralleled his artistic development. His first major publication came in 1867 with *Tiger-Lilies,* a novel that he had begun writing in late 1863 or early 1864. The story line and characters are of less interest for our purposes than what the novel reveals about Lanier's grounding in English and German Romanticism, particularly his tendency to view social development in terms of dualities caught in dynamic tension. Lanier's early training in German historicism ultimately led him to interpret the shattering dislocations caused by the Civil War as part of a dialectical process that was propelling the South in a radically new direction. In a novel entitled *John Lockwood's Mill* that he began in 1868 but never completed, Lanier observed that the end of the war "wrought one transformation especially magical" in that "a land of leisure became suddenly a land of labor. A people which had dreamed away half a life, instantly began to work away the other half. Idleness became the one crime, in a country where, for years, Leisure had been the popular pride."[75]

Unlike most Georgians of his social station, the idea of work did not trouble Lanier. Polite society had discovered poverty but even the departure of the negro cooks into the night did not trouble the aspiring novelist, who described the introduction of "the fairer daughters of the family" to a new occupation "an advent of the dawn!" The problem was that the "happy resoluteness" and "cheerful energy" evident in the spring of 1866 was gone by 1868 and a million workers stood idle: "For at the close of the war, our one hope for the Future, our one forgetfulness of the Past, our one refuge from the starving Present, was Labor. And, today, we cannot labor, for there is here neither reward nor demand for labor. Our hope, our forgetfulness, our solace, has been drowned in some vile muddle or other of politics in which we had no part and no interest: our life is filled with the intolerable gloom of idleness, in order that some vile party or other may retain or acquire its offices and its patronages."[76]

In his Reconstruction prose and poetry, such as his unpublished story "Bombs from Below: Wanted Engineers!" and a poem entitled "The Raven Days," Lanier continued to vent his pain and anger toward the North. A poem that he published in 1868 entitled "Laughter in the Senate" contrasted the South's hunger and despair with the sounds of merrymaking in the distance. In the piece, "tyrants" crush the hope that peace would bring cheerful aid from the victors, who quickly had forgotten "how fresh is the pall / Over their dead and ours." Although largely ignored today, all three pieces hint that Lanier's subsequent calls for agrarian reform reflected his distrust of the North as well as his romantic pastoral vision.[77]

In an address that he delivered before the Furlow Masonic Female College at the end of June 1869 in Americus, Georgia, Lanier stated his hope that the wealth of "our mineral mountains" would liberate southern agriculture from the "hostile combinations of European capital," although the North's "taunting arrogance" was delaying the restoration of prosperity. One of the key social questions left unanswered in the war's aftermath was the role to be played by women, "the heart, the one-flower, the sole passion, the only beloved, of society." Lanier voiced his deep fear that "a time may come when you will no longer be lovable, when we *can not* love you, and when, by consequence, chaos *will* come again." What worried Lanier was that southern women would heed the calls of "certain deluded sisters" in Europe and the North and begin "crying for the vote and for women to become lawyers, physicians, and ministers." If women acquired the vote and moved into the professions, they would be the same as men, "and men do not love men." A woman's place was in the home. In Lanier's words, "*that society which keeps its homes pure is invulnerable to all those serpents, physical, moral, political, social, religious, that creep and crawl about the world.*" He voiced his hope that heroic southern women would reject the latest temptation of Eve: "Ah, I do not forget, that I speak to the mothers of the heroes of the Southern Confederacy!"[78]

Speaking directly to the link between domesticity and the preservation of southern manhood, Lanier spoke glowingly of the Confederate "sweethearts whose contempt for cowardice and admiration for bravery were at once the most dreadful punishment of the coward and the most thrilling inspiration of the brave." Surely wives and mothers who had made clothing to protect soldiers from the cold, fed and gave drink to the troops, nursed the sick and wounded, comforted the imprisoned, and tended faithfully to the graves of the dead would reject the "unnatural propositions" of "the legion of female suffrage" when it at last moved south. It was time, in other words, for the southern lady to get back on her domestic pedestal and let men attend to the world of work and politics.[79]

Next Lanier turned his attention to the impact of the late war on the South's agricultural system. The substitution of free labor for slave labor had come so quickly as to nearly "paralyze all of our industrial energies." Unfortunately, the "spectre of free labor" had marched down from the North in bad company: "Under its feet, lay the dead body of our political independence. Trooping behind its back came a fearful retinue. Poverty, lawlessness, marital demoralization, political incapacity, physical indolence, domestic improvidence, agricultural ignorance, moral profligacy in awful twinhood with religious fanaticism; all these stalked along in the twain of free labor, as they had been the supple courtiers of this seemingly dreadful king." In response, the South "theorized upon it." Public communications predicted the death of the planting interests in the South and many farmers sold out and migrated to Brazil, Cuba, Central America, and California. The common belief had been that the freedmen would never work and that cotton would never again pay because of Egyptian and East Indian competition, even if the farmer managed to survive the "perennial hosts" of boll-worms, army-worms, caterpillars, droughts, freshets, and fevers.[80]

"But what has been the real result?" he asked. Starting again with nothing, "without implements, without stock, without labor, without money, without anything but scarred hands and scarred hearts, we started to work." After four years, old railroads had been repaired and "scores of new ones" started, children were going to schools and colleges, and prophecies in the newspapers of agricultural failure had been replaced by "practical discussions" of fencing, fertilizers, improved seeds, and new varieties of breeding stock. Assuming the prophetic voice that characterized much of his subsequent poetry, Lanier stated that "in entire explanation of all these marvels, we sell two hundred and fifty million dollars' worth of cotton in one year!" Southern cotton was not only superior in quality to that produced abroad, it was predicted that the Pacific Railroad would shortly "bring us multitudes of laborers, whose competition will forever check any absurd demands of our present farm-hands." Some were even beginning to whisper among themselves that "*perhaps after all, Cotton Is King.*" Still, patience was in order in such trying times of political hardship. As Lanier warned his audience, "Let us not forget, for instance, to accept and digest the unpalatable truth that we, here in the South, are among the crudest theorizers in the world."[81]

In 1871 Lanier stated poetically his case for farm revitalization in "Thar's More in the Man Than Thar Is in the Land," the first of three cracker dialect poems to appear in print in rapid succession. In the poem Lanier told the story of a foolish farmer in Middle Georgia:

> I knowed a man, which he lived in Jones
> Which Jones is a country of red hills and stones,
> And he lived pretty much by gittin' of loans,
> And his mules was nuthin' but skin and bones,
> And his hogs was flat as his corn-bread pones,
> And he had 'bout a thousand acres o' land.

After concluding that there was no living to be had in the land, Jones sells out to a farmer named Brown for a dollar and fifty cents an acre and heads for Texas, "whar cotton would sprout / By the time you could plant it in the land." Unfortunately, the cost of the trip and a small plot of land leaves Jones broke. Meanwhile, farmer Brown moves to the Jones farm in Middle Georgia:

> And he rolled up his breeches and bared his arm,
> And he picked all the rocks from off'n the groun',
> And he rooted it up and he plowed it down,
> Then he sowed his corn and his wheat in the land.

When Jones returns busted from Texas five years later, fat farmer Brown invites him in for a plate of smoking hot vittles:

> And when he had filled hisself and the floor
> Brown looked at him sharp and riz and swore
> That, "whether men's land was rich or poor
> Thar was more in the man than thar was in the land."[82]

That Lanier recognized the difficulty of getting the message of agricultural reform through to Georgia farmers was shown in two pieces he wrote in 1870–71 entitled "Jones's Private Argyment" and "9 From 8." Back from Texas, farmer Jones joins the chorus against taking out loans to buy meat and essentials only to find trouble when prices fall. Nevertheless, he reasons that if everyone else plants corn, cotton prices will rise sky high, so he plants cotton anyway. In "9 From 8" a farmer laments the mathematics of "crap-leens" and his inability to escape the grasp of merchants, while the poet points out that such an equation always "Leaves nuthin'—and none to carry."[83]

Though he had yet to achieve his full potential as a poet, all of the components of Lanier's pastoral critique of capitalism were in place by 1871. In the first stanza of "The Homestead," Lanier applauded the restoration of home rule:

> The State spread out her arms and said:
> My Children, Hate to-day is dead,
> And Love and Law, together wed,
> Sit on the hills to rule you.

The debate that followed in Georgia as elsewhere in the South over the next two decades essentially boiled down to choosing the appropriate road for the "New South." Would the South rebuild itself in the image of the victorious North, hereafter symbolized by Lanier as Trade? Would the South turn back to the past by wedding itself to King Cotton? Or would the South seek a new road? In "The Homestead," Lanier resurrected a standard antebellum theme by championing domesticity as the foundation of republican virtue, but gave the old formula a new twist. In the aftermath of failed Confederate nationalism, Lanier called for a return to rural republican simplicity but located the yeoman rather than the plantation household at the center of his vision.[84]

Lanier had yet to resolve his ambivalent feelings toward the former slaves, however, and was not ready to make the leap of faith to a biracial yeoman republic. When Congress debated a new civil rights bill introduced by Charles Sumner in 1874, Lanier rushed yet another cracker dialect poem into print, which one critic considers his "bitterest denunciation" of Reconstruction. Written on a train in Virginia, "Civil Rights" delivered the basic warning that if the Yankees were going to force conflict by pushing social equality for African Americans in the South, whites would take their revenge on blacks before surrendering their own existence.[85]

The poem describes a Sunday visit by Old Uncle Johnny Stiles to his neighbor "Jeems." Just as Stiles was "startin' out to learn to like 'em some agin," "them Yankees" began stirring up more trouble. Recalling the loss of his son in the late war and the damage wrought by "Sherman's folks," Stiles was finding it hard to swallow the latest civil rights. He had "tried to see it right" by admitting wrong on both sides and explained to Jeems that he "didn't want no war at fust," but had answered the call of duty to "old Georgy." It was hard to treat an old enemy "brotherlee" however:

> When every nigger's son is schooled (I payin' of the tax,
> For not a mother's son of 'em has more than's on ther backs),
> And when they crowds and stinks me off from the gittin' to the polls,
> While Congress grinds ther grain, as 'twere, 'thout of takin no tolls;
> And when I stands aside and waits, and hopes that things will mend,
> Here comes this Civil Rights and says, this fuss shan't have no end!

To Stiles it seemed that "j'est when the water's roughest, here of late," the Yankees had thrown black and white in the South "from off the Ship of State" into the "ragin' sea" with but one rotten plank to hold, laughing to see whether both would drown "or live by makin' fight!" A man of responsibility, Stiles intended to gather his grain and feed his family, but made clear his determination to resist:

> I tell you, Jeems, I *kin* not help it—*maybe* "its" a sin;
> *By God! Ef they don't fling a rope, I'll push the nigger in!*[86]

Lanier's national breakthrough as a poet came in 1875 when *Lippincott's Magazine* published "Corn." The impact of the depression of 1873 undoubtedly made the poem's theme of rural decline and decay within a rapacious commercial world ring true to a wide audience. In the piece, Lanier contended that the "incalculable tides" of trade had swept away the happiness born of communion with God and tradition and thrust the "steadfast dweller on the selfsame spot" into oblivion. In consequence, the restless-hearted and barbarian children of a forlorn land had abandoned their old to die on the neglected and scarified hills of Georgia. "Scorning the slow reward of patient grain," the farmer, Lanier's metaphor for the South, had sold his soul and soil to "coquette Cotton," but like "a foolish Jason on a treacherous sea" had reaped only misery rather than quick gain. "Lulled by smooth rippling loans," the farmer had turned his fields into "a gambler's hell," staking everything on "games of Buy-and-Sell" that left him at the mercy of the market and begging at the banker's door the next year. Enslaved by the crop-lien system and impervious to the truth that only the majesty of corn, sown "with antique sinew and with modern art," could restore life to the land, the farmer "nursed his cotton" and "cursed his grain" in a vain endeavor to clear his cloud of debt:

> At last
> He woke to find his foolish dreaming past,
> And all his best-of-life the easy prey
> Of squandering scamps and quacks that lined his way
> With vile array,
> From rascal statesman down to petty knave;
> Himself, at best, for all his bragging brave,
> A gamester's catspaw and a banker's slave.[87]

Lanier resumed his critique of capitalism in "The Symphony." Everywhere the poet looked, the pressures of trade were tightening upon the poor, who were toiling like beasts in the mills, mines, and fields. Lamenting the death of Christian charity, Lanier could only cry, "O Trade! O Trade! would thou wert dead!" Ignoring the needs of the heart, the song of Nature, and the love of Christ, trade for the sake of trade alone was akin to "war grown miserly," an inhumane struggle that denied to man the leisure to pursue Art and Beauty. In its mature form, Lanier's agrarian ideal can thus be seen as an outgrowth of a romantic vision in which the simple yeoman assumes the medieval knight's quest for spiritual harmony. The dark side of trade was that it treated land only as something to exploit for profit rather than as a perennial source of human renewal. Moreover, by electing to serve Mammon, the farmer had turned a deaf ear to the song of Nature. While every man was not an artist, all men could experience Art through communion with Nature. Lanier's belief in the redemptive quality of subsistence farming had become more than the prescription for material success advertised in his earlier dialect poems. Simply stated, Lanier equated getting back to Nature with the transcendent love of Christ. Corn fed the hunger of body and soul by freeing the individual from the restraints of time.[88]

Most Georgia farmers were unwilling or simply unable to transcend the earthly domain of King Cotton. The Civil War and Reconstruction had unleashed a revolution in the countryside that forced planters, merchants, yeoman farmers, and former slaves into unaccustomed roles. In retrospect, it is not surprising that the commercial transformation of rural Georgia was replete with conflict and hardship. The merger of planters and merchants into a new ruling class was a difficult transition, as was the transformation of the white yeoman majority and former slaves into a rural proletariat. Both were interrelated processes subject to the agency of everyone involved and influence of outside forces beyond the ability of most Georgians to comprehend fully. Nevertheless, the destruction of slavery did not destroy Georgia's plantation economy. By accepting a junior partnership in the national corporate order, the landed elite preserved and expanded its local economic power and reasserted its statewide political dominance. Sharecropping, tenancy, and the notorious crop lien may well have been logical economic choices for planters and merchants after the war, but the restoration of plantation society came at a heavy price. For small farmers of both races, the dream of self-sufficient independence was fading fast. As Reconstruction drew to an end, many Georgians heralded the arrival of a New South. Having prospered during the years of Republican rule, Atlanta in particular seemed positioned for a new leadership role as a broker between Yankee capitalism and the Georgia countryside. Still recovering from the back-to-back storms of the Civil War and Reconstruction, rural Georgians had less reason to be optimistic because yet another storm was gathering in the distance. King Cotton was back on his throne but there was trouble brewing in his realm.

PART THREE

The Restoration

CHAPTER SIX

Back in Tall Cotton

The New South or the Same Old South?

Speaking in November 1900 through his yeoman philosopher Billy Sanders, Joel Chandler Harris expressed his hope that the South would not abandon its ideological heritage as it entered an uncertain future: "What's the use of our advanced civilization an' our mor'l progress, I'd like to know if we can't patch up our philosophy so's it'll gallop along with ever'thing else?" Harris's outlook in 1900 contrasted sharply with the robust optimism that he had brought to Henry Grady's New South crusade in 1876. Soon after joining the staff of the Atlanta *Constitution* that year, Harris had begun using his Uncle Remus folktales and local color sketches to promote the New South program for economic revitalization. Over the years, however, Harris had grown disenchanted with the moral decay that he associated with urban life. Ironically, by serving as a bridge between plantation society and New South modernization, his literary efforts lent substantial support to the growing bourgeois spirit that was gradually undermining the paternalistic ideals that he shared with most postbellum Georgia writers. Although the plantation regime in Georgia had weathered Reconstruction and the farmer revolt, the aging "Philosopher of Shady Dale" had become doubtful whether the South could withstand the storm of progress he saw gathering on the horizon at the turn of the century. As one of the foremost southern writers of his generation, Harris's efforts to reconcile the Old South and the New South set the tone for other Georgia authors who were trying to come to grips with the turbulent closing decades of the nineteenth century.[1]

The restoration of home rule in Georgia in late 1871 demonstrated the tough resiliency of the plantation regime, although its long-term prospects remained uncertain. Later that decade the Radical Republican attempt to force liberal capitalism on the South ended with the Compromise of 1877, an agreement whereby the Republican Party gained four more years of control of the White House in exchange for removing the remaining obstacles to the restoration of the Democratic Party's regional political hegemony. Simply stated, the Republican Party's base in the South and black social and political rights were sacrificed on the alter of political and economic expediency. In the words of one historian, the deal was possible because "Southern planters no longer represented a threat to the expansion of northern capitalism."[2]

Having consolidated its power with a new constitution that protected planter interests, Georgia's Bourbon leadership undoubtedly anticipated brighter days ahead in 1877. For the most part, the landed elite's labor problem had been brought under control by sharecropping and the crop lien, which tied farm labor to the land in the cotton belt, while appeals to white supremacy and the Lost Cause already showed promise as a means of providing the ideological cohesion necessary to maintain planter dominance of local and statewide politics. Challenges to planter interests, however, came in rapid succession from the New South movement, the Southern Farmers' Alliance, and the Populist Party. Many historians have overestimated the immediate threat of the New South program to planter interests in the late nineteenth century, but the farmer revolt presented a direct challenge to the status quo by dividing the planter class into warring factions, alienating substantial numbers of white yeoman farmers from the Democratic Party, and appealing to black farmers to join its crusade.[3]

The rapid postwar transformation of American entrepreneurial capitalism, which had glorified the small, independent producer as the backbone of the republic, into urban-industrial corporate capitalism affected much of the rural United States like a tornado. While farmers everywhere struggled to survive the storm, rural Georgia was particularly hard hit by social unrest. Ultimately, the largest planter faction joined forces with New South leaders and town merchants to defeat the grassroots challenge from the countryside. A classic example of accommodation between landed elites and their dependent merchant allies in response to capitalist modernization, the plantation regime survived by abandoning the white yeomanry and disfranchising landless blacks. By the turn of the century, rural blacks were caught in a terrible web of Jim Crow paternalism and race hatred, while a growing number of white farmers found themselves dispossessed of their land and political influence. Yet try as it might to restore its antebellum glory, the plantation regime was a shadow of its old self, its domain a backwater in a nation on the verge of becoming a major international power.[4]

When it became increasingly evident that the New South dream of a full partnership within American capitalism was not forthcoming and the Populists began to push an agenda calling for the radical restructuring of the corporate order to protect small agricultural producers, the stage was set for a judicious Bourbon compromise reflected in the ideological adjustments evident in the work of New South authors like Charles Henry Smith and Joel Chandler Harris. In addition, a curious anomaly becomes apparent after 1880, for while rural life dominated contemporary literature, both the Farmers' Alliance and the Populists are notable mostly by their absence from the published literary record. With the exception of two polemical novels by Populist leaders, the groundswell of grassroots political unrest that erupted in Georgia after Reconstruction seemingly escaped the notice of literary observers who prided themselves on their intimate ties with the countryside.[5]

The most likely explanation for this omission lies in the destabilization of the political and racial status quo feared by conservative planters, merchants, and their middle-class spokesmen. Nor should the Atlanta *Constitution*'s importance in Georgia's postbellum literary revival be overlooked because of its commitment to the New South program of agricultural reform and conservative politics. By driving New South elites and conservative planters together, the Populists revealed the superficiality of many of their presumed differences, which perhaps explains why Smith and Harris could simultaneously champion the white yeomanry, plantation paternalism, and the New South program for agricultural reform. Both were committed to the restoration of social order and hopeful that something akin to the hierarchical arrangements of the Old South could be preserved.

Broadly speaking, the industrial revolution that transformed the United States into an urban nation in the late nineteenth century was an uneven process of development with many regional variations. As Raymond Williams has shown, the contrast in pastoral literature between the city and the country carries positive and negative connotations. The country is not only defined as the source of natural life, organic harmony, peace, and innocence, it is presented as the home of much ignorance and backwardness.

On the other hand, the city is portrayed as the center of achievement and culture, as well as violence and excessive worldliness. As postbellum Georgia authors such as Joel Chandler Harris and Richard Malcolm Johnston intuitively understood, memories of the Old South had tremendous appeal as an island of stability, a mythical time when planters and yeomen supposedly stood united.[6]

Nostalgia for lost rural traditions represented a cultural rejection of unsettling changes in social relations, a process seen most vividly by urban observers with one foot in the rural past. Thus while the city provided career opportunities for men like Smith and Harris, they could not conceal their profound sense of loss. Both remained close enough to the land to witness the social impact of the commercial expansion of the tyranny of King Cotton. The weakened land was made to produce more cotton than ever, while the volume of human misery grew in direct proportion. Although Smith and Harris argued that overproduction of cotton was a major problem in Georgia, they also believed that urbanization was destroying the cohesiveness of southern culture. Analogous to capitalism itself, the city symbolized the end of childhood in a wasteland devoid of the structure of feeling many authors associated with the Old South. This identification of the idea of the country with childhood is a recurring literary theme that speaks strongly to the emotional and intellectual impact of capitalist urbanization on generations of rural Georgians after the Civil War, as well as to the longevity of the plantation regime.[7]

Still, it is important to remember that the future of plantation society was anything but certain in the closing decades of the nineteenth century. By shattering the dominance of the planter class, the Civil War and Reconstruction had created a window of opportunity for alternative visions for the South's future. Thus when the poet Sidney Lanier turned to the census reports while researching an essay for *Scribner's Monthly*, he took heart in the tremendous growth in the number of small farms recorded between 1860 and 1880. Proudly proclaiming that "the New South means small farming," Lanier misread the data as indicative of planter decline because of the census bureau's failure to distinguish between tenant farmers and small landowners. First published in October 1880, "The New South" reiterated Lanier's romantic belief that all cultural expression was rooted in the land. Lanier contrasted "the quiet rise of the small farmer" in the South with the trend toward large, corporate wheat farms in the West, which he described as "mining for wheat" or "a manufacturing business" rather than farming. Foreshadowing the Populists, Lanier defined the problem as striking the appropriate balance between the corporation, which he labeled the spirit of control, and the small farmer, who represented the spirit of independence. Diversified small farms were needed to preserve civic virtue and a rich community life. Lanier's attachment to the Jeffersonian ideal was rooted more in his romantic vision than personal experience. Writing from a clippings file he had accumulated while living in Baltimore, he heralded the advent of scientific farming and the emerging political unity of small farmers, white and black, a rather dramatic departure from the harsh racism that had colored much of his work in the past. Lanier wrote that when small farmers finally recognized their community of interests, "whatever now remains of the color-line must surely disappear out of the Southern political situation." Consistent with the message of his earlier poetry, Lanier rooted his vision of agrarian utopia in the reclamation of the rolling hills of Middle Georgia.[8]

Other observers placed their hopes for the future in the dramatic rise of Atlanta from the ashes after the Civil War. Even the South Carolina poet Paul Hamilton Hayne, who had taken refuge in the pine barrens near Augusta after being impoverished by the war, got caught up in the New South excitement over industrial expansion, albeit briefly. In a piece published in the Atlanta *Constitution* in 1881 entitled "The Exposition Ode," Hayne heralded the liberating power of "the steam-god's fiery passion," although he soon became disillusioned with the New South movement because the industrial machine was under northern control. The year before his death in 1886, Hayne wrote in "To the New South" that industrial development should not come at the expense of what was worth preserving in the older agrarian tradition. "Foul not the fairness of your natal nest," he warned.[9]

The foremost champion of industrial development as a panacea for Georgia's economic ills was Henry W. Grady, the New South editor of the Atlanta *Constitution.* In a series of widely acclaimed speeches in the late 1880s, Grady outlined a program for economic development that he believed would enable the South to escape its colonial dependence on the North. When examined closely, however, it becomes evident that his program for economic revitalization, which emphasized the expansion of cotton mills and smaller home industries, agricultural diversification to lessen Georgia's dependence on imported foodstuffs and fertilizers, and sectional reconciliation to attract outside capital, presented less of a threat to the plantation regime than many observers thought at the time or later. The preservation of white supremacy and the Solid South completed Grady's formula for planter survival through cooperation with urban business interests.[10]

Grady's disdain for the South's colonial economy did not blind him to political reality in Georgia, where cotton remained king and the planters were a force with which to be reckoned. Neither should his appeals for sectional reconciliation and northern capital be interpreted exclusively as a sign of capitulation. Standing between the planter elite and Yankee capitalism, Grady envisioned industrial development as a means of restoring southern independence. Moreover, the term *colonial* communicated a strong ideological message in a nation with a rich anticolonial heritage and suggested that the North remained an unjust imperial oppressor. Use of the term by southern authors also lent credence to the argument that the Civil War had not simply been a rebellion within an indivisible Union. In addition, emphasizing the South's colonial status told the people at home that their political leaders, past and present, were not responsible for their poverty and regional underdevelopment.

White supremacy was not only necessary to preserve the Solid South, Grady understood as well that any program for industrial development that threatened planter interests had little chance for success. He also realized that class conflict between the landed elite and the yeomanry would undermine the New South program. Not surprisingly, the authors in the literary revival of the 1880s who were associated with the Atlanta *Constitution* championed antebellum planters and small farmers alike, as well as blacks who accepted their traditional place in the hierarchical order. For this reason, New South literary spokesmen like Smith and Harris felt a strong kinship with local color writers like Richard Malcolm Johnston who glorified antebellum plantation life. As had Augustus B. Longstreet and William Tappan Thompson, the authors who led Georgia's literary revival in the 1880s rejected the aristocratic style of the Virginia plantation tradition for a "frontier" plantation ideal that united all landed whites in democratic harmony. Stories that applauded the friendly social interaction between planters and small farmers were more than simple nostalgia or an effort to create a literary photograph of a vanishing landscape. Georgia's postbellum plantation romancers and local color writers were active participants in a broader search for order in a social system dangerously adrift.

Although she is best remembered as a Civil War diarist and botanist, Eliza Frances Andrews published three novels between 1876 and 1882. Writing under the gender-neutral pseudonym, Elzey Hay, Andrews drew upon her wartime experiences as a refugee in Southwest Georgia in *A Family Secret,* a Civil War plantation romance published by J. B. Lippincott in 1876. In the novel Andrews displays a strong talent for landscape detail and recreates the privileged social world of the southern elites who flocked to Georgia's plantation frontier to escape the war. Relying upon stock romance characters, including a gallant Confederate officer of noble Virginian birth, a mysterious belle of initially questionable albeit equally exalted heritage, a planter villain of tainted blood, an earthy cracker, and a New England scoundrel minister, *A Family Secret* follows an interesting if pretty much predictable story line as a multitude of obstacles standing between the hero and heroine are removed en route to a happy ending that finds young love at last triumphant. Of greater historical interest are the author's exploration of class relationships and portrait of Southwest Georgia's "piney woods" plantation society.[11]

Modeled after Albany, "South Ambury" is the center of a thriving cotton culture and a warehousing and distribution center for the Confederacy. After traveling by rail through the winter piney-woods tangle of forest, wiregrass, cotton fields, and clearings "where the old, dead pines, bleached and blistered by the almost tropical sun of that far Southern region, and twisted by its storms into a thousand fantastic shapes, stretch their wasted arms to heaven," the reader finally arrives in the little town, where the great cotton warehouses surrounding the depot dominate the landscape and "a general aspect of lintiness" prevails.[12]

Andrews portrayed the surrounding countryside as a primitive land dominated by great plantations of many thousand acres under the control of a few wealthy families. The frontier character of the scene is indicated by its class structure, for the plantations include vast domains of uncultivated land peopled by "mean whites." Neither are there signs of the democratic harmony proclaimed by Georgia's more famous postbellum authors. Jim Chance, for example, a character who shows the influence of Longstreet, expresses his contempt when he sees the hero and heroine, Colonel Audley Malvern and Ruth Harfleur, pass in a light carriage: "This here's the rich men's quarrel, and they may do their own fightin'. 'Taint none of my bisness if the d——d niggers does git sot free. Ef things goes as they say they're like to do now, some folks what holds their heads high enough to-day will be brought down to bite the dust afore long, and some other folks I knows on won't be sorry fur it, neither. . . . Ef the derned niggers does git sot up, them what owns 'em 'll git sot down,—that's one comfort."[13]

In Andrews's social universe, outward appearances were a poor indicator of personal worth in the absence of honor and noble blood. The heroine's uncle, George Bruen, for example, is a rustic whose sprawling frontier dwelling is rough on the outside but spacious and warm within, its genuine aristocratic character revealed by fine furnishings passed down through the generations. The two surest signs of noble blood were equestrianship and the kind treatment of servants. The main villain, Julian Harfleur, is the region's wealthiest planter, but the slaves on his magnificent estate are poorly clad and cowed "in glaring contrast with the greasy contentment that beamed in the shining black faces of George Bruen's dependents." Strikingly handsome in spite of his advanced years, Harfleur is the offspring of French creoles who had fled St. Domingo during Toussaint L'Ouverture's revolt. A man of "dark, terrible beauty that made the beholder shudder," his almost perfectly white hair contrasts strongly with "the dark olive of his complexion." Leaving the possibility of tainted blood unstated, Andrews hints early in the story that the Harfleur "family secret" lies in her father's past rather than Ruth's, whose legitimacy remains in question until the novel's denouement.[14]

After a rather disappointing second novel in 1879 entitled *A Mere Adventurer,* Andrews authored another plantation romance in 1882, entitled *Prince Hal; or, The Romance of a Rich Young Man.* Set in the fall-line plantation culture of her youth, the story follows a similar story line to *A Family Secret* in that the plot revolves around the mysterious origins of an aristocratic hero thought to be of humble birth throughout much of the romance, although the loyalty of a free negro "mammy" figure named Maum Miley to the child prior to his being taken under the wing of a rich planter foreshadows his true ancestry. Andrews also provides a glimpse into the education and social world of the children of Georgia's leading antebellum planter families. Of additional interest is her description of the Old South as a premodern society, which she portrayed as a beloved yet "cursed" time with "a glamour of romance" that "the cold verities of history will never dispel."[15]

The novel's focus on the manners and values of antebellum society communicated the message that redemption of virtue was possible through sacrifice and dedication. Accordingly, the title character redeems his sullied honor by making the ultimate sacrifice on the blood-stained field of Chickamauga. This didactic tone is even more apparent in Mary Ross Banks's largely forgotten *Bright Days in the Old Plantation Time,* a lightly embellished memoir published in 1882 that recalls her childhood visits to her grandmother's plantation near Griffin, Georgia. The town-raised daughter of a wealthy merchant-planter, Banks wrote to give her grandchildren "a correct view" of plantation slavery, hoping as well to rid northern children of the false impression that slaves had been treated as "mere beasts of burden" rather than with kindness. Her best chapter recalls a corn-shucking, which a favorite servant calls "de mos' consequenshus time en de whole year 'cep' Chris'mus and fofe-er-Jewly." Similar sentimental reminiscences of childhood appear in Montgomery M. Folsom's *Scraps of Song and Southern Scenes: A Collection of Humorous and Pathetic Poems and Descriptive Sketches of Plantation Life in the Backwoods of Georgia,* which he dedicated to Henry Grady.[16]

By far the foremost champion of antebellum rural life in Middle Georgia was Hancock County's Richard Malcolm Johnston. Born in 1822 near Powelton into a solid planter family, Johnston's formal education included field schools, the Powelton Academy, and Mercer University in Penfield. Prior to the war, he vacillated between a legal career and teaching, an experience which provided material for his literary endeavors later in life. At one point, Johnston was a law partner of Linton Stephens, Alexander H. Stephen's younger half-brother. When he was defeated for a circuit judgeship by Garnett Andrews in 1857, he accepted a professorship at the University of Georgia that he held when the war began in 1861. Returning to his plantation in Hancock County, Johnston opened "Rockby," a select boarding school for boys. He also served briefly during the war on the staff of Governor Joseph E. Brown. Johnson moved to Baltimore after the war, where his friend Sidney Lanier encouraged his literary ambitions. Bert Hitchcock describes Johnston as the embodiment of the courteous Old South plantation gentleman and a bridge between the antebellum humor and postbellum local color traditions. In addition to several editions of *Dukesborough Tales,* his most famous work, he wrote four novels and six collections of stories.[17]

Johnston never strayed far from the themes he explored in *Dukesborough Tales,* which included schooling, law, marriage, death, religion, paternalism, and the psychological conflict within rural families arising over such issues as land greed. Hitchcock argues that the unchanging focus of his work was the life of the common people between the 1820s and 1840s. As defined by Johnston in an essay entitled "Middle Georgia Rural Life" that appeared in *Century Magazine* in March 1892, the common people included families that owned between two hundred and one thousand acres and between one and fifty slaves, figures that communicate considerable ambiguity. His stories and novels reveal clearly that Johnston's ideal of the common man was a small planter in a democratic slaveholding republic. As he remembered Middle Georgia in his autobiography, "patrician rule" had been necessary in newly settled communities "yet community existence formed itself on a basis approaching as nearly approximate equality as was possible" given the "individual differences distinctive in all minds."[18]

Johnston's most famous story is "The Goosepond School," the lead story in the 1871 edition of *Dukesborough Tales.* In the story Johnston made his case for humane and liberal education by describing the downfall of Israel Meadows, an unschooled and sadistic master of a plantation field school. Like Powelton, Dukesborough was a village that had started without much plan or direction. Beginning with a blacksmith shop, the town had grown gradually along a winding road by adding a small store, a few family residences, and a church. Since then the village had suffered "the most absolute decay that I have known ever to befall any village." Like the Old South, "It had run its race, like all other things, places, and persons, that have lived out their lives and run their races." The other stories in the first edition of *Dukesborough Tales* examine the workings of the Superior Court in antebellum times, corporal punishment in education, the marriage pursuits of a scoundrel, the trials of a poor widow and her children, a wandering minstrel, a salt hoarder during the war, and the courtship of an old bachelor.[19]

In 1883, the same year that the second edition of *Dukesborough Tales* launched his national literary career, Johnston fleshed out the topography of Dukesborough in *Old Mark Langston: A Tale of Duke's Creek,* a rather flat novel set in the late 1820s that recreates the same themes of his earlier stories. In the novel, Johnston continued his exploration of the impact of greed on familial and community harmony, a theme he developed further in several of the stories in *Mr. Absalom Billingslea and Other Georgia Folk.* In "Mr. Thomas Chivers's Boarder," he related how the paternalistic code worked within planter society. The story revolves around the local response to a planter who overworks his slaves and refuses to treat his wife and daughter with proper respect, behavior that violates the moral standards of the community.[20]

In "Moll and Virgil," one of his few stories that revolves almost exclusively around slaves, Johnston reiterated his belief that the vast majority of planters in Middle Georgia had been kind and beloved masters. In the story, two elderly slaves labor tirelessly to free their master after he is falsely convicted of stealing a horse and imprisoned in Milledgeville. An old sheriff delivers the paternalistic moral late in the tale: "I'm gittin' to be of a old man, an' have knowed right smart o' people in my time, white folks *an'* niggers, an' my expeunce of niggers is that in gen'l, whar a man treat 'em right, an' have been raised 'ith 'em, they ain't a more thankfuler ner 'fectionate creeters than them, ner them that'll take bigger resks fer 'em."[21]

In his essay "Middle Georgia Rural Life," Johnston asserted that the paternalistic ideal was still at work in 1892. Recalling the kind treatment they had received while slaves, freedmen in Middle Georgia had been less troublesome than elsewhere. As Johnston explained, "On many a plantation in Middle Georgia freedmen and their families are dwelling now as they dwelt before the war." Taken together, two racial anecdotes offer a return to paternalism as an alternative to the impersonal world of working for shares on the free labor market. When his former master asks why he had quit working for another farmer, an "old-time negro" replies:

> Well now, Marse Jack, I gwine up en tell you jes how 't is. I wuck fer dah man all las' year, en I make him a good crop. Well, now, de troof is, I did git f'om him a few, but, min' you, jes only a few, merlasses en tobarker, en one hat, en a pa'r o' shoes, en one little thing en 'nother. Well, den, Chris'mus come, en he say, "Jim, I gwine make out our count." En den he tuck he piece o' paper, en he pen, en he ink-vial, en he 'gin a-settin' down, en when he thoo wid dat job, he 'gin a-addin' up, en a-put'n' down, en a-kyar'n'; en he kyar'd, en he kep' on a-kyar'n', ontwel, bless your soul and body! Marse Jacky, when he got thoo, he done kyar's off all what was a-comin' to me! En so I makes up my min', I does, to leff dar, en pewoose myself back to you, whar I knows dey not gwine be no sich kyar'n' as dem.

It is uncertain what Johnston thought in Baltimore of the farmer revolt that was raging in the region around Hancock County in 1892, but his little anecdote communicates more than his expressed purpose of recreating the picturesque language of an "old-time negro." By returning to his former place in the paternal hierarchy, the old man frees himself from a postwar system more exploitative than slavery.[22]

After publishing a second novel in 1889 entitled *Ogeechee Cross-Firings,* Johnston released a collection of stories that had first appeared in *Harper's Magazine, Harper's Weekly, Harper's Bazaar, The Century,* and *The Cosmopolitan.* Published in 1891, *The Primes and Their Neighbors: Ten Tales of Middle Georgia* differs from most of his earlier work in that it includes a story set during Reconstruction. Entitled "Travis and Major Jonathan Wilby," the tale takes place outside Hancock County across the Oconee River and revolves around an old bachelor named Jonathan Wilby, who had owned a good plantation and several slaves before the war. Fond of the good life, hunting with hounds, and traveling, Wilby had run up debts that the narrator explains would have been inconsequential but for the war. Although against secession he had answered the call of duty, leaving his plantation under the care of his slave foreman Travis, a strong and steady man ten years his senior who had been his childhood nurse. Johnston states that had it not been for Travis's industry and economy, his master's debts would have been even larger. Moreover, Travis had taken good advantage of the custom of giving slaves small plots of land for cotton cultivation in addition to their gardens. At the war's beginning, Travis had already put aside four hundred dollars. While he tended to the plantation, Wilby served well during the war, rising to the rank of major.[23]

Some years later, the narrator, while traveling to visit a gentleman named Bass who lives nearby, chances to meet the Major at his home when bad roads and nightfall necessitate stopping at the next farm he sees in search of lodging. The house is a nice, white, two-story mansion in the midst of a grove of red oaks. Seated on the piazza with a book on his lap, the Major naturally offers him the best in southern hospitality, glad to enjoy a meal and conversation with a cultured guest. Something of a recluse, the Major lives largely within his books, his particular interest being stories about General Lee and the war, the outcome of which he accepts as God's will. That evening, the Major describes his war experiences and the hard times that had followed, as well as the excellent care given his land by Travis, whom he nonetheless considers a bit too free with his whip when dealing with their black hands.

The next morning after a substantial breakfast, Travis escorts the narrator the remaining distance to the Bass plantation and fills in the missing details of the Major's story. Just before the war, Bass's daughter had pledged herself to Wilby, but in his absence had fallen under the spell of a deserter dressed as a colonel. After running off with the scoundrel, she had returned home and died while giving birth to a stillborn child. When "Marse Jon'than" came home on furlough, he had been crushed by the news and returned immediately to the war, where he received a terrible head wound. Still despondent after the war, he had gone to Augusta to try and raise money to cover his debts. Meanwhile, acting through Henry Bass, his "servant" had purchased Wilby's plantation with fifteen hundred dollars of his own money and paid off the Major's remaining debt through careful crop management. When he finally found Marse Jon'than, he carried the desperately ill hero home and nursed him back to health. The narrator recalls that the Major's perfect demeanor as a gentleman had prevented him from realizing that his life was an illusion. The whole community respected the Major so much that everyone kept the truth concealed, knowing that it would break his heart. Moreover, Travis and his wife thought of the land as belonging to the old man and continued to serve him faithfully.

On one level "Travis and Major Jonathan Wilby" can be read simply as nostalgic glorification of plantation slavery. Yet the fact that Travis allows his former master to live out his declining years under the illusion that he still owns his land affords an interesting twist on the spread of tenancy and sharecropping through Middle Georgia. Considered in conjunction with his essay on Middle Georgia, the story also can be interpreted as voicing an ideological response to the racial conflict spawned by the farmer revolt in which the author posits paternalism as an alternative to the interracial political cooperation advocated by Populist leaders. From his vantage point in Baltimore, Johnston must have looked upon events in Middle Georgia in the 1890s with serious concern, although he never addressed the situation directly in his stories and novels of the period. Still, it is perhaps no coincidence that he fleshed out his ideal of a slaveholding republic in his 1893 novel, *Widow Guthrie*.[24]

Considered his best novel because of his insightful treatment of the psychological impact of bad marriages and familial conflict in plantation society, Johnston dedicated the work "to those survivors among the associates of my youth to whom, as to me, the old Georgia seems to have been more happy than the new." As sentimentally portrayed by Johnston, the Middle-Georgia frontier in 1828 was devoid of poverty and class conflict, an egalitarianism born of the need for mutual cooperation against the Indians that was reinforced by slavery. Under such conditions, "it behooved people within degrees" to set aside personal and "even family distinctions," which led "the uncultured poor man" to feel a freedom equal to that of his wealthier neighbors.[25]

Following in the tradition established nearly six decades before by Longstreet, Johnston rejected the condescending class attitudes often associated with the wealthy, arguing instead for an easy and benign interaction beneficial to all classes. Although infrequent, antebellum marriages between men and women of different class origins had usually "lowered not as much as they exalted" and had produced a race characterized by "true manhood and true womanhood." Johnston acknowledged that there had been "an aristocracy of excellent type" in rural Georgia, but maintained that the "broad line between the white man and the negro" had produced genuine democratic unity. He depicted the aristocratic element as follows: "In its very highest representatives it was least ostentatious. Its graciousness was not misunderstood by the humble, and they not often sought to overleap barriers to entirely equal intercourse which, not convention, but nature and different fortune and opportunities had raised. No man could feel himself to be more of a freeman than the white man of middle Georgia sixty years ago."[26]

Johnston completed his description of Middle Georgia's happy state of affairs before the Civil War by voicing his praise for the old plantation's paternalistic race relations, where "close contiguity to their owners gave rise to humanity and fidelity." Nowhere was "domestic and community police upon a scale of less vigilance or greater security than on plantations." A slave named Lizy in *Widow Guthrie* explains, "Marster know his niggers ain' gwine steal from him," while his dogs protected the premises from intruders. Reports to the contrary in antebellum journals aside, such assertions of harmony stood in stark contrast to Georgia's troubled race relations in 1893.[27]

Unlike Richard Malcolm Johnston, who abandoned the country for the city after the Civil War, Charles Henry Smith quit the city in 1877 and bought a farm near Cartersville. Determined to give his children the benefits of a solid, rural upbringing, Smith devoted the next ten years of his life to farming, although he continued to make his primary livelihood on the lecture circuit and by writing a weekly column in the Atlanta *Constitution* with few interruptions until his death in 1903. After 1877 Smith also transformed Bill Arp into a folksy, literate, rural commentator who directed his comments toward family life, farming, the common people, and the Old South. Yet as his most recent biographer has observed, Smith was anything but a contented country sage. A reluctant supporter of Henry Grady's New South program at best, Smith rejected cities as corrupt and immoral and believed that New South society lacked the Old South's traditional virtues of "hard work, morality, and self-reliance." In David B. Parker's words, "Arp's writings on his family and farm, the Georgia folk, and the past were an implicit criticism of the new order."[28]

Like Grady, Smith championed the ideal of an independent and self-sufficient South, which perhaps explains why he bought into the New South crusade. He believed that railroad expansion and expanded manufacturing would benefit farmers, as would scientific farming and crop diversification. Still, it was one thing to transform Bill Arp into an agricultural reformer; swallowing the entire New South agenda was another matter altogether. An unreconstructed rebel to the end, Smith never accepted the idea of sectional reconciliation and equated the New South with all the bad features of Yankee materialism, such as crime, idleness, vice, and new roles for women out of step with the Old South's "goodly heritage."[29]

Parker sees three stages in the evolution of Smith's racial thought. During Reconstruction his outlook was characteristically harsh, although the restoration of home rule in the South restored temporarily his faith in paternalism. Around 1890, however, Smith became increasingly vitriolic. In response to the widespread rejection by so-called "new issue negroes" of his Old South notions of proper racial etiquette, Smith began voicing his agreement with the popular white notion that blacks were lapsing into degeneracy as a race. Rejecting education for blacks beyond agricultural and technological training for a life of labor, Smith argued that the solution to black crime was good moral training and the revival of the whipping post. As did many white Georgians, Smith blamed the rising tide of racial violence in the early 1890s on blacks and advocated lynching in response to presumed outrages against white women. Nevertheless, Smith never accepted completely what Joel Williamson has labeled the radical racist outlook. Essentially a conservative at heart, Smith drew a distinction between "good negroes" and "brutes" and even argued that only the intelligent and qualified of both races should be allowed to vote.[30]

Smith's emergence as an agricultural reformer can be traced in several of the essays included in his 1884 anthology, *Bill Arp's Scrap Book: Humor and Philosophy.* In "Smoking the Pipe of Peace," he contrasted the joys of farming to town life, although he lamented the plague of flies, bugs, animals, and weeds that hindered his efforts to make a good crop. But compared to life in the crowded city and the endless pursuit of money, life in the country was sweet: "I like farmin. Its an honest, quiet life, and it does me so much good to work and get all over in a swet of perspiration. I enjoy my umble food and my repose, and get up every mornin' renewed and rejuvenated like an eagle in his flight, or words to that effect." Unlike the miserable existence endured by lawyers, doctors, and clerks in the city, "who were all penned up like convicts in a chain-gang," farming was a life of freedom and variety, where one could stop most any time to chat with a neighbor or go hunting without worrying about the consequences.[31]

One of the major components of the New South program for agricultural diversification was livestock raising, although Smith soon discovered that the distance between theory and practice was greater than he had initially anticipated. In "The Stricken Sheep," Arp described his problems with local dogs. Left unchained at night, the animals preyed on sheep and domestic fowl. Although his loss of five sheep was bad enough, he reported that a neighbor had lost over a hundred sheep in less than two years before abandoning the enterprise. Arp vowed to kill every dog that came on his premises thereafter and to run for the legislature himself if the next candidate did not take a stand against dogs. Like the fence law struggles, the dog issue revealed class divisions in the Georgia countryside. Depending upon their dogs for hunting and protection but disinclined to feed them regularly, many rural Georgians simply let the animals fend for themselves. In spite of Bill Arp's folksy dialect, Smith's stance on the dog issue accorded more with the interests of the landlord class than the upcountry yeomanry.[32]

Reflecting his farm's location near Cartersville in the northwestern upcountry, Smith's ideal New South farmer was a humble yeoman named Cobe, who had "a chunk of a cow and a sow and pigs, and about enough old rickety furniture to move in one wagon load" along with his wife and six well-mannered if lightly educated children who lived on "corn-bread and taters." In Arp's opinion, such folk were the country's best hope because they were hard-working and productive. Dependable in war, the children of the poor yeomanry were "running this Southern country now." From their ranks were drawn the best merchants in the cities, as well as the best mechanics, railroad men, and bankers, even if they did "spell hog with a double g." In "The Old Man and His Son Conclude to Avoid the Ethiopian and to Gather Their Own Crop," Arp described his ideal of the good life as "a smart and diligent man with good land" and a few thousand dollars invested in stocks to provide enough income to educate his children, visit relatives, provide his wife and daughters with a few luxuries like new bonnets and "red ear-rings," and "have a little missionary money left." Smith deemed outside investments "highly necessary" because even an experienced man had to deal with "a thousand little leaks in farmin" that only capital could remedy. Every "aspirin man" he knew in the towns and cities hoped one day to return to the land.[33]

In "Beautiful Snow and New Year's Calling," Smith made yet another appeal for agricultural diversification. After the first snow, Arp reported that he had planted eight acres of clover and planned to "sow some red-top and timothy, for grass is better than cotton, and oats are better than corn." Last year, he continued, one acre had yielded over three tons worth seventy dollars in the field, without baling. The moral of the story was as follows: "I wish our farmers would try the grasses, for it does look like agricultural suicide to see car after car of Tennessee hay unloading at our depot every winter and selling for $25 a ton. I reckon our farmers know their business, but it looks curious to me to see them running everything into cotton, and selling it for a *big pile* of money, and then paying half of it out for labor and most all the rest for corn and hay to make another crop with." In the next paragraph, Arp's description of a visit to Rome made clear just how formidable an opponent cotton was to New South agricultural diversification. Smith wrote that he had never seen the like in his life, "for you can hardly see the town for the cotton."[34]

In an essay entitled "Nobody Growing Rich, But Many Scronging to Keep Up Appearances," Smith also expressed his belief that the young men of the postbellum era would never equal the giants who had led plantation society during the time of slavery. Nevertheless, freedom had opened the door of opportunity for humbler men by breaking down the social barriers of antebellum society. Success in making money had replaced statesmanship and great learning. Although sorry that greed had destroyed honor in politics, Smith took comfort in the rise of the common people in a world where all classes were becoming more alike in the white community.[35]

Ironically, Smith's racism prevented him from seeing a critical contradiction in the New South program for agricultural reform. While he wanted to free the white yeoman farmer from the tyranny of cotton, his ideal of the "good negro" was rooted in plantation slavery. Simply stated, as long as the plantation regime controlled black labor in the old cotton belt, white yeoman farmers could do little to prevent cotton from following the railroads into new markets, especially when new commercial fertilizers made the crop even more attractive. Although sympathetic to the small farmer's plight, Smith's acceptance of Henry Grady's argument that white solidarity was essential to regional political solidarity doomed his New South appeals for agricultural reform from the start. It would not be the last time that racism undermined the prospects for real change in the Georgia countryside.

In "Races and Human Nature," Smith restated his longstanding belief that northerners were simply incapable of understanding "the great Southern problem." In Bill Arp's words, "The Yankee never will know what the negro is, for he never knew him in a state of slavery." Though it remained unclear how a new generation of white southerners would fare any better with blacks who had never known slavery, Smith contended that philanthropists were wasting their time but welcomed their money. He also criticized southerners who argued that slavery had "perished under the condemnation of God and man," stating that "if the nigger is any better off now than he used to be, I can't see." Smith loved the "old darkeys" like children, not as his equals but as his dependents. When relations between whites and blacks were otherwise, he had "no use for the nigger." Education for citizenship was a humbug and a proven failure. Whereas government was a natural vocation for the Anglo-Saxon race, he continued, blacks were natural laborers and servants who became unhappy fools and vagabonds when treated otherwise. He had no desire to restore slavery but philanthropists were deceiving "the negro when they flatter him with a capacity equal to whites in fitness to invent, or to govern, or to rise to the heroic or the sublime." Smith thought their money would be better spent on the education of poor white children.[36]

As Smith revealed in another essay, the paternalistic practices he had learned under slavery still governed his relations with his black farmhands. In "The Negro" he wrote that he was satisfied with the improvement of "country niggers" since Reconstruction because they were conscious of their inferiority and accepted the command of their natural superiors. Unlike the white man, blacks rarely cheated or swindled anyone, although they were prone to "small pilfering," a minor transgression Mrs. Arp overlooked to prevent hurting their feelings. Smith simply could not imagine life otherwise: "But for hard work, contented work, humble work, who could take their place on the farms and on the drays, and the steamboats and the railroads? Who would do the white man's bidding with so little murmuring and so much cheerfulness? The negro is still an important factor in our southern homes and southern industries, and I hope he will remain. He is grafted on the southern tree."[37]

Had Smith's racial stance evolved no further, his glorification of the so-called old-time negro would locate him well within the conservative tradition, which is an impression communicated by the pieces in *The Farm and the Fireside: Sketches of Domestic Life in War and Peace* (1892) and *Bill Arp from the Uncivil War to Date* (1903). Both books suggest that Smith tried to escape the social turmoil of the 1890s by seeking refuge in the nostalgic landscape of memory, an interpretation out of step with many of his uncollected writings in the Atlanta *Constitution.* Parker makes the convincing argument that Smith largely abandoned the paternalistic outlook that colored his sketches in the 1880s and moved toward a more radical stance that condemned blacks as dangerously degenerate. One could even argue that his disillusionment with the New South movement produced a virulent racism akin to that of Thomas E. Watson's in the aftermath of Populism.[38]

Unlike many of his white contemporaries like Smith, whose racial attitudes hardened in response to the political turmoil unleashed by the Populists, Joel Chandler Harris remained true to plantation paternalism throughout his literary career. Biographers and literary historians have variously portrayed Harris as a New South ideologue, a plantation romancer, and a champion of the white yeomanry, but he is best understood as a man who was trying to bridge two worlds in transition. As historian Eric Foner has observed, one cannot understand fully the ongoing efforts to reconstruct plantation society without giving careful consideration to the parallel transformations wrought in the North by urbanization and industrialization. In spite of his modest claim that he was little more than a cornfield journalist, Harris was a gifted author and an astute observer of the social transformation of the American South in the late nineteenth century. The primary concern to which Harris directed much of his social commentary for over three decades was the changing relationship between town and country in a time of urban-industrial expansion.[39]

Harris was a man of substantial literary ambition and a careful student of the South's literary forms and traditions. He was aware of the didactic function of folklore in the black community, as well as literature's parallel purpose in Victorian society. Thus his skills as a collector of African American folktales should not obscure the fact that his Uncle Remus stories were framed carefully to deliver ideological messages to adult white audiences. His description of Uncle Remus as a composite of several slaves he had known in his youth on Joseph Addison Turner's plantation near Eatonton is sometimes cited as evidence of the character's authenticity. His professed self-identification with the character aside, Remus did not speak through Harris so much as Harris spoke through Remus. Uncle Remus was first and foremost a literary construction, as were his less notable literary archetypes Billy Sanders and Aunt Minervy Ann. All three characters were convenient mouthpieces through which an otherwise reticent public speaker communicated his thoughts regarding significant social issues.[40]

Harris consistently defined himself as a conservative plantation paternalist throughout his long tenure as a New South spokesman for the Atlanta *Constitution.* As he proclaimed in a December 1877 piece entitled "The Old Plantation," "Now that the problem of slavery, which even before the desperate cast of the die in 1861 had begun to perplex the more thoughtful of the Southern people, is successfully (but O, how cruelly!) solved, even the bare suggestion of its reestablishment is unsavory; but the memory of the old plantation will remain green and gracious forever." Like Charles Henry Smith, Harris was uncomfortable with New South materialism and urban life, but he was appalled by the rising tide of racial intolerance in the 1890s. Harris respected the humanity and character of African Americans, but should also be recognized as a white supremacist whose perceptions had been shaped by slavery. Ironically, the animal tales that were part of the oral literature of resistance to slavery were appropriated by Harris to affirm the hierarchical social relations of plantation society against the market values and practices of modern bourgeois society.[41]

Harris began writing dialect stories shortly after joining the Atlanta *Constitution*'s staff in October 1876. Originally casting Uncle Remus as an old Atlanta Negro, Harris soon transformed the character into a defender of the old plantation regime. After an article in *Lippincott's Magazine* awakened him to the literary potential of folklore, Harris published his first plantation fable in the *Constitution* in July 1879, a tale entitled "The Story of Mr. Rabbit and Mr. Fox as Told by Uncle Remus." During the next three decades, Harris published more than 180 folktales in book-length collections.[42]

The publication of *Uncle Remus: His Songs and His Sayings* in 1880 established his national literary reputation, although he modified some of his early sketches from the *Constitution* in deference to northern readers. The underlying theme of the stories set in Atlanta is that African Americans would be better off back on the plantation. In "Race Improvement," Remus praises the gradual return of young black men to their "proper" place. Compelled by hunger and the law, they were learning the true meaning of freedom. In Remus's words, "You slap de law onter a nigger a time er two, an' larn 'im dat he's got fer to look atter his own rashuns an' keep out'n udder fokes's chick'n-coops, an' sorter coax 'im inter de idee dat he's got ter feed 'is own chilluns, an' I be blessed ef you ain't got 'im on risin' groun'." In "The Emigrants," Remus sees a forlorn-looking black family preparing to board a train for Alabama. When he learns that they have no money, vittles, or relatives in "Tallypoosy," Remus lets them know in no uncertain terms that Alabama is not the promised land, telling the father that he would be better off on the chain-gang. In "As to Education," Remus voices the opinion that education was ruining young blacks: "Put a spellin'-book in a nigger's han's, en right den er dar' you loozes a plow-hand." All three stories deliver a conservative labor message that Georgia planters would have applauded.[43]

Harris was hardly the first Georgia author to create a black champion of paternalism, although his had the most lasting impact. Few white southern readers would have been surprised to read that the venerable old man had "nothing but pleasant memories of the discipline of slavery," or that he had "all the prejudices of caste and pride of family that were the natural results of the system." Nor would they have found fault with his description of the relationship between the old man and the little boy as "the product of that practical reconstruction which has been going on to some extent since the war in spite of the politicians." Yet when Remus unfolds "the mysteries of plantation lore" to the little boy, he reveals his creator's hesitancy to give up the heritage of plantation slavery. In essence, Harris was searching for a way to make the social arrangements of contemporary plantation society acceptable outside the South.[44]

What made Joel Chandler Harris unique among southern authors was his refusal to cast Uncle Remus as a minstrel in black face. Remus is a complex character and anything but a mindless lackey, which reflects the authenticity of the folktales and his creator's empathetic outlook. Still, it is important to distinguish between the content of the frames and the actual folktales when analyzing the Uncle Remus stories. Simply stated, the dominant voice in the frames is white, while the tales offer a different perspective on plantation life. In "Why Mr. Possum Loves Peace," for example, Brer Possum and Brer Coon decide to take a walk through the settlement after supper. Seeing Mr. Dog in the distance, they begin discussing their alternatives in the face of danger. Brer Possum vows to stand by his friend when Brer Coon decides to fight. But when Mr. Dog attacks, nature takes over and Brer Possum plays dead. Brer Coon wins the contest, for one dog could no more count on defeating an adult raccoon than an unarmed white man on subduing a slave encountered on the road at night. Afterward, Brer Coon shuns his cowardly companion until Brer Possum explains that the only reason he had rolled over on his back was because he was "de most ticklish chap w'at you ever laid eye on" and had laughed himself senseless when Mr. Dog put his nose "down yer 'mong my ribs."[45]

A careful student of the antebellum humorists, Harris understood the importance of establishing an authentic setting in the frame to set the proper stage for the fable. In this instance, Uncle Remus transfers a hot coal from the palm of his callused hand to his clay pipe, a reflection of a life of labor that is "viewed by the little boy with undisguised admiration." Brothers in slavery, Brer Possum and Brer Coon are allegorical characters, just as his title "Mr." reflects the dog's domestication by man. There were several lessons that slave children might have drawn from the original fable. In the face of danger, one could flee, surrender, or fight. Self-reliance was valuable because solidarity often evaporated quickly in a world where whites enjoyed superior force. Whereas standing one's ground brought greater prestige and might be successful in certain situations, surrender carried a heavy price but was sometimes necessary for survival. As Uncle Remus explains in another tale, "In dis worl', lots er folks is gotter suffer fer udder folks sins. Looks like hit's mighty onwrong; but hit's des dat away."[46]

For this reason the animals in the fables all accept oppression and injustice as part of the natural order of things. In a world where the strong usually dominate, the weak survive through craft and cunning. Thus it is Brer Rabbit who represents the independent man, not Brer Wolf. Yet even the heroic rabbit must recognize his limitations to survive, a lesson that the "creetur" community forces upon him on more than one occasion. As Remus explains in "Mr. Rabbit Meets His Match Again," "Dey ain't no smart man, 'cep' w'at dey's a smarter." Wherever one turns in the tales, the reality of white power looms large.[47]

Uncle Remus speaks with authority because he accepts his place in the hierarchical order of plantation society. Although postbellum sharecropping and tenancy were characterized by the decentralized residential arrangements demanded by African American families, his cabin is still adjacent to the big house. As an integral member of his white family, Remus naturally tries to prevent the little boy from associating with poor-white neighbors. When the little boy violates the family code by playing with the Favers children anyway, it is Remus who disciplines him. Like Brer Rabbit, however, there are limits to the old man's authority. After Remus reprimands him in the frame of "Why Mr. Possum Has No Hair on His Tail," the little boy bribes him out of his silence with a long piece of candle, a seemingly inconsequential but highly significant act. The candle puts the old man back into his place by dramatizing his dependence on his white family for the basic necessities of life. The act illustrates reciprocity as well. His personal associations with blacks had imparted to the little boy a trace of "negro nature" because he had purloined the candle with which he purchases absolution and another story from Remus.[48]

Harris returned to the theme of caste and class relations three years later in *Nights with Uncle Remus: Myths and Legends of the Old Plantation.* In the frame of "How Brother Fox Was Too Smart," Remus catches the little boy climbing in a big red-oak tree and lectures him about copying the Favers children. Significantly, Remus also rejects the social attitudes of the boy's Yankee father: "Yo' pa, he got de idee dat some folks is good ez yuther folks; but Miss Sally, she know better. She know dat dey ain't no Favers 'pon de top side er de yeth w'at kin hol' der han' wid de Abercrombies in p'int er breedin' en raisin'." Part of Miss Sally's family since long before her birth, Remus feels secure enough to dispute the judgment of her husband. And while the Favers "allers did hate niggers kaze dey ain't had none," Remus feels equally safe within the protective web of paternalism. Just the year before last, he explains, the boy's Uncle James had warned Jim Favers that if he touched "one er his niggers, he'd slap a load ez buck shot in 'im." Although Remus crosses the color line by speaking against whites, one is a transplanted Yankee and the others are of lowly social origin. The underlying message is that a return to plantation paternalism was the solution to the South's race problem.[49]

Harris framed the closing tales in *Nights with Uncle Remus* by preparations for Christmas on the plantation, a time for celebration and the renewal of paternalistic bonds. In honor of the marriage of Daddy Jack and 'Tildy, a large platform normally used for sunning wheat and seed cotton is decorated for a dance, while mounds of lightwood are strategically placed for illumination. Feeling excluded from the fun, the little boy is near tears on the back piazza until Uncle Remus arrives. Captain of the corn-pile at shuckings, the most stout at log-rolling, the swiftest with a hoe, and the neatest with a plow, Remus is greeted with universal affection and respect by the plantation hands, who still consider him their leader. For the little boy's benefit, Remus tells the fiddler to put his instrument aside because they are going to sing as in the old times. Gathering the best singers around him, Remus sets the rhythm by slapping his left hand on his leg and breast, while the others keep time with their feet. The Christmas song, a strong, sweet melody of a hundred voices soon brings tears to the eyes of the company at the big house, which includes men and women who have toured the capitals of Europe. Several songs later the little boy is fast asleep and Remus gathers him up into his strong arms and carries him off to bed, singly softly all the way.[50]

Though one of the most sentimental Uncle Remus stories, "The Night before Christmas" communicates effectively the continuity of the plantation. Antebellum planters had exploited the Christmas celebration to demonstrate the moral superiority of slavery to doubting visitors. After the war, the seasonality of cotton production turned landlords away from wage labor arrangements during spring cultivation and the late fall harvest because there was no incentive to work harder at the precise moment when the failure to do so was courting disaster. In addition to providing incentives for accelerated production, such rituals also reinforced traditional patterns of deference and reciprocity within the structure of local authority in rural communities.[51]

In *Free Joe and Other Georgian Sketches,* which was published in 1887, Harris reiterated his commitment to paternalism. Set in 1850 in the Middle Georgia village of Hillsborough, "Free Joe and the Rest of the World" traces the tragic demise of a "black atom" whose "peculiar condition" had made him more helpless than a slave. Feared by whites because he represents the potential for insurrection, Free Joe is also despised by blacks because he remains aloof, realizing instinctively that whites will not tolerate closer affinity with the slave community. Unlike the happy slaves, Free Joe rarely laughs and never sings or dances. After being forcibly separated from his slave wife, Joe slowly pines away in the woods, the victim of a cruel slaveholder who had violated the paternalistic ethos. On one level, the story can be read as a harsh indictment of the cruelty of slavery. As a poor-white fortune-teller who had befriended Joe explains, "Niggers is niggers . . . an' you can't rub it out; yit I lay I've seed a heap of white people lots meaner'n than Free Joe." Notably, however, Harris traces Joe's tragic fall to his emancipation from slavery, a supposedly "natural" condition for blacks characterized by laughing, singing, and dancing. Harris's seemingly subversive critique of slavery loses its edge when his paternalistic outlook is recalled.[52]

The most effective piece of New South propaganda in *Free Joe and Other Georgian Sketches* is "Aunt Fountain's Prisoner." Many years removed from the village of Rockville, the narrator recalls his surprise one day upon seeing an advertisement for "gilt-edged" butter from the Jersey farm on the Tomlinson Place, a large plantation that had been owned before the war by the area's wealthiest family. Recalling that Judge Addison Tomlinson and his wife had been the standard bearers of local society, the narrator explains that he had been shocked to see that the advertisement had been signed by Ferris Trunion, a transparent play on words Harris used to deliver the moral of the story.[53]

When an opportunity presents itself for a business trip from Atlanta to the village, the narrator gladly returns to the scene of his youth. Upon his arrival, he is pleasantly surprised by the vast changes in Rockville, which is full of new faces, new enterprises, and "a bustle" that "must have caused queer sensations" among older citizens who were accustomed to a slower pace of life. The narrator's wistful longing for the romance and traditions of small town life and the old plantation yet admiration for the energy of the New South convey Harris's own ambivalence in the late 1880s.

Aunt Fountain had been a Tomlinson slave who sold ginger-cakes and persimmon beer in Rockville before the war. After quickly renewing his acquaintance with her ginger-cakes, which have unfortunately "lost their old-time relish," the narrator is joined by Aunt Fountain for a visit to the Tomlinson place. Along the way she fills in the gaps in his knowledge of the area's history since the war. During Sherman's invasion, she had come across a Yankee soldier trapped under his horse at the bottom of a deep gully. Drawn to the man by his humor and grace under duress, she had freed both man and horse and hurried back to the big house for help. The haughty mistress of the house had been hesitant to aid the injured invader but her beautiful daughter, Miss Lady, had fulfilled her Christian duty in spite of her animosity toward Yankees.

Miraculous indeed had been the transformations that transpired during Trunion's slow recovery. Though the old judge had lost his mind during the war, Trunion's presence on the piazza had restored him to his senses. Aunt Fountain recalls how she had chastised her proud mistress: "You see how you bin cuttin' up 'roun' dat sick w'ite man wid yo' biggity capers, en yit de Lord retch down en make Marster soun' en well time de yuther w'ite man tetch 'im." The South, in other words, would be foolish to reject a helping hand from the victorious North.[54]

By this point in the narrative, the formula is more or less complete. Compelled to remain by his host's gracious southern hospitality, Trunion turns out to be the plantation's salvation. The merger of all that was noble in the Old South with his Yankee ingenuity, modern work ethic, and capital enables the family to hold onto its land during Reconstruction. Naturally, Trunion and Miss Lady fall in love and are married. Though Mrs. Tomlinson never fully accepts her Yankee son-in-law, she revels in her spirited grandson. Moreover, Trunion's knack for farming eventually wins over his neighbors, especially after he demonstrates how to cultivate bermuda grass, the cotton farmer's nemesis, to feed fine, profitable diary herds. The appropriate moral of the story was "that one may be a Yankee and a Southerner too, simply by being a large-hearted, whole-souled American."[55]

Notwithstanding such messages, Harris still felt uncomfortable enough with some elements in the New South formula to voice serious misgivings. Although casting Trunion as a practical and progressive modern man, Harris reminded his readers that even a Yankee could take pride in aristocratic lineage. Moreover, in a story entitled "Trouble on Lost Mountain," the mountain signifies the cultural purity of the premodern white yeomanry, while a railroad is the snake of progress that defiles the garden. In other words, whereas one story in *Free Joe and Other Georgian Sketches* presents the New South movement as the salvation of the plantation, another portrays economic expansion into the hill country as an unqualified evil.[56]

Unlike Sidney Lanier, who envisioned a retreat into domesticity in the aftermath of the Civil War, Harris took a more expansive albeit essentially conservative view of the place of women in the New South. In an 1890 essay entitled "The Women of the South," Harris took issue with three stereotypes that he believed prevailed in the North: "One is that the stage representations of negro character are true to life; another is that the poor white trash of the South are utterly worthless and thriftless; and the other is that the white women of the South lived in a state of idleness during the days of slavery, swinging and languishing in hammocks, while bevies of pickaninnies cooled the tropical air with long-handled fans made of peacock tails."[57]

Harris asserted that the wives and daughters of antebellum planters had been the "busiest women the world has ever seen." In the paragraphs that follow, Harris described the contributions of women to the "intelligent management" of the "commissary and sanitary departments of the plantation." Perhaps reflecting the fact that his own limited experience with plantation life had occurred during the Civil War, Harris argued that the success of the plantation depended on the energy, industry, and apt management of the mistress, which were qualities essential to "the comfort and moral discipline of the establishment." As eulogized by Harris, the plantation lady of Middle Georgia was remarkable indeed:

> These Southern women were the outgrowth of the plantation system, the result of six or seven generations of development. On that system they placed the impress of their humanity and refinement; and the outcome of it is seen in the condition of the negro race to-day. In the sphere of their homes and in their social relations they exercised a power and influence that has no parallel in history. As they were themselves, so they trained their daughters to be, and the Southern women of to-day still possess the characteristics that made their mothers and grandmothers beautiful and gracious; still possess the refinement that built up a rare civilization amid unpromising surroundings; still possess the energy and patience and gentleness that wrought order and discipline on the plantations.[58]

But what of the New South? "As the vine was, so must the fruit be," he wrote. Changing times, however, dictated "that certain of these characteristics should be modified or amplified according as the circumstances of an environment altogether new may demand." Compelled by circumstance after the Civil War "to seek a wider and more profitable field for her talent, her energy and her industry than the home and the fireside afford," the New South woman had demonstrated that she was "amply able to take care of herself." In addition to influencing the direction taken by literature and the arts since the Civil War, women had made their mark in the trades, professions, and business as stenographers, typists, and clerks. The New South woman was "to be found, in short, wherever there is room for her, and her field is always widening."[59]

Harris thought that the New South woman would "exercise a mellowing and restraining influence on the ripping and snorting age just ahead of us—the rattling and groaning age of electricity," but he was less certain what role she would play in the woman's rights movement in the future. Although Harris was less forthright than Sidney Lanier had been two decades earlier, his conservative leanings are evident in the following passage: "Just now she has no aptitude in that direction. She has been taught to believe that the influences that are the result of a happy home-life are more powerful and more important elements of politics than the casting of a ballot; and in this belief she seems to be at one with an overwhelming majority of American women—the mothers and daughters who are the hope and pride of the Republic." The New South woman, "Conservative in all other directions," was "inclined to be somewhat radical in her crusade against rum," but tended "to fret and grieve" when public opinion and the "wheels of legislation" failed to address her temperance work. All told, the New South woman's past devotion, suffering, privation, and self-sacrifice had "consecrated her to the future" and "taught her the blessings of charity in its largest and last interpretation."[60]

After publishing *Daddy Jake the Runaway and Short Stories Told after Dark* in 1889, in which he stated his belief that slave resistance had been justified in the rare absence of paternalism, Harris returned to the New South in *Balaam and His Master, and Other Sketches and Stories,* which appeared in 1891 while the Populist revolt was escalating in Middle Georgia. Several stories in the collection reveal that Harris was still juggling his loyalties to the New South movement and the Old South and searching for bridges to bring both together. In "A Conscript's Christmas," he expressed his sympathy for yeoman resistance to the conscript law during the Civil War, possibly because he saw the legacy of division between the upcountry yeomanry and planters in the cotton belt as contributing to the contemporary political conflict in Georgia. In the title story, Harris predictably argued that blacks had been exceptionally loyal before and after the war. In "Ananias," he also alluded to two stories from the Bible to make the point that blacks were essential to the southern way of life and should not be feared and distrusted.[61]

Harris's efforts to reconcile plantation paternalism and New South modernization is also evident in "The Old Bascom Place," a story that delineates a comprehensive formula for agricultural diversification. Set in Hillsborough in 1876, the story begins when an old farmer notices an elderly gentleman and a beautiful young woman looking toward the old Bascom place, which now belongs to Francis Underwood, an enterprising young northerner. At one time near the pinnacle of plantation society, the Bascom family had fallen on hard times after the war. In dire financial straits, Judge Bascom had accepted a minor position with the carpetbag government in Atlanta during Reconstruction, although his action had resulted in ostracism back home. Some time thereafter, his young wife and brother-in-law had secured power of attorney and sold the Bascom estate. At this point in the story, Judge Bascom becomes haunted by the desire to regain control of the old plantation. After the death of his wife, he returns to Hillsborough with his daughter Mildred, who supplements his tiny pension by operating a primary school and giving music lessons.[62]

Underwood, the stereotypically thrifty and energetic Yankee farmer, is the most complete archetype of a New South farmer that Harris constructed in his fiction:

> He had a dairy farm stocked with the choicest strains of Jersey cattle, and he shipped hundreds of pounds of golden butter all over the country every week in the year; he bred Percheron horses for farm-work and trotting-horses for the road; he had a flourishing farm on which he raised, in addition to his own supplies, a hundred or more bales of cotton every year; he had a steam saw-mill and cotton-gin; he was a contractor and builder; and he was also an active partner in the largest store in Hillsborough. Moreover he took a lively interest in the affairs of the town.

With the exception of his Yankee origins, Underwood is little removed from the town-country elite who rose to prominence in the Georgia countryside in the early twentieth century. What makes this an Old South romance is that the plantation ethos is revitalized by the union of Francis and Mildred in matrimony. Like Trunion in "Aunt Fountain's Prisoner," Underwood is a true gentleman who receives the stamp of approval from a faithful black servant who recognizes him as "quality folk" in spite of his sectional origins. Like Richard Malcolm Johnston's Major Wilby, Judge Bascom finally slips into a world of illusion. At the request of a local doctor, the Underwoods take the Bascoms into their home. Returned to his ancestral estate, Judge Bascom dies a happy man. Though Mildred gives up her name in marriage, "the old name still clings to Underwood's domain." In other words, Harris portrays the New South as simply the Old South reborn.[63]

Yet by 1891 many Georgia farmers were finding it difficult to relate to either the New South or the Old South. The financial problems associated with the commercial expansion of cotton production, such as overproduction, falling crop prices, indebtedness at high interest, a contracted money supply, high costs for essential goods and services, and extortionate railroad fees, led many farmers to seek political relief outside the two-party system, especially after the Democratic Party and the so-called Farmers' Alliance legislature in 1890 failed to deliver promised reforms. As a character in Charles C. Post's 1891 novel *Congressman Swanson* explains, "We have tried 'em both and they have promised and promised, but they never do anything."[64]

In 1885, Post had abandoned his journalistic career in Indiana because of poor health and moved to Douglasville, Georgia. Reflecting his earlier involvement with the Indiana Grange and Greenback Party, Post lent his talents to the cause of farm reform after arriving in Georgia by serving as a lecturer for the Douglas County Farmers' Alliance. Later he joined with Thomas E. Watson to found the *People's Party Paper,* Georgia's leading Populist newspaper. The basic argument Post made in *Congressman Swanson* was that both the Democratic and Republican parties had sold out to large corporations. For this reason, he concluded that genuine relief for workers, farmers, and small businessmen would come only through a third party committed to changes such as monetary and banking reforms, the nationalization of the railroads, and a subtreasury plan to break the stranglehold that speculators had on agricultural markets by creating a national system of crop warehouses and low-interest federal loans for farmers.[65]

Late in his novel Post introduced a character by the name of Deacon William Bascomb, otherwise known as "Uncle Billy Bowlegs." "A former slave who tends a few acres of rented land on shares," Uncle Billy's sole possession is a steer that he had raised from a little calf. Between Christmas and the October cotton harvest, Uncle Billy lives on credit arranged by his landlord with the local merchant, where he purchases his humble fare of corn meal, side meat, and cane molasses. Post observed that Uncle Billy was not the only victim of the crop lien system because his landlord's credit line was secured by a mortgage note on his land. Caught in a vicious cycle, the landlord passes on the annual accumulation of interest on his own purchases to Uncle Billy, who in turn eats up his "crop in advance of gathering it." As Post explained, "If the landlord and Uncle Billy could ever get ahead enough to pay cash for what they live on there would be some chance for them to at least keep even."[66]

Post traced the depressed condition of the southern countryside to wartime requisitions and damage, the collapse of the Confederacy's currency, and the end of slavery. After Lee's surrender, he explained, Confederate soldiers had to start over again with nothing but their land and at best a mule, steer, or horse. Because planters had to rebuild and support their former slaves or see them starve, the "mortgage note-system of credit" had evolved. In addition to the problem of high interest rates, planters had to absorb a heavy markup ranging from fifteen to fifty percent on the goods they purchased and were forced to sell their cotton during the late fall harvest when the market was flooded and prices were low. As a result, speculators reaped the profits that should have gone to planters and laborers.

The downward thrust of the credit system ultimately drove the planter into tenancy on his own land, or in search of "a piece of cheap, wild land somewhere" where he could begin anew. The end result in either case was that the planter "will never live in anything better than a rough board house; will never drive a top buggy, never have a piano or an organ in the house, nor send his children to school more than three months in the year."[67]

Foreshadowing the national platform of the People's Party in 1892, Post advocated a return to the greenback system that had been in operation in the United States at the end of the Civil War to alleviate the problem of farmer indebtedness. Essentially, Post took the position that an expansion of the volume of currency in circulation would generate inflationary pressures on crop prices and make it easier for farmers to liquidate their debts. Post also related how the Farmers' Alliance had formed a cotton bagging manufacturing cooperative to break the monopoly held by the Bagging Trust on jute. He noted that it was strange that "the Alliance received little or no encouragement from the country merchants" in its "fight against one of the most dangerous and oppressive monopolies in the country." As he lamented, "It is indeed most unfortunate for all the people that the systems of exchange of the world have been such as to cause those who assist the wealth producers in exchanging the various commodities which they produce to imagine that their own interests are directly antagonistic to those of the men and women who produce the wealth."[68]

When farmers established cooperative stores to purchase their supplies "at first hands," Post explained that it had created harsh feelings among merchants toward the Alliance. "Possessed of almost unlimited capital, and unscrupulous in the use of means through which to accomplish their ends," the Bagging Trust also fought the Alliance by convincing the Liverpool Exchange, "the leading cotton market of the world," not to purchase cotton unless it was wrapped with jute. Fortunately, Post continued, American cotton buyers refused to go along with the boycott orchestrated by the Trust. Covered in such wrappings as cotton bagging and even coarse cloth "woven out of pine straw," the cotton was re-wrapped in jute when it was pressed into larger bales for international shipment. Such had been "the spirit shown by the planters" gathered in the Alliance by the "tens of thousands" that "the back of the Jute Trust was broken in a single season" and prices returned to a reasonable level.[69]

Undoubtedly hoping to sustain commitment to the Populist cause among rural readers, Post voiced his anger that the fight with the Bagging Trust had turned many of the Alliance's former leaders in the towns and cities against the organization and driven them back into the folds of the Democratic and Republican parties. The hard lesson that their former leaders had exploited the Alliance to obtain office or personal advantage convinced "the wealth-producers of all sections" of the nation that they must create a new party "whose motto should be that of equal rights to all and special privileges to none." In Post's confident words, a People's Party, "pledged to the securing of equal and exact justice to all men, a party of the people, redolent of life and eager for action, stepped into the arena and offered battle to the plutocracy of the world."[70]

As befitting a movement rooted in the Alliance tradition of popular political education, Post undoubtedly hoped that rural voters and urban workers would be inspired by his trenchant analysis of the farm problem and endorse the party platform by marching to the polls to vote the Populist ticket. The note of optimism at the conclusion of *Congressman Swanson* reflected the hopes and aspirations of thousands of rural Georgians who joined the Populist crusade to preserve a republican way of life rooted in farm ownership. Firmly in control of the Democratic Party, the Bourbon coalition of conservative planters and merchants had other ideas. Defeated in its initial bid for national political power in 1892, the Populist Party was reinvigorated by the Depression of 1893. The Democratic Party diffused the grassroots assault on the Solid South by incorporating a free silver plank into its own national platform in 1896. In Georgia, where Thomas E. Watson resisted fusion with the Democracy, the Bourbon coalition crushed the farmer revolt through direct intimidation of the black vote in the cotton belt, election fraud in Populist strongholds, and exploitation of white racial fears.

Although Joel Chandler Harris addressed issues such as free silver in his editorials in the Atlanta *Constitution,* one finds few direct allusions to the farmer revolt in his book-length anthologies. Harris sympathized with the plight of white yeoman farmers, but he was committed to the restoration of social stability in the countryside and hopeful that a middle ground could be found within the Democratic Party between Populist biracial political cooperation and the racial apocalypse predicted by a growing number of white extremists. Thus it is almost certain that the Old South's shotgun wedding to the New South received his blessing. Moreover, the overall tone of *On the Plantation: A Story of a Georgia Boy's Adventures during the War,* an autobiographical novel that he published in 1892, suggests strongly that he was still searching for social consensus in a time of turmoil. As he had in many of his earlier stories, Harris incorporated sympathetic portrayals of Confederate deserters, runaway slaves, and the Yankee invaders into the narrative. Significantly, the novel ends with the narrator's explanation that Mink the runaway had become a tenant on the plantation after the war, had eventually bought a little farm of his own, and had prospered, the clear ideological message being that a black farmer's dream of land ownership was best realized through cooperation with the established social order.[71]

That same year Harris published another volume in the Uncle Remus series entitled *Uncle Remus and His Friends: Old Plantation Stories, Songs and Ballads with Sketches of Negro Character.* In "Death and the Negro Man," the plantation Remus narrates the story of a disagreeable black man who did not want to work. When his master and overseer hear him express his hope that "Gran'sir Death" would come and take them away, they decide "dat dey gwine ter play a prank on dat nigger man." One night after midnight his master dresses in a white quilt and pillowcase with two eye holes cut in it and comes to the man's cabin. The sight of death at his door frightens the man into the woods for "mighty nigh a week," but also transforms him into such an outstanding worker that his master refuses to "take lev'm hunder'd dollars for 'im,—cash money, paid down in his han'!" Sensitive to the negative impact of memories of the Ku Klux Klan on northern public opinion, Harris sanitized white terrorism by treating it as a harmless form of labor control, implying that fear was a necessary and effective motivation to work because blacks were superstitious and did not understand the nature of free labor. As Remus explains to the little boy in another tale, "Creeturs is creeturs. You er what you is, en you can't be no is-er; I'm what I am en I can't be no am-er. It all done been fix, en I ain't see nobody yit what kin onfix it."[72]

As he had done in *Uncle Remus: His Songs and His Sayings,* Harris continued to voice his support for plantation paternalism through his increasingly famous literary creation. As before, when Remus speaks out in the frame of a story against social equality, it is really Harris talking. What conservative defenders of the status quo feared most in 1892 was that black voters would answer the Populist Party's call for interracial political cooperation. Not surprisingly, the urban Remus delivers the message in "Intimidation of a Colored Voter" that blacks should stay away from the polls rather than divide the white vote.[73]

Consistent with his defense of plantation paternalism, Harris cast African Americans in the urban Remus stories as childlike primitives who were lost in the city. Because they were presumably confused by modern technological innovations such as telephones, phonographs, and streetcars, and often abused by white courts and juries when they became "too uppity" for their own good, Harris believed that blacks would be better off on the old plantation. Known as a "white-folks' nigger" in the kitchen, the urban Remus has no use for "new issue" blacks without roots in plantation slavery. Neither is he sympathetic to the "African Exodus" movement that some white observers advanced as a solution to the New South's race problem. As he explains to Miss Sally's cook, "What I gwine to do in Affiky? I ain't no Affikin nigger." In yet another story entitled "William Henry at School," Remus proclaims that his grandson's most serious flaw was that he was not in touch with the land: "He got town nigger blood in 'im, dat boy is, en he ain't never gwine res' satisfied twel he git in de chain-gang." Harris framed the issue of the labor shortage in terms of free will by advocating that urban blacks voluntarily return to the countryside, perhaps missing the irony that landlords frequently exploited convict labor to accomplish much the same purpose, especially during times of peak labor demand.[74]

Unlike Harris, whose racial outlook was shaped by plantation slavery, Maurice Thompson was raised on a small farm in the Cherokee hills of North Georgia. In the early 1850s his family moved from Indiana to a small farm in the Coosawattee River valley near Calhoun. Thompson's biographer considers it unlikely that his family owned slaves. After wartime service with the Sixty-Third Regiment of Georgia Volunteers, Thompson returned to Indiana and pursued careers in law and the railroad business. During the 1870s, he began writing local color stories, although many remained unpublished until the 1890s.[75]

What distinguishes Thompson's North Georgia fiction is his frank exploration of the racial fear and hostility that characterized the 1890s. Originally published in the *Independent* in January 1892, his poem "A Voodoo Prophecy" acknowledged the past wrongs of slavery and its legacy of suffering, yet voiced a deep revulsion toward African Americans. His mind possessed by the "black and terrible memory" of the evils of slavery, "the prophet of the dusky race" predicts dark days ahead. Rejecting white assertions that slavery had lifted Africans to "a higher life," the prophet expresses his longing for his primitive past:

> Was I a heathen? Ay, I was—am still
> A fetich worshipper; but I was free
> To loiter or to wander at my will,
> To leap and dance,
> To hurl my lance,
> And breathe the air of savage liberty.

Miscegenation would be the African race's final revenge against its hated white oppressor:

> You, seed of Abel, proud of your descent,
> And arrogant, because your cheeks are fair,
> Within my loins an inky curse is pent
> To flood
> Your blood
> And stain your skin and crisp your golden hair.

Thompson warned in the poem's last stanza that only the preservation of white supremacy would stop the savage hordes of the "Prince of Darkness" from destroying civilization and ruling the world.[76]

Thompson's best remembered work is *Stories of the Cherokee Hills,* which appeared in 1898. Written mostly in the 1870s but revised for magazine publication in the late 1880s and early 1890s, Thompson's "color-line" stories examine the impact of slavery on mountain whites. Although most owned no slaves, Thompson explained that the plantations in the fertile valleys below often affected their lives. In "A Race Romance," an old bachelor named Brimson struggles to resolve the conflict between his treasured egalitarian ideals and his determination to protect his investment in a slave named Rory whom he had purchased at a sheriff's sale to prevent his acquisition by a New Orleans slavetrader. Brimson hates slavery and believes in racial equality, but he "cayn't stan' the expense" of freeing the man. When he treats Rory as an equal, his neighbors ostracize him. Fiercely independent, the old mountaineer learns how to read and write so he can prepare Rory for freedom. But Brimson's efforts prove inadequate to Rory's "barbaric nature," which "seemed to deepen and broaden apace with his educational acquirements." Encouraged by Brimson to assert his rights after emancipation, Rory loses "his childlike simplicity" and lapses into savagery. Isolated in a mountain pocket, a likely metaphor for the South, the old mountaineer grows weaker every year. Rory's devolution into barbarism eventually results in his dominance over his former master.[77]

The final story in *Stories of the Cherokee Hills* can be read as an allegory of the Populist movement in North Georgia. "The Balance of Power" revolves around a political struggle between an ambitious young lawyer of honest mountaineer heritage named Tom Banister and a planter-politician named Colonel Mobley Sommerton. Standing between the two are Phyllis Somerton, who is in love with her father's upstart political rival, and Barnaby the freedman, who sometimes works as a household servant for the Sommertons. Barnaby is also widely regarded as a political boss among the few blacks who live in the town of Elijay. In a one-party town a "pretended rather than a real prejudice" is the key to electoral success. Candidates play the race card to convince white voters that their opponents are popular among blacks. A veteran of the legislature and a master of political trickery, Sommerton bribes Barnaby, who also accepts money from Phyllis and Tom. The morning of the convention, Sommerton is stunned when Tom delivers the speech he had prepared for the occasion and wins the election by one vote. Tom confesses, however, that the Colonel's promise to deed his plantation to Phyllis if he lost had motivated his lapse into larceny. Withdrawing his name from nomination, he moves that Sommerton be nominated by universal proclamation, reconciliation follows, and everyone lives happily ever after. The wedding of the cracker upstart to the planter's daughter brings political harmony. White solidarity restores the real balance of power, although the potential for future divisiveness remains because Barnaby still has the black vote in his pocket along with two coins.[78]

As illustrated by Harris in *Uncle Remus and His Friends,* the farmer revolt revived interest in Georgia in African colonization societies. Unlike Harris, Louis Beauregard Pendleton advocated African colonization as the solution to the South's race problem. Born in Ware County in 1861, Pendleton is remembered primarily as the author of adventure stories for boys, including one dedicated "To That Bright Star of the New South—Henry Woodfin Grady." One of the major dilemmas faced by the proponents of New South industrial development was finding a way to reconcile their need for low-cost wage labor with the landed elite's determination to preserve a large pool of dependent farm labor. Although a Jim Crow compromise eventually settled the issue, the battle between the Populists and conservative Democrats for the black vote led many white observers to conclude that a racial apocalypse was looming in the near future unless radical action was taken as soon as possible. It was within this social context that Pendleton published *The Sons of Ham: A Tale of the New South* in 1895.[79]

Set in the 1880s in the little interior town of Barcelona, which Pendleton apparently modeled on Waycross, the novel begins when a young lawyer named Robert Morton comes to the defense of a Yankee damsel in distress who had come south for her health and to relieve strain on her large family's finances. A minor but important character in the story by the name of Francie Black is Pendleton's mouthpiece for denouncing northern misconceptions about the New South. Although "expecting to find the most intense heat, a landscape composed almost entirely of immense steaming cotton-fields, [and] a people who, for the most part, lay around in a state of semi-coma," Black instead finds Georgians to be hard-working farmers, carpenters, merchants, and clerks. As her friend Colonel Sanford explains, such misconceptions simply indicated that "greed of gain" was universal and that a hot climate was not an obstacle to progress. Moreover, having read about "the down-trodden negro" and expecting to see daily evidence of white oppression, Black is quite surprised to discover that blacks live in "perfect freedom" from molestation in Barcelona, "although she was quickly made aware that a most intense race antipathy really existed."[80]

A "mushroom" community transformed during the Civil War by the arrival of coastal refugees who looked down upon the "homespun provincials," Barcelona is still characterized by rigid social divisions twenty-five years later. Many native crackers have prospered by adapting to new conditions and the old guard is "losing ground in corresponding ratio." Friendships exist between the two classes, but intermarriage seldom occurs. What keeps the white community united is the presence of a common danger, "real or fancied." Nearly equal in size to the white community, the black community is perceived as a "growing menace," although individuals are seldom treated as enemies.[81]

Shifting the scene to a tournament and ball, Pendleton stages a discussion of the race problem between Colonel Sanford and a young Yankee named Mr. Shepherd. The grizzled old veteran argues that the black man had always been a curse upon the South's prosperity. Not only had "thrifty foreign immigrants" avoided the South on his account, the region's inability to assimilate its black population meant that "we can only look forward to an indefinite extension of the inevitable struggle between two opposing factors, two hostile races, in one country." Had the South's slaves been white serfs, he explains, fusion would have followed emancipation.

After staining a continent with the blood of the red man and revealing their determination to "shut the Golden Gate against the yellow man," northerners should be able to see that blacks are "hopelessly inferior" and were "never intended to inhabit a common country with the whites" except as slaves. Colonel Sanford concludes by telling Shepherd that the North simply did not realize that racial solidarity must come before partisan politics and that colonization was the South's only salvation, even if it resulted in temporary agricultural dislocation.[82]

Only one black character in the novel is portrayed sympathetically. Not surprisingly, she is an old mammy archetype who is dedicated to an Old South family in tragic decline. Still, *The Sons of Ham* affords a rare literary glimpse into life in a small Georgia town's black district in the late nineteenth century, although Pendleton burlesqued the scene for racist comic effect. The day after the tournament ball, a group of visitors from Philadelphia decides to explore Barcelona's black neighborhoods. Walking along the narrow back street of the business district they pass a few restaurants, a cobbler's shop, and a fish market. Drawn to a saloon, they see "a large wire cage containing four dogs, two raccoons, a goat, a monkey, and a grinning, full-grown young negro." At the sight of such a peculiar advertisement, one of them exclaims that "Darwin would have gone half-way round the world to see this . . . a case of natural selection ready to his hand."[83]

Next the scene shifts to the "Neck," a teeming residential suburb that includes two churches, a public hall, a few schoolhouses, many comfortable little dwellings, and a large number of "cheerless hovels." In the front yard of one stands Josephine Witherspoon, "a fat blooming matron of thirty summers." Josephine is "a celebrated laundress" who supports her children and her younger husband Cicero, "a conscienceless vagabond" who works just enough to evade the vagrant law when not stealing from whites. A woman of "easy conscience" herself, Josephine enjoys the chickens, melons, and potatoes that Cicero pilfers, but she will not brook his infidelity.[84]

Rather than working in the shade of the China-tree in the rear of her house, Josephine prefers the heat of the hot October sun in the front yard, where she can gossip with passersby while tending to the steaming garments in her wash-pot. Among those who pass her yard that afternoon is Mrs. Simpson, a white woman who lives with her husband and children on a small farm just outside of town. Natives of New Jersey who had come south after the Civil War because of the milder climate, the Simpsons have fallen on hard times. A bricklayer by trade idled by poor health, Mr. Simpson is a man of some intelligence who resents being too poor to send his children to school while local blacks attend free. For the benefit of northern readers, Pendleton explained that the school fund came from a tax on white property distributed per capita, irrespective of race. Since the fund was inadequate, "no educated white man could be found to open a school without further remuneration," whereas the black community was willing to accept lower standards. The net effect according to Pendleton was that the law discriminated against poor whites who could not afford the tuition to attend white schools. By drawing such a contrast between deprived whites and presumably shiftless blacks, Pendleton implied that removal of the black population would open the door of opportunity to northern migrants and bring genuine educational progress to the South.[85]

When Josephine catches Cicero with a jezebel named Rosetta Hightower, she attacks them both with her battling-stick. Seeking revenge, Rosetta visits Mammy Nanny, the local "trick-doctor," to buy a love potion for Cicero and a hex on his wife. A woman of considerable local repute because of the efficacy of her magic, the old conjure woman demands two dollars and a chicken for her services. The literate if superstitious daughter of a prosperous carpenter, Rosetta had never before found it necessary "to go into service." Yet when neither her father nor friends will lend her the money, she begins canvassing Barcelona's white neighborhoods in search of a family to exploit, which provides Pendleton an opportunity to lament the South's servant problem.[86]

Securing a position as a nurse, Rosetta works diligently just long enough to get an advance against her month's wages, steals a chicken, and heads for Mammy Nanny's. She has no problem administering the love potion to Cicero, but she oversleeps and is seen putting the spell-box on Josephine's doorstep at dawn. Outraged, Josephine takes Rosetta "up fo' de Mare" for "bad-mouthing" her. The scene at the full mayor's court the next morning stages Pendleton's argument that the black vote had corrupted southern politics.[87]

According to Pendleton, one of the consequences of the social upheaval caused by the war was that the bottom rail had truly been placed on top. Ignorant and incompetent, Mayor Adam Brown is a man of humble origin who had married above himself and risen to power through the support of poor voters. After threatening both women with the chain-gang if they disturb the peace again, Brown dismisses the case. Watching the mayor in action, Colonel Sanford explains to Robert Morton that Brown exemplifies "the evils resulting from the disorderly association of two races in one State." Without the bought black vote, Pendleton believed that such men would never have risen to power. Although most rejected his colonization crusade, landed elites rapidly perfected more convenient ways to "reform" Georgia politics in the aftermath of Populism.[88]

Pendleton realized that one of the biggest obstacles to African colonization was planter resistance to the loss of black labor. Appropriately, Morton overhears Sanford and a prominent planter in animated conversation in the center of a small crowd. In response to the Colonel's call for wholesale removal of the black population, the planter asks, "Who is goin' to plough my fields, and pick my cotton, and do the cuttin' and dippin' on my turpentine farm?" After admitting that the transition to white foreign labor would be difficult, the Colonel argues that the inconvenience would be a small price to pay for a better world for their children and grandchildren. Willing to leave the matter to Providence, the planter replies, "Let our children control 'em as we control 'em. This is a white man's country and always will be." Given the black race's higher rate of reproduction and improvements in education and organization, the Colonel replies, the fight to preserve the status quo would eventually evolve into "a desperate struggle for existence" that one race would lose. He also observes that amalgamation was the only way for "two distinct races to exist on terms of equality and friendship under one government," a solution to the race problem that "not a man or woman of either race in the whole country" would accept for a moment. What "the people of the outside world" failed to realize was that blacks had been waging "silent but ceaseless and inexorable warfare" against the dominant race ever since emancipation. Refusal to take action amounted to cutting "our children's throats rather than suffer from a temporary disorganization of labor." When Colonel Sanford attends a debating society meeting about colonization in the public hall in the Neck, a wealthy planter labels him a dangerous labor agitator. Indeed, most Georgia planters considered African colonization ludicrous. Black labor had been the foundation of the plantation economy for over a century; conservative landowners saw little reason to abandon the status quo in the 1890s.[89]

In the end, Pendleton resorted to sensationalism to drive home his argument by concluding *The Sons of Ham* with a race war. While such scenes became common in Georgia literature in the twentieth century, Pendleton was the first Georgia author to incorporate a full-blown riot into a novel. After the Colonel's son is robbed and murdered, a white mob lynches an innocent black tenant farmer. Two months later, racial violence explodes when the town marshal is killed while trying to arrest a "colored outlaw" who is subsequently cornered with his followers in a nearby swamp. When the rumor spreads that armed blacks are preparing to come to the outlaw's rescue, the governor dispatches the Georgia Hussars and infantry companies from the surrounding counties prepare to march. Meanwhile, white vigilantes invade Barcelona's black section and attack local blacks of questionable character. Order is eventually restored, but the tragedy leaves Colonel Sanford extremely discouraged about the future prospects of his cause. Lacking sympathy from the North, resisted from within by powerful planters, and condemned to live among ignorant, poverty-stricken, and easily corrupted blacks amid the "fires of race hate," he bemoans the perilous times ahead for the South.[90]

Although Pendleton's scheme for African colonization went largely ignored, it does reveal the potential challenge to planter interests inherent in the New South modernization program. Moreover, the level of racial violence in Georgia remained high for decades. If nothing else, the fixation upon the South's race problem among Georgia authors in the late nineteenth century reveals the depth of white southern resistance to the dictates of free labor capitalism. After the Democratic Party delivered a fatal blow to the Populists in Georgia in 1896, the black vote became in C. Vann Woodward's apt phrase a "sectional scapegoat" in the drive to reconcile estranged whites to the restoration of the status quo. Determined to diffuse permanently the potential for grassroots resistance, the planter-merchant coalition instituted an apartheid system that resulted in the near total disfranchisement of black voters through the white primary, poll tax, and property and literacy qualifications, so-called reforms that drove large numbers of poor whites from the polls as well. White supremacy, race-baiting, and the myth of Reconstruction and the Lost Cause were then offered as a "magical formula" to justify the preservation of the plantation economy, although it proved a costly victory for white paternalists. The fusion of the plantation regime with the New South movement also lent greater legitimacy to racist extremists and eroded further the remaining vestiges of antebellum paternalism, a transition in social relations that received national legal sanction in 1896 when the Supreme Court handed down its verdict in *Plessy v. Ferguson.* Separate but equal not only reflected a new racist consensus in the United States, it signaled the doom of paternalism. In the absence of intimacy, reciprocity in productive relations became an anachronism, a slow decline captured in the South's literary record in seemingly endless accounts of barbaric violence and alienation that foreshadowed the final collapse of the plantation system decades later.[91]

Literary defenders of plantation paternalism remained, but their arguments began to sound increasingly hollow. Even the most nostalgic authors like Eugenia Jones Bacon were affected by the hardening racial climate at the turn of the century. Raised on a plantation in Liberty County, Bacon published *Lyddy: A Tale of the Old South* in 1898 to erase misconceptions about slavery that she identified with the lasting popularity of Harriet Beecher Stowe's *Uncle Tom's Cabin.* The only flaw that clouds the virtue of her saintly black heroine is her imperfect sexual morality, which Bacon implied was characteristic of her race. After tracing the decline of plantation paternalism since the Civil War, Bacon stated that miscegenation rather than slavery had been the Old South's original sin. Moreover, the problem was spreading throughout the nation. In Bacon's words, "The admixture of colour was a dreadful curse on southern estates. Now, one has but to note the coppery-tinged children in large northern cities, to realize that this evil has not abated." Ironically, in spite of her spirited defense of paternalism, Bacon concluded that segregation was necessary to prevent further race-mixing.[92]

As he had done throughout his long career, Joel Chandler Harris continued to bridge the Old and New Souths, albeit with more and more reluctance. There are ample clues in the literary output of his declining years to suggest that Harris believed that plantation slavery had offered a better quality of life than was available in the New South at the turn of the century. Significantly, he persisted in dismissing Reconstruction as an ignoble crusade and in whitewashing the Ku Klux Klan, maintaining all along that the freedmen had been misled by a misguided minority of fanatics among the federal occupation forces. Although few had remained as loyal as his literary archetypes Uncle Remus and Aunt Minervy Ann, Harris thought it wrong to keep punishing "grown children" who had been momentarily led astray decades before. In the words of a white household manager in his novel *Gabriel Tolliver: A Story of Reconstruction,* "Everything they know, everything they do, everything they say—everything—they have larnt from the white folks. Study a nigger right close, an' you'll ketch a glimpse of how white folks would look an' do wi'out the'r trimmin's." What troubled Harris most was his fear that without the old planter aristocracy to protect blacks and teach common whites the distinction between the good life and the vulgar pursuit of money, the Old South's values and traditions would gradually fade. As another character bemoans late in the novel:

> You will have plenty of company in the money-grabbing business before long. I can see signs of it now, and every time I think of it I feel sorry for our young men, yes, and our young women, and the long generations that are to come after them. . . . You remember how, before the war, we used to sneer at the Yankees for their money-making proclivities? Well, it won't be very long before we'll beat them at their own game; and then our politicians will thrive, for each and all of them will have their principles dictated by Shylock and his partners.[93]

Though an advocate of agricultural diversification since the 1880s, Harris had never really contested the centrality of cotton in the New South's economy. He apparently accepted the New South crusade for mill development in rural areas as a way to lessen the South's colonial dependence on northern factories, albeit with some hesitation. In his 1896 novel *Sister Jane: Her Friends and Acquaintances,* for example, he included a less than flattering description of a cotton factory and its ragged white work force that revealed his growing disillusionment with the New South. Long an admirer of the yeoman independence of upcountry whites, it is unclear whether Harris considered mill village paternalism a step forward or backward, even if New South boosters advertised it as a major social reform. In either case, Harris obviously thought mill work more suitable for whites. As Aunt Minervy Ann makes clear in a later story, working the land under white supervision was the proper labor for blacks.[94]

In a series of articles in *The Saturday Evening Post* in early 1904, Harris stated that he was not as pessimistic as his fellow southerners who lamented the demise of the "old-time darky" because the younger generation at the close of the Civil War "had not only come in direct contact with the discipline of the plantation, but had fallen under the immediate influence of their forbears." He argued further that "the negro has been steadily growing better" and "he is beginning to realize that the best interests of all the members of the community in which he lives are also his best interests." Nor did Harris fear amalgamation, race war, and educational improvements for African Americans. Deeming it patently unfair to compare black educational progress with that of whites, Harris argued that the Negro was "only about three centuries from a state of barbaric slavery in Africa compared with which his term of servitude in the United States was Christian freedom." Harris declared that he remained hopeful in spite of individual cases of brutality, cruelty, and bestiality within the black population, stating that "the overwhelming majority of the negroes in all parts of the South, especially in the agricultural regions, are leading sober and industrious lives." That such a statement would have been regarded by many as liberal at the time is a sobering reminder of just how oppressive the racial climate had become in the early twentieth century.[95]

The following year Harris reported in *Told By Uncle Remus* that Uncle Remus had retired as a storyteller after the little boy grew up and moved to Atlanta. Eventually, the old man's white family had rejoined him on the old plantation in Putnam County. Troubled by the sickly appearance and ways of her city-raised grandson, Miss Sally enlists the aid of her old friend, who takes the boy on his knee. Bookish, frail, and more quiet than his father had been, the boy is "a source of perpetual wonder to Uncle Remus," an effeminate child whose overly protective mother rejects Miss Sally's traditional matriarchal role in the familial hierarchy. As Miss Sally laments, "A grandmother doesn't count for much these days unless there is illness."[96]

Harris idealized the plantation household as a complete organic entity, a universe wherein the lives of whites and blacks were interwoven in nearly perfect harmony. For Harris, urban life was draining the vitality of whites and blacks alike. White men who had come to maturity on the old plantation consequently found themselves out of touch with their sons, while blacks wandered the streets tragically adrift. In the twilight of his literary career, Harris came to see the city as the harbinger of a crisis of generations that was threatening to destroy the South's identity by dissolving the fabric of social relations that had once characterized rural life. When the city finally emerged triumphant over the countryside, the bottom rail would indeed be on top. A world where faithful servants and grandmothers were no longer needed and mothers kept their sons out of the healthy sunshine for fear of freckles was alien to Joel Chandler Harris.

A somewhat quixotic Remus rises to the challenge and sallies forth to rescue Miss Sally's grandson from the demons of modernity. Yet even after he coaxes the lad onto his knee, Uncle Remus finds it difficult to reach the child within. The first step in bringing the little boy back into harmony with nature is to get him in touch with Brer Rabbit, or to teach him that some defiance and laughing until he sprains his "goozle-um" or throws his "th'oat-latch outer j'int" is healthy. In the opening frame of "Why Mr. Cricket Has Elbows on His Legs," the little boy's mother punishes him for wiping his mouth on his sleeve by shutting him in the parlor, which makes Miss Sally feel like a mother-in-law rather than a grandmother because she had given him the forbidden molasses candy in the first place. Made aware of her transgression by Remus, the boy's tearful mother allows him to go with the old man to fetch a load of corn. Along the way, Remus tells the boy the story of Grandaddy Cricket, a tale of the old plantation days when everything was bigger and better. On the return ride, the noisy wagon scares up a rabbit, which reminds Remus of a tale from the time when his great-grandaddy's great-grandaddy had lived, a form of redemptive nostalgia that helps the boy get in touch with his past. When Remus compares the present unfavorably with bygone days, it is not simply wistful longing. His stories enable the boy to tap into the fertile springs of his imagination, a fountain of youth that cleanses his soul of the pernicious effects of growing up in "'Lantamafantarum." When one recalls that the Remus stories were not really for children, it becomes evident that the boy is a metaphor for the South.[97]

At long last, Harris had resolved the outstanding dilemma of his literary career. In the final analysis, there was no substitute for plantation paternalism. Too long on the dangerous road of progress, he concluded that the New South needed to find its way back to the briar patch before it was too late. His rejection of the New South reflected the triumph of the Lost Cause ideology at the fin de siècle. To paraphrase his fellow Georgian Mildred L. Rutherford of the United Daughters of the Confederacy, the New South was simply the Old South remade. A sturdy hybrid transformed by the ravages of time into a colonial nabob, King Cotton nonetheless continued to reign in the Empire State of the South as it entered a new century.[98]

EPILOGUE

A "November Cotton Flower"

The Lost Cause Revival of the Plantation Regime

Speaking before a meeting of the United Daughters of the Confederacy (UDC) in November 1912, the Lost Cause patriot and educator Mildred Lewis Rutherford pronounced sentence on the New South: "Henry Grady was a very young man when he went to Boston and spoke of 'the new South.' He did not know how the people of the Old South would feel about that. There is no new South. The South of today is the South of yesterday remade to fit the new order of things." In an address entitled "The South in the Building of the Nation," Rutherford urged her UDC sisters to write the true history of the South. Though she advocated further reconciliation with the North, the education of the next generation of white southerners was too important to entrust to Yankee publishers.[1]

As historian-general of the UDC, Rutherford set out systematically to purge the historical record of every piece of falsehood and slander about the South that had accumulated over the years, especially in textbooks. The word slavery, for example, had only crept into the southern vocabulary with the abolition crusade "during the old plantation days." According to Rutherford, however, "They were our people, our negroes, part of our very homes." Nor did participating in the violence of the Ku Klux Klan during Reconstruction stain the honor of the heroic Confederate soldier, who had been compelled by necessity "to establish the political supremacy of the white man in the South." Neither did Rutherford see any contradiction in pledging loyalty to two flags, describing the Confederate flag as emblematic of southern patriotism: "Four years it waved its precious folds above a righteous cause, and when we furled it, it was because we were overpowered and not because we were conquered. Silently and reverently we laid that flag away, that our children and children's children coming after us might revere it; it will teach them the principles for which our fathers fought—states' rights and constitutional liberty."[2]

Born of defeat in war and anger over the perceived excesses of Reconstruction, the Lost Cause ideology offered a middle ground where country and urban elites could find common cause after the demise of Populism in Georgia. An ideological rationalization for life on the periphery of American capitalism as well as an expression of heartfelt commitment to the cultural heritage of the antebellum South, the Lost Cause was a tacit admission in spite of its militant Confederate rhetoric that the North's dominance was in fact complete. As Numan V. Bartley has observed, "If Populism could not turn back the tide of Yankee values and capitalist market relationships, then mythology, religion, and white supremacy would have to serve." It remained problematic, however, how long the plantation regime could isolate itself from the transforming influence of the larger market society.[3]

Historians who profess continuity within capitalism in the nineteenth-century South often fail to take the Lost Cause ideology seriously, sometimes dismissing it rather quickly as "itself a lost cause." In such interpretations, the rhetoric of the New South represents an effort by pragmatic conservatives to create a white work force so that the region could restore its prosperity within the free market system. While true to an extent, such interpretations invert a vital relationship by downplaying the centrality of the Lost Cause ideology to the preservation of the hegemony of plantation society. Reinforced by the bailing wire of capitalistic credit mechanisms, legal chicanery, force, and racism, plantation agriculture derailed the arrival of a modern diversified economy in Georgia until well into the twentieth century.[4]

The Lost Cause ideology became a vital component in the preservation of a plantation zone within a modern capitalist state, although compromises had to be made with increasingly affluent New South merchants who supported the plantation ethos but were the advance agents of market society values in a quasi-colonial system. The dilemma facing Georgia's landlord class was how to encourage economic development without losing its control of plantation labor and the political process. Tragically, the Lost Cause was anything but a romantic fantasy, for it was the planter-merchant coalition's feeble offering to the white yeomanry for its heroic sacrifices in the Civil War and subsequent loss of a life of sturdy independence on the land. Silenced politically by the demise of Populism, the white yeomanry continued to slide into a state of dependency that paralleled the condition of black sharecroppers, a nether world between freedom and slavery.

By glorifying the plantation ideal and white supremacy, the Lost Cause creed helped to rally the white masses to their new captains in much the same way that their fathers had rallied to the flag during the so-called War Between the States. When the old leaders expired, new captains appeared to keep the cause alive. The Lost Cause remained a living cause as long as the planter-merchant elite stood tall in the saddle. But in truth the plantation regime was more fragile than Lost Cause ideologues liked to admit. By the beginning of the twentieth century, King Cotton had become a "November Cotton Flower" who had risen from the ashes of defeat to reclaim his throne, but his days in the sun were numbered.[5]

As Rollin G. Osterweis has observed, the Lost Cause was firmly rooted in literary expression in the postbellum South. Chivalric planters, southern belles, Confederate knights, and "obliging old Uncle Remus" all served to enlist the ideals of the Old South in the service of postbellum social and political realities. Thus it is simply wrong to dismiss postbellum plantation literature as nostalgia. Georgia's literary revival in the 1880s cannot be divorced from the broader social context. The pastoral writings of postbellum Georgia authors like Richard Malcolm Johnston, Charles Henry Smith, and Joel Chandler Harris were well within the romantic tradition of criticizing contemporary social conditions by contrasting them with an idealized past. Trusting in the power of literary expression to ameliorate unwanted social change, Georgia authors looked to the past to help reshape a world amid profound transformation. Most enlisted their pens in the defense of plantation society. Their memories of the Civil War and Reconstruction still fresh, it is not surprising that they longed for the relative harmony of their antebellum childhoods and turned away from the unrest that troubled the Georgia countryside in the late nineteenth century.[6]

The anti-urban thrust in the writings of Smith and Harris also reflected the subordination of the New South creed into the Lost Cause ideology. Conservative Democrats appealed to the Lost Cause in the 1890s to counter the Populist Party's strength in rural Georgia by offering patriotism and paternalism as an alternative to interracial political cooperation. Two memoirs of antebellum plantation life and the war published in 1892 were unrepentant about glorifying the old regime, a form of militant literary remembrance that coincided with the Populist Party's foray into national politics that year. In *Plantation Life before Emancipation,* the Reverend R. Q. Mallard stated vigorously his belief that "no laboring population in the world had been better off than the southern slaves." The son-in-law of the late Reverend Charles C. Jones of Liberty County, Mallard considered life in the city a poor substitute for the invigorating childhood he had known on the plantation, where Christian paternalism had created "affectionate relations" between the races lost after emancipation. Mallard also proclaimed that Uncle Remus had a real counterpart in old Liberty County.[7]

Whereas Mallard claimed to have "no harsh or angry feelings" against either the North or blacks, Mary A. H. Gay blamed the war on fifty years of "insults and taunts" by Yankee politicians and abolitionists. Motivated by her reverence for the Lost Cause and determination to speak the truth as she saw it, Gay's memoir was part of a wider effort to redeem the Old South and preserve a distinctive southern identity. Divorced from the contemporary social context, *Life in Dixie during the War* comes across as little more than angry nostalgia. Yet when cast in the light of the political struggle that was raging in the Georgia countryside in 1892, it becomes clear that Gay's memoir lent ideological support to the status quo and thus contributed to the ideological triumph of the plantation regime after the demise of the Populists.[8]

By the turn of the century, the Lost Cause had evolved into the mature ideological voice of a plantation regime that had survived a century of conflict intact if substantially hybridized by the experience. Many Georgia authors in the coming decades correctly portrayed the city as the major threat remaining to the security of the status quo in the countryside, a situation that reflected the South's commercial relationship with the industrial North. The collapse of Populism had signaled the restoration of Bourbon dominance in Georgia. Moreover, the national triumph of corporate capitalism and the Republican Party had consolidated the South's position in the American economy as a plantation zone for much of the next century.

It is significant that contemporary literary sources suggest that life in rural Georgia in the early twentieth century was neither isolated nor static. Long before the revolution unleashed by agricultural mechanization and scientific farming in the mid-twentieth century, new consumer goods such as the automobile and the telephone had begun to transform the countryside. The abandonment by landlords of their old plantation homes for the comforts and conveniences of town life further eroded the vestiges of paternalism that remained imbedded in the culture of rural productive relations. Most Georgia authors in the first decades of the new century would continue to draw their primary inspiration from life on the land, but the growing conflict between town and country set the stage for the creation of a new literary landscape, albeit one that was also rooted deeply in the past.[9]

Compared to the depressed circumstances of the late nineteenth century, the first two decades of the new century were a time of relative prosperity in rural Georgia. Although his mantle had been made sooty by the smokestacks that symbolized the imperial ascendancy of Big Business in American life, King Cotton continued to reign in Georgia. One of the primary functions of the Lost Cause ideology was to teach the formerly independent white yeomen to bend the knee to their new master, even when he pushed them into tenancy or off the land altogether. Yet at the same time that the landed elite was consolidating its power in the countryside and small towns, urbanization was continuing to erode the economic foundations of the plantation economy, albeit ever so slowly. The rise in town-country conflict took many forms, the most spectacular and tragic being the Atlanta riot in 1906, an event from his childhood recreated later by Walter F. White in his novel *Flight*. Urban growth was luring away rural workers at the precise moment that landlords needed surplus labor to take full advantage of the expanding market for cotton, while making it more difficult to control those who remained on the land.[10]

To be sure, Georgia's cities and towns continued to function primarily as entrepôts that orchestrated the outward flow of staple crops and natural resources and the inward flow of foodstuffs and manufactured goods. As islands of modernity within a transitional society wedded to tradition, cities nonetheless accelerated the cultural transformation of the countryside, a process often bemoaned by twentieth-century Georgia authors. Lured by its hypnotic lights and exotic attractions, rubes and bumpkins were drawn to the city, milked of their life's blood, and left desolate, a literary theme with deep antebellum roots made even more poignant by the loss of meaning that twentieth-century authors often associated with urban existence. Violence, alienation, sexual licentiousness, and godlessness awaited those cast from the garden.

A basic consensus once existed among historians of the American South that the period between 1870 and 1930 was characterized by the dominance of longstanding cultural traditions. The literary sources of the period, however, portray it as a time of unsettling change. People clung tenaciously to the old ways precisely because they knew that the world of their fathers was fading fast. The context of their lives was changing even if their basic routines remained the same. In other words, rural Georgia was still a backwater, but it was no longer isolated from a brave new world that simultaneously inspired wonder and fear.[11]

Weakened by the unwelcome arrival of the voracious boll weevil, the plantation regime staggered through the 1920s and collapsed on tobacco road in the Great Depression. Critical rather than laudatory about southern social relations, many among the rising generation of Georgia authors began to advocate liberal change. As had the Civil War eighty years before, World War II marked a great turning point in the life of the plantation regime. A Second Reconstruction followed in which federally financed mechanization depopulated the countryside, a modern enclosure movement that in turn inspired a successful attack against Jim Crow in the South. By the 1970s, King Cotton was dead in Georgia and his former realm once again covered with pines.

Plantation society defined the universe of Georgia authors for nearly two centuries. Even the literature of the surreal highways and byways of the contemporary era is rooted in its rich soil and shaped by its historical traditions and ideological assumptions. Most authors in modern Georgia still look to the past for literary inspiration. Nevertheless, the plantation has finally gone with the wind, albeit a century late. Accordingly, the literary landscape of Georgia authors has increasingly become a shadow world, a reflection of distant if not ancestral memories rather than reality. Unlike the postbellum period, when the destruction of the Confederacy and emancipation spawned a literature dedicated to the resurrection of the plantation system, or the long decline of the traditional South that followed and sparked an explosion of literary genius so powerful as to be labeled a rebirth, modern Georgia is rapidly losing its feel for the land. This is not to argue that the city is incapable of inspiring literary greatness or that the genre of southern literature is dead. As they have for generations, the contradictions of capitalism will continue to generate pastoral longings.

In the nineteenth century Georgia writers fashioned a reactionary literature of resistance dedicated to preserving the class, racial, and gender arrangements of plantation society. Cotton production still dictated the fundamental rhythms of life in Georgia at the beginning of the twentieth century, but emancipation and the destruction of the white yeomanry were social changes too profound to paper over forever by ideological appeals to domesticity and the Lost Cause. Widespread lamentation about the servant problem in the literary record likewise speaks to the impact of emancipation on plantation society and the tenacious hold of traditional race and gender relations in southern households. Historically the cornerstone of plantation society, paternalism was in universal retreat but continued to buffer racist extremism as long as the landed elite retained its stranglehold on state and local politics. The realm of King Cotton was still a white man's country, but the winds of change were gathering once again on the distant horizon. The future of plantation society seemed secure enough in 1912 that Mildred Rutherford stated with assurance that the New South was simply the Old South remade. No more. At the dawn of a new millenium, many among those who continue to feel the compelling urge to tell about the South have begun to wonder whether it still exists. But that is yet another story, the moral of which remains to be told.

NOTES

PROLOGUE: Georgia Scenes Revisited

1. As the sociologist Immanuel Wallerstein has written in another context, "What of the cultural sphere? Was there no place for ideas, values, science, art, religion, language, passion, and color? Of course there was, for cultures are the ways in which people clothe their politico-economic interests and drives in order to express them, hide them, extend them in space and time, and preserve their memory." See *The Modern World-System II: Mercantilism and the Consolidation of the European World-Economy, 1600–1750* (New York: Academic Press, 1980), 65.

2. See Raymond Williams, *Culture and Society, 1780–1950* (1958; reprint, New York: Harper and Row, 1966), 280, 313; and C. Vann Woodward, revised edition, *The Burden of Southern History* (Baton Rouge: Louisiana State University Press, 1968).

3. Karl Polanyi, *The Great Transformation: The Political and Economic Origins of Our Time* (1944; reprint, Boston: Beacon Press, 1957), 186.

4. See Williams, *Culture and Society,* 130; and *The Country and the City* (London: Chatto and Windus, 1973), 2, 37. Also see John Merrington, "Town and Country in the Transition to Capitalism," *New Left Review* 93 (1975), 71–92.

5. Williams, *The Country and the City,* 146–47; and Margaret Mitchell, *Gone with the Wind* (New York: Macmillan Publishing Company, 1936).

6. Williams, *The Country and the City,* 82–83. Speaking of the English landowning class in a passage that also speaks to postbellum Georgia, Williams observed that "in its actual inhumanity, it could be recognized only with difficulty by men linked to and dependent on it, and the great majority of the poor and oppressed were without a connecting voice to make clear the recognition which was their daily experience. Thus a humane instinct was separated from society; it became a sympathy and a pity, *after* the decisive social events. The real ruling class could not be put in question, so they were seen as temporarily absent, or as the good old people succeeded by the bad new people—themselves succeeding themselves."

7. See Barrington Moore Jr., *Social Origins of Dictatorship and Democracy: Lord*

and Peasant in the Making of the Modern World (Boston: Beacon Press, 1966), 492.

8. Raymond Williams, *Marxism and Literature* (New York: Oxford University Press, 1977), 166; V. N. Volosinov, *Marxism and the Philosophy of Language,* translated by Ladislav Matejka and I. R. Titunik (Cambridge: Harvard University Press, 1986), 9–11. Also see Mikhail Bakhtin, *Problems of Dostoevsky's Poetics,* edited and translated by Caryl Emerson with an introduction by Wayne C. Booth (Minneapolis: University of Minnesota Press, 1984), 5–46; *The Dialogic Imagination: Four Essays,* edited by Michael Holquist and translated by Caryl Emerson and Michael Holquist (Austin: University of Texas Press, 1981); Bryan D. Palmer, *Descent into Discourse: The Reification of Language and the Writing of Social History* (Philadelphia: Temple University Press, 1990); and especially Richard Gray, *The Life of William Faulkner* (Oxford: Blackwell Publishers, 1994).

9. See Quinten Hoare and Geoffrey Nowell Smith, editors and translators, *Selections from the Prison Notebooks of Antonio Gramsci* (New York: International Publishers, 1971), 5–23; and T. J. Jackson Lears, "The Concept of Cultural Hegemony: Problems and Possibilities," *American Historical Review* 90 (1985), 567–93.

10. Raymond Williams, *Keywords: A Vocabulary of Culture and Society* (New York: Oxford University Press, 1976). Also see E. P. Thompson, *The Making of the English Working Class* (New York: Pantheon Books, 1963); *Whigs and Hunters: The Origin of the Black Act* (New York: Pantheon Books, 1975); and *Customs in Common: Studies in Traditional Popular Culture* (New York: New Press, 1993).

11. The relevant literature is voluminous and often difficult reading, but see Fredric Jameson, *Postmodernism; or, The Cultural Logic of Late Capitalism* (Durham: Duke University Press, 1991); Raymond Boudon, *The Analysis of Ideology,* translated by Malcolm Slater (Chicago: University of Chicago Press, 1989); Roland Barthes, *Mythologies,* selected and translated by Annette Lavers (New York: Hill and Wang, 1972); Michel Vovelle, *Ideologies and Mentalities,* translated by Eamon O'Flaherty (Chicago: University of Chicago Press, 1990); Clifford Geertz, *The Interpretation of Cultures: Selected Essays* (New York: Basic Books, 1973), 193–233; and Dominick LaCapra and Stephen L. Kaplan, eds., *Modern European Intellectual History: Reappraisals and New Perspectives* (Ithaca: Cornell University Press, 1982).

12. Terry Eagleton, *Ideology: An Introduction* (London; Verso, 1991), 1–9.

13. *Ibid.,* 56.

14. Moore, *Social Origins of Dictatorship and Democracy,* 486–91. For a broader treatment of southern literary defensiveness, see Fred Hobson, *Tell about the South: The Southern Rage to Explain* (Baton Rouge: Louisiana State University Press, 1983).

15. Charles A. Beard and Mary R. Beard, *The Rise of American Civilization,* volume II (New York: Macmillan Company, 1930), 52–121.

CHAPTER ONE: Breaking New Ground

1. John Melish, *Travels through the United States of America, in the Years 1806 and 1807, and 1809, 1810, and 1811* (1815; reprint, Belfast: J. Smyth, 1818), 39. Melish was born in 1771 and died in 1822. Also see Mills B. Lane, ed., *The Rambler in Georgia* (Savannah: Beehive Press, 1973), 16.

2. Melish, *Travels,* 40–41.

3. *Ibid.,* 41.

4. *Ibid.,* 43–44. Hereinafter spellings of placenames have occasionally been altered to reflect modern usage.

5. *Ibid.,* 44.

6. *Ibid.,* 46–47.

7. *Ibid.,* 47–48.

8. *Ibid.,* 48–49.

9. *Ibid.,* 49–50.

10. *Ibid.,* 50–51.

11. *Ibid.,* 53.

12. *Ibid.,* 263.

13. *Ibid.,* 264–66.

14. *Ibid.,* 267.

15. Lane, *The Rambler,* ix–xxxiv. Also see Jack K. Williams, "Georgia As Seen by Ante-Bellum English Travelers," *Georgia Historical Quarterly* 32 (1948), 158–74; "Travel in Ante-Bellum Georgia as Recorded by English Visitors," *Georgia Historical Quarterly* 33 (1949), 191–205; and "An Evaluation of Seventeen British Travelers to Ante-Bellum Georgia," *Georgia Historical Quarterly* 35 (1951), 307–18. For an older but still useful overview of the period covered in this chapter, see Everett Dick, *The Dixie Frontier: A Social History* (1948; reprint, Norman: University of Oklahoma Press, 1993). The standard bibliographical reference is Thomas D. Clark, *Travels in the Old South: A Bibliography,* 3 volumes (Norman: University of Oklahoma Press, 1956–59).

16. Ulrich B. Phillips, *Life and Labor in the Old South* (1929; reprint, Boston: Little, Brown and Company, 1941), 218–20.

17. Mary Louise Pratt, "Scratches on the Face of the Country; or, What Mr. Barrow Saw in the Land of the Bushmen," in Henry Louis Gates Jr., ed. *"Race," Writing, and Difference* (Chicago: University of Chicago Press, 1986), 139–40.

18. *Ibid.,* 140–41.

19. *Ibid.,* 142–43.

20. *Ibid.,* 143–45.

21. For an excellent discussion of the scientific travel writings of the period, see Pamela Regis, *Describing Early America: Bartram, Jefferson, Crèvecoeur, and the Rhetoric of Natural History* (Dekalb: Northern Illinois University Press, 1992).

22. Pratt associates the isolated narrator, or stranger in a strange land, in the sentimental style of traveler account with bourgeois society, an experiential voice emanating from alienation from the private domestic sphere. In particular, female narrators characteristically bemoan the loss of the comforts of home. Yet even such dramas of "personal survival" can be seen as imperial in their effect on the audience in that they represented a call to arms of sort, a demand for the imposition of civilized order on an otherwise barbaric landscape. This was especially true when the issue of slavery was inserted into the narrative. For a brief overview of the importance of slavery in the genre, see James M. Woods, "In the Eye of the Beholder: Slavery in the Travel Accounts in the Old South, 1790–1860," *Southern Studies* 1 (1990), 33–59.

23. In addition to the three articles by Williams cited earlier, see Phillips, *Life and Labor,* 140–59.

24. William I. Hair, "Stagecoaches and Public Accommodations in Antebellum Georgia," *Georgia Historical Quarterly* 68 (1984), 326; and Basil Hall, *Travels in North America in the Years 1827 and 1828,* volume II (Philadelphia: Carey, Lea and Carey, 1829), 247.

25. Hair, "Stagecoaches in Georgia," 327–28.

26. Bernhard, Karl, duke of Saxe-Weimar-Eisenbach, *Travels through North America, during the years 1825 and 1826,* volume II (Philadelphia: Carey, Lea and Carey, 1828), 17–18; and Mary C. Simms Oliphant et al., eds., *The Letters of William Gilmore Simms,* volume I (Columbia: University of South Carolina Press, 1952), 23–24.

27. Adam Hodgson, *Remarks during a Journey through North America in the Years 1819, 1820, and 1821, in a Series of Letters* (New York: Samuel Whiting, 1823), 144–45; and Bernhard, *Travels,* volume II, 18. Also see Frank L. Owsley, *Plain Folk of the Old South* (Baton Rouge: Louisiana State University Press, 1949), 23–89; and James Oakes, *The Ruling Race: A History of American Slaveholders* (New York: Alfred A. Knopf, 1982), 69–95.

28. Excerpted from C. D. Arfwedson, *The United States and Canada* (London: 1834), in Lane, *The Rambler,* 102–4.

29. Tyrone Power, *Impressions of America, during the Years 1833, 1834, and 1835,* volume II (London: Richard Bentley, 1836), 123–24.

30. Oakes, *The Ruling Race,* 79; Eugene D. Genovese, *The World the Slaveholders Made: Two Essays in Interpretation* (1969; reprint, New York: Vintage Books, 1971); Joan E. Cashin, *A Family Venture: Men and Women on the Southern Frontier* (Baltimore: Johns Hopkins University Press, 1991); and Robert Manson Myers, ed., *The Children of Pride: A True Story of Georgia and the Civil War* (New York: Yale University Press, 1972), 485–88.

31. Power, *Impressions,* 125–27.

32. Hall, *Travels,* II, 248–49; and Charles Joseph Latrobe, *The Rambler in North*

America: MDCCCXXXII–MDCCCXXXIII, second edition, volume II (London: R. B. Seeley and W. Burnside, 1836), 54.

33. Hall, *Travels,* II, 253–55.

34. Sir Charles Lyell, *A Second Visit to the United States of North America,* volume II (New York: Harper and Brothers, 1849), 20–21. Lyell had briefly visited Georgia in the winter of 1841–42. See *Travels in North America, in the Years 1841–2; with Geological Observations on the United States, Canada, and Nova Scotia,* volume I (New York: Wiley and Putnam, 1845), 122–35.

35. James Silk Buckingham, *The Slave States of America,* volume I (London and Paris: Fisher, Son, and Co., 1842), 513.

36. *Ibid.,* 245.

37. *Ibid.,* 210–11; and Una Pope-Hennessey, ed., *The Aristocratic Journey, Being the Outspoken Letters of Mrs. Basil Hall, Written during a 14-Months' Sojourn in America, 1827–28* (New York: G. P. Putnam's Sons, 1931), 235–37. Also see Lewis Gray, *History of Agriculture in the Southern United States to 1860,* volume I (Washington, D.C.: Carnegie Institution, 1933), 484; and J. Wayne Flynt, *Dixie's Forgotten People: The South's Poor Whites* (Bloomington: Indiana University Press, 1980), 9.

38. Owsley, *Plain Folk,* 1–22.

39. Frederika Bremer, *The Homes of the New World: Impressions of America,* translated by Mary Howitt, volume I (London: Arthur Hall, Virtue, and Co., 1853), 374–76.

40. Emily P. Burke, *Pleasure and Pain: Reminiscences of Georgia in the 1840's* (1850; reprint, Savannah: Beehive Press, 1978), 76–82.

41. *Ibid.,* 81. Also see Keith L. Bryant Jr., "The Role and Status of the Female Yeomanry in the Antebellum South: The Literary View," *Southern Quarterly* 18 (1980), 73–88.

42. *Ibid.,* 80–82.

43. Frederick Law Olmsted, *A Journey in the Seaboard States, with Remarks on Their Economy* (New York: Dix and Edwards, 1856), 413. Also see *A Journey in the Backcountry* (New York: Mason Brothers, 1860); and *The Cotton Kingdom: A Traveller's Observations on Cotton and Slavery in the American Slave States,* 2 volumes (New York: Mason Brothers, 1861).

44. Olmsted, *A Journey in the Seaboard States,* 413–14.

45. *Ibid.,* 414.

46. *Ibid.,* 414. Olmsted had reached the conclusion by 1860 that "the present agitation of the country results less from the labors of the abolitionists than from the conceit, avarice, and folly of wealthy owners of slaves." The following year he came out in favor of forcing the South into line. See *A Journey in the Back Country,* vii; and *The Cotton Kingdom,* 8.

47. Buckingham, *The Slave States,* II, 154–57.

48. *Ibid.,* 167; and Charles Lanman, *Adventures in the Wilds of the United States*

and British American Provinces, volume I (Philadelphia: John W. Moore, 1856), 360–63.

49. Stephen Hahn, *The Roots of Southern Populism: Yeoman Farmers and the Transformation of the Georgia Upcountry, 1850–1890* (New York: Oxford University Press, 1983); and David F. Wieman, "Farmers and the Market in Antebellum America: A View from the Georgia Upcountry," *Journal of Economic History* 47 (1987), 627–47.

50. Carlton H. Rogers, *Incidents of Travel in the Southern States and Cuba* (New York: R. Craighead, 1862), 261–62.

51. Buckingham, *The Slave States,* II, 122–23.

52. *Ibid.,* 88–94; and Richard N. Wright, "Ambivalent Bastions of Slavery: The 'Peculiar Institution' on College Campuses in Antebellum Georgia," *Georgia Historical Quarterly* 80 (1996), 467–85. To his pleasant surprise, Buckingham attended a "very brilliant party" hosted by the president of the university for the professors, senior students, and the leading families in Athens. Literally overwhelmed by the charm and beauty of the young ladies present, Buckingham expressed doubt whether any town of comparable size and population in England or France could produce as much feminine beauty, general intelligence, and elegance of manners as he witnessed that evening, which he considered a rare deviation from the general character of town society in the South.

53. Oliphant, *The Letters of William Gilmore Simms,* I, 17–22; Power, *Impressions,* II, 117–31; Bernhard, *Travels,* II, 13; and George William Featherstonaugh, *Excursion through the Slave States, from Washington on the Potomac to the Frontier of Mexico; with Sketches of Popular Manners and Geological Notices* (1844; reprint, New York: Negro Universities Press, 1968), 155.

54. Hall, *Travels,* II, 258–59; Pope-Hennessey, *The Aristocratic Journey,* 237; James Stuart, *Three Years in North America,* volume II (New York: J. and J. Harper, 1833), 82; and Bremer, *The Homes of the New World,* I, 329–34.

55. Hodgson, *Remarks,* 135–38; and Melish, *Travels,* 50–51, 264–66.

56. Pope-Hennessey, *The Aristocratic Journey,* 227–28; and E. J. Hobsbawm and George Rudé, *Captain Swing: A Social History of the Great English Agricultural Uprising of 1830* (New York: W. W. Norton and Company, 1968).

57. Stuart, *Three Years,* II, 81–82; and Buckingham, *The Slave States,* II, 50.

58. Buckingham, *The Slave States,* II, 46–50.

59. Hall, *Travels,* II, 261–64; Pope-Hennessey, *The Aristocratic Journey,* 238–40; Basil Hall, *Forty Etchings, from Sketches Made with the Camera Lucida in North America, in 1827 and 1828* (Edinburgh: Cadell and Co., 1829); and F. Nash Boney, "A British 'Grand Tour' of Crackerland: Basil and Margaret Hall View Frontier Georgia in 1828," *Georgia Historical Quarterly* 74 (1990), 277–92.

60. Stuart, *Three Years,* II, 84–87.

61. Power, *Impressions,* II, 132–39; the quotation is on 138. Barely a decade old

when Buckingham passed through, Columbus still had the reputation of being a rough place. Nor had the legal system improved much. Returning in May 1839 after two months of traveling westward and settling back into his lodgings at the Oglethorpe Hotel, Buckingham heard talk of a recent case of arson that was unusual in that slaves had not been implicated in the subsequent investigation. To cover up fraudulent land transfers from the Cherokees, a group of conspirators reportedly had burned the courthouse to destroy incriminating documents. Apparently, the conspirators had done their work too well because a rush of unrelated lawsuits had followed. See *The Slave States,* I, 514.

62. Buckingham, *The Slave States,* I, 246–47; and Lyell, *A Second Visit,* 34–37. Lyell also reported that black operators were excluded from the Columbus mills. Racial exclusion in the cotton mills that Buckingham had visited in 1839 in Augusta and Athens was less rigid, although he observed a trend in that direction. Each of the three mills on the Oconee River in Athens employed approximately the same ratio of free to slave labor. Whereas one mill owner owned his black workers, the other two hired slaves from local planters for a monthly wage. None of the three reported any racial problems among their workers, proof in Buckingham's eyes of the lower level of "prejudice of color" in the South relative to the North, an argument that propagandists on both sides of the debate over slavery found useful. One mill owner told Buckingham that blacks and whites could do the same job, but slaves were more expensive because they were paid the same wage but had to be fed as well. The same man expressed the hope that white immigration would soon result in an all-white work force in the cotton mills. See *The Slave States,* I, 169; and II, 111–14.

63. Olmsted, *A Journey in the Seaboard States,* 547–49.

64. Robert S. Starobin, *Industrial Slavery in the Old South* (New York: Oxford University Press, 1970), viii; and Buckingham, *The Slave States,* II, 113.

65. Buckingham, *The Slave States,* II, 114–16; Oakes, *The Ruling Race,* 91–92; Elizabeth Fox-Genovese, *Within the Plantation Household: Black and White Women of the Old South* (Chapel Hill: University of North Carolina Press, 1988), 70–82; and Eugene D. Genovese, *The Political Economy of Slavery: Studies in the Economy and Society of the Slave South* (1964; reprint, New York: Vintage Books, 1967). Stephanie McCurry argues that the shared interest of white men in maintaining inequitable gender arrangements in rural households provided further ideological cohesion in the political culture of the South Carolina low country. See *Masters of Small Worlds: Yeoman Households, Gender Relations, and the Political Culture of the Antebellum South Carolina Low Country* (New York: Oxford University Press, 1995).

66. Genovese, *The Political Economy of Slavery,* 17–18; *The World the Slaveholders Made,* 124–25; and Numan V. Bartley, *The Creation of Modern Georgia* (Athens: University of Georgia Press, 1983), 16–29.

67. Drew Gilpin Faust, ed., *Ideology of Slavery: Proslavery Thought in the Ante-*

bellum South, 1830–1860 (Baton Rouge: Louisiana State University Press, 1981); Larry E. Tise, *Proslavery: A History of the Defense of Slavery in America, 1701–1840* (Athens: University of Georgia Press, 1987); William S. Jenkins, *Pro-Slavery Thought in the Old South* (Chapel Hill: University of North Carolina Press, 1935); Malcolm Bell Jr., *Major Butler's Legacy: Five Generations of a Slaveholding Family* (Athens: University of Georgia Press, 1987), 102–5; T. Reed Ferguson, *The John Couper Family at Cannon's Point* (Macon: Mercer University Press, 1994), 159–73; Amelia Matilda Murray, *Letters from the United States, Cuba and Canada* (New York: G. P. Putnam and Company, 1856), 216–26; and Frances Anne Kemble, *Journal of a Residence on a Georgia Plantation in 1838–1839* (1863; reprint, Athens: University of Georgia Press, 1984), 341–42. Margaret Hall was a notable exception, describing Couper as "a person of very formal manners, but it is merely manner and goes no further than the very surface." What was worse, Couper not only shared her husband's "low estimation of women," he was a "staunch American and republican" who had recently taken a sixteen-year-old bride. To her disgust, Couper articulated the belief that only by marrying young and cultivating his bride's mind could a man get "a rational companion in his wife." See Pope-Hennessey, *An Aristocratic Journey*, 232–34.

68. Hall, *Travels*, II, 211, 223, 260; Lyell, *A Second Visit*, I, 262, 268–69; and Buckingham, *The Slave States*, 134. The relevant literature on plantation slavery is voluminous. In addition to the sources previously cited, see Ulrich B. Phillips, *American Negro Slavery* (1918; reprint Baton Rouge: Louisiana State University Press, 1966); Ralph B. Flanders, *Plantation Slavery in Georgia* (Chapel Hill: University of North Carolina Press, 1933); Kenneth M. Stampp, *The Peculiar Institution: Slavery in the Ante-Bellum South* (1956; reprint, New York: Vintage Books, 1989); Eugene D. Genovese, *Roll, Jordan, Roll: The World the Slaves Made* (New York: Random House, 1974); Gavin Wright, *The Political Economy of the Cotton South* (New York: W. W. Norton, 1978); Robert William Fogel, *Without Consent or Contract: The Rise and Fall of American Slavery* (New York: W. W. Norton, 1989); James Oakes, *Slavery and Freedom: An Interpretation of the Old South* (New York: Alfred A. Knopf, 1990); Joseph P. Reidy, *From Slavery to Agrarian Capitalism in the Cotton Plantation South: Central Georgia* (Chapel Hill: University of North Carolina Press, 1992); and Peter Kolchin, *American Slavery, 1619–1877* (New York: Hill and Wang, 1993). Recent studies that focus specifically on the rice coast include Julia F. Smith, *Slavery and Rice Culture in Low Country Georgia, 1750–1860* (Knoxville: University of Tennessee Press, 1985); Peter A. Coclanis, *The Shadow of a Dream: Economic Life and Death in the South Carolina Low Country, 1670–1920* (New York: Oxford University Press, 1989); Betty Wood, *Women's Work, Men's Work: The Informal Slave Economies of Georgia* (Athens: University of Georgia Press, 1995); Mart A. Stewart, *"What Nature Suffers to Groe": Life, Labor, and Landscape on the Georgia Coast, 1680–1920* (Ath-

ens: University of Georgia Press, 1996); and William Dushinberre, *Them Dark Days: Slavery in the American Rice Swamps* (New York: Oxford University Press, 1996).

69. Hall, *Travels,* II, 233–40; Genovese, *The World the Slaveholders Made,* 97–99, and *Roll, Jordan, Roll,* 49–70.

70. Lyell, *A Second Visit,* I, 261–62; Olmsted, *A Journey in the Seaboard States,* 420–21; Charles Hoffman and Tess Hoffman, *North by South: The Two Lives of Richard James Arnold* (Athens: University of Georgia Press, 1988), xiii–xxii; George Lewis, *Impressions of America and American Churches: From the Journal of the Rev. G. Lewis* (1848; reprint, New York: Negro Universities Press, 1968), 127–29; and Genovese, *The World the Slaveholders Made,* 96.

71. Olmsted, *A Journey in the Seaboard States,* 421–22; Hall, *Travels,* II, 233; Fox-Genovese, *Within the Plantation Household,* 216–24; Stampp, *The Peculiar Institution,* 282–95; and Lawrence W. Levine, *Black Culture and Black Consciousness: Afro-American Folk Thought from Slavery to Freedom* (New York: Oxford University Press, 1977).

72. Lyell, *A Second Visit,* I, 264; and Smith, *Slavery and Rice Culture,* 113–40.

73. Genovese, *Roll, Jordan, Roll,* 3–7; and Kolchin, *American Slavery,* 111–27.

74. Genovese, *Roll, Jordan, Roll,* 6; and Olmsted, *A Journey in the Seaboard States,* 448–49.

75. Olmsted, *A Journey in the Seaboard States,* 449–61; Smith, *Slavery and Rice Culture,* 141–65; George A. Rogers and R. Frank Saunders Jr., *Swamp Water and Wiregrass: Historical Sketches of Coastal Georgia* (Macon: Mercer University Press, 1984); Hoffman and Hoffman, *North by South,* xvii; Hall, *Travels,* II, 232–33; and Lyell, *A Second Visit,* I, 263–65.

76. Olmsted, *A Journey in the Seaboard States,* 439–46.

77. Lanman, *Adventures,* II, 147–50; and Stampp, *The Peculiar Institution,* 67–73.

78. Buckingham, *The Slave States,* I, 131–32; Bartley, *Creation,* 23; Lyell, *A Second Visit,* I, 267; and Olmsted, *A Journey in the Seaboard States,* 436–38.

79. Olmsted, *A Journey in the Seaboard States,* 426–29; and Hoffman and Hoffman, *North by South,* 165–78.

80. Buckingham, *The Slave States,* I, 131–32; Olmsted, *A Journey in the Seaboard States,* 421; and Genovese, *Roll, Jordan, Roll,* 327–65.

81. Lyell, *A Second Visit,* I, 262–63; Buckingham, *The Slave States,* I, 132, 223; Olmsted, *A Journey in the Seaboard States,* 431–36; Smith, *Slavery and Rice Culture,* 61–63; and Stampp, *The Peculiar Institution,* 54–60.

82. Olmsted, *A Journey in the Seaboard States,* 479–81; Genovese, *Roll, Jordan, Roll,* 613–21; Stampp, *The Peculiar Institution,* 86–140; Smith, *Slavery and Rice Culture,* 183–206; Ralph B. Flanders, "Planter Problems in Ante-Bellum Georgia," *Georgia Historical Quarterly* 14 (1930), 17–40, and *Plantation Slavery,* 213–31.

83. Lyell, *A Second Visit,* I, 265–66; Olmsted, *A Journey in the Seaboard States,*

438–39, 484–88; Phillips, *Life and Labor,* 305–27; Flanders, *Plantation Slavery,* 133–43; and Smith, *Slavery and Rice Culture,* 64–75. One of the best sources on coastal Georgia overseers is James M. Clifton's anthology of the Manigault family papers. See *Life and Labor on Argyle Island: Letters and Documents of a Savannah River Rice Plantation, 1833–1867* (Savannah: Beehive Press, 1978).

84. Hall, *Travels,* II, 224–25, 233–34.

85. *Ibid.,* 243; Latrobe, *The Rambler,* II, 19–20; and Bremer, *The Homes of the New World,* I, 382–83.

86. Nehemiah Adams, *A South-Side View of Slavery; or, Three Months at the South in 1854* (Boston: T. R. Marvin, 1855), 15, 18. Also see the introduction by Mills Lane in Nehemiah Adams, *A South-Side View of Slavery* (Savannah: Beehive Press, 1974), vii–liv.

87. Adams, *South-Side* (1855), 24–43, 47–60, 116, 201.

88. Murray, *Letters,* 211–25.

89. At one point, Parsons acted as an agent for a Savannah commission house, while superintending mill construction and production for a lumbering company upon another. See Charles Grandison Parsons, *Inside View of Slavery; or, A Tour among the Planters* (Boston: John B. Jewett and Company, 1855), xi–xii, 12–31; and Lane in Adams, *South-Side* (1974), viii–ix.

90. Rogers, *Incidents of Travel,* 234; and Parsons, *Inside,* 65–66, 135–49; the quotation is on 65.

91. Parsons, *Inside,* 150–85, 206–15.

92. *Ibid.,* 254–85.

93. *Ibid.,* 296–300.

94. Fred Hobson, *Tell about the South: The Southern Rage to Explain* (Baton Rouge: Louisiana State University Press, 1983), 3–16.

CHAPTER TWO: Tending the Rich Crop

1. Pamela Regis, *Describing Early America: Bartram, Jefferson, Crèvecoeur, and the Rhetoric of Natural History* (Dekalb: Northern Illinois University Press, 1992), 2–39.

2. Peter Kolchin, *American Slavery, 1619–1877* (New York: Hill and Wang, 1993), 182.

3. William Gilmore Simms, *Guy Rivers: A Tale of Old Georgia,* 2 vols. (New York: Harper and Brothers, 1834); Mary C. Simms Oliphant et al., eds., *The Letters of William Gilmore Simms,* volume I (Columbia: University of South Carolina Press, 1952), 55; and John H. Goff, "The Sandtown Trail," *Atlanta Historical Bulletin* 11 (1966), 34–52. Although the infamous John A. Murrell influenced Simms's portrayal of outlaws in his border romances, he was not the model for Guy Rivers. See

Mary Ann Wimsatt, *The Major Fiction of William Gilmore Simms* (Baton Rouge: Louisiana State University Press, 1989), 93–98, 121–27. Also see Simms, *Guy Rivers: A Tale of Georgia,* ed. John Caldwell Guilds (Fayetteville: University of Arkansas Press, 1993), xv–xxi, 449–76; John Caldwell Guilds, *Simms: A Literary Life* (Fayetteville: University of Arkansas Press, 1992); Charles S. Watson, *From Nationalism to Secession: The Changing Fiction of William Gilmore Simms* (Westport: Greenwood Press, 1993); and Susan J. Tracy, *In the Master's Eye: Representations of Women, Blacks, and Poor Whites in Antebellum Southern Literature* (Amherst: University of Massacchusetts Press, 1995).

4. William Gilmore Simms, *Guy Rivers: A Tale of Old Georgia,* revised edition (Chicago and New York: Belford, Clarke and Co., 1885), 7–12; E. Merton Coulter, *Auraria: The Story of a Georgia Gold-Mining Town* (Athens: University of Georgia Press, 1956), 54–56; Auraria *Western Herald,* I (1), 9 April 1833; and Oliphant, *The Letters,* I, 287–88, 295–302. Simms made his first trip to the Southwest in 1824–25 to visit his father in Mississippi. After his father died in 1830, Simms made another trip to the Southwest the following year to settle his estate. This trip was more widely publicized because Simms, the young editor of the Charleston *City Gazette,* submitted a series of ten travel letters entitled "Notes of a Small Tourist" for publication in the editorial correspondence column. When his stage broke down on 6 March 1831, Simms stayed overnight at the plantation of Captain Henry Crowell on the west bank of the Flint River, a visit that Crowell's daughter recorded in her album. One finds the following passage of interest in the album: "On his return from North Georgia, on the border, near where Atlanta now stands, he again visited us, travelling at least one hundred miles out of his way to do so; my father's residence being in what is now Taylor County, thirty miles west of the city of Macon. He remained with us for several days, that we might assist him in the frontier legends, vernacular, etc. Immediately, upon the publication of the work, *Guy Rivers,* he sent us each a copy." Quoted by William Stanley Hoole in "A Note on Simms's Visits to the Southwest," *American Literature* 6 (1934), 334–36. Also see Hampton M. Jarrell, "Simms's Visits to the Southwest," *American Literature* 5 (1933), 29–30. Simms made good use of his travels by stage through Middle Georgia in an unsigned novelette in 1852 in which he incorporated humor scenes borrowed from Augustus Baldwin Longstreet and William Tappan Thompson, including a horse race, gander pulling, and circus. See William Gilmore Simms, *As Good as a Comedy; or, The Tennessean's Story* (Philadelphia: A. Hart, 1852); Mary Ann Wimsatt, "William Gilmore Simms," in Louis D. Rubin Jr., ed., *The History of Southern Literature* (Baton Rouge: Louisiana State University Press, 1985), 115; and Wimsatt, *The Major Fiction,* 195–202.

5. *Guy Rivers* (1834), 35.

6. *Guy Rivers* (1885), revised edition, 53.

7. *Ibid.,* 60–64.

8. *Ibid.*, 99–103.
9. *Ibid.*, 108–10.
10. *Ibid.*, 69.
11. *Ibid.*, 68–98.
12. *Ibid.*, 140–53.
13. *Ibid.*, 144–46.
14. *Ibid.*, 169.
15. *Ibid.*, 190.
16. *Ibid.*, 286.
17. As quoted by Jay B. Hubbell, *The South in American Literature, 1697–1900* (Durham, Duke University Press, 1954), 666. Also see Augustus Baldwin Longstreet, *Georgia Scenes, Characters, Incidents, etc. in the First Half Century of the Republic, by a Native Georgian* (Augusta: S. R. Sentinel, 1835).
18. For two examples see Thomas Daniel Young, Floyd C. Watkins, and Richard Croom Beatty, eds., *The Literature of the South,* revised edition (Glenview: Scott, Foresman and Company, 1968); and Hugh Ruppersburg, ed., *Georgia Voices, Volume One: Fiction* (Athens: University of Georgia Press, 1992).
19. Hubbell's emphasis on the supposedly middle-class character of Middle Georgia served two purposes. First, it reflected the general rejection by consensus historians after World War II of the work of the Georgia-born historian Ulrich B. Phillips, who had portrayed the Old South as a region dominated by large planters. Second, it lent support to the underlying purpose of his book, which was to claim for southern literature its rightful place within the nation's literary heritage. See Hubbell, *The South in American Literature,* 667, 691; and Ulrich B. Phillips, *American Negro Slavery* (1918; reprint, Baton Rouge: Louisiana State University Press, 1966). Also see Hubbell's *Southern Life in Fiction* (Athens: University of Georgia Press, 1960); and Frank Lawrence Owsley, *Plain Folk of the Old South* (Baton Rouge: Louisiana State University Press, 1949). Clement Eaton also emphasized the middle-class character of the South in *The Growth of Southern Civilization, 1790–1860* (New York: Harper and Row Publishers, 1961), but subsequently modified his position in *The Waning of the Old South Civilization, 1860–1880's* (Athens: University of Georgia Press, 1968). Among recent literary historians, Louis D. Rubin Jr. has consistently championed the middle-class thesis. For example, see *The Edge of the Swamp: A Study in the Literature and Society of the Old South* (Baton Rouge: Louisiana State University Press, 1989). Contemporary historians who share a similar outlook include F. Nash Boney, *Southerners All* (Macon: Mercer University Press, 1984); and James Oakes, *The Ruling Race: A History of American Slaveholders* (New York: Alfred A. Knopf, 1982).
20. See Eugene D. Genovese, *The Political Economy of Slavery: Studies in the Economy and Society of the Slave South* (1964; reprint, New York: Vintage Books, 1967); *The World the Slaveholders Made: Two Essays in Interpretation* (1969; reprint,

New York: Vintage Books, 1971); and *Roll, Jordan, Roll: The World the Slaves Made* (New York: Random House, 1974). Also see Numan V. Bartley, *The Creation of Modern Georgia* (Athens: University of Georgia Press, 1983). The foremost literary historian who emphasizes the centrality of plantation slavery in southern culture is Lewis P. Simpson. See, for example, *The Brazen Face of History: Studies in the Literary Consciousness in America* (Baton Rouge: Louisiana State University Press, 1980), 67–83.

21. The quotation is from Ulrich B. Phillips, *Life and Labor in the Old South* (1929; reprint, Boston: Little, Brown and Company, 1941), 351. The position of the literati in plantation society perhaps accounts for the paradox noted by Merrill Maguire Skaggs that southern literature "insists on a democratic society while preserving the conventions associated with a socially rigid society in which whites must be classified as aristocrats or trash." See *The Folk of Southern Fiction* (Athens: University of Georgia Press, 1972), 251. For a conflicting view of the role of town professionals in southern society, see Oakes, *The Ruling Race,* 123–50. Many historians argue that hegemonic conditions exist when an articulate, class-conscious elite infuses the social order with its values, mores, prejudices, and aspirations. Backed by the power of the state and economic coercion, the primary instruments of ideological transmission are religion, law, education, and the family. See Eugene D. Genovese, *"Slavery Ordained of God": The Southern Slaveholders' View of Biblical History and Modern Politics* (Gettysburg: Gettysburg College, 1985); and *The Slaveholders' Dilemma: Freedom and Progress in Southern Conservative Thought, 1820–1860* (Columbia: University of South Carolina Press, 1992). Also see Elizabeth Fox-Genovese and Eugene D. Genovese, *Fruits of Merchant Capital: Slavery and Bourgeois Property in the Rise and Expansion of Capitalism* (New York: Oxford University Press, 1983). The work of Drew Gilpin Faust is especially insightful regarding the ideological character of southern literary expression. See *A Sacred Circle: The Dilemma of the Intellectual in the Old South, 1840–1860* (Baton Rouge: Louisiana State University Press, 1977); *The Creation of Confederate Nationalism: Ideology and Identity in the Civil War South* (Baton Rouge: Louisiana State University Press, 1989); *Southern Stories: Slaveholders in Peace and War* (Columbia: University of Missouri Press, 1992); and (ed.) *Ideology of Slavery: Proslavery Thought in the Antebellum South, 1830–1860* (Baton Rouge: Louisiana State University Press, 1981). Related works include William S. Jenkins, *Pro-Slavery Thought in the Old South* (Chapel Hill: University of North Carolina Press, 1935); and Larry E. Tise, *Proslavery: A History of the Defense of Slavery in America, 1701–1840* (Athens: University of Georgia Press, 1987).

22. E. P. Thompson, "Patrician Society, Plebeian Culture," *Journal of Social History* 7 (1974), 382–405; "Eighteenth-Century English Society: Class Struggle without Class?" *Social History* 3 (1978), 133–65; and *Customs in Common: Studies in Traditional Popular Culture* (New York: New Press, 1993). Also see the various

works of Raymond Williams, including *Culture and Society, 1780–1950* (1958; reprint, New York: Harper and Row, 1966); T. J. Jackson Lears, "The Concept of Cultural Hegemony: Problems and Possibilities," *American Historical Review* 90 (1985), 567–93; and Alexander Saxton, *The Rise and Fall of the White Republic: Class Politics and Mass Culture in Nineteenth-Century America* (New York: Verso, 1990).

23. See Steven Hahn, *The Roots of Southern Populism: Yeoman Farmers and the Transformation of the Georgia Upcountry, 1850–1890* (New York: Oxford University Press, 1983), 86–90. For more on the unique historical evolution of the yeomanry in the United States, see Allan Kulikoff, *The Agrarian Origins of American Capitalism* (Charlottesville: University Press of Virginia, 1992).

24. See Ritchie Devon Watson Jr., *Yeoman Versus Cavalier: The Old Southwest's Fictional Road to Rebellion* (Baton Rouge: Louisiana State University Press, 1993); Joseph Vincent Ridgely, *Nineteenth-Century Southern Literature* (Lexington: University Press of Kentucky, 1980); and William R. Taylor, *Cavalier and Yankee: The Old South and American National Character* (New York: George Braziller, 1961).

25. Daniel Joseph Singal argues that the humor stories that began to appear after the nullification crisis in 1833 "were designed primarily to warn readers of the dangerous men lurking at the bottom of Southern society, especially in the raw frontier areas of the deep South." See *The War Within: From Victorian to Modernist Thought in the South, 1919–1945* (Chapel Hill: University of North Carolina Press, 1982), 19. Also see James E. Kibler Jr.'s introduction to Augustus Baldwin Longstreet, *Georgia Scenes,* reprint edition (Nashville: J. S. Saunders and Company, 1992), xiii.

26. The framework story was a traditional narrative device used by Longstreet and other southern humorists in which a well-educated gentleman-narrator introduced antebellum readers to customs, events, and behaviors common to frontier life that were no longer acceptable in polite society. Safely ensconced within moralistic introductions and conclusions, and tempered by occasional editorial commentary, the rough-and-tumble world of the backcountry folk thus became a favorite literary topic in genteel circles. In his excellent study of four nineteenth-century Georgia writers, Robert L. Phillips Jr. observes that "Longstreet's narrators were refined, well-educated, rather elderly gentlemen. They knew the Georgia frontier as well as its settled areas; they knew the poor farmers and the wealthy aristocrats. They lived in Middle Georgia during the time that it was being settled, when it was being transformed from a raw, backwoods society to a more civilized culture, and they had definite notions about how Middle Georgia civilization should develop." See "The Novel and the Romance in Middle Georgia Humor and Local Color: A Study of Narrative Method in the Works of Augustus Baldwin Longstreet, William Tappan Thompson, Richard Malcolm Johnston, and Joel Chandler Harris" (Ph.D. dissertation, University of North Carolina, 1971), 84. Also see James D. Wilson's profile of Longstreet in Kenneth Coleman and Charles Stephen Gurr, eds., *Dictionary of Georgia Biography,* II (Athens: University of Georgia Press, 1983), 632–33;

Young, Watkins, and Beatty, *The Literature of the South,* 97–100; and Hennig Cohen and William B. Dillingham, eds., *Humor of the Old Southwest,* second edition (1964; reprint, Athens: University of Georgia Press, 1975), xiv–xxvi. The quotation is from Mary Ann Wimsatt and Robert L. Phillips, "Antebellum Humor," in Louis D. Rubin Jr., ed., *The History of Southern Literature,* 136–56.

27. See Fitz R. Longstreet, ed., *Stories with a Moral: Humorous and Descriptive of Southern Life a Century Ago* (Philadelphia: John C. Winston Company, 1912). Although he sold the *State Rights' Sentinel* in 1836, Longstreet continued to publish sketches in the Augusta *Mirror,* the *Southern Miscellany,* which was edited by William Tappan Thompson, and William Gilmore Simms's literary magazine, *The Magnolia.* His last major publication was serialized in 1859 in the *Southern Field and Fireside* before its publication in 1864 as *Master William Mitten; or, A Youth of Brilliant Talents, Who Was Ruined by Bad Luck* (reprint, Macon: J. W. Burke and Company, 1889). Licensed to preach by the Methodist Church in 1829, Longstreet accepted a ministerial appointment in 1838, and later served as president of Emory College in Oxford, Georgia, Centenary College in Louisiana, the University of Mississippi, and the University of South Carolina. He died in Mississippi in 1870. For biographical information, see Hubbell, *The South in American Literature,* 666–69; O. P. Fitzgerald, *Judge Longstreet: A Life Sketch* (Nashville: Publishing House of the Methodist Episcopal Church South, 1891); Richard Harwell's introduction to the Beehive Press edition of *Georgia Scenes* (Savannah: Beehive Press, 1975); Kimball King, *Augustus Baldwin Longstreet* (Boston: Twayne Publishers, 1984), 1–52; John Donald Wade, *Augustus Baldwin Longstreet: A Study of the Development of Culture in the South* (New York: Macmillan Company, 1924); and James B. Meriwether, "Augustus Baldwin Longstreet: Realist and Artist," *Mississippi Quarterly* 35 (1982), 351–64. Also see M. Thomas Inge, ed., *The Frontier Humorists: Critical Views* (Hamden: Archon Books, 1975), especially Franklin J. Meine, "Tall Tales of the Southwest," 15–31, and Walter Blair, "Southern Humor," 45–82. For a marvelous piece of detective work that brings together all of Longstreet's Georgia scenes, see David Rachels, ed., *Augustus Baldwin Longstreet's Georgia Scenes Completed* (Athens: University of Georgia Press, 1998). For a comparative study that places Longstreet's humor within national trends, see Henry O. Robertson Jr., "The Prism of Laughter: Antebellum Humorists in Regional Perspective" (Ph.D. dissertation, Louisiana State University, 1997), 1–93, 271–94. For an older but still useful survey of early Georgia periodicals, see Bertram H. Flanders, *Early Georgia Magazines: Literary Periodicals to 1865* (Athens: University of Georgia Press, 1944).

28. See the preface (no pagination) to King, *Augustus Baldwin Longstreet;* and Meriwether, "Augustus Baldwin Longstreet," 361.

29. See John Mayfield, "The Theatre of Public Esteem: Ethics and Values in Longstreet's *Georgia Scenes,*" *Georgia Historical Quarterly* 75 (1991), 567; and Kibler, *Georgia Scenes,* xviii.

30. As quoted from Oscar Penn Fitzgerald's 1891 biography of Longstreet by Harwell in *Georgia Scenes,* xviii–xix. Writing on 10 April 1836 to Thomas Willis White, editor of the *Southern Literary Messenger,* about a second volume of Georgia Scenes that he never actually completed, Longstreet stated that "the leading object of the Georgia Scenes, is to enable those who come after us, to see us *precisely as we are.* If my life be spared; they will [be] carried through all ranks of society. I have often desired to see the Greeks and Romans, as they saw each other—To be present at their amusements—hear their wits and wags—enter their dwellings—see their tables—look into their schools &c. &c. The time will come, perhaps, when the same desire will be felt to know all about us; and to gratify that desire, I am now writing." See J. R. Scafidel, "The Letters of Augustus Baldwin Longstreet" (Ph.D. dissertation, University of South Carolina, 1976), 98–103.

31. *Georgia Scenes,* Beehive Press edition, 80–90. Hereinafter, all quotations and references cited in this chapter come from this edition unless otherwise noted.

32. *Ibid.,* 124–34.

33. *Ibid.,* 56–70. The standard study of southern honor is Bertram Wyatt-Brown's *Southern Honor, Ethics and Behavior in the Old South* (New York: Oxford University Press, 1982).

34. *Georgia Scenes,* 57–59.

35. *Ibid.,* 59. To quote Robert L. Phillips Jr., "Longstreet had no faith in the common, uneducated frontiersman or farmer and little faith in the goodness of human nature in general. The crudeness of the lower orders of society could be presented but only for the humor or moral benefit to be derived, and when the lower orders became a challenge to the political hegemony of the upper classes, the narrator's didacticism grows loud." See "The Novel and the Romance in Middle Georgia Humor and Local Color," 148.

36. *Georgia Scenes,* 60–61. Also see Elliott J. Gorn, "'Gouge and Bite, Pull Hair and Scratch': The Social Significance of Fighting in the Southern Backcountry," *American Historical Review* 90 (1985), 18–43; and Kenneth S. Greenberg, *Honor and Slavery: Lies, Duels, Noses, Masks, Dressing as a Woman, Gifts, Strangers, Baseball, Hunting, and Gambling in the Old South* (Princeton: Princeton University Press, 1996).

37. *Georgia Scenes,* 65–68.

38. *Ibid.,* 70.

39. See Mikhail Bakhtin, *Problems of Dostoevsky's Poetics,* edited and translated by Caryl Emerson with an introduction by Wayne C. Booth (Minneapolis: University of Minnesota Press, 1984), 115–22; *Rabelais and His World,* translated by Helene Iswolsky (Cambridge: M.I.T. Press, 1968); Clifford Geertz, *The Interpretation of Cultures: Selected Essays* (New York: Basic Books, 1973), 412–53; and Ted Ownby, *Subduing Satan: Religion, Recreation, and Manhood in the Rural South, 1865–1920* (Chapel Hill: University of North Carolina Press, 1990).

40. Geertz, *The Interpretation of Cultures*, 432–33.

41. *Ibid.*, 435–36.

42. *Georgia Scenes*, 20–55, 173–84.

43. *Ibid.*, 135–47; the quotation is on 135. Phillips summarizes the social views Longstreet communicated through Baldwin and Hall: "A conservative, virile, and moral refinement is what the narrators appreciate; the frivolous accomplishments of polite society are worthless if they are not based on solid character developed with a full appreciation of the soil, of hard work, and an understanding that barbarity and crudeness exist." See "The Novel and the Romance in Middle Georgia Humor and Local Color," 110–11.

44. *Georgia Scenes*, 7–19. Longstreet made much the same point in "The Song," in which he expressed his preference for the native songs of Scotland and Ireland over the classical music popular in European aristocratic circles. Longstreet believed that the folk traditions of the frontier were more in harmony with the South's native soul. See *Georgia Scenes*, 70–79.

45. *Ibid.*, 91–124. For relative discussions of gender roles in the antebellum South, see Elizabeth Fox-Genovese, *Within the Plantation Household: Black and White Women of the Old South* (Chapel Hill: University of North Carolina Press, 1988); Catherine Clinton, *The Plantation Mistress: Women's World in the Old South* (New York: Pantheon, 1982); Jean E. Friedman. *The Enclosed Garden: Women and Community in the Evangelical South, 1830–1900* (Chapel Hill: University of North Carolina Press, 1985); Anne Firor Scott, *The Southern Lady: From Pedestal to Politics, 1830–1930* (Chicago: University of Chicago Press, 1970); Carol Bleser, ed., *In Joy and Sorrow: Women, Family and Marriage in the Victorian South, 1830–1900* (New York: Oxford University Press, 1991); Keith L. Bryant Jr., "The Role and Status of the Female Yeomanry in the Antebellum South: The Literary View," *Southern Quarterly* 18 (1980), 73–88; and Harland D. Hagler, "The Ideal Woman in the Antebellum South: Lady or Farmwife?," *Journal of Southern History* 46 (1980), 405–17. Two studies that examine the ideological functions of southern domesticity as evidenced in literature are Minrose C. Gwin, *Black and White Women of the Old South: The Peculiar Sisterhood in American Literature* (Knoxville: University of Tennessee Press, 1985); and Elizabeth Moss, *Domestic Novelists in the Old South: Defenders of Southern Culture* (Baton Rouge: Louisiana State University Press, 1992).

46. *Georgia Scenes*, 91–93.

47. *Ibid.*, 108. Longstreet's public support for nullification during the tariff fight can be traced through a series of letters that he published in newspapers in 1832. In a letter addressed to "Seneca" published in the Augusta *Chronicle* on 13 October 1832, he stated that his firebrand rhetoric was directed toward redeeming "Southern honor" from the tariff policies of the North. Longstreet argued that the "actual sufferings" done to Georgians by the tariff were such as to "*justify* her in hazarding the perils of War for relief; if she cannot obtain it, and speedily too, by peaceful

means." As for those who advised a more cautious approach, Longstreet stated that "such a course, in nine cases out of ten, would make resistance absolutely hopeless. ONCE MORE—and I would proclaim it with the trumpet's voice—ONCE MORE, BE IT KNOWN TO ALL WHO COMPLAIN OF GEORGIA'S TEMERITY, THAT SIXTEEN YEARS HAVE ROLLED AWAY SINCE SHE BEGAN TO ARGUE, PETITION, AND REMONSTRATE AGAINST THE RESTRICTIVE SYSTEM: DURING ALL WHICH TIME, THE MONSTER HAS BEEN GROWING MORE VENOMOUS, HIDEOUS, AND VORACIOUS!" See Scafidel, "The Letters of Augustus Baldwin Longstreet," 5–36; the quotation is on 23.

48. *Georgia Scenes,* 114.

49. Augustus Baldwin Longstreet, *Georgia Scenes* (Atlanta: Cherokee Publishing Company, 1971), 130. Arguing from a Jungian perspective, Alan Henry Rose maintains that the use of African American characters in southern humor creates "a profoundly ambivalent situation." Because racial images "contained compellingly powerful subjective associations" that were taboo to express in the South, the solution was to censor blacks from the narrative or rely on stereotypes. The fact that Mrs. Slang beats Rose reveals Longstreet's ambivalence because he cannot let condemnation of white on black violence go without qualification, and therefore dehumanizes Rose by denying to her the ability to reason. Rose concludes that "it is a measure of the importance attached to reestablishing conventional antebellum racial attitudes that in order to portray the black in this reassuring stereotype Longstreet sacrifices narrative consistency in his tale, abandoning his rigorously detached satire for the sake of an intrusive conjectural slur on the nature of the black intellect." See *Demonic Vision: Racial Fantasy and Southern Fiction* (Hamden: Archon Books, 1976), 19–38.

50. *Georgia Scenes,* 133. Like many defenders of plantation slavery, Longstreet's racism was linked intimately with his sense of Christian obligation toward Africa. The slaveholder's imperial world view is especially evident in a piece entitled "Africa.—1832" by Georgia poet Samuel J. Cassels:

From Northern Barbar to the Southern cape,
From Western Guinea to the Mozambique;
Dark superstition holds her bloody sway,
And death is gorged with many a welcome prey.
Her kings are despots, and her gods are fiends,
Her worship orgies, and her music screams;
Around her palace hang the skulls of foes,
And heads on heads lie thick around her doors.
Her inner forests hear the clash of arms,
Her coasts and cities shake with dire alarms;
Her winds blow hatred, and her rain is blood,
Her leagues are ruptures, and her friendships rude.
Satan's dread kingdom spreads from far to near,

Whose sum is darkness, and whose hope, despair;
And with an iron rod of mountain weight,
He breaks the nations here both small and great.
Where, then, O Afric, shall they help be found?
Oh tell us where? If not in gospel-sound?
Earth's cold charity but looks and passes by;
And reason renewed but heaves a sigh—
Mere Science yields her glimm'ring light in vain,
Her strength is weakness and her mercy pain.
But *Gospel Truth* can break they chains apart,
Disperse they gloom and sanctify they heart;
Its still surall voice shall turn they screams to joy,
Break down thy temples and thy tongues employ.

See Samuel J. Cassels, *Providence and Other Poems* (Macon: Griffin and Purse, 1838); and Lawrence Huff's biographical profile of Cassels in Coleman and Gurr, *Dictionary of Georgia Biography,* I, 178–80.

51. *Stories with a Moral,* 50–87. Also see Watson, *Yeoman Versus Cavalier,* 59–60.

52. *Stories with a Moral,* 87.

53. See Henry Prentice Miller, "The Life and Works of Wiliam Tappan Thompson" (Ph.D. dissertation, University of Chicago, 1942); and "The Background and Significance of Major Jones's Courtship," *Georgia Historical Quarterly* 30 (1946), 267–96. Miller's dissertation has been superseded by Herbert Phinehas Shippey's excellent study, "William Tappan Thompson: A Biography and Uncollected Writings" (Ph.D. dissertation, University of South Carolina, 1991). Also see Shippey's essay on Thompson in Coleman and Gurr, *Dictionary of Georgia Biography,* II, 974–76; and Hubbell, *The South in American Literature,* 669–72.

54. After Thompson moved back to Augusta, he published *Chronicles of Pineville: Embracing Sketches of Georgia Scenes, Incidents and Characters* (Philadelphia: Carey and Hart, 1845). Afterward he moved to Baltimore, where he published *John's Alive; or, The Bride of a Ghost, and Other Sketches* in 1846 (Philadelphia: David McKay, 1883); and *Major Jones's Sketches of Travel: Comprising the Scenes, Incidents, and Adventures in His Tour from Georgia to Canada* (Philadelphia: T. B. Peterson and Brothers, 1848). Returning to Georgia, he established the Savannah *Daily News* with John M. Cooper in 1850, which he edited until his death in 1882, excluding a brief stint in the military following Sherman's invasion of Georgia. Joel Chandler Harris, who joined Thompson at the *Daily News* in 1870, later wrote that *Major Jones's Courtship* was in nearly every household in rural America and rivaled *Uncle Tom's Cabin* in popularity. The publication history of Thompson's writings is somewhat confusing, largely because of errors or misprints passed along in subsequent printings by different publishers. In this chapter, I follow the dates established by

Miller in his 1942 study. The editions I used are *Major Jones's Courtship: Detailed, with Other Scenes, Incidents, and Adventures, in a Series of Letters, by Himself* (Philadelphia: Carey and Hart, 1844); *Major Jones's Courtship: Detailed, with Other Scenes, Incidents, and Adventures, in a Series of Letters, by Himself. Revised and Enlarged. To Which Are Added Thirteen Humorous Sketches* (New York: D. Appleton and Company, 1872); and *Major Jones's Sketches of Travel: Comprising the Scenes, Incidents, and Adventures in His Tour from Georgia to Canada* (Philadelphia: T. B. Peterson and Brothers, 1848).

55. *Chronicles of Pineville,* 5–7; and Cohen and Dillingham, *Humor of the Old Southwest,* 121–22.

56. *Major Jones's Courtship* (1844), 11–21.

57. *Ibid.,* 21–30; the quotation is on 21–22.

58. *Ibid.,* 31, 153–61; the quotation is on 156–57.

59. *Ibid.,* 158–59.

60. *Ibid.,* 160.

61. Herbert Shippey also concludes that Thompson anticipates the work of postbellum local color writers. See "William Tappan Thompson," 132.

62. *Major Jones's Courtship* (1844), 66, 78–79.

63. *Major Jones's Courtship* (1872), 214–22. In "Beginning to Practice; or, Cousin Pete's First Case of Cholera," a story that Thompson published in the Savannah *Morning News* that reveals the impact of the city's frequent epidemics on his literary imagination, slaves are simply the victims of the Major's cousin's foray into the medical profession without the necessary training. Pete learns a tragic and expensive lesson when he kills five of his slaves while playing doctor, the moral of the tale being that the sons of planters were better off on the land. *Ibid.,* 207–13. In an anonymous sketch entitled "Happy Domestics" that he published in the *Southern Miscellany,* Thompson gave what Herbert Shippey describes as "a conventional pro-slavery description of slaves satisfied in their bondage." Shippey also concludes that African Americans rarely appear in his early fiction except in "a stereotyped manner." See "William Tappan Thompson," 125–26. Ironically, slaves actually helped to inspire southwestern humor "by acting out the trickster style from their African heritage." In the words of Johanna Nichol Shields, "Humorists copied, exaggerated, and published these curious exchanges between power and wit, tainting them with racism while capturing them in form." See "White Honor, Black Humor, and the Making of a Southern Style," *Southern Cultures* 1 (1995), 420–30. Also see David R. Roediger, *The Wages of Whiteness: Race and the Making of the American Working Class* (New York: Verso, 1991); and Eric J. Sundquist, *To Wake the Nations: Race in the Making of American Literature* (Cambridge: Belknap Press of Harvard University Press, 1993). While president of Emory College, Longstreet played a leading role in the breakup of the Methodist Church over the issue of slavery in 1845. His *Letters on the Epistle of Paul to Philemon; or, The Connection of*

Apostolical Christianity with Slavery (Charleston: B. Jenkins, 1845) epitomized proslavery thought. See Richard N. Wright, "Ambivalent Bastions of Savery: The 'Peculiar Institution' on College Campuses in Antebellum Georgia," *Georgia Historical Quarterly* 80 (1996), 475.

64. According to Shippey, the *Southern Miscellany* published a Major Jones letter during early April 1844 in an issue that was subsequently lost. Reprinted in the New Orleans *Daily Tropic* and the Albany *Evening Journal* (N.Y.), the sketch recounts a trip by Major Jones to Augusta, where he shakes hands with Henry Clay. Because Clay actually stopped in Augusta during his campaign, Shippey argues that it is possible that Thompson actually met his political idol there. See "William Tappan Thompson," 130–31.

65. *Georgia Scenes,* 184; *Chronicles of Pineville,* 136–60; and *Major Jones's Courtship* (1872), 274–80. Thompson's drinking sketch with the most interesting historical setting is "Boss Ankles, the Man What Got Blowed Up with a Sky-Racket," which appeared in the *Family Companion and Ladies' Mirror* in 1842. In the Pineville of old, storekeepers kept a barrel of free whiskey or rum in their back rooms to attract customers. A storekeeper named Mr. Harley doled out such generous samples that his establishment was especially popular. By noon on Saturdays, otherwise shy country folk, wiregrass boys, and torrid clay-eaters, even some women, would be in their cups and ready to fight. On their way out of town that night, many would fall asleep under the china trees. Awakened from their stupor by the sun the next day, they would often discover that they had been victimized by village pranksters who had sheared their clothing, painted their faces, or cropped their hair to the skin. In "The Anti-Rail-Rode Man," a comic look at moral authoritarianism in the days "when Judge Lynch exercised a broad jurisdiction," Thompson tells the story of the first time anyone successfully resisted vigilante justice in Pineville. When the local boys decide to ride John Borum, "a very turbulent, desperate, dare-devil sort of fellow" when drunk, out of town on a rail, they quickly think better of the plan when he confronts them with a bag of powder and a hot cigar. See *Chronicles of Pineville,* 39–58, 179–86. Also see Stanley K. Schultz, "Temperence Reform in the Antebellum South: Social Control and Urban Order," *South Atlantic Quarterly* 83 (1984), 323–39; Ian R. Tyrrell, *Sobering Up: From Temperance to Prohibition in Antebellum America, 1800–1860* (Westport: Greenwood Press, 1979); and "Drink and Temperance in the Old South: An Overview and Interpretation," *Journal of Southern History* 48 (1982), 485–510.

66. Cohen and Dillingham, *Humor of the Old Southwest,* 203–4; and William Stanley Hoole, *Alias Simon Suggs: The Life and Times of Johnson Jones Hooper* (Tuscaloosa: University of Alabama Press, 1952).

67. William T. Porter, ed., *The Big Bear of Arkansas, and Other Tales* (Philadelphia: T. B. Peterson, 1843), 62–79.

68. *Ibid.,* 64.

69. *Ibid.*, 65.

70. *Ibid.*, 69–70.

71. *Ibid.*, 71.

72. *Ibid.*, 75. Johanna Nichol Shields argues that the Simon Suggs stories explore the complex mentality that sought "to perpetuate both slavery and freedom in a progressive world." Shields also contends that the Georgia genesis story evidences Hooper's rejection of paternalism as a foundation for southern society, observing that the Reverend Suggs is a harsh patriarch who abuses his white and black "sons" alike. Unlike the more developed southeastern states, the southwestern frontier was a place where the common man, however "dirty and disreputable," could still evade the restrictions plantation society placed upon his freedom, while slavery simultaneously provided opportunity for social mobility to those who exercised their native wit and talent. See Johanna Nichol Shields, "A Sadder Simon Suggs: Freedom and Slavery in the Humor of Johnson Hooper," *Journal of Southern History* 56 (1990), 641–64.

73. See James E. Kibler's essay in Coleman and Gurr, *Dictionary of Georgia Biography,* II, 594–96; and Thomas A. Burke, ed., *Polly Peablossom's Wedding, and Other Tales* (Philadelphia: A. Hart, 1851), 13–23, 76–88.

74. Lamar in Burke, *Polly Peablossom's Wedding,* 21.

75. *Ibid.*, 76. In his postbellum memoir, Judge Garnett Andrews sets the story in Rabun Gap. See *Reminiscences of an Old Georgia Lawyer* (1870; reprint, Atlanta: Cherokee Publishing Company, 1984), 92. According to Hubbell, the story is often linked to "Colonel Quagg's Conversion" by Charles Dickens. See *The South in American Literature,* 661. The Reverend Francis Robert Goulding, a Georgia author who specialized in adventure stories for boys, incorporated the tale into *Nacoochee; or, Boy-life from Home,* the second volume in his trilogy entitled *The Woodruff Stories* (Philadelphia: Claxton, Remsen and Haffelfinger, 1880), 154–69. For relevant discussions of the role of evangelical religion in the Old South, see Friedman, *The Enclosed Garden;* Anne C. Loveland, *Southern Evangelicals and the Social Order, 1800–1860* (Baton Rouge: Louisiana State University Press, 1988); Donald G. Mathews, *Slavery and Methodism: A Chapter in American Morality, 1780–1845* (Princeton: Princeton University Press, 1965); Samuel S. Hill, ed., *Varieties of Southern Religious Experience* (Baton Rouge: Louisiana State University Press, 1988); Wayne Mixon's essay, "Georgia," in Samuel S. Hill, ed., *Religion in the Southern States: A Historical Study* (Macon: Mercer University Press, 1983), 77–100; Edgar T. Thompson's essay, "God and the Solid South," in Samuel S. Hill et al., *Religion and the Solid South* (Nashville: Abingdon Press, 1972), 57–91; and Christopher H. Owen, *The Sacred Flame of Love: Methodism and Society in Nineteenth-Century Georgia* (Athens: University of Georgia Press, 1998).

76. Lamar in Burke, *Polly Peablossom's Wedding,* 77–78.

77. *Ibid.*, 85–86.

78. Burke, *Polly Peablossom's Wedding,* 44–48.

79. See R. M. Charlton's "Bingo. A Georgia Sketch," Burke's "'Doing' a Sheriff. A Georgia Sketch," and the anonymously authored "Practical Jokes and Bad Liquor" in Burke, *Polly Peablossom's Wedding,* 61–66, 98–101, 132–36.

80. Lane in Burke, *Polly Peablossom's Wedding,* 28–40; the quotation is on 29–30.

81. *Ibid.,* 40.

82. The letters were collected and published as *A Voice from the South: Comprising Letters from Georgia to Massachusetts, and to the Southern States* (Baltimore: Western Continent Press, 1847). The letters have also been collected in Scafidel, "The Letters of Augustus Baldwin Longstreet," 276–89, which is the source used in this study.

83. Scafidel, "The Letters of Augustus Baldwin Longstreet," 278–79.

84. *Ibid.,* 305. According to the U.S. Manuscript Census Returns, Longstreet himself owned nineteen slaves in 1840, ten in 1850, and seven in 1860. See Robertson, "The Prism of Laughter," 271–94.

85. Thompson, *Major Jones's Sketches of Travel,* 5–6.

86. *Ibid.,* 7–10; the quotation is on 9.

87. *Ibid.,* 11–13.

88. *Ibid.,* 13–14; the quotation is on 14.

89. *Ibid.,* 14–17; the quotation is on 17. Also see George M. Frederickson, *The Black Image in the White Mind: The Debate on Afro-American Character and Destiny, 1817–1914* (New York: Harper and Row, 1971), 1–164.

90. *Major Jones's Sketches of Travel,* 18–26; the quotation is on 20.

91. *Ibid.,* 23.

92. Shippey, "William Tappan Thompson," 138; and Thompson, *Major Jones's Sketches of Travel,* 192.

93. David L. Roath, *Zara: A Romance* (Athens: Christy, Kelsea and Burke, 1851), 15. Little is known about Roath other than he lived in Athens in the 1850s, edited a periodical called *Roath's Monthly Magazine* in 1853, served as ordinary of Richmond County from 1862 to 1866, and was clerk of the city court in Augusta from 1865 to 1866. See Robert M. Willingham Jr.'s essay in Coleman and Gurr, *Dictionary of Georgia Biography,* II, 845–46. Roath also authored a mundane collection of derivative sketches entitled *The Five Love Adventures of Solomon Slug and Other Sketches* (New York: Bruce and Brother, 1852). While the title story is an enjoyably ludicrous account of a rogue's unsuccessful schemes to marry money that shows Roath's talent for comic characterization and settings, the other sketches are unmemorable.

94. *Zara,* 15–17.

95. *Ibid.,* 36–37.

96. *Ibid.,* 51.

97. *Ibid.*, 93.

98. *Ibid.*, 97.

99. *Ibid.*, 104–5.

100. Francis James Robinson, *Kups of Kauphy: A Georgia Book in Warp and Woof. Containing Tales, Incidents, etc. of the "Empire State of the South," with a Slight Sketch of That Well-Known and Eccentric "Colored Gemman," OLD JACK* (Athens, 1853). The only extant copy is in the Special Collections Library, Duke University, although several sketches are reprinted in Cohen and Dillingham, *Humor of the Old Southwest,* 332–35.

101. According to tradition, "Old Jack" was the same waiter mentioned by Thompson in *Major Jones's Courtship.* See Hubbell, *The South in American Literature,* 660, 671; and Wimsatt and Phillips in Rubin, *The History of Southern Literature,* 152. For a thoughtful treatment of African American character types in American literature, see Catherine Starke, *Black Portraiture in American Fiction: Stock Characters, Archetypes, and Individuals* (New York: Basic Books, 1971).

102. *Kups of Kauphy,* 106–7.

103. Caroline Lee Hentz, *The Planter's Northern Bride,* with an introduction by Rhoda Coleman Ellison (1854; reprint, Chapel Hill: University of North Carolina Press, 1970).

104. See F. N. Boney's introduction to John Brown, *Slave Life in Georgia. A Narrative of the Life, Sufferings, and Escape of John Brown, a Fugitive Slave* (1855; reprint, Savannah: Beehive Press, 1972), vii–xxi; and Frances Foster Smith, *Witnessing Slavery: The Development of Ante-Bellum Slave Narratives,* second edition (Madison: University of Wisconsin Press, 1994).

105. Brown, *Slave Life in Georgia,* 22–24.

106. *Ibid.*, 35–37, 40–53, 143–64. Also of interest is William and Ellen Craft's account of their flight from Macon to freedom. See *Running a Thousand Miles for Freedom; or, The Escape of William and Ellen Craft from Slavery* (1860; reprint, New York: Arno Press, 1969). After making their way to England, the Crafts remained active in the abolitionist movement. With the help of Boston abolitionists, they purchased a plantation in Bryan County, Georgia, in 1874 and started the Woodville Co-operative Farm School, which they modeled on the Ockham school in Surrey, England, where they had taught carpentry and needlecrafts for three years. Financed by Lady Byron and Lord Lovelace and administered by Lady Lovelace, Lord Byron's daughter, the Ockham school was founded in 1835 upon the principle that a combination of practical vocational and academic training was the best remedy for agricultural unrest. Although both the Woodville plantation and school initially did quite well, the project met with strong local opposition from Richard Arnold's heirs almost from the beginning. Chronically short of capital, the school floundered in the 1890s. The land was sold at public auction just before William Craft's death in 1900. See R. J. M. Blackett, "Fugitive Slaves in Britain: The Odyssey of

William and Ellen Craft," *Journal of American Studies* 12 (1978), 41–62; and Charles Hoffmann and Tess Hoffmann, *North by South: The Two Lives of Richard James Arnold* (Athens: University of Georgia Press, 1988), 261.

107. See Ebenezer Starnes, *The Slaveholder Abroad; or, Billy Buck's Visit, with His Master, to England. A Series of Letters from Dr. Pleasant Jones to Major Joseph Jones, of Georgia* (Philadelphia: J. B. Lippincott, 1860); and Allen D. Candler and Clement A. Evans, eds., *Cyclopedia of Georgia,* III (1906; reprint, Spartanburg: Reprint Company, 1972), 359.

108. Harrison Berry, *Slavery and Abolitionism, As Viewed by a Georgia Slave* (Atlanta: Franklin Printing House, 1861), which is reprinted in Maxwell Whiteman, ed., *Afro-American History Series,* volume VII (Wilmington: Scholarly Resources, 1972); the quotation is on 26. Whereas Whiteman argues that Berry probably did not write *Slavery and Abolitionism,* Clarence Mohr reaches a different conclusion in his excellent study of slavery in Georgia during the Civil War. Mohr makes the provocative argument that Berry considered "planter paternalism a fragile shield against persecution in times of crisis," and that he was voicing his dissent in the only language that white society would tolerate without losing his credibility in an increasingly hostile racial environment. See *On the Threshold of Freedom: Masters and Slaves in Civil War Georgia* (Athens: University of Georgia Press, 1986), 5–64; and "Harrison Berry: A Black Pamphleteer in Georgia during Slavery and Freedom," *Georgia Historical Quarterly* 67 (1983), 189–205.

CHAPTER THREE: Lay-By Time

1. See Paul E. Johnson and Sean Wilentz, *The Kingdom of Matthias: A Story of Sex and Salvation in Nineteenth-Century America* (New York: Oxford University Press, 1994), 6; Charles Sellers, *The Market Revolution: Jacksonian America, 1815–1846* (New York: Oxford University Press, 1991); and Ronald J. Zboray, *A Fictive People: Antebellum Economic Development and the American Reading Public* (New York: Oxford University Press, 1993).

2. Elizabeth Fox-Genovese, *Within the Plantation Household: Black and White Women of the Old South* (Chapel Hill: University of North Carolina Press, 1988).

3. See Elizabeth Moss, *Domestic Novelists in the Old South: Defenders of Southern Culture* (Baton Rouge: Louisiana State University Press, 1992), 1–29; the quotation is on 14.

4. Caroline Lee Hentz, *The Planter's Northern Bride,* with an introduction by Rhoda Coleman Ellison (1854; reprint, Chapel Hill: University of North Carolina Press, 1970), vii–xxii; and Moss, *Domestic Novelists,* 106–20.

5. Hentz, *The Planter's Northern Bride* (1970), 4–6.

6. *Ibid.,* 23.

7. *Ibid.*, 27–28.
8. *Ibid.*, 32.
9. *Ibid.*, 84–85.
10. *Ibid.*, 150–65; the quotation is on 150.
11. *Ibid.*, 203.
12. *Ibid.*, 204.
13. *Ibid.*, 208–9.
14. *Ibid.*, 231–32.
15. *Ibid.*, 232–34.
16. *Ibid.*, 279–88.
17. *Ibid.*, 303, 304.
18. *Ibid.*, 312.
19. *Ibid.*, 317.
20. *Ibid.*, 321–22.
21. *Ibid.*, 324–25.
22. *Ibid.*, 325–26.
23. *Ibid.*, 327–28.
24. *Ibid.*, 330–31.
25. *Ibid.*, 332–35.
26. *Ibid.*, 339.
27. *Ibid.*, 342.
28. *Ibid.*, 360.
29. *Ibid.*, 452–53.
30. *Ibid.*, 509.
31. *Ibid.*, 578–79.
32. Moss, *Domestic Novelists,* 62–63. In the words of one historian, "The southern white woman, in life and often in the literature of the period, was fully obligated to uphold moral virtue in the domestic sphere—a sphere enlarged in southern society to include the plantation." See Minrose C. Gwin, *Black and White Women of the Old South: The Peculiar Sisterhood in American Literature* (Knoxville: University of Tennessee Press, 1985), 22. Also see Steven M. Stowe, *Intimacy and Power in the Old South: Ritual in the Lives of the Planters* (Baltimore: Johns Hopkins University Press, 1987), x.
33. Robert Manson Myers, ed., *The Children of Pride: A True Story of Georgia and the Civil War* (New York: Yale University Press, 1972), xi–xvii.
34. Fox-Genovese, *Within the Plantation Household,* 242–52.
35. *Ibid.*, 247. In Stowe's words, "The planters' reliance on letters to inspire, comfort, and control is the chief example of the way in which a certain form of language is a window on both the social order and an individual's perceptions." See *Intimacy and Power,* 3.
36. Fox-Genovese, *Within the Plantation Household,* 31; Fox-Genovese defines

the household as "a basic social unit in which people, whether voluntarily or under compulsion, pool their income and resources." Also see Catherine Clinton, *The Plantation Mistress: Woman's World in the Old South* (New York: Partheon, 1982), 16–58, 164–65; and Jean E. Friedman, *The Enclosed Garden: Women and Community in the Evangelical South, 1830–1900* (Chapel Hill: University of North Carolina Press, 1985), 21–38.

37. Cornelia Jones Pond, *Life on a Liberty County Plantation: The Journal of Cornelia Jones Pond,* edited by Josephine Martin (Darien, Georgia: Darien *News,* 1974), 2–3, 67–68; the quotation is on 2.

38. Emily P. Burke, *Pleasure and Pain: Reminiscences of Georgia in the 1840's* (1850; reprint, Savannah: Beehive Press, 1978), 32–36.

39. See James I. Robertson's introduction to Dolly Lunt Burge, *The Diary of Dolly Lunt Burge* (Athens: University of Georgia Press, 1962), vii–xv. Also see Christine Jacobson Carter, ed., *The Diary of Dolly Lunt Burge* (Athens: University of Georgia Press, 1997).

40. Burge, *The Diary,* 16.

41. *Ibid.,* 36–40, 42, 55–56, 62, 65, 67–69. Also see Ulrich B. Phillips, *American Negro Slavery* (1918; reprint, Baton Rouge: Louisiana State University Press, 1966), 205–27; and *Life and Labor in the Old South* (1929; reprint, Boston: Little, Brown, and Company, 1941), 91–111; Ralph B. Flanders, *Plantation Slavery in Georgia* (Chapel Hill: University of North Carolina Press, 1933), 55–93; Lewis C. Gray, *History of Agriculture in the Southern United States to 1860,* II (Washington, D.C.: Carnegie Institution, 1933), 691–720; James C. Bonner, *A History of Georgia Agriculture, 1732–1860* (Athens: University of Georgia Press, 1964), 47–60; Kenneth M. Stampp, *The Peculiar Institution: Slavery in the Antebellum South* (1956; reprint, New York: Vintage Books, 1989), 45–46; and Clement Eaton, *The Growth of Southern Civilization, 1790–1860* (New York: Harper and Row Publishers, 1961), 25–48.

42. Phillips, *Life and Labor,* 3. In Stampp's words, the fruits of the slave system were "determined not by the climate, not by the soil, but by the kinds of seeds sown by men." See *The Peculiar Institution,* 27.

43. Burge, *The Diary,* 30, 40, 42, 66–67.

44. Myers, *The Children of Pride,* 85–88; the quotation is on 86.

45. *Ibid.,* 88–91.

46. James M. Clifton, ed., *Life and Labor on Argyle Island* (Savannah: Beehive Press, 1978), 8–9, 53–54, 94, 99; Jeffrey R. Young, "Ideology and Death on a Savannah River Rice Plantation, 1833–1867: Paternalism Amidst 'a Good Supply of Disease and Pain,'" *Journal of Southern History* 59 (1993), 673–706; Myers, *The Children of Pride,* 113–14; Burge, *The Diary,* 38, 54; and Virginia Ingraham Burr, ed., *The Secret Eye: The Journal of Ella Gertrude Clanton Thomas, 1848–1880,* with an introduction by Nell Irvin Painter (Chapel Hill: University of North Carolina Press, 1990), 157–58.

47. Clifton, *Life and Labor,* 54, 69–70.

48. Myers, *The Children of Pride,* 183–86, 240–46, 255–58, 263–71, 306, 309–10.

49. *Ibid.,* 109–10; and George A. Rogers and R. Frank Saunders Jr., *Swamp Water and Wiregrass: Historical Sketches of Coastal Georgia* (Macon: Mercer University Press, 1984), 43–59.

50. Susan M. Kollock, ed., "Letters of the Kollock and Allied Families, 1826–1884" (Part II), *Georgia Historical Quarterly* 34 (1950), 39–41; Burge, *The Diary,* 63–64; Una Pope-Hennessey, ed., *The Aristocratic Journey, Being the Outspoken Letters of Mrs. Basil Hall, Written during a 14-Months' Sojourn in America, 1827–28* (New York: G. P. Putnam's Sons, 1931), 229–30; Anne Firor Scott, *The Southern Lady: From Pedestal to Politics, 1830–1930* (Chicago: University of Chicago Press, 1970), 3–79; Sally G. McMillen, *Southern Women: Black and White in the Old South* (Arlington Heights: Harlan Davidson, 1992); and Fox-Genovese, *Within the Plantation Household,* 225–30.

51. Myers, *The Children of Pride,* 7–36.

52. *Ibid.,* 112–13, 317–19; Rebecca Latimer Felton, *Country Life in Georgia in the Days of My Youth* (Atlanta: Index Printing Company, 1919), 52–53; Burr, *The Secret Eye,* 169; and Pond, *Life on a Liberty County Plantation,* 67–71. Also see Stowe, *Intimacy and Power,* 125; and Sally G. McMillen, *Motherhood in the Old South* (Baton Rouge: Louisiana State University Press, 1990).

53. Burke, *Pleasure and Pain,* 71.

54. *Ibid.,* 72–75; Amelia Akehurst Lines, *To Raise Myself a Little: The Diaries and Letters of Jennie, a Georgia Teacher, 1851–1886,* edited with an introduction by Thomas Dyer (Athens: University of Georgia Press, 1982), 61, 100, 107–11, 125–35; and Burge, *The Diary,* 1–20.

55. Pond, *Life on a Liberty County Plantation,* 7–25; and Myers, *The Children of Pride,* 1709.

56. Felton, *Country Life,* 58–62, 71–72; and John E. Talmadge, *Rebecca Latimer Felton: Nine Stormy Decades* (Athens: University of Georgia Press, 1960), 1–10.

57. William Dallam Armes, ed., *The Autobiography of Joseph LeConte* (New York: D. Appleton and Company, 1903), 5–33; and Lester D. Stephens, *Joseph LeConte: Gentle Prophet of Evolution* (Baton Rouge: Louisiana State University Press, 1982), 1–15.

58. Armes, *The Autobiography of Joseph LeConte,* 22–23; and Myers, *The Children of Pride.* The standard study of the cotton factorage system is Harold D. Woodman, *King Cotton and His Retainers: Financing and Marketing the Cotton Crop of the South, 1800–1925* (Lexington: University of Kentucky Press, 1968).

59. Myers, *The Children of Pride;* Marion Alexander Boggs, ed., *The Alexander Letters, 1787–1900* (1910; reprint, Athens: University of Georgia Press, 1980), 133–37, 140–50; Fox-Genovese, *Within the Plantation Household,* 212–16; and Clinton, *The*

Plantation Mistress, 123–38. For an excellent overview of the topic, see Christie Anne Farnham, *The Education of the Southern Belle: Higher Education in the Antebellum South* (New York: New York University Press, 1994).

60. Burr, *The Secret Eye,* 118–21, and Painter's introduction, 3–5. Also see Clinton, *The Plantation Mistress,* 59–86.

61. Myers, *The Children of Pride,* 563–69, 573–74; and Burr, *The Secret Eye,* 145–46. Also see Stowe, *Intimacy and Power,* 96–105.

62. Myers, *The Children of Pride,* 326–27; Burr, *The Secret Eye,* 135–36; and Felton, *Country Life,* 72.

63. Boggs, *The Alexander Letters,* 164–65; and Burr, *The Secret Eye,* 122.

64. Felton, *Country Life,* 53; and Burr, *The Secret Eye,* 141–42. Also see Clinton, *The Plantation Mistress,* 139–63.

65. Burr, *The Secret Eye,* 158–59; and Burge, *The Diary,* 15, 28.

66. Boggs, *The Alexander Letters,* 38–43, 190–91; Felton, *Country Life,* 49; Myers, *The Children of Pride,* 69–71, 98–103, 265–66; and Burge, *The Diary,* 54, 60–61. Also see Sally G. McMillen, "Antebellum Southern Fathers and the Health Care of Children," *Journal of Southern History* 60 (1994), 513–32.

67. Fox-Genovese, *Within the Plantation Household,* 44; Eugene D. Genovese and Elizabeth Fox-Genovese, "The Religious Ideals of Southern Slave Society," *Georgia Historical Quarterly* 70 (1986), 1–16; Friedman, *The Enclosed Garden,* xi–xvi, 3–20; and James Oakes, *The Ruling Race: A History of American Slaveholders* (New York: Alfred A. Knopf, 1982), 96–122. Also see Mitchell Snay, *Gospel of Disunion: Religion and Separatism in the Antebellum South* (New York: Cambridge University Press, 1993); Albert J. Raboteau, *Slave Religion: The 'Invisible Institution' in the Antebellum South* (New York: Oxford University Press, 1978); John B. Boles, ed., *Masters and Slaves in the House of the Lord: Race and Religion in the American South, 1740–1870* (Lexington: University Press of Kentucky, 1988); and Frederick A. Bode, "A Common Sphere: White Evangelicals and Gender in Antebellum Georgia," *Georgia Historical Quarterly* 79 (1995), 775–809.

68. Dickson D. Bruce Jr., *And They All Sang Hallelujah: Plain Folk Camp-Meeting Religion, 1800–1845* (Knoxville: University of Tennessee Press, 1974), 4, 36–95.

69. Burke, *Pleasure and Pain,* 92–96. Also see the description of a Methodist camp meeting attended by Frederika Bremer near Charleston, South Carolina, in 1850 in *The Homes of the New World: Impressions of America,* I, translated by Mary Howitt (London: Arthur Hall, Virtue, and Co., 1853), 313–25.

70. Burke, *Pleasure and Pain,* 93.

71. *Ibid.,* 47–50; Burge, *The Diary,* 6; Lines, *To Raise Myself a Little,* 61, 86, 98–101; and Burr, *The Secret Eye,* 126–31.

72. Burr, *The Secret Eye,* 167–69, and Painter's introduction, 66–67; Clinton,

The Plantation Mistress, 87–109; and Fox-Genovese, *Within the Plantation Household,* 334–71.

73. Stowe, *Intimacy and Power,* xv.

74. See John A. Scott's introduction to Frances Anne Kemble, *Journal of a Residence on a Georgian Plantation in 1838–1839* (1863; reprint, Athens: University of Georgia Press, 1984), ix–lxi; Malcolm Bell Jr., *Major Butler's Legacy: Five Generations of a Slaveholding Family* (Athens: University of Georgia Press, 1987), 106, 255–310, 489–94; J. C. Furnas, *Fanny Kemble: Leading Lady of the Nineteenth-Century Stage* (New York: Dial Press, 1982), 194–228; Margaret Armstrong, *Fanny Kemble: A Passionate Victorian* (New York: Macmillan Company, 1938), 207–52; and Jean E. Friedman's essay on Kemble in Kenneth Coleman and Charles Stephen Gurr, eds., *Dictionary of Georgia Biography,* II (Athens: University of Georgia Press, 1983), 569–71.

75. Scott in Kemble, *Journal,* lviii–lix; and Bell, *Major Butler's Legacy,* 127.

76. Elizabeth Fox-Genovese, *Within the Plantation Household,* 146–91, 290–333; Jacqueline Jones, *Labor of Love, Labor of Sorrow: Black Women, Work and the Family, from Slavery to the Present* (1985; reprint, New York: Vintage Books, 1986), 11–43; and Deborah Gray White, *Ar'n't I a Woman? Female Slaves in the Plantation South* (New York: W. W. Norton and Company, 1985).

77. Kemble, *Journal,* 65–66, 156–57.

78. *Ibid.,* 205–6, 208, 214, 222, 245; the quotation is on 245. Jacqueline Jones argues that concern for the well-being of slave families and children declined throughout the South during the cotton boom years from 1830 to 1860, a period characterized by a decline in slave fertility, increase in miscarriage rates, dissolution of slave families during the massive, forced migration to the Lower South, and greater workloads for women in the fields. See *Labor of Love, Labor of Sorrow,* 15, 19–20.

79. Kemble, *Journal,* 95–96, 132–40, 207, 247, 270; Jones, *Ar'n't I a Woman?,* 91–118, 142–60; and Herbert G. Gutman, *The Black Family in Slavery and Freedom, 1750–1925* (1976; reprint, New York: Vintage Books, 1977).

80. Kemble, *Journal,* 201, 233–34.

81. *Ibid.,* 80, 210, 215–16, 240–41; and White, *Ar'n't I a Woman?,* 79–86.

82. Kemble, *Journal,* 67–70, 74–76, 97–100, 130, 145–46, 194, 275; Stampp, *The Peculiar Institution,* 296–321, 317–18; Julia F. Smith, *Slavery and Rice Culture in Low Country Georgia, 1750–1860* (Knoxville: University of Tennessee Press, 1985), 59–60; and Albert E. Cowdry, *This Land, This South: An Environmental History* (Lexington: University Press of Kentucky, 1983), 25–43.

83. Kemble, *Journal,* 59–60, 92–94, 106–7, 118–19, 261–62, 294; the quotation is on 107; also see Eugene D. Genovese, *Roll, Jordan, Roll: The World the Slaves Made* (New York: Random House, 1974), 161–68.

CHAPTER FOUR: A Harvest of Fire

1. Letter from E. P. Alexander to his sister Clifford dated Washington Territory, 11 November 1860. See Marion Alexander Boggs, ed., *The Alexander Letters, 1787–1900* (1910; reprint, Athens: University of Georgia Press, 1980), 218–20.

2. Charles Henry Smith, *Bill Arp, So Called. A Side Show of the Southern Side of the War* (New York: Metropolitan Record Office, 1866), 19; James C. Austin, *Bill Arp* (New York: Twayne Publishers, 1969), 19; and T. Conn Bryan, *Confederate Georgia* (Athens: University of Georgia Press, 1953), 1–32.

3. Jay B. Hubbell, *The South in American Literature, 1607–1900* (Durham: Duke University Press, 1954), 454; Michelle Cutliff Ticknor, ed., *The Poems of Francis Orray Ticknor* (New York: Neale Publishing Company, 1911); Garland Greever, ed., *Sidney Lanier: Tiger-Lilies and Southern Prose,* volume V in Charles R. Anderson, general editor, *The Centennial Edition of the Works of Sidney Lanier* (Baltimore: Johns Hopkins Press, 1945); and Kittrell J. Warren, *Life and Public Services of an Army Straggler,* edited by Floyd C. Watkins (1865; reprint, Athens: University of Georgia Press, 1961). To be sure, the city of Columbus could lay some claim to Alabama's Augusta Jane Evans and her influential war novel, *Macaria; or, Altars of Sacrifice,* which will be examined later in this chapter.

4. See Elisabeth Muhlenfeld, "The Civil War and Authorship," in Louis D. Rubin Jr., ed., *The History of Southern Literature* (Baton Rouge: Louisiana State University Press, 1985), 178–87; and George C. Rable, *Civil Wars: Women and the Crisis of Southern Nationalism* (Urbana: University of Illinois Press, 1989), 39–49. One should not, however, allow revolutionary rhetoric to detract from the conservative character of the Confederacy's bid for political independence. See James M. McPherson, *Battle Cry of Freedom: The Civil War Era* (New York: Ballantine Books, 1988), 202–75.

5. See Drew Gilpin Faust, *Mothers of Invention: Women of the Slaveholding South in the American Civil War* (1996; reprint, New York: Vintage Books, 1997); and *The Creation of Confederate Nationalism: Ideology and Identity in the Civil War South* (Baton Rouge: Louisiana State University Press, 1988). Also see Catherine Clinton and Nina Silber, eds., *Divided Houses: Gender and the Civil War* (New York: Oxford University Press, 1992); and Helen M. Cooper, Adrienne Anslander, and Susan Merrill Squier, eds., *War, Gender, and Literary Representation* (Chapel Hill: University of North Carolina Press, 1989).

6. Three years later the prospect of defeat and the loss of her family's wealth led her to question the capacity of the southern people for self-government and whether slavery was right. See Virginia Ingraham Burr, *The Secret Eye: The Journal of Ella Gertrude Clanton Thomas, 1848–1889,* with an introduction by Nell Irvin Painter (Chapel Hill: University of North Carolina Press, 1990), 183–86, 237–39; and Faust, *Mothers of Invention,* 9–19.

7. Rev. C. C. Jones to Hon. Charles C. Jones Jr., 27 October 1860 and 15 November 1860. Robert Manson Myers, ed., *The Children of Pride: A True Story of Georgia and the Civil War* (New Haven: Yale University Press, 1972), 625, 628–29.

8. Mrs. Mary Jones to Hon. Charles C. Jones Jr., 3 January 1861; and Mrs. Mary S. Mallard to Mrs. Mary Jones, 25 January 1861. Myers, *The Children of Pride,* 641, 645–46.

9. By early 1863, Jones simply referred to Union troops as "the abolitionists." See Hon. Charles C. Jones Jr. to Rev. C. C. Jones, 28 January 1861; and Col. Charles C. Jones Jr. to Rev. and Mrs. C. C. Jones, 3 March 1863. Myers, *The Children of Pride,* 648, 1034.

10. Lt. Charles C. Jones Jr. to Rev. and Mrs. C. C. Jones, 9 November 1861; and Rev. C. C. Jones to Lt. Charles C. Jones Jr., 24 March 1862. Myers, *The Children of Pride,* 791–93, 865–67.

11. Rev. C. C. Jones to Lt. Charles C. Jones Jr., 28 May 1862. Myers, *The Children of Pride,* 897.

12. Lt. Charles C. Jones Jr. to Rev. C. C. Jones, 27 September 1862; and Rev. John Jones to Mrs. Mary S. Mallard, 1 July 1864. Myers, *The Children of Pride,* 966–68, 1189–90. Barrington Moore labels the Civil War "the last revolutionary offensive on the part of what one may legitimately call urban or bourgeois capitalist democracy." Moore argues that slavery had become an obstacle to the political and social democracy needed to weld the West to the Northeast's market economy and free northern capitalists from their dependence on southern landlords. In the words of Numan V. Bartley, "While Georgians were in revolt, northern Republicans enacted a hard money banking system, a high tariff, and other 'reforms' to promote the interests of bankers, industrialists, and merchants to the North at the expense of the less developed sections to the South and West." See Barrington Moore Jr., *Social Origins of Dictatorship and Democracy: Lord and Peasant in the Making of the Modern World* (Boston: Beacon Press, 1966), 111–55; and Numan V. Bartley, *The Creation of Modern Georgia* (Athens: University of Georgia Press, 1983), 31.

13. James L. Roark, *Masters without Slaves: Southern Planters in the Civil War and Reconstruction* (New York: W. W. Norton and Company, 1977), vii–xii.

14. Rev. C. C. Jones to Lt. Charles C. Jones Jr., 18 February 1862. Myers, *The Children of Pride,* 848–49. For an excellent brief overview of the Confederacy, see Emory M. Thomas, *The Confederate Nation, 1861–1865* (New York: Harper and Row, 1979).

15. Myers, *The Children of Pride,* 674–78, 681–82, 777–78, 806–12, 830–34, 850–51, 878–79, 893–94; Burr, *The Secret Eye,* 191–94, 209–20, 234–35, 239–40; and Cornelia Jones Pond, *Life on a Liberty County Plantation: The Journal of Cornelia Jones Pond,* edited by Josephine Bacon Martin (Darien: Darien *News,* 1974), 90–95.

16. Rable, *Civil Wars,* 106; and Burr, *The Secret Eye,* 193, 203–4.

17. Myers, *The Children of Pride,* 959–1065; Edgeworth Bird to Sallie Bird, 9 July 1863, in John Rozier, ed., *The Granite Farm Letters: The Civil War Correspondence of Edgeworth and Sallie Bird* (Athens: University of Georgia Press, 1988), 119–23; and George W. Peddy to Kate Peddy, 11 November 1863 and 20 January 1864. George P. Cuttino, ed., *Saddle Bag and Spinning Wheel: Being the Civil War Letters of George W. Peddy, M.D. and His Wife Kate Featherston Peddy* (Macon: Mercer University Press, 1981), 189, 198–99.

18. Smith, *Bill Arp, So Called,* 31–34, 52–66, 72–83, 119–22; David C. Parker, "Bill Arp, Joe Brown, and the Confederate War Effort," *Georgia Historical Quarterly* 73 (1989), 79–87; and *Alias Bill Arp: Charles Henry Smith and the South's "Goodly Heritage"* (Athens: University of Georgia Press, 1991), 51–76; Bryan, *Confederate Georgia,* 80–100; and Rable, *Civil Wars,* 75–89.

19. Steven Hahn, *The Roots of Southern Populism: Yeoman Farmers and the Transformation of the Georgia Upcountry, 1850–1890* (New York: Oxford University Press, 1983), 116–33; Bryan, *Confederate Georgia,* 137–55; and Lewis N. Wynne and Guy Porcher Harrison, "'Plain Folk' Coping in the Confederacy: The Garrett-Asbell Letters," *Georgia Historical Quarterly* 72 (1988), 102–18.

20. Rable, *Civil Wars,* 71.

21. Rozier, *The Granite Farm Letters,* 10–16, 32–35, 58, 67–70, 76, 153.

22. Peddy, *Saddle Bag and Spinning Wheel,* 121–22; and Faust, *Mothers of Invention,* 114–23.

23. Peddy, *Saddle Bag and Spinning Wheel,* 11–12, 15, 30–31, 107–9, 128–30, 197, 201.

24. Mary A. H. Gay, *Life in Dixie during the War* (1892; 1897 edition reprint, Atlanta: Darby Printing Company, 1979), 36–51, 94–97, 108–12; Pond, *Life on a Liberty County Plantation,* 97–98; Peddy, *Saddle Bag and Spinning Wheel,* 107–8, 122–24, 137–38, 223–24; Rozier, *The Granite Farm Letters,* 152–55; Spencer Bidwell King Jr., ed., *Ebb Tide: As Seen through the Diary of Josephine Clay Habersham, 1863* (Athens: University of Georgia Press, 1958), 92–94; Rable, *Civil Wars,* 91–144; Elizabeth Fox-Genovese, *Within the Plantation Household: Black and White Women of the Old South* (Chapel Hill: University of North Carolina Press, 1988), 202–10; Bryan, *Confederate Georgia,* 174–200; and Faust, *Mothers of Invention,* 20–29, 92–112.

25. Gay, *Life in Dixie,* 104–7, 113, 170–92.

26. Dolly Lunt Burge, *The Diary of Dolly Lunt Burge,* edited by James I. Robertson Jr. (Athens: University of Georgia Press, 1962), 75.

27. Burge, *The Diary,* 78–79; and Rev. C. C. Jones to Lt. Charles C. Jones, 14 March 1862. Myers, *The Children of Pride,* 858–61.

28. Burge, *The Diary,* 80–81; Myers, *The Children of Pride,* 949–57, 1014–18, 1059–61; and Pond, *Life on a Liberty County Plantation,* 98–101; the quotation is on

98. Also see Mary Elizabeth Massey, *Ersatz in the Confederacy: Shortages and Substitutes on the Southern Homefront* (Columbia: University of South Carolina Press, 1993); and Faust, *Mothers of Invention*, 45–51.

29. Burge, *The Diary*, 90, 98–99; and Rozier, *The Granite Farm Letters*, 153.

30. Myers, *The Children of Pride*, 870, 878–79, 881–83, 909–10, 1040–44, 1067; and Burge, *The Diary*, 84–85.

31. Rozier, *The Granite Farm Letters*, 80–82, 105–6; Burr, *The Secret Eye*, 205; Rebecca Latimer Felton, *Country Life in Georgia in the Days of My Youth* (Atlanta: Index Printing Company, 1919), 88; and King, *Ebb Tide*, 33, 115.

32. T. Conn Bryan, ed., "A Georgia Woman's Civil War Diary: The Journal of Minerva Leah Rowles McClatchey, 1864–65," *Georgia Historical Quarterly* 60 (1967), 197–216; the quotation is on 205.

33. *Ibid.*, 207–8, 211; and Gay, *Life in Dixie*, 271–73.

34. Smith, *Bill Arp, So Called*, 21–23; and Rable, *Civil Wars*, 57, 202–20.

35. Myers, *The Children of Pride*, 844–47; Burr, *The Secret Eye*, 200–220; King, *Ebb Tide*, 24–25, 36–52; Peddy, *Saddle Bag and Spinning Wheel*, 167–68, 201–2, 208–10, 267; Joseph LeConte, *'Ware Sherman: A Journal of Three Months' Personal Experience in the Last Days of the Confederacy* (Berkeley: University of California Press, 1937), 22–23; and Faust, *Mothers of Invention*, 179–84.

36. Augusta Jane Evans, *Macaria; or, Altars of Sacrifice*, edited with an introduction by Drew Gilpin Faust (1864; reprint, Baton Rouge: Louisiana State University Press, 1992), ix–xxvi. Also see Faust, *Mothers of Invention*, 168–78; Elizabeth Moss, *Domestic Novelists in the Old South: Defenders of Southern Culture* (Baton Rouge: Louisiana State University Press, 1992), 28–29, 35–37, 153–94; and Anne Goodwyn Jones, *Tomorrow Is Another Day: The Woman Writer in the South, 1859–1936* (Baton Rouge: Louisiana State University Press, 1981), 51–91.

37. See Faust's introduction to Evans, *Macaria*, xxi.

38. Jay B. Hubbell, *The South in American Literature, 1607–1900* (Durham: Duke University Press, 1954), 610–16.

39. Evans, *Macaria*, 299.

40. *Ibid.*, 300–301.

41. *Ibid.*, 302, 304.

42. *Ibid.*, 307–8.

43. *Ibid.*, 308.

44. *Ibid.*, 328.

45. *Ibid.*, 335.

46. *Ibid.*, 364–65.

47. *Ibid.*, 366–67.

48. *Ibid.*, 367–68.

49. *Ibid.*, 380–81.

50. *Ibid.*, 414.

51. Faust, *Mothers of Invention,* 173–77.

52. Eugene D. Genovese, *Roll, Jordan, Roll: The World the Slaves Made* (New York: Random House, 1974), 97–112; Leon F. Litwack, *Been in the Storm So Long: The Aftermath of Slavery* (New York: Alfred A. Knopf, 1980), 4; Jacqueline Jones, *Labor of Love, Labor of Sorrow: Black Women, Work, and the Family, from Slavery to the Present* (1985; reprint, New York: Vintage Books, 1986), 47–51; Bryan, *Confederate Georgia,* 118–36; and Paul D. Escott, "The Context of Freedom: Georgia's Slaves during the Civil War," *Georgia Historical Quarterly* 58 (1974), 79–104. Drew Gilpin Faust makes the telling point that the domesticity of slavery made the seemingly private world of household relations central to public life in the South. In her words, "The direct exercise of control over slaves was the most fundamental and essential political act in the Old South." See *Mothers of Invention,* 54.

53. Smith, *Bill Arp, So Called,* 24–30; the two letters are reproduced in their original dialect form in Charles Henry Smith, *Bill Arp's Peace Papers* (New York: G. W. Carleton and Company, 1873), 27–34.

54. Clarence L. Mohr, *On the Threshold of Freedom: Masters and Slaves in Civil War Georgia* (Athens: University of Georgia Press, 1986), 68–96; Peddy, *Saddle Bag and Spinning Wheel,* 74–76; and Rozier, *The Granite Farm Letters,* 126–33, 148, 154–55; the quotation is on 133.

55. James M. Clifton, ed., *Life and Labor on Argyle Island: Letters and Documents of a Savannah River Rice Plantation, 1833–1867* (Savannah: Beehive Press, 1978), 319, 341–42.

56. Myers, *The Children of Pride,* 925–26, 928–30, 933–40.

57. *Ibid.,* 940. The letters that detail the Jones family's efforts to remove their slaves inland are on 793–94, 797–99, 805–6, 865–67, 885–89, 959–68, 976–80, 984, 986–87, 994–95, 1015–18, 1064–65. Also see Mohr, *On the Threshold of Freedom,* 210–32.

58. Roark, *Masters without Slaves,* 35–108.

59. Exceptions include the early seizure of the sea islands, sporadic raids along the coast, and a pair of dramatic attacks against the Western and Atlantic Railroad. For more on Sherman's invasion of Georgia, see Joseph Glatthaar, *The March to the Sea and Beyond: Sherman's Troops in the Savannah and Carolinas Campaign* (New York: New York University Press, 1985); John F. Marszalek, *Sherman: A Soldier's Passion for Order* (New York: Random House, 1993), 259–316; and Lee B. Kennett, *Marching through Georgia: The Story of Soldiers and Civilians during Sherman's Campaign* (New York: HarperCollins, 1995). Contemporary accounts of Sherman's invasion from the northern perspective include David P. Conyngham, *Sherman's March through the South, with Sketches and Incidents of the Campaign* (New York: Sheldon and Company, 1865); and Richard Harwell and Phillip Racine, eds., *The Fiery Trail: A Union Officer's Account of Sherman's Last Campaign* (Knoxville: University of Tennessee Press, 1986).

60. Rable, *Civil Wars,* 154–80; and Bryan, *Confederate Georgia,* 156–73.

61. Peddy, *Saddle Bag and Spinning Wheel,* 251–54, 284. For an enlightening discussion of the issue of wartime sexuality and pregnancies, see Faust, *The Mothers of Invention,* 123–29.

62. Bryan, "A Confederate Woman's Civil War Diary," 199; Myers, *The Children of Pride,* 1173–75; and Charles Henry Smith, *Bill Arp's Scrap Book: Humor and Philosophy* (Atlanta: Jas. P. Harrison and Company, 1884), 36–41, 51–56.

63. Bryan, "A Confederate Woman's Civil War Diary," 200–203.

64. *Ibid.,* 208–10. Also see Mills Lane, ed., *Times That Prove People's Principles: Civil War in Georgia, a Documentary History* (Savannah: Beehive Press, 1993), 163–71.

65. Mills Lane, ed., *"War Is Hell!" William T. Sherman's Personal Narrative of His March through Georgia* (Savannah: Beehive Press, 1974), 129, 148.

66. *Ibid.,* 149. Also see Edmund Drago, "How Sherman's March through Georgia Affected the Slaves," *Georgia Historical Quarterly* 57 (1973), 361–75.

67. *"War Is Hell!"* 150–53; Marszalek, *Sherman,* 306; Faust, *Mothers of Invention,* 200; and Glatthaar, *The March to the Sea,* 72–76. The extensive kinship network that linked elite families throughout Georgia and the South assured rapid dissemination of stories of rape and pillage by Sherman's men. Even women who escaped the wrath of the Union army during its march to the sea still felt insecure afterward. See Clifford Hull to Louisa Gilmer, Washington, Georgia, 7 December 1864, in Boggs, *The Alexander Letters,* 281–85. An admittedly fierce Lost Cause partisan, Mary Gay labeled Sherman "the born leader of the most ruthless, Godless band of men ever organized in the name of patriotism." See *Life in Dixie,* 168.

68. Rable, *Civil Wars,* 167; and Rozier, *The Granite Farm Letters,* 189–228.

69. Myers, *The Children of Pride,* 1220–48. Cornelia Jones Pond's postwar memoir, *Life on a Liberty County Plantation,* is also useful, especially 109–19. Also see George A. Rogers and R. Frank Saunders Jr., "The Scourge of Sherman's Men in Liberty County, Georgia," in *Swamp Water and Wiregrass: Historical Sketches of Coastal Georgia* (Macon: Mercer University Press, 1984), 61–72.

70. Myers, *The Children of Pride,* 1226–27.

71. *Ibid.,* 1227–28; and Faust, *Mothers of Invention,* 196–207.

72. Myers, *The Children of Pride,* 1229–41.

73. *Ibid.,* 1242–48.

74. LeConte, *'Ware Sherman,* 14–74; and Lester D. Stephens, *Joseph LeConte: Gentle Prophet of Evolution* (Baton Rouge: Louisiana State University Press, 1982), 74–91.

75. Myers, *The Children of Pride,* 1253–67; Rable, *Civil Wars,* 181–201; Mohr, *On the Threshold of Freedom,* 99–119; Burr, *The Secret Eye,* 220; and Faust, *Mothers of Invention,* 40–45, 244–45.

76. Eliza Frances Andrews, *The War-Time Journal of a Georgia Girl, 1864–1865*

(New York: D. Appleton and Company, 1908), 19–127. Also see the introduction to Spencer B. King Jr.'s edited edition of *The War-Time Journal* (1960; reprint, Atlanta: Cherokee Publishing Company, 1976), vii–xviii; and Charlotte A. Ford, "Eliza Frances Andrews, Practical Botanist, 1840–1931," *Georgia Historical Quarterly* 70 (1986), 63–80.

77. Andrews, *The War-Time Journal of a Georgia Girl,* 32–35.

78. *Ibid.,* 54, 61.

79. *Ibid.,* 83–102.

80. Burge, *The Diary,* 105–6.

81. Gay, *Life in Dixie,* 203, 207–42, 255–63; Bryan, "A Georgia Woman's Civil War Diary," 212; Pond, *Life on a Liberty County Plantation,* 121–24; and Burge, *The Diary,* 107.

82. Burge, *The Diary,* 109–10; Bryan, "A Georgia Woman's Civil War Diary," 212–13; and Andrews, *The War-Time Journal of a Georgia Girl,* 145–55.

83. Litwack, *Been in the Storm So Long,* 167–220; George P. Rawick, ed., *The American Slave: A Composite Autobioigraphy,* volume XII (Westport: Greenwood Publishing Company, 1972), 262; Burr, The *Secret Eye,* 8–9, 236, 238–39, 252–53; Andrews, *The War-Time Journal of a Georgia Girl,* 127; Burge, *The Diary,* 113; and Rable, *Civil Wars,* 221–39. Also see William A. Byrne, "'Uncle Billy' Sherman Comes to Town: The Free Winter of Black Savannah," *Georgia Historical Quarterly* 79 (1995), 91–116.

84. Bryan, "A Georgia Woman's Civil War Diary," 213–14; Myers, *The Children of Pride,* 694–96, 722–29, 855–61, 921–24, 971–73; and Mrs. George J. Kollock to W. W. Kollock, 17 September 1863, in Susan M. Kollock, ed., "Letters of the Kollock and Allied Families, 1826–1884," *Georgia Historical Quarterly* 34 (1950), 313.

85. Gay, *Life in Dixie,* 78–86; King, *Ebb Tide,* 35–36; Myers, *The Children of Pride,* 1141–43, 1267–69; Bryan, "A Georgia Woman's Civil War Diary," 214; and Andrews, *The War-Time Journal of a Georgia Girl,* 172–73.

86. Andrews, *The War-Time Journal of a Georgia Girl,* 67, 171; Smith, *Bill Arp, So Called,* 143; and Burr, *The Secret Eye,* 260–62.

CHAPTER FIVE: Reclaiming the Scorched Earth

1. Sidney Lanier, *Poems of Sidney Lanier,* edited by Mary Day Lanier (1916; reprint, Athens: University of Georgia Press and Middle Georgia Historical Society, 1967), 233. Also see Eric Foner, *Reconstruction: America's Unfinished Revolution, 1863–1877* (New York: Harper and Row, 1988), 11. Several biographers have observed that the poem refers to the wedding of John Basil Lamar's daughter Augusta to the older James Monroe Ogden, but the poem clearly works best as an allegory of the war. As Aubrey Harrison Starke points out, Goodman Death, Grooms-

man Grief, and Bridesmaid Pain are from *Pilgrim's Progress.* See *Sidney Lanier: A Biographical and Critical Study* (Chapel Hill: University of North Carolina Press, 1933), 73.

2. Lanier, *Poems,* 243; and Garland Greever, ed., *Sidney Lanier: Tiger-Lilies and Southern Prose,* volume V in *The Centennial Edition of the Works of Sidney Lanier,* Charles R. Anderson, general editor (Baltimore: Johns Hopkins Press, 1945), xxxvii, 200–203.

3. Greever, *Sidney Lanier: Tiger-Lilies,* 201.

4. *Ibid.,* 201. For more on the theme of miscegenation, see Joel Williamson, *New People: Miscegenation and Mullattoes in the United States* (New York: Free Press, 1980).

5. *Ibid.,* 201–2. For an introduction to the extensive historical literature about the meaning of freedom to former slaves, see Eric Foner, *Nothing But Freedom: Emancipation and Its Legacy* (Baton Rouge: Louisiana State University Press, 1983); and *Reconstruction,* 77–123; Herbert G. Gutman, *The Black Family in Slavery and Freedom, 1750–1925* (1976; reprint, New York: Vintage Books, 1977), 185–229, 363–431; and Jacqueline Jones, *Labor of Love, Labor of Sorrow: Black Women, Work and the Family, from Slavery to the Present* (1985; reprint, New York: Vintage Books, 1986), 52–78.

6. Greever, *Sidney Lanier: Tiger-Lilies,* 202.

7. *Ibid.,* 202–3.

8. Charles Henry Smith, *Bill Arp, So Called. A Side Show of the Southern Side of the War* (New York: Metropolitan Record Office, 1866), 132–38; the quotation comes from *Bill Arp's Scrap Book: Humor and Philosophy* (Atlanta: Jas. P. Harrison and Company, 1884), 57–58. Also see David B. Parker, *Alias Bill Arp: Charles Henry Smith and the South's "Goodly Heritage"* (Athens: University of Georgia Press, 1991), 51–76; and James C. Austin, *Bill Arp* (New York: Twayne Publishers, 1969), 23–26, 54, 97.

9. Smith, *Bill Arp's Scrap Book,* 58–59.

10. Smith, *Bill Arp, So Called,* 144; and Whitelaw Reid, *After the War: A Southern Tour* (Cincinnati: Moore, Wilstach and Baldwin, 1866), iii–iv, 9. Foner's definitive study of Reconstruction is without question the best place to start one's study of the period, but also see Lewis Nicholas Wynne, *The Continuity of Cotton: Planter Politics in Georgia, 1865–1892* (Macon: Mercer University Press, 1986); Charles L. Flynn Jr., *White Land, Black Labor: Caste and Class in Late Nineteenth-Century Georgia* (Baton Rouge: Louisiana State University Press, 1983); Numan V. Bartley, *The Creation of Modern Georgia* (Athens: University of Georgia Press, 1983), 31–77; Alan Conway, *The Reconstruction of Georgia* (Minneapolis: University of Minnesota Press, 1966); and C. Mildred Thompson, *Reconstruction in Georgia* (1915; reprint, Savannah: Beehive Press, 1972).

11. Reid, *After the War,* 131–35.

12. *Ibid.,* 136–37.

13. *Ibid.*, 137–38.

14. *Ibid.*, 143–44.

15. *Ibid.*, 145–46. For more on the role of northern teachers in Georgia during Reconstruction, see Jacqueline Jones, *Soldiers of Light and Love: Northern Teachers and Georgia Blacks, 1865–1873* (1980; reprint, Athens: University of Georgia Press, 1992).

16. Reid, *After the War,* 146–51.

17. *Ibid.*, 151–52; and Robert Manson Myers, ed., *The Children of Pride: A True Story of Georgia and the Civil War* (New Haven: Yale University Press, 1972), 1306–7.

18. Reid, *After the War,* 153–54.

19. *Ibid.*, 355–57. Also see Sidney Andrews, *The South since the War: As Shown by Fourteen Weeks of Travel and Observation in Georgia and the Carolinas* (Boston: Ticknor and Fields, 1866), 338–44; John Richard Dennett, *The South As It Is, 1865–1866,* edited by Henry M. Christman (Athens: University of Georgia Press, 1968), 267–68; and Edward King, *The Great South: A Record of Journeys in Louisiana, Texas, The Indian Territory, Missouri, Arkansas, Mississippi, Alabama, Georgia, Florida, South Carolina, North Carolina, Kentucky, Tennessee, Virginia, and Maryland* (Hartford: American Publishing Company, 1875), 350–57.

20. Reid, *After the War,* 357–60.

21. *Ibid.*, 361–63.

22. My biographical sketch of Dennett is drawn from Christman's introduction to *The South As It Is,* v–xi.

23. Andrews, *The South since the War,* 237–87; and Wynne, *The Continuity of Cotton,* 1–6.

24. Andrews, *The South since the War,* 288–300.

25. *Ibid.*, 301–17, 325–31.

26. *Ibid.*, 354–55, 365–66; and Dennett, *The South As It Is,* 264–65.

27. Dennett, *The South As It Is,* 273–74.

28. Wynne, *The Continuity of Cotton,* 7–28. The term *laborlords* was coined by Gavin Wright in *Old South, New South: Revolutions in the Southern Economy since the Civil War* (New York: Basic Books, 1986), 17–50. Also see Foner, *Reconstruction,* 124–25; Leon F. Litwack, *Been in the Storm So Long: The Aftermath of Slavery* (New York: Alfred A. Knopf, 1980), 379–86; Paul A. Cimbala, "On the Front Line of Freedom: Freedmen's Bureau Officers and Agents in Reconstruction Georgia, 1865–1868," *Georgia Historical Quarterly* 76 (1992), 577–611; and Cimbala, *Under the Guardianship of the Nation: The Freedmen's Bureau and the Reconstruction of Georgia, 1865–1870* (Athens: University of Georgia Press, 1997).

29. Andrews, *The South since the War,* 321–23.

30. Dennett, *The South As It Is,* 268–71.

31. *Ibid.*, 275–77, 280–81.

32. Robert Somers, *The Southern States since the War* (London: Macmillan and Co., 1871), 62–102.

33. See Immanuel Wallerstein, *The Modern World-System: Capitalist Agriculture and the Origins of the European World Economy in the Sixteenth Century* (New York: Academic Press, 1974); *The Modern World-System II: Mercantilism and the Consolidation of the European World-Economy, 1600–1750* (New York: Academic Press, 1980); and *The Modern World-System III: The Second Era of Great Expansion of the Capitalist World-Economy, 1730–1840s* (San Diego: Academic Press, 1989). An insightful application of Wallerstein's model to the American South can be found in Jack Temple Kirby, *Rural Worlds Lost: The American South, 1920–1960* (Baton Rouge: Louisiana State University Press, 1987), 25–50.

34. King, *The Great South*, i.

35. *Ibid.*, 346–48.

36. *Ibid.*, 350–54.

37. *Ibid.*, 358–62; the quotation is on 362.

38. *Ibid.*, 363.

39. *Ibid.*, 364–67; the quotation is on 367.

40. *Ibid.*, 371.

41. *Ibid.*, 373.

42. *Ibid.*, 371–72.

43. *Ibid.*, 372.

44. *Ibid.*, 374; Andrews, *The South since the War*, 318–20, 348–50, 361; Dennett, *The South As It Is*, 278–79; and Nell Irvin Painter's introduction to Virginia Ingraham Burr's *Secret Eye: The Journal of Ella Gertrude Clanton Thomas, 1848–1889* (Chapel Hill: University of North Carolina Press, 1990), 10–11. Also see George C. Rable, *Civil Wars: Women and the Crisis of Southern Nationalism* (Urbana: University of Illinois Press, 1989), 240–64; and Jean E. Friedman, *The Enclosed Garden: Women and Community in the Evangelical South, 1830–1900* (Chapel Hill: University of North Carolina Press 1985), 107–8.

45. See Painter in Burr, *The Secret Eye*, 33, 51–52; Jones, *Labor of Love, Labor of Sorrow*, 52–57; Flynn, *White Land, Black Labor*, 15; C. Vann Woodward, *Origins of the New South, 1877–1913* (1951; reprint, Baton Rouge: Louisiana State University Press, 1971), 209; and Eliza Frances Andrews, *The War-Time Journal of a Georgia Girl, 1864–1865* (New York: D. Appleton and Company, 1908), 198. Also see Mary M. Johnston-Miller, "Heirs to Paternalism: Elite Women and Their Servants in Alabama and Georgia, 1861–1874" (Ph.D. dissertation, Emory University, 1994).

46. Dolly Lunt Burge, *The Diary of Dolly Lunt Burge*, edited by James I. Robertson Jr. (Athens: University of Georgia Press, 1962), 111–13; and Burr, *The Secret Eye*, 264–77. Also see Myers, *The Children of Pride*, 1273–77.

47. Andrews, *The War-Time Journal of a Georgia Girl*, 213, 251, 254, 258–59, 267, 282, 288, 338.

48. *Ibid.*, 234–36, 252, 270–72, 275–77, 286, 292–93, 303; and Myers, *The Children of Pride*, 1281–83.

49. Andrews, *The War-Time Journal of a Georgia Girl,* 254–56, 314–17; the quotation is on 316.

50. *Ibid.,* 373–81.

51. Litwack, *Been in the Storm So Long,* 399–45. The historical literature on the evolution of the sharecropping system in the American South is vast. In addition to the relevant sections of the works cited previously, see Jay R. Mandle, *The Roots of Black Poverty: The Southern Plantation Economy after the Civil War* (Durham: Duke University Press, 1978); and Mandle, *Not Slave, Not Free: The African American Economic Experience since the Civil War* (Durham: Duke University Press, 1992); Jonathan Wiener, *Social Origins of the New South: Alabama, 1860–1885* (Baton Rouge: Louisiana State University Press, 1978); and Wiener, "Class Structure and Economic Development in the American South, 1865–1955," *American Historical Review* 84 (1979), 970–92; Robert P. Brooks, *The Agrarian Revolution in Georgia, 1865–1912* (Madison: University of Wisconsin Press, 1914); and Harold D. Woodman, *New South, New Law: The Legal Foundations of Credit and Labor Relations in the Postbellum Agricultural South* (Baton Rouge: Louisiana State University Press, 1995).

52. Russell Duncan, *Freedom's Shore: Tunis Campbell and the Georgia Freedmen* (Athens: University of Georgia Press, 1986); Thomas F. Armstrong, "From Task Labor to Free Labor: The Transition along Georgia's Rice Coast, 1820–1880," *Georgia Historical Quarterly* 64 (1980), 432–47; Armstrong, "Georgia Lumber Workers, 1880–1917: The Social Implications of Work," *Georgia Historical Quarterly* 67 (1983), 435–50; Mart A. Stewart, *"What Nature Suffers to Groe": Life, Labor, and Landscape on the Georgia Coast, 1680–1920* (Athens: University of Georgia Press, 1996), 193–224; and Mark V. Wetherington, *The New South Comes to Wiregrass Georgia, 1860–1910* (Knoxville: University of Tennessee Press, 1994).

53. See Paul Cimbala, "The Freedmen's Bureau, the Freedmen and Sherman's Grant in Reconstruction Georgia, 1865–1867," *Journal of Southern History* 55 (1989), 597–632; Frances Butler Leigh, *Ten Years on a Georgia Plantation since the War* (1883; reprint, New York: Negro Universities Press, 1969); Malcolm Bell Jr., *Major Butler's Legacy: Five Generations of a Slaveholding Family* (Athens: University of Georgia Press, 1987), 388–474, 493–94; and Jean Friedman's essay on Leigh in Coleman and Gurr, *Dictionary of Georgia Biography,* II, 614–16. Frances Leigh and her sister, Sarah Wister, sold off the bulk of the Butler estate in the first decade of the twentieth century. Sarah Wister's son, the author Owen Wister, sold what remained of the estate in 1923.

54. Leigh, *Ten Years,* 1–24. For a broader treatment of the issue of black mobility in the postbellum era, see William Cohen, *At Freedom's Edge: Black Mobility and the Southern White Quest for Racial Control, 1861–1915* (Baton Rouge: Louisiana State University Press, 1991).

55. Leigh, *Ten Years,* 24–38.

56. *Ibid.,* 48–59.

57. Bartley, *The Creation of Modern Georgia,* 46; and Charles Henry Smith, *Bill*

Arp's Peace Papers (New York: G. W. Carleton and Company, 1873), 148–55. Also see Foner, *Reconstruction,* 425–44; Flynn, *White Land, Black Labor,* 29–56; David M. Chalmers, *Hooded Americanism: The History of the Ku Klux Klan* (1965; reprint, Chicago: Quadrangle Paperbacks, 1968), 2–19; and George C. Rable, *But There Was No Peace: The Role of Violence in the Politics of Reconstruction* (Athens: University of Georgia Press, 1984). For more detailed treatments of Georgia's Republican Party during Reconstruction, see Olive H. Shadgett, *The Republican Party in Georgia: From Reconstruction through 1900* (Athens: University of Georgia Press, 1964); and Elizabeth Studley Nathans, *Losing the Peace: Georgia Republicans and Reconstruction* (Baton Rouge: Louisiana State University Press, 1969).

58. Leigh, *Ten Years,* 66–71.

59. *Ibid.,* 73–77; and Woodward, *Origins,* 180–84.

60. Leigh, *Ten Years,* 76. Also see E. P. Thompson, "Time, Work Discipline and Industrial Capitalism," *Past and Present* 38 (1967), 56–97.

61. Leigh, *Ten Years,* 79.

62. *Ibid.,* 81–97, 112–16, 131–32. Also see Patricia K. Hunt, "Clothing as an Expression of History: The Dress of African-American Women in Georgia, 1880–1910," *Georgia Historical Quarterly* 76 (1992), 459–71.

63. *Ibid.,* 97–112, 132–37. Ella Clanton Thomas was rare among white Georgians in that she appreciated the strong desire among the freedmen for the vote. See Burr, *The Secret Eye,* 293–97. Also see Bartley, *The Creation of Modern Georgia,* 59–69.

64. Smith, *Bill Arp's Peace Papers,* 178–85; the quotation is on 181.

65. *Ibid.,* 183–84. Also see Foner, *Reconstruction,* 170.

66. Mary Lennox, *Ante Bellum. Southern Life As It Was* (Philadelphia: J. B. Lippincott, 1868), v. Born Mary Louise Redd in Greensboro, Georgia, and orphaned at an early age, she married James Carter Cook Jr. of Columbus in 1844 when she was nineteen. See Clason Kyle, "Who Was Mary Lennox?," Columbus *Sunday Ledger-Enquirer Magazine,* 28 July 1968, 10–12.

67. Lennox, *Ante Bellum,* 36.

68. *Ibid.,* 37–38.

69. *Ibid.,* 92–93.

70. *Ibid.,* 48, 60–73, 103–17; the quotation is on 48.

71. *Ibid.,* 59.

72. *Ibid.,* 307–8.

73. *Ibid.,* 320–22.

74. For more on Lanier, see Edwin Mims, *Sidney Lanier* (Boston: Houghton, Mifflin and Company, 1905); Starke, *Sidney Lanier: A Biographical and Critical Study,* 1–70; Lincoln Lorenz, *The Life of Sidney Lanier* (New York: Coward-McMann, 1935); Greever, *Sidney Lanier: Tiger-Lilies,* vii–lx; Charles R. Anderson, ed., *Sidney Lanier: Poems and Poem Outlines,* volume I in *The Centennial Edition of the Works of Sidney Lanier* (Baltimore: Johns Hopkins Press, 1945), xxi–xc; Edd Winfield Parks, *Sidney Lanier: The Man, the Poet, the Critic* (Athens: University of

Georgia Press, 1968); Jack De Bellis, *Sidney Lanier* (New York: Twayne Publishers, 1972); and Wayne Mixon's essay on Lanier in Kenneth Coleman and Charles Stephen Gurr, eds., *Dictionary of Georgia Biography,* II (Athens: University of Georgia Press, 1983), 604–5.

75. See *Tiger-Lilies. A Novel* (New York: Hurd and Houghton, 1867), which is reprinted in Greever, *Sidney Lanier: Tiger-Lilies,* 1–193, as is *John Lockwood's Mill,* 231–46; the quotation is on 231.

76. Greever, *Sidney Lanier: Tiger-Lilies,* 233. Writing from Macon on 16 December 1867 to Milton H. Northrup, a northern friend from his days as a student at Oglethorpe College, Lanier spoke of the poverty and distress in the South: "My Dear Boy, some members of my family, who used to roll in wealth, are, every day, with their own hands, ploughing the little patch of ground which the war has left them, while their wives do the cooking and washing. This, in itself, I confess I do not regret: being now a confirmed lunatic on the dignity of labor andc." See Charles R. Anderson and Aubrey H. Starke, eds., *Sidney Lanier: Letters, 1857–1868,* volume VII in the *Centennial Edition of the Works of Sidney Lanier* (Baltimore: Johns Hopkins Press, 1945), 358–59.

77. Greever, *Sidney Lanier: Tiger-Lilies,* 204–8; and Lanier, *Poems,* 221, 223.

78. Greever, *Sidney Lanier: Tiger-Lilies,* 247–64; the highlighted quote is on 252.

79. *Ibid.,* 252–53.

80. *Ibid.,* 254–55; the quotation is on 254.

81. *Ibid.,* 255–56.

82. Lanier, *Poems,* 180–82. According to De Bellis, "Such 'cracker barrel philosophy' typifies the dialect poems, but the rustic epigram shows that man superintends the enclosed garden and that the state of nature reflects man's nature. Pastoral values have been asserted for the first time in the cause of social amelioration." See *Sidney Lanier,* 57. Also see Lucinda Hardwick MacKethan, *The Dream of Arcady: Place and Time in Southern Literature* (Baton Rouge: Louisiana State University Press, 1980), 18–35.

83. Lanier, *Poems,* 177–79, 183–84. The physician-poet Francis Orray Ticknor also lent his support to the cause of agricultural diversification in 1869 in "King Korn." In the poem, Ticknor observed that "Many a fool is born to rule / A realm that he couldn't feed." He also shared Lanier's belief that a self-sufficient yeomanry was the solution to the labor shortage. In "Land and Labor," Ticknor described the complaint that labor was scarce and land too cheap as an absurdity:

> Your labor too high! *who,* ever, was known
> To utter that cry for a work of his own?
> Too much for a darkey! *How* much for the hint?
> He might be a "gold mine"—might I be the mint?

See Michelle Cutliff Ticknor, ed., *The Poems of Francis Orray Ticknor* (New York: Neale Publishing Company, 1911), 117–20; and Jay B. Hubbell, *The South in American Literature, 1607–1900* (Durham: Duke University Press, 1954), 474–76. In still another dialect poem written in 1870–71 but unpublished until 1945, Lanier defended his region against charges of extralegal terrorism. See "Them Ku Klux" in Anderson, *Sidney Lanier: Poems and Poem Outlines,* 191–94.

84. Anderson, *Lanier: Poems and Poem Outlines,* 25–28.

85. *Ibid.,* 40–42, 340–41.

86. *Ibid.,* 41–42. De Bellis sees the poem as a turning point in the evolution of Lanier's racial thought, arguing that Lanier's first impulse was to destroy blacks even if it meant going against everything in which he believed. Because this went against the grain for Lanier, he began to seek a corrective to the South's mistaken racial assumptions. See *Sidney Lanier,* 60.

87. Lanier, *Poems,* 53–59. In his ledger, Lanier wrote that those who considered it folly to try and help the wretched poor became "tradesmen, bankers, belly-gods, corporation-men, paying open respect to the laws which protect their property and secret disrespect to the laws which protect other men's property. They subscribe to churches because religion is conservative and because church-affinities bring custom." As quoted in Anderson, *Lanier: Poems and Poem Outlines,* 372–73.

88. Lanier, *Poems,* 60–70. Applauding the "entire *absence,* in every thing you write, of *Trade* in any of its forms," Lanier had written to Paul H. Hayne on 17 April 1872, "Trade, Trade, Trade: pah are we not all sick? . . . 'Tis an old spider that has crawled all over our modern life, and covered it with a flimsy web that conceals the Realities." Lanier went on to assert that the commercial spirit had killed chivalry, hatched the Jacquerie in the fourteenth century, spawned John Brown in the nineteenth century, and broken "the saintly heart of Robert Lee." See Charles R. Anderson and Aubrey H. Starke, eds., *Sidney Lanier: Letters, 1869–1873,* volume VIII in the *Centennial Edition of the Works of Sidney Lanier* (Baltimore: Johns Hopkins Press, 1945), 223–24. Writing during the Great Depression, Starke saw the significance of "The Symphony" as protest, not poetry: "With its evidence of Lanier's reaction against gross materialism and too pure transcendentalism, and his attempt to direct the attention of poetry to the practical problems of the world, it is the most succinct evidence we possess of Lanier's concern with the predominant movement of his century, the industrial revolution as social fact and as philosophical ideal." See *Sidney Lanier,* 210. Two years later, Lanier used humor to drive home much the same message in "The Hard Times in Elfland," a long Christmas poem that portrays Santa Claus as being reduced to a thin, sickly, and seedy stranger after being suckered by a slick railroad man. See *Poems,* 159–67.

CHAPTER SIX: Back in Tall Cotton

1. The quotation is from "Mark and Mack, and the Philosophy of the Trusts," *World's Work,* November 1900, as reprinted in Julia Collier Harris, ed., *Joel Chandler*

Harris: Editor and Essayist (Chapel Hill: University of North Carolina Press, 1931), 198. Also see T. J. Jackson Lears, *No Place of Grace: Antimodernism and the Transformation of American Culture, 1880–1920* (New York: Pantheon Books, 1981).

2. See Numan V. Bartley, *The Creation of Modern Georgia* (Athens: University of Georgia Press, 1983), 69.

3. *Ibid.*, 75–102. For more on the transformation of Georgia agriculture and the farmer response in the late nineteenth century, see C. Vann Woodward, *Tom Watson: Agrarian Rebel* (1938; reprint, New York: Oxford University Press, 1975); and Woodward, *Origins of the New South, 1877–1913* (1951; reprint, Baton Rouge: Louisiana State University Press, 1971); Robert C. McMath Jr., *Populist Vanguard: A History of the Southern Farmers' Alliance* (1975; reprint, New York: W. W. Norton and Company, 1977); and McMath, *American Populism: A Social History, 1877–1898* (New York: Hill and Wang, 1993); Lawrence Goodwyn, *Democratic Promise: The Populist Moment in America* (New York: Oxford University Press, 1976); Bruce Palmer, *Man Over Money: The Southern Populist Critique of American Capitalism* (Chapel Hill: University of North Carolina Press, 1980); Barton C. Shaw, *The Wool-Hat Boys: Georgia's Populist Party* (Baton Rouge: Louisiana State University Press, 1984); Steven Hahn, *The Roots of Southern Populism: Yeoman Farmers and the Transformation of the Georgia Upcountry, 1850–1890* (New York: Oxford University Press, 1983); William F. Holmes, ed., *American Populism* (Lexington: D. C. Heath and Company, 1994); Holmes, "Populism: In Search of Context," *Agricultural History* 64 (1990), 26–58; Michael Schwartz, *Radical Protest and Social Structure: The Southern Farmers' Alliance and Cotton Tenancy, 1880–1890* (New York: Academic Press, 1976); John D. Hicks, *The Populist Revolt: A History of the Farmers' Alliance and the People's Party* (Minneapolis: University of Minnesota Press, 1931); Robert P. Brooks, *The Agrarian Revolution in Georgia, 1865–1912* (Madison: University of Wisconsin Press, 1914); Peter Temin, "Patterns of Cotton Agriculture in Post-Bellum Georgia," *Journal of Economic History* 43 (1983), 661–64; and David F. Wieman, "The Economic Emancipation of the Non-Slaveholding Class: Upcountry Farmers in the Georgia Cotton Economy," *Journal of Economic History* 45 (1985), 71–94.

4. In addition to the relevant sections of the works cited in the previous note, see Edward L. Ayers, *The Promise of the New South: Life after Reconstruction* (New York: Oxford University Press, 1992); Dewey W. Grantham, *The South in Modern America: A Region at Odds* (New York: HarperCollins Publishers, 1994); Howard N. Rabinowitz, *Race Relations in the Urban South, 1865–1890* (New York: Oxford University Press, 1978); and Rabinowitz, *The First New South, 1865–1920* (Arlington Heights: Harlan Davidson, 1992); Charles L. Flynn Jr., *White Land, Black Labor: Caste and Class in Late Nineteenth-Century Georgia* (Baton Rouge: Louisiana State University Press, 1983); Lewis Nicholas Wynne, *The Continuity of Cotton: Planter Politics in Georgia, 1865–1892* (Macon: Mercer University Press, 1986); Dwight B.

Billings, *Planters and the Making of a "New South"* (Chapel Hill: University of North Carolina Press, 1979); Jay R. Mandle, *The Roots of Black Poverty: The Southern Plantation Economy after the Civil War* (Durham: Duke University Press, 1978); Barrington Moore Jr., *Social Origins of Dictatorship and Democracy* (Boston: Beacon Press, 1966); Jonathan Wiener, *Social Origins of the New South: Alabama, 1860–1885* (Baton Rouge: Louisiana State University Press, 1978); and Wiener, "Class Structure and Economic Development in the American South, 1865–1955," *American Historical Review* 84 (1979), 970–92; C. Vann Woodward, *The Strange Career of Jim Crow,* third revised edition (New York: Oxford University Press, 1974); Joel Williamson, *The Crucible of Race: Black-White Relations in the American South since Emancipation* (New York: Oxford University Press, 1984); Gerald David Jaynes, *Branches without Roots: Genesis of the Black Working Class in the American South, 1862–1882* (New York: Oxford University Press, 1986); William H. Harris, *The Harder We Run: Black Workers since the Civil War* (New York: Oxford University Press, 1982); and Horace Calvin Wingo, "Race Relations in Georgia, 1872–1908" (Ph.D. dissertation, University of Georgia, 1969).

5. See Thomas M. Norwood, *Plutocracy; or, American White Slavery, a Politico-Social Novel* (New York: American News Company, 1888); and Charles C. Post, *Congressman Swanson* (Chicago: Charles H. Sergel and Company, 1891). Although Charles Henry Smith sometimes addressed the farmer revolt in the Atlanta *Constitution,* he excluded these pieces from his book-length Bill Arp anthologies. See David B. Parker, *Alias Bill Arp: Charles Henry Smith and the South's "Goodly Heritage"* (Athens: University of Georgia Press, 1991). The populist poetry mentioned by Woodward in his biography of Tom Watson remains uncollected. See *Tom Watson,* 256–57. Also see Thomas E. Watson, *The Life and Speeches of Thomas E. Watson* (Thomson, Georgia: Jeffersonian Publishing Company, 1911).

6. Raymond Williams, *Culture and Society, 1780–1950* (1958; reprint, New York: Harper and Row, 1966); and *The Country and the City* (London: Chatto and Windus, 1973). For a discussion of the relevance of Williams's work to the American South, see Michael J. Cassity, "Southern Workers and Social Change: Concepts and Prospects," *Georgia Historical Quarterly* 62 (1978), 200–212.

7. Williams, *The Country and the City,* 82, 165, 297.

8. See "The New South," in Garland Greever, ed., *Sidney Lanier: Tiger-Lilies and Southern Prose,* volume V in *The Centennial Edition of the Works of Sidney Lanier,* Charles R. Anderson, general editor (Baltimore: Johns Hopkins Press, 1945), 334–58. Also see Woodward, *Origins,* 175–76; Jay B. Hubbell, *The South in American Literature, 1607–1900* (Durham: Duke University Press, 1954), 758–77; Wayne Mixon, *Southern Writers and the New South Movement, 1865–1913* (Macon: Mercer University Press, 1980), 1–72; and Lucinda Hardwick MacKethan, *The Dream of Arcady: Place and Time in Southern Literature* (Baton Rouge: Louisiana State University Press, 1980), 18–35.

9. As quoted in Woodward, *Tom Watson,* 87. Also see Mixon, *Southern Writers and the New South Movement,* 13–22; and Hubbell, *The South in American Literature,* 743–57. For more on the dramatic transformation of Atlanta, see James Michael Russell, *Atlanta, 1847–1890: City Building in the Old South and the New* (Baton Rouge; Louisiana State University Press, 1988); Harold E. Davis, *Henry Grady's New South: Atlanta, a Brave and Beautiful City* (Tuscaloosa: University of Alabama Press, 1990); and Don H. Doyle, *New Men, New Cities, New South: Atlanta, Nashville, Charleston, Mobile, 1860–1910* (Chapel Hill: University of North Carolina Press, 1990).

10. Bartley, *The Creation of Modern Georgia,* 83–87; Woodward, *Tom Watson,* 113–28; Raymond B. Nixon, *Henry W. Grady: Spokesman of the New South* (New York: Alfred Knopf, 1943); Ferald J. Bryan, *Henry Grady or Tom Watson?: The Rhetorical Struggle for the New South, 1880–1890* (Macon: Mercer University Press, 1994); Doris Lanier, "Henry W. Grady and the Piedmont Chautauqua [1888–91]," *Southern Studies* 23 (1984), 216–42; and Harold E. Davis, "Henry Grady, the Atlanta Constitution, and the Politics of Farming in the 1880s," *Georgia Historical Quarterly* 71 (1987), 571–600. Also see Henry Grady, *The New South: Writings and Speeches of Henry Grady,* with an introduction by Mills Lane (Savannah: Beehive Press, 1971).

11. Eliza Frances Andrews, *A Family Secret* (Philadelphia: J. B. Lippincott, 1876); and Charlotte A. Ford, "Eliza Frances Andrews, Practical Botanist, 1840–1931," *Georgia Historical Quarterly* 70 (1986), 63–80.

12. Andrews, *A Family Secret,* 29–30.

13. *Ibid.,* 17.

14. *Ibid.,* 71–72.

15. Eliza Frances Andrews, *A Mere Adventurer* (Philadelphia: J. B. Lippincott, 1879); and *Prince Hal; or, The Romance of a Rich Young Man* (Philadelphia: J. B. Lippincott, 1882), 25–26.

16. Mary Ross Banks, *Bright Days in the Old Plantation Time* (Boston: Lee and Shepard Publishers, 1882), 1–2, 114–32; and Montgomery M. Folsom, *Scraps of Song and Southern Scenes: A Collection of Humorous and Pathetic Poems and Descriptive Sketches of Plantation Life in the Backwoods of Georgia* (Atlanta: Charles P. Byrd, 1889).

17. Richard Malcolm Johnston, *Autobiography of Col. Richard Malcolm Johnston* (Washington: Neale Company, 1900); and Bert Hitchcock, *Richard Malcolm Johnston* (Boston: Twayne Publishers, 1978). Also see Hitchcock's essay in Kenneth Coleman and Charles Stephen Gurr, eds., *Dictionary of Georgia Biography,* I (Athens: University of Georgia Press, 1983), 541–43; Clement Eaton, *The Waning of the Old South Civilization, 1860–1880's* (Athens: University of Georgia Press, 1968), 13–18; Hubbell, *The South in American Literature,* 777–82; Corliss H. Edwards Jr., "Richard Malcolm Johnston's View of the Old-Field School," *Georgia Historical Quarterly* 50 (1966), 382–90; and Robert L. Phillips Jr., "The Novel and the Ro-

mance in Middle Georgia Humor and Local Color: A Study of Narrative Method in the Works of Augustus Baldwin Longstreet, William Tappan Thompson, Richard Malcolm Johnston, and Joel Chandler Harris" (Ph.D. dissertation, University of North Carolina, 1971), 226–312.

18. L. Moody Simms Jr., "Richard Malcolm Johnston on Rural Life in Middle Georgia," *Georgia Historical Quarterly* 58 (1974), 181–92; and Johnston, *Autobiography,* 81. Phillips observes that "while Johnston believed that antebellum Middle Georgia society was almost perfect democracy and while middle class farmers were his favorite people, his narrator came from the upper level of society." See "The Novel and the Romance in Middle Georgia Humor and Local Color," 252. It also seems likely that Sidney Lanier, his literary mentor in Baltimore, communicated to Johnston his view of the yeomanry as a source of moral redemption in the South.

19. Richard Malcolm Johnston, *Dukesborough Tales* (Baltimore: Turnbull Brothers, 1871). The story "The Goosepond School" first appeared in 1857 as "Five Chapters of a History" in W. T. Porter's *Spirit of the Times* and was reprinted in *Georgia Sketches* in 1864. The 1883 edition of *Dukesborough Tales* contained all of his previous stories. All of the editions of *Dukesborough Tales* were different. See Phillips, "The Novel and the Romance in Middle Georgia Humor," 229–30.

20. Richard Malcolm Johnston, *Old Mark Langston: A Tale of Duke's Creek* (New York: Harper and Brothers, 1883); and *Mr. Absalom Billingslea and Other Georgia Folk* (1887; reprint, New York: Books for Libraries Press, 1970).

21. Johnston, *Mr. Absalom Billingslea,* 413.

22. As quoted from Simms, "Richard Malcolm Johnston on Rural Life in Middle Georgia," 190.

23. Richard Malcolm Johnston, *Ogeechee Cross-Firings* (New York: Harper and Brother, 1889); and *The Primes and Their Neighbors: Ten Tales of Middle Georgia* (New York: D. Appleton and Company, 1891), 136–60.

24. Richard Malcolm Johnston, *Widow Guthrie* (New York: D. Appleton and Company, 1893). Johnston's other works include *Mr. Billy Downs and His Likes* (New York: Charles L. Webster, 1892); *Mr. Fortner's Marital Claims* (New York: D. Appleton, 1892); *Little-Ike Templin and Other Stories* (1884; reprint, Freeport, New York: Books for Libraries Press, 1972); *Old Times in Middle Georgia* (New York: Macmillan Company, 1897); and *Pearce Amerson's Will* (Chicago: Way and Williams, 1898).

25. Johnston, *Widow Guthrie,* 1, 215.

26. *Ibid.,* 216–17.

27. *Ibid.,* 217–18.

28. James C. Austin, *Bill Arp* (New York: Twayne Publishers, 1969), 27–78; Margaret Gillis Figh, "Life in Nineteenth-Century Georgia As Reflected in Bill Arp's Works," *Georgia Historical Quarterly* 35 (1951), 16–22; and Parker, *Alias Bill Arp,* xviii–xix, 31–47.

29. Parker, *Alias Bill Arp,* 96–111, 131–47.

30. *Ibid.,* 112–30. Also see David B. Parker, "Bill Arp and Blacks: The Forgotten Letters," *Georgia Historical Quarterly* 67 (1983), 336–49; and Williamson, *The Crucible of Race.*

31. Charles Henry Smith, *Bill Arp's Scrap Book; Humor and Philosophy* (Atlanta: Jas. P. Harrison and Company, 1884), 72–83.

32. *Ibid.,* 81–86.

33. *Ibid.,* 112–17, 121–25.

34. *Ibid.,* 130–34.

35. *Ibid.,* 140–46.

36. *Ibid.,* 152–56.

37. *Ibid.,* 217–20, 312–14.

38. Charles Henry Smith, *The Farm and Fireside: Sketches of Domestic Life in War and Peace* (Atlanta: Constitution Publishing Company, 1892); and Smith, *Bill Arp from the Uncivil War to Date* (Atlanta: Hudgins Publishing Company, 1903).

39. Hugh T. Keenan, ed., *Dearest Chums and Partners, Joel Chandler Harris's Letters to His Children: A Domestic Biography* (Athens: University of Georgia Press, 1993), xvii–xxxii; R. Bruce Bickley Jr., ed., *Critical Essays on Joel Chandler Harris* (Boston: G. K. Hall and Company, 1981); and Bickley, *Joel Chandler Harris* (1978; reprint, Athens: University of Georgia Press, 1987); Paul M. Cousins, *Joel Chandler Harris, a Biography* (Baton Rouge: Louisiana State University Press, 1968); Alvin F. Harlow, *Joel Chandler Harris: Plantation Storyteller* (New York: Julian Messner, 1941); Julia Collier Harris, *The Life and Times of Joel Chandler Harris* (Boston: Houghton Mifflin Company, 1918); Robert Lemuel Wiggins, *The Life of Joel Chandler Harris: From Obscurity in Boyhood to Fame in Early Manhood* (Nashville: Publishing House Methodist Episcopal Church, South, 1918); and Harry Aubrey Toulmin Jr., *Social Historians* (Boston: Gorham Press, 1911), 133–64. Also see Hubbell, *The South in American Literature,* 782–95; George M. Frederickson, *The Black Image in the White Mind: The Debate on Afro-American Character and Destiny, 1817–1914* (New York: Harper and Row, 1971), 198–227; MacKethan, *The Dream of Arcady,* 61–85; Phillips, "The Novel and the Romance in Middle Georgia Humor," 313–459; Wayne Mixon, "Joel Chandler Harris, the Yeoman Tradition, and the New South Movement," *Georgia Historical Quarterly* 61 (1977), 308–17; and Mixon, *Southern Writers and the New South Movement,* 73–84.

40. Stella Brewer Brookes, *Joel Chandler Harris: Folklorist* (Athens: University of Georgia Press, 1950); Florence E. Baer, *Sources and Analogues of the Uncle Remus Tales* (Helsinki: Suomalainen Tiedeakatemia Academia Scientiarum Finnica, 1980); John A. Burrison, *"The Golden Arm": The Folk Tale and Its Literary Use by Mark Twain and Joel C. Harris,* Research Paper Number 19 (Atlanta: Georgia State College, 1968); and Catherine Starke, *Black Portraiture in American Fiction: Stock Characters, Archetypes, and Individuals* (New York: Basic Books, 1971).

41. See Harris, *Joel Chandler Harris: Editor and Essayist,* 89–92.

42. Hereinafter unless otherwise noted, citations relative to the Uncle Remus folktales refer to Joel Chandler Harris, *The Complete Tales of Uncle Remus,* compiled by Richard Chase (Boston: Houghton Mifflin Company, 1955), whereas references to related sketches are drawn from contemporary editions of his work.

43. Joel Chandler Harris, *Uncle Remus: His Songs and His Sayings* (1880; reprint, New York: D. Appleton and Company, 1893), 202–4, 208–9, 222–23.

44. Like Henry Grady, Harris considered sectional reconciliation necessary because the South needed northern help for economic development. In light of his new audience of northern readers, Harris modified a sketch entitled "Uncle Remus as a Rebel" that had appeared earlier in the Atlanta *Constitution* in October 1877. Retitled "A Story of the War," the sketch is set in Putnam County during Sherman's march to the sea. In the original version, Remus kills a Yankee sharpshooter to save his master's life, whereas in the new version the man only loses an arm. After being nursed back to health, the Yankee marries the planter's daughter, symbolically rejoining the North and South in wedlock. Thus resurrected from the dead, "Mars John" becomes the little boy's father in the Remus stories. Even after Harris became disillusioned with the New South movement in the 1890s, he continued to champion sectional reconciliation. See Harris, *The Complete Tales,* xxvi–xxvii; and *Uncle Remus: His Songs and His Sayings,* 175–85. For insightful discussions of the issue of sectional reunion, see John C. Inscoe, "The Confederate Homefront Sanitized: Joel Chandler Harris' *On the Plantation* and Sectional Reconciliation," *Georgia Historical Quarterly* 76 (1992), 652–74; Nina Silber, *The Romance of Reunion: Northerners and the South, 1865–1900* (Chapel Hill: University of North Carolina Press, 1993); and Joyce Appleby, "Reconciliation and the Northern Novelist, 1865–1880," *Civil War History* 10 (1964), 117–29. Also see Paul Buck's older but still useful study, *The Road to Reunion, 1865–1900* (Boston: Little, Brown, 1937).

45. Harris used the traditional literary device of introductory and concluding frames to establish narrative distance between the authorial voice evident in the dialogue between Uncle Remus and the little boy and the African American folktales that he incorporated into his stories. Harris, *The Complete Tales,* 9–12.

46. *Ibid.,* 57.

47. *Ibid.,* 69–71. Also see Lawrence W. Levine, *Black Culture and Black Consciousness: Afro-American Folk Thought from Slavery to Freedom* (New York: Oxford University Press, 1977), 81–135.

48. Harris, *The Complete Tales,* 87–90.

49. *Ibid.,* 130–33.

50. *Ibid.,* 402–7. Also see Harris, *On the Plantation,* 104–21.

51. In predominantly white yeoman districts, the rituals of celebration reinforced patriarchal arrangements within kinship networks and reinforced community cohesion by providing work and food for less fortunate neighbors. See Gavin

Wright, *Old South, New South: Revolutions in the Southern Economy since the Civil War* (New York: Basic Books, 1986), 91; Roger D. Abrahams, *Singing the Master: The Emergence of African-American Culture in the Plantation South* (New York: Pantheon, 1992); and Floyd C. Watkins and Charles Hubert Watkins, *Yesterday in the Hills* (Athens: University of Georgia Press, 1982). In the title sketch of *Mingo, and Other Sketches in Black and White* a faithful old black man and an old yeoman woman join forces to provide a better future for her granddaughter, the orphan of a tragic union between parents from different social classes. The two old-timers put aside their racial differences to restore the child to her proper social station. In "Blue Dave," a runaway slave finds redemption when he rescues the son of a Putnam County plantation mistress, whereas "A Piece of Land" details the much-deserved downfall of a rich planter whose greed for land had driven him into a life of crime. In "A Bold Deserter," a story in an 1898 collection entitled *Tales of the Home Folks in Peace and War,* a simple yeoman deserter becomes a war hero, rises to the rank of colonel, and marries a rich planter's daughter, whereas in "The Baby's Christmas" a faithful black mammy arranges the reunion of a class-divided old planter family in a vulgar mansion on Peachtree Street "in the city whose name has come to be identified with all that is progressive in the South." Viewed together these stories communicate Harris's ongoing reverence for traditional hierarchical social relations. See Joel Chandler Harris, *Mingo, and Other Sketches in Black and White* (1884; reprint, New York: McKinlay, Stone and Mackenzie, 1912); 3–35, 171–234, 237–73; and *Tales of the Home Folks in Peace and War* (New York: McKinlay, Stone and Mackenzie, 1898), 184–214, 377–416.

52. Joel Chandler Harris, *Free Joe and Other Georgia Sketches* (New York: Charles Scribner's Sons, 1887), 1–20. Writing to Harris from the executive mansion on 21 October 1901, Theodore Roosevelt stated that he doubted if there was "a more genuinely pathetic tale in all our literature." Roosevelt also appreciated what Harris's writings contributed to the cause of sectional reconciliation: "I know of course the ordinary talk is that an artist should be judged purely by his art; but I am rather a Philistine and like to feel that the art serves a good purpose." See Joel Chandler Harris Collection, Box 9, Folder 9, Special Collections, Robert W. Woodruff Library, Emory University.

53. Harris, *Free Joe and Other Georgia Sketches,* 72–98. Like Hillsborough, Rockville is modeled on the town of Eatonton where Harris spent his childhood.

54. *Ibid.,* 92.

55. *Ibid.,* 98. *Free Joe and Other Georgian Sketches* also contains two other stories that communicate the theme of sectional reunion. In "Little Compton" (21–71), two friends from Hillsborough, a rich planter's son and a Yankee storekeeper, choose different sides when the Civil War begins, only to meet again at the height of Pickett's Charge at Gettysburg, where both lose an arm. Returning together to Hillsborough, the storekeeper saves the town and his friend's life from Sherman's

army, the New South message being that southern planters should restore their antebellum friendship with northern businessmen. In "Azalia" (138–236), the daughter of a deceased Boston abolitionist comes to Georgia for her health in 1873 and marries a planter who had been a general in the Confederate army.

56. *Ibid.*, 99–137.

57. Joel Chandler Harris, "The Women of the South," in *Southern Historical Society Papers,* XVIII (Richmond: Virginia Historical Society, 1890), 277–81; the quotation is on 277.

58. *Ibid.*, 279. Perhaps reflecting his own humble origins and New South ideological bent, Harris's devotion to the plantation mistress did not transfer completely to the antebellum plantation system, but it came close. As he wrote on the next page: "I know of no more beautiful or romantic civilization than that which blossomed under the plantation system, and yet, in the natural order of things, it would have inevitably have run to caste distinctions. It had social ideals that were impracticable, and it had literary ideals that were foolish; nevertheless, after everything had been said, caste distinctions under the plantation system would have been less distasteful than those which are now in process of organization in some parts of the country."

59. *Ibid.*, 280–81.

60. *Ibid.*, 281.

61. Joel Chandler Harris, *Daddy Jake the Runaway and Short Stories Told after Dark* (1889; reprint, New York: Century Company, 1907); and Harris, *Balaam and His Master, and Other Sketches and Stories* (1891; reprint, New York: McKinlay, Stone and Mackenzie, 1919), 45–112, 7–44, 113–48. In Acts 5:1–11, a man who holds back part of his gift to the church is rebuked by Peter and dies. Thereafter understood as synonymous with liar, the name conveys the belief common among southern whites in the late nineteenth century that African Americans were untrustworthy. Yet in Acts 9:10–22, it is a Christian named Ananias who restores Paul's sight during his conversion, which is the meaning suggested by Harris when a former master finally comes to see Ananias as a good and faithful servant even in freedom.

62. Harris, *Balaam and His Master,* 192–293.

63. *Ibid.*, 222.

64. See Post, *Congressman Swanson,* 29. Also see William F. Holmes, "The Southern Farmers' Alliance: The Georgia Experience," *Georgia Historical Quarterly* 72 (1988), 627–53.

65. See the essay on Post by William F. Holmes in Coleman and Gurr, *Dictionary of Georgia Biography,* II, 806–7.

66. Post, *Congressman Swanson,* 316–25.

67. *Ibid.*, 322–23.

68. *Ibid.*, 331.

69. *Ibid.*, 332–34. Also see William F. Holmes, "The Southern Farmers' Alliance and the Jute Cartel," *Journal of Southern History* 60 (1994), 59–80.

70. Post, *Congressman Swanson*, 334–36.

71. Wayne Mixon, "The Ultimate Irrelevance of Race: Joel Chandler Harris and Uncle Remus in Their Time," *Journal of Southern History* 56 (1990), 457–80; and Joel Chandler Harris, *On the Plantation: A Story of a Georgia Boy's Adventures during the War* (1892; reprint, Athens: University of Georgia Press, 1980).

72. Joel Chandler Harris, *Uncle Remus and His Friends: Old Plantation Stories, Songs and Ballads with Sketches of Negro Character* (Boston: Houghton Mifflin Company, 1892); and *The Complete Remus*, 494–96, 512.

73. Harris, *Uncle Remus and His Friends*, 238–42.

74. *Ibid.*, 219–24, 262–70, 292–300, 315–45. For more on convict labor, see Alex Lichtenstein, *Twice the Work of Free Labor: The Political Economy of Convict Labor in the New South* (New York: Verso, 1996); Elizabeth A. Taylor, "The Origin and Development of the Convict Lease System in Georgia," *Georgia Historical Quarterly* 26 (1942), 113–28; and Taylor, "The Abolition of the Convict Lease System in Georgia," *Georgia Historical Quarterly* 26 (1942), 273–87. Bridges Smith, a journalist with whom Harris had worked years earlier in Macon, returned repeatedly to the theme of convict labor in a series of "darky" humor sketches he published in the Macon *Telegraph* that reflected his experiences with the magistrate's court during his tenure as mayor of Macon from 1899 to 1907. He later published his collected sketches as *100 Stories in Black: A Collection of Bright, Breezy, Humorous Stories of the Colored Race As Seen in the Sunny South* (New York: J. S. Ogilvie Publishing Company, 1910).

75. Otis B. Wheeler, *The Literary Career of Maurice Thompson* (Baton Rouge: Louisiana State University Press, 1965), 3–37.

76. *Ibid.*, 98–103.

77. In another story entitled "Ben and Judas," which is an allegory about the Civil War and Reconstruction, a master and slave united since birth briefly reverse roles in the watermelon patch sixty years later before resuming their accustomed positions across the color line. Maurice Thompson, *Stories of the Cherokee Hills* (Boston: Houghton, Mifflin and Company, 1898), 34–77, 98–103.

78. *Ibid.*, 216–55. Also see Gerald H. Gaither, *Blacks and the Populist Revolt: Ballots and Bigotry in the "New South"* (Tuscaloosa: University of Alabama Press, 1977).

79. Louis Beauregard Pendleton, *The Sons of Ham: A Tale of the New South* (Boston: Roberts Brothers, 1895). Published biographical information on Pendleton is scarce. See Lucien Lamar Knight, *Biographical Dictionary of Southern Authors* (1929; reprint, Detroit: Gale Research Company, 1978), 338; and Bertha Sheppard Hart, *Introduction to Georgia Writers* (Macon: J. W. Burke Company, 1929), 140,

309. Pendleton's other works include *King Tom and the Runaways: The Story of What Befell Two Boys in a Georgia Swamp* (New York: D. Appleton and Company, 1890); *In the Okefenokee: A Story of War Time and the Great Georgia Swamp* (Boston: Roberts Brothers, 1895); *In the Wire-Grass* (New York: D. Appleton and Company, 1889); *Captain Ted: A Boy's Adventures among Hiding Slackers in the Great Georgia Swamp* (New York: D. Appleton and Company, 1918); and *Echo of Drums* (New York: Sovereign House, 1938).

80. Pendleton, *The Sons of Ham,* 12–14.

81. *Ibid.,* 17–18.

82. *Ibid.,* 43–49.

83. *Ibid.,* 64–66.

84. *Ibid.,* 67–71.

85. *Ibid.,* 71–74.

86. *Ibid.,* 80–94. For more on the social implications of the servant problem in the urban South, see Tera W. Hunter, "Domination and Resistance: The Politics of Wage Household Labor in New South Atlanta," *Labor History* 34 (1993), 205–20; and Hunter, *To 'Joy My Freedom: Southern Black Women's Lives and Labors after the Civil War* (Cambridge: Harvard University Press, 1997).

87. Pendleton, *The Sons of Ham,* 95–97.

88. *Ibid.,* 98–106.

89. *Ibid.,* 146–48, 173–91. Ironically, black nationalists subverted the idea of repatriation to Africa to their own purposes. See Edwin S. Redkey, *Black Exodus: Black Nationalist and Back-to-Africa Movements, 1890–1910* (New Haven: Yale University Press, 1969).

90. Pendleton, *The Sons of Ham,* 192–207, 270–96, 326–28. For related discussions of racist violence in postbellum Georgia, see W. Fitzhugh Brundage, "The Varn Mill Riot of 1891: Lynchings, Attempted Lynchings, and Justice in Ware County, Georgia," *Georgia Historical Quarterly* 77 (1994), 257–80; and *Lynching in the New South: Georgia and Virginia, 1880–1930* (Champaign: University of Illinois Press, 1993), 103–39.

91. Woodward, *The Strange Career of Jim Crow,* 82.

92. Eugenia Jones Bacon, *Lyddy: A Tale of the Old South* (New York: Continental Publishing Co., 1898), 9–11, 285–86; and Knight, *Biographical Dictionary of Southern Authors,* 16. Also see *Lyddy: A Tale of the Old South,* with an introduction by Lucinda Hardwick MacKethan (Athens: University of Georgia Press, 1998).

93. Joel Chandler Harris, *Gabriel Tolliver: A Story of Reconstruction* (New York: McClure, Phillips and Co., 1902), 114, 189; the quotation is on 403–4. Many of the same themes appear in his 1899 publication *The Chronicles of Aunt Minervy Ann* (1899; reprint, New York: Charles Scribner's Sons, 1907). The seeming triumph of crass materialism led Harris to conclude that the Civil War and Reconstruction had weakened severely the nation's democratic heritage, which is one reason he consid-

ered the assassination of Abraham Lincoln so tragic. Harris believed that no other American leader could have healed the nation of its sectional wounds while guiding the ship of state through the troubled waters of postwar industrialization. As his cracker philosopher Billy Sanders explains in "The Kidnapping of President Lincoln," if the "plain people of the South" had really known Lincoln, the war would not have lasted very long. See Joel Chandler Harris, *On the Wings of Occasions* (New York: Doubleday, Page and Co., 1900), 123–243. Joel Chandler Harris, *Sister Jane: Her Friends and Acquaintances* (Boston: Houghton and Mifflin and Company, 1896), 31.

94. A story entitled "Miss Puss's Parasol" recounts Aunt Minervy Ann's visit to Atlanta to see the State Fair. Having served "Marse Tumlin" since before the Civil War, she refuses wages for her domestic services back home in Middle Georgia. Aunt Minervy Ann relates to the narrator that her husband Hamp had been prospering because of the good cotton market. During Reconstruction, Hamp had dabbled foolishly in local politics until she put him back into his "proper place." Hamp's good fortune also reflected the harmonious relationship between industrialists and cotton growers at the turn of the century. As she explains, "Marse Tumlin say de reason cotton wuth so much mo' is bekaze dey so many new cotton fac'tries been put up. Ef dat de case, I dunner why de white folks don't go ahead an' put up ten a day. Ef dey make cotton wuth mo' it look like ter me dat dey'd have one at eve'y cross-road." See Joel Chandler Harris, *The Making of a Statesman and Other Stories* (New York: McClure, Phillips and Co., 1902), 217–47; the quotation is on 221. For an introduction to the increasingly extensive literature on the postbellum transformation of the South's textile industry, see Patrick J. Hearden, *Independence and Empire: The New South's Cotton Mill Campaign, 1865–1901* (DeKalb: Northern Illinois University Press, 1982); Cathy McHugh, *The Labor System in the Southern Cotton Textile Industry, 1880–1915* (New York: Oxford University Press, 1988); I. A. Newby, *Plain Folk in the New South: Social Change and Cultural Persistence, 1880–1915* (Baton Rouge: Louisiana State University Press, 1989); Allen Tullos, *Habits of Industry: White Culture and the Transformation of the Carolina Piedmont* (Chapel Hill: University of North Carolina Press, 1989); and Douglas Flamming, *Creating the Modern South: Millhands and Managers in Dalton Georgia, 1884–1984* (Chapel Hill: University of North Carolina Press, 1993).

95. The *Saturday Evening Post* articles are reproduced in Julia Collier Harris, *Joel Chandler Harris: Editor and Essayist*, 114–59.

96. Harris, *The Complete Tales*, 579–86.

97. *Ibid.*, 586–604.

98. In an article he wrote for *Uncle Remus's Magazine* just months before his death in 1908, Harris rejected the "state paternalism" of the new generation of reformers in the Progressive movement, arguing that direct parental involvement was the only genuine source of moral order and correct social behavior. See "Mr. Billy

Sanders Discusses Fathers and Sons" in Julia Collier Harris, *Joel Chandler Harris: Editor and Essayist,* 230–37; and Bartley, *The Creation of Modern Georgia,* 105–6.

EPILOGUE: A "November Cotton Flower"

1. Mildred Lewis Rutherford, *Four Addresses* (Birmingham: Mildred Rutherford Historical Circle, 1916), 13–14. Born in Athens, Georgia, in 1851, Rutherford was associated with the Lucy Cobb Institute there for more than forty years. Also see Virginia Clare, *Thunder and Stars: The Life of Mildred Rutherford* (Atlanta: Oglethorpe University Press, 1941); and Bessie Mell Lane's essay in Kenneth Coleman and Charles Stephen Gurr, *Dictionary of Georgia Biography,* II (Athens: University o1 Georgia Press, 1983), 863–64.

2. In a second speech delivered before the UDC in New Orleans in November 1912, Rutherford quoted the following piece of verse to inspire her sisters:

> Though we were overpowered, we were not degraded,
> Southern laurels have never faded;
> All is not lost unto us,
> Only baseness can undo us.
> Kneeling at your country's altar
> Teach your children not to falter
> Till the right shall rule in Dixie.

See Rutherford, *Four Addresses,* 3–15; the quotation is on 11; the poem is on 45. Also see Fred Arthur Bailey, "The Textbooks of the 'Lost Cause': Censorship and the Creation of Southern State Histories," *Georgia Historical Quarterly* 75 (1991), 507–33; and Bailey, "Mildred Lewis Rutherford and the Patrician Cult of the Old South," *Georgia Historical Quarterly* 78 (1994), 509–35. Also see H. E. Gulley, "Women and the Lost Cause: Preserving a Confederate Identity in the American Deep South," *Journal of Historical Geography* 19 (1993), 125–41.

3. See Numan V. Bartley, *The Creation of Modern Georgia* (Athens: University of Georgia Press, 1983), 103–12; the quotation is on 103.

4. See, for example, Laurence Shore, *Southern Capitalists: The Ideological Leadership of an Elite, 1832–1885* (Chapel Hill: University of North Carolina Press, 1986).

5. Wilbur J. Cash, *The Mind of the South* (1941; reprint, New York: Vintage Books, 1969), 112–15; Paul Gaston, *The New South Creed: A Study in Southern Mythmaking* (Baton Rouge: Louisiana State University Press, 1970); Rollin G. Osterweis, *The Myth of the Lost Cause, 1865–1900* (Hamden: Archon Books, 1973); Charles Reagan Wilson, *Baptized in Blood: The Religion of the Lost Cause, 1865–1920* (Athens: University of Georgia Press, 1980); John David Smith, *An Old Creed for the New South: Proslavery Ideology and Historiography, 1865–1918* (Westport: Greenwood Press, 1985); Gaines M. Foster, *Ghosts of the Confederacy: Defeat, the Lost Cause, and*

the Emergence of the New South, 1865–1913 (New York: Oxford University Press, 1987); and Fred Hobson, *Tell about the South: The Southern Rage to Explain* (Baton Rouge: Louisiana State University Press, 1983), 85–128. The phrase "November Cotton Flower" was a poetic term coined by Jean Toomer to dramatize the tragic beauty inherent in the southern black peasantry's pending disappearance under the onslaught of modernity. See *Cane* (1923; reprint, New York: Harper and Row, 1969).

6. Osterweis, *The Myth of the Lost Cause,* ix–xi. Also see Wayne Mixon, *Southern Writers and the New South Movement, 1865–1913* (Macon: Mercer University Press, 1980); C. Vann Woodward, *Origins of the New South, 1877–1913* (1951; reprint, Baton Rouge: Louisiana State University Press, 1971), 164–68; and Lucinda Hardwick MacKethan, *The Dream of Arcady: Place and Time in Southern Literature* (Baton Rouge: Louisiana State University Press, 1980).

7. R. Q. Mallard, *Plantation Life before Emancipation* (Richmond: Whittet and Shepperson, 1892), 36, 54–73. Also see Charles C. Jones Jr., *Negro Myths from the Georgia Coast: Told in the Vernacular* (Boston: Houghton, Mifflin and Company, 1888).

8. Mary A. H. Gay, *Life in Dixie during the War* (1892; 1897 edition reprint, Atlanta: Darby Printing Company, 1979), 15; and Bartley, *The Creation of Modern Georgia,* 105–8.

9. Although there are signs in their writings of the accelerating conflict between Victorian and Modernist values, the three most prolific Georgia writers in the early twentieth century adhered to the literary forms and assumptions of the nineteenth century. The best place to begin one's study of Corra Harris, Will N. Harben, and Harry Stillwell Edwards is with their novels and short stories, but also see Karen Coffing, "Corra Harris and the *Saturday Evening Post:* Southern Domesticity Conveyed to a National Audience, 1900–1930," *Georgia Historical Quarterly* 79 (1995), 367–93; Coffing, "Southern Womanhood Preached to a National Audience: Corra Harris, Author and Novelist" (Ph.D. dissertation, Kent State University, 1992); John E. Talmadge, *Corra Harris, Lady of Purpose* (Athens: University of Georgia Press, 1968); Walter Blackstock, *Corra Harris: An Analytical Study of Her Novels* (Tallahassee: Florida State University, 1955); Doris Lanier, "Harry Stillwell Edwards: Chronicler of the South," *Atlanta History: A Journal of Georgia and the South* 31 (1987), 30–41; Wayne Mixon, "Hillbilly Heretic: Will N. Harben's Challenge to the Old-Time Religion," in Charles Reagan Wilson, ed., *Cultural Perspectives on the American South, volume* V (New York: Gordon and Beach, 1991), 17–29; James K. Murphy, *Will N. Harben* (Boston: Twayne Publishers, 1979); Robert Bush, "Will N. Harben's Northern Georgia Fiction," *Mississippi Quarterly* 20 (1976), 103–17; and Nelle Edwards Smith, *Harry Stillwell Edwards: A Man . . . Not without Honor* (Macon: Eneas Africanus Press, 1969).

10. Walter Francis White, *Flight* (New York: Alfred A. Knopf, 1926); Charles Crowe, "Racial Violence and Social Reform: Origins of the Atlanta Race Riot of

1906," *Journal of Negro History* 53 (1968), 234–56; and Crowe, "Racial Massacre in Atlanta, September 22, 1906," *Journal of Negro History* 54 (1969), 150–73. Also see Gregory Mixon, "'Good Negro-Bad Negro': The Dynamics of Race and Class in Atlanta during the Era of the 1906 Riot," *Georgia Historical Quarterly* 81 (1997), 593–621.

11. For an interpretation that emphasizes change over continuity during the period, see Edward L. Ayers, *The Promise of the New South: Life after Reconstruction* (New York: Oxford University Press, 1992). For more on the transformation of southern agriculture in the twentieth century, see Pete Daniel, *Breaking the Land: The Transformation of Cotton, Tobacco, and Rice Cultures since 1880* (Urbana: University of Illinois Press, 1985); Daniel, *Standing at the Crossroads: Southern Life in the Twentieth Century* (New York: Hill and Wang, 1986); Gavin Wright, *Old South, New South: Revolutions in the Southern Economy since the Civil War* (New York: Basic Books, 1986); Jack Temple Kirby, *Rural Worlds Lost: The American South, 1920–1960* (Baton Rouge: Louisiana State University Press, 1987); and Gilbert C. Fite, *Cotton Fields No More: Southern Agriculture, 1865–1980* (Lexington: University Press of Kentucky, 1984). For an older but still useful introduction to the transformation of agriculture in modern Georgia, see Willard Range, *A Century of Georgia Agriculture, 1850–1950* (Athens: University of Georgia Press, 1954).

BIBLIOGRAPHY

PRIMARY SOURCES

Adams, Nehemiah. *A South-Side View of Slavery; or, Three Months at the South in 1854.* Boston: T. R. Marvin, 1855.

———. *A South-Side View of Slavery.* Savannah: Beehive Press, 1974.

Anderson, Charles R., ed. *Sidney Lanier: Poems and Poem Outlines.* Volume I in *The Centennial Edition of the Works of Sidney Lanier.* Baltimore: Johns Hopkins Press, 1945.

Anderson, Charles R., and Starke, Aubrey H., eds. *Sidney Lanier: Letters, 1857–1868.* Volume VII in the *Centennial Edition of the Works of Sidney Lanier.* Baltimore: Johns Hopkins Press, 1945.

———, eds. *Sidney Lanier: Letters, 1869–1873.* Volume VIII in the *Centennial Edition of the Works of Sidney Lanier.* Baltimore: Johns Hopkins Press, 1945.

Andrews, Eliza Frances. *A Family Secret.* Philadelphia: J. B. Lippincott, 1876.

———. *A Mere Adventurer.* Philadelphia: J. B. Lippincott, 1879.

———. *Prince Hal; or, The Romance of a Rich Young Man.* Philadelphia: J. B. Lippincott, 1882.

———. *The War-Time Journal of a Georgia Girl, 1864–1865.* New York: D. Appleton and Company, 1908.

———. *The War-Time Journal* (1960). Edited with an introduction by Spencer B. King Jr. Reprinted: Atlanta: Cherokee Publishing Company, 1976.

Andrews, Garnett. *Reminiscences of an Old Georgia Lawyer* (1870). Reprinted: Atlanta: Cherokee Publishing Company, 1984.

Andrews, Sidney. *The South since the War: As Shown by Fourteen Weeks of Travel and Observation in Georgia and the Carolinas.* Boston: Ticknor and Fields, 1866.

Armes, William Dallam, ed. *The Autobiography of Joseph LeConte.* New York: D. Appleton and Company, 1903.

Bacon, Eugenia Jones. *Lyddy: A Tale of the Old South.* New York: Continental Publishing Co., 1898.

———. *Lyddy: A Tale of the Old South.* With an introduction by Lucinda Hardwick MacKethan. Athens: University of Georgia Press, 1998.

Banks, Mary Ross. *Bright Days in the Old Plantation Time.* Boston: Lee and Shepard Publishers, 1882.

Bernhard, Karl, duke of Saxe-Weimar-Eisenbach. *Travels through North America, during the Years 1825 and 1826.* 2 vols. Philadelphia: Carey, Lea and Carey, 1828.

Berry, Harrison. *Slavery and Abolitionism, As Viewed by a Georgia Slave.* Atlanta: Franklin Printing House, 1861. Reprinted in Maxwell Whiteman, ed. *Afro-American History Series.* Volume VII. Wilmington: Scholarly Resources, 1972.

Boggs, Marion Alexander, ed. *The Alexander Letters, 1787–1900* (1910). Reprinted: Athens: University of Georgia Press, 1980.

Bremer, Frederika. *The Homes of the New World: Impressions of America.* 3 vols. Translated by Mary Howitt. London: Arthur Hall, Virtue, and Co., 1853.

Brown, John. *Slave Life in Georgia. A Narrative of the Life, Sufferings, and Escape of John Brown, a Fugitive Slave* (1855). Edited with an introduction by F. N. Boney. Reprinted: Savannah: Beehive Press, 1972.

Bryan, T. Conn, ed. "A Georgia Woman's Civil War Diary: The Journal of Minerva Leah Rowles McClatchey, 1864–65." *Georgia Historical Quarterly* 60 (1967), 197–216.

Buckingham, James Silk. *The Slave States of America.* 2 vols. London and Paris: Fisher, Son, and Co., 1842.

Burge, Dolly Lunt. *The Diary of Dolly Lunt Burge.* Edited with an introduction by James I. Robertson Jr. Athens: University of Georgia Press, 1962.

Burke, Emily P. *Pleasure and Pain: Reminiscences of Georgia in the 1840's* (1850). Reprinted: Savannah: Beehive Press, 1978.

Burke, Thomas A., ed. *Polly Peablossom's Wedding, and Other Tales.* Philadelphia: A. Hart, 1851.

Burr, Virginia Ingraham, ed. *The Secret Eye: The Journal of Ella Gertrude Clanton Thomas, 1848–1889.* With an introduction by Nell Irvin Painter. Chapel Hill: University of North Carolina Press, 1990.

Carter, Christine Jacobson, ed. *The Diary of Dolly Lunt Burge.* Athens: University of Georgia Press, 1997.

Cassels, Samuel J. *Providence and Other Poems.* Macon: Griffin and Purse, 1838.

Clifton, James M., ed. *Life and Labor on Argyle Island: Letters and Documents of a Savannah River Rice Plantation, 1833–1867.* Savannah: Beehive Press, 1978.

Cohen, Hennig, and Dillingham, William B., eds. *Humor of the Old Southwest* (1964). Second edition. Reprinted: Athens: University of Georgia Press, 1975.

Conyngham, David P. *Sherman's March through the South, with Sketches and Incidents of the Campaign.* New York: Sheldon and Company, 1865.

Craft, William, and Craft, Ellen. *Running a Thousand Miles for Freedom; or, The Escape of William and Ellen Craft from Slavery* (1860). Reprinted: New York: Arno Press, 1969.

Cuttino, George P., ed. *Saddle Bag and Spinning Wheel: Being the Civil War Letters of George W. Peddy, M.D., and His Wife Kate Featherston Peddy.* Macon: Mercer University Press, 1981.

Dennett, John Richard. *The South As It Is, 1865–1866.* Edited by Henry M. Christman. Athens: University of Georgia Press, 1968.

Evans, Augusta Jane. *Macaria; or, Altars of Sacrifice* (1864). With an introduction by Drew Gilpin Faust. Reprinted: Baton Rouge: Louisiana State University Press, 1992.

Featherstonaugh, George William. *Excursion through the Slave States, from Washington on the Potomac to the Frontier of Mexico; with Sketches of Popular Manners and Geological Notices* (1844). Reprinted: New York: Negro Universities Press, 1968.

Felton, Rebecca Latimer. *Country Life in Georgia in the Days of My Youth.* Atlanta: Index Printing Company, 1919.

Folsom, Montgomery M. *Scraps of Song and Southern Scenes: A Collection of Humorous and Pathetic Poems and Descriptive Sketches of Plantation Life in the Backwoods of Georgia.* Atlanta: Charles P. Byrd, 1889.

Gay, Mary A. H. *Life in Dixie during the War* (1892). 1897 edition reprinted: Atlanta: Darby Printing Company, 1979.

Goulding, Francis Robert. *The Woodruff Stories* (1870). Reprinted: Philadelphia: Claxton, Remsen and Haffelfinger, 1880.

Grady, Henry. *The New South: Writings and Speeches of Henry Grady.* With an introduction by Mills Lane. Savannah: Beehive Press, 1971.

Greever, Garland, ed. *Sidney Lanier: Tiger-Lilies and Southern Prose.* Volume V in Charles R. Anderson, general editor. *The Centennial Edition of the Works of Sidney Lanier.* Baltimore: Johns Hopkins Press, 1945.

Hall, Basil. *Travels in North America in the Years 1827 and 1828.* 2 vols. Philadelphia: Carey, Lea, and Carey, 1829.

———. *Forty Etchings, from Sketches Made with the Camera Lucida in North America, in 1827 and 1828.* Edinburgh: Cadell and Co., 1829.

Harris, Joel Chandler. *Uncle Remus: His Songs and His Sayings* (1880). Reprinted: New York: D. Appleton and Company, 1893.

———. *Mingo, and Other Sketches in Black and White* (1884). Reprinted: New York: McKinlay, Stone, and Mackenzie, 1912.

———. *Free Joe and Other Georgia Sketches.* New York: Charles Scribner's Sons, 1887.

———. *Daddy Jake the Runaway and Short Stories Told after Dark* (1889). Reprinted: New York: Century Company, 1907.

———. "The Women of the South." In *Southern Historical Society Papers.* Volume XVIII. Richmond: Virginia Historical Society, 1890.

———. *Balaam and His Master, and Other Sketches and Stories* (1891). Reprinted: New York: McKinlay, Stone, and Mackenzie, 1919.

———. *On the Plantation: A Story of a Georgia Boy's Adventures during the War* (1892). Reprinted: Athens: University of Georgia Press, 1980.

———. *Uncle Remus and His Friends: Old Plantation Stories, Songs and Ballads with Sketches of Negro Character.* Boston: Houghton Mifflin Company, 1892.

———. *Sister Jane: Her Friends and Acquaintances.* Boston: Houghton and Mifflin and Company, 1896.

———. *Tales of the Home Folks in Peace and War.* New York: McKinlay, Stone and Mackenzie, 1898.

———. *The Chronicles of Aunt Minervy Ann* (1899). Reprinted: New York: Charles Scribner's Sons, 1907.

———. *On the Wings of Occasions.* New York: Doubleday, Page and Co., 1900.

———. *Gabriel Tolliver: A Story of Reconstruction.* New York: McClure, Phillips and Co., 1902.

———. *The Making of a Statesman and Other Stories.* New York: McClure, Phillips and Co., 1902.

———. *The Complete Tales of Uncle Remus.* Compiled by Richard Chase. Boston: Houghton Mifflin Company, 1955.

Harris, Julia Collier. *The Life and Times of Joel Chandler Harris.* Boston: Houghton Mifflin Company, 1918.

———, ed. *Joel Chandler Harris: Editor and Essayist.* Chapel Hill: University of North Carolina Press, 1931.

Harwell, Richard, and Racine, Phillip, eds. *The Fiery Trail: A Union Officer's Account of Sherman's Last Campaign.* Knoxville: University of Tennessee Press, 1986.

Hentz, Caroline Lee. *The Planter's Northern Bride* (1854). With an introduction by Rhoda Coleman Ellison. Reprinted: Chapel Hill: University of North Carolina Press, 1970.

Hodgson, Adam. *Remarks during a Journey through North America in the Years 1819, 1820, and 1821, in a Series of Letters.* New York: Samuel Whiting, 1823.

Johnston, Richard Malcolm. *Dukesborough Tales.* Baltimore: Turnbull Brothers, 1871.

———. *Old Mark Langston: A Tale of Duke's Creek.* New York: Harper and Brothers, 1883.

———. *Little-Ike Templin and Other Stories* (1884). Reprinted: Freeport, New York: Books for Libraries Press, 1972.

———. *Mr. Absalom Billingslea and Other Georgia Folk* (1887). Reprinted: New York: Books for Libraries Press, 1970.

———. *Ogeechee Cross-Firings.* New York: Harper and Brother, 1889.

———. *The Primes and Their Neighbors: Ten Tales of Middle Georgia.* New York: D. Appleton and Company, 1891.

———. *Mr. Billy Downs and His Likes.* New York: Charles L. Webster, 1892.

———. *Mr. Fortner's Marital Claims.* New York: D. Appleton, 1892.

———. *Widow Guthrie.* New York: D. Appleton and Company, 1893.

———. *Old Times in Middle Georgia.* New York: Macmillan Company, 1897.

———. *Pearce Amerson's Will.* Chicago: Way and Williams, 1898.

———. *Autobiography of Col. Richard Malcolm Johnston.* Washington: Neale Company, 1900.

Jones, Charles C., Jr. *Negro Myths from the Georgia Coast: Told in the Vernacular.* Boston: Houghton, Mifflin and Company, 1888.

Keenan, Hugh T., ed. *Dearest Chums and Partners, Joel Chandler Harris's Letters to His Children: A Domestic Biography.* Athens: University of Georgia Press, 1993.

Kemble, Frances Anne. *Journal of a Residence on a Georgian Plantation in 1838–1839* (1863). With an introduction by John A. Scott. Reprinted: Athens: University of Georgia Press, 1984.

King, Edward. *The Great South: A Record of Journeys in Louisiana, Texas, the Indian Territory, Missouri, Arkansas, Mississippi, Alabama, Georgia, Florida, South Carolina, North Carolina, Kentucky, Tennessee, Virginia, and Maryland.* Hartford: American Publishing Company, 1875.

King, Spencer Bidwell, Jr., ed. *Ebb Tide: As Seen through the Diary of Josephine Clay Habersham, 1863.* Athens: University of Georgia Press, 1958.

Kollock, Susan M., ed. "Letters of the Kollock and Allied Families, 1826–1884." *Georgia Historical Quarterly* 33 (1949), 331–54; 34 (1950), 36–63, 126–56, 227–57, 313–27; 35 (1951), 60–75.

Lane, Mills B., ed. *The Rambler in Georgia.* Savannah: Beehive Press, 1973.

———. *"War Is Hell!" William T. Sherman's Personal Narrative of His March through Georgia.* Savannah: Beehive Press, 1974.

———. *Times That Prove People's Principles: Civil War in Georgia, a Documentary History.* Savannah: Beehive Press, 1993.

Lanier, Sidney. *Tiger-Lilies. A Novel.* New York: Hurd and Houghton, 1867.

———. *Poems of Sidney Lanier* (1916). Edited by Mary Day Lanier. Reprinted: Athens: University of Georgia Press and Middle Georgia Historical Society, 1967.

Lanman, Charles. *Adventures in the Wilds of the United States and British American Provinces.* 2 vols. Philadelphia: John W. Moore, 1856.

Latrobe, Charles Joseph. *The Rambler in North America: MDCCCXXXII–MDCCCXXXIII.* 2 vols. Second edition. London: R. B. Seeley and W. Burnside, 1836.

LeConte, Joseph. *'Ware Sherman: A Journal of Three Months' Personal Experience in the Last Days of the Confederacy.* Berkeley: University of California Press, 1937.

Leigh, Frances Butler. *Ten Years on a Georgia Plantation since the War* (1883). Reprinted: New York: Negro Universities Press, 1969.

Lennox, Mary. *Ante Bellum. Southern Life As It Was.* Philadelphia: J. B. Lippincott, 1868.

Lewis, George. *Impressions of America and American Churches: From the Journal of the Rev. G. Lewis* (1848). Reprinted: New York: Negro Universities Press, 1968.

Lines, Amelia Akehurst. *To Raise Myself a Little: The Diaries and Letters of Jennie, a*

Georgia Teacher, 1851–1886. Edited with an introduction by Thomas Dyer. Athens: University of Georgia Press, 1982.

Longstreet, Augustus Baldwin. *Georgia Scenes, Characters, Incidents, etc. in the First Half Century of the Republic, by a Native Georgian.* Augusta: S. R. Sentinel, 1835.

———. *Georgia Scenes* (1835). Reprinted: Atlanta: Cherokee Publishing Company, 1971.

———. *Georgia Scenes* (1835). With an introduction by Richard Harwell. Reprinted: Savannah: Beehive Press, 1975.

———. *Georgia Scenes* (1835). With an introduction by James E. Kibler Jr. Reprinted: Nashville: J. S. Saunders and Company, 1992.

———. *Letters on the Epistle of Paul to Philemon; or, The Connection of Apostolical Christianity with Slavery.* Charleston: B. Jenkins, 1845.

———. *A Voice from the South: Comprising Letters from Georgia to Massachusetts, and to the Southern States.* Baltimore: Western Continent Press, 1847.

———. *Master William Mitten; or, A Youth of Brilliant Talents, Who was Ruined by Bad Luck* (1864). Reprinted: Macon: J. W. Burke and Company, 1889.

Longstreet, Fitz R., ed. *Stories with a Moral: Humorous and Descriptive of Southern Life a Century Ago.* Philadelphia: John C. Winston Company, 1912.

Lyell, Sir Charles. *Travels in North America, in the Years 1841–2; with Geological Observations on the United States, Canada, and Nova Scotia.* 2 vols. New York: Wiley and Putnam, 1845.

———. *A Second Visit to the United States of North America.* 2 vols. New York: Harper and Brothers, 1849.

Mallard, R. Q. *Plantation Life before Emancipation.* Richmond: Whittet and Shepperson, 1892.

Melish, John. *Travels through the United States of America, in the Years 1806 and 1807, and 1809, 1810, and 1811* (1815). Reprinted: Belfast: J. Smyth, 1818.

Mitchell, Margaret. *Gone with the Wind.* New York: Macmillan Publishing Company, 1936.

Murray, Amelia Matilda. *Letters from the United States, Cuba and Canada.* New York: G. P. Putnam and Company, 1856.

Myers, Robert Manson, ed. *The Children of Pride: A True Story of Georgia and the Civil War.* New York: Yale University Press, 1972.

Norwood, Thomas M. *Plutocracy; or, American White Slavery, a Politico-Social Novel.* New York: American News Company, 1888.

Oliphant, Mary C. Simms, et al., eds. *The Letters of William Gilmore Simms.* Volume I (1830–44). Columbia: University of South Carolina Press, 1952.

Olmsted, Frederick Law. *A Journey in the Seaboard States, with Remarks on Their Economy.* New York: Dix and Edwards, 1856.

———. *A Journey in the Backcountry.* New York: Mason Brothers, 1860.

———. *The Cotton Kingdom: A Traveller's Observations on Cotton and Slavery in the American Slave States.* 2 vols. New York: Mason Brothers, 1861.

Parsons, Charles Grandison. *Inside View of Slavery; or, A Tour among the Planters.* Boston: John B. Jewett and Company, 1855.

Pendleton, Louis Beauregard. *In the Wire-Grass.* New York: D. Appleton and Company, 1889.

———. *King Tom and the Runaways: The Story of What Befell Two Boys in a Georgia Swamp.* New York: D. Appleton and Company, 1890.

———. *In the Okefenokee: A Story of War Time and the Great Georgia Swamp.* Boston: Roberts Brothers, 1895.

———. *The Sons of Ham: A Tale of the New South.* Boston: Roberts Brothers, 1895.

———. *Captain Ted: A Boy's Adventures among Hiding Slackers in the Great Georgia Swamp.* New York: D. Appleton and Company, 1918.

———. *Echo of Drums.* New York: Sovereign House, 1938.

Pond, Cornelia Jones. *Life on a Liberty County Plantation: The Journal of Cornelia Jones Pond.* Edited by Josephine Bacon Martin. Darien, Georgia: Darien *News,* 1974.

Pope-Hennessey, Una, ed. *The Aristocratic Journey, Being the Outspoken Letters of Mrs. Basil Hall, Written during a 14-Months' Sojourn in America, 1827–28.* New York: G. P. Putnam's Sons, 1931.

Porter, William T., ed. *The Big Bear of Arkansas, and Other Tales.* Philadelphia: T. B. Peterson, 1843.

Post, Charles C. *Congressman Swanson.* Chicago: Charles H. Sergel and Company, 1891.

Power, Tyrone. *Impressions of America, during the Years 1833, 1834, and 1835.* 2 vols. London: Richard Bentley, 1836.

Rachels, David, ed. *Augustus Baldwin Longstreet's Georgia Scenes Completed.* Athens: University of Georgia Press, 1998.

Rawick, George P., ed. *The American Slave: A Composite Autobioigraphy.* Volume XII. Westport: Greenwood Publishing Company, 1972.

Reid, Whitelaw. *After the War: A Southern Tour.* Cincinnati: Moore, Wilstach and Baldwin, 1866.

Roath, David L. *Zara: A Romance.* Athens: Christy, Kelsea and Burke, 1851.

———. *The Five Love Adventures of Solomon Slug and Other Sketches.* New York: Bruce and Brother, 1852.

Robinson, Francis James. *Kups of Kauphy: A Georgia Book in Warp and Woof. Containing Tales, Incidents, etc. of the "Empire State of the South," with a Slight Sketch of That Well-Known and Eccentric "Colored Gemman," OLD JACK.* Athens, Georgia: 1853.

Rogers, Carlton H. *Incidents of Travel in the Southern States and Cuba.* New York: R. Craighead, 1862.

Rozier, John, ed. *The Granite Farm Letters: The Civil War Correspondence of Edgeworth and Sallie Bird.* Athens: University of Georgia Press, 1988.

Ruppersburg, Hugh, ed. *Georgia Voices, Volume One: Fiction.* Athens: University of Georgia Press, 1992.

Rutherford, Mildred Lewis. *Four Addresses.* Birmingham: Mildred Rutherford Historical Circle, 1916.

Scafidel, J. R. "The Letters of Augustus Baldwin Longstreet." Ph.D. dissertation, University of South Carolina, 1976.

Simms, William Gilmore. *Guy Rivers: A Tale of Old Georgia.* 2 vols. New York: Harper and Brothers, 1834.

———. *Guy Rivers: A Tale of Old Georgia.* Revised edition. Chicago and New York: Belford, Clarke and Co., 1885.

———. *Guy Rivers: A Tale of Georgia.* Edited by John Caldwell Guilds. Fayetteville: University of Arkansas Press, 1993.

———. *As Good as a Comedy; or, The Tennessean's Story.* Philadelphia: A. Hart, 1852.

Smith, Bridges. *100 Stories in Black: A Collection of Bright, Breezy, Humorous Stories of the Colored Race As Seen in the Sunny South.* New York: J. S. Ogilvie Publishing Company, 1910.

Smith, Charles Henry. *Bill Arp, So Called. A Side Show of the Southern Side of the War.* New York: Metropolitan Record Office, 1866.

———. *Bill Arp's Peace Papers.* New York: G. W. Carleton and Company, 1873.

———. *Bill Arp's Scrap Book: Humor and Philosophy.* Atlanta: Jas. P. Harrison and Company, 1884.

———. *The Farm and Fireside: Sketches of Domestic Life in War and Peace.* Atlanta: Constitution Publishing Company, 1892.

———. *Bill Arp from the Uncivil War to Date.* Atlanta: Hudgins Publishing Company, 1903.

Somers, Robert. *The Southern States since the War.* London: Macmillan and Co., 1871.

Starnes, Ebenezer. *The Slaveholder Abroad; or, Billy Buck's Visit, with His Master, to England. A Series of Letters from Dr. Pleasant Jones to Major Joseph Jones, of Georgia.* Philadelphia: J. B. Lippincott, 1860.

Stuart, James. *Three Years in North America.* 2 vols. New York: J. and J. Harper, 1833.

Thompson, Maurice. *Stories of the Cherokee Hills.* Boston: Houghton, Mifflin and Company, 1898.

Thompson, William Tappan. *Major Jones's Courtship: Detailed, with Other Scenes, Incidents, and Adventures, in a Series of Letters, by Himself.* Philadelphia: Carey and Hart, 1844.

———. *Chronicles of Pineville: Embracing Sketches of Georgia Scenes, Incidents and Characters.* Philadelphia: Carey and Hart, 1845.

———. *Major Jones's Sketches of Travel: Comprising the Scenes, Incidents, and Adventures in His Tour from Georgia to Canada.* Philadelphia: T. B. Peterson and Brothers, 1848.

———. *Major Jones's Courtship: Detailed, with Other Scenes, Incidents, and Adventures, in a Series of Letters, by Himself. Revised and Enlarged. To Which Are Added Thirteen Humorous Sketches.* New York: D. Appleton and Company, 1872.

———. *John's Alive; or, The Bride of a Ghost, and Other Sketches.* Philadelphia: David McKay, 1883.

Ticknor, Michelle Cutliff, ed. *The Poems of Francis Orray Ticknor.* New York: Neale Publishing Company, 1911.

Toomer, Jean. *Cane* (1923). Reprinted: New York: Harper and Row, 1969.

Warren, Kittrell J. *Life and Public Services of an Army Straggler* (1865). Edited by Floyd C. Watkins. Reprinted: Athens: University of Georgia Press, 1961.

Watson, Thomas E. *The Life and Speeches of Thomas E. Watson.* Thomson, Georgia: Jeffersonian Publishing Company, 1911.

White, Walter Francis. *Flight.* New York: Alfred A. Knopf, 1926.

Wynne, Lewis N., and Harrison, Guy Porcher. "'Plain Folk' Coping in the Confederacy: The Garrett-Asbell Letters." *Georgia Historical Quarterly* 72 (1988), 102–18.

Young, Thomas Daniel, Watkins, Floyd C., and Beatty, Richard Croom, eds. *The Literature of the South.* Revised edition. Glenview: Scott, Foresman and Company, 1968.

SECONDARY SOURCES

Abrahams, Roger D. *Singing the Master: The Emergence of African-American Culture in the Plantation South.* New York: Pantheon, 1992.

Appleby, Joyce. "Reconciliation and the Northern Novelist, 1865–1880." *Civil War History* 10 (1964), 117–29.

Armstrong, Margaret. *Fanny Kemble: A Passionate Victorian.* New York: Macmillan Company, 1938.

Armstrong, Thomas F. "From Task Labor to Free Labor: The Transition along Georgia's Rice Coast, 1820–1880." *Georgia Historical Quarterly* 64 (1980), 432–47.

———. "Georgia Lumber Workers, 1880–1917: The Social Implications of Work." *Georgia Historical Quarterly* 67 (1983), 435–50.

Austin, James C. *Bill Arp.* New York: Twayne Publishers, 1969.

Ayers, Edward L. *The Promise of the New South: Life after Reconstruction.* New York: Oxford University Press, 1992.

Baer, Florence E. *Sources and Analogues of the Uncle Remus Tales.* Helsinki: Suomalainen Tiedeakatemia Academia Scientiarum Finnica, 1980.

Bailey, Fred Arthur. "The Textbooks of the 'Lost Cause': Censorship and the Creation of Southern State Histories." *Georgia Historical Quarterly* 75 (1991), 507–33.

———. "Mildred Lewis Rutherford and the Patrician Cult of the Old South." *Georgia Historical Quarterly* 78 (1994), 509–35.

Bakhtin, Mikhail. *Rabelais and His World.* Translated by Helene Iswolsky. Cambridge: M.I.T. Press, 1968.

———. *The Dialogic Imagination: Four Essays.* Edited by Michael Holquist and translated by Caryl Emerson and Michael Holquist. Austin: University of Texas Press, 1981.

———. *Problems of Dostoevsky's Poetics.* Edited and translated by Caryl Emerson with an introduction by Wayne C. Booth. Minneapolis: University of Minnesota Press, 1984.

Barthes, Roland. *Mythologies.* Selected and translated by Annette Lavers. New York: Hill and Wang, 1972.

Bartley, Numan V. *The Creation of Modern Georgia.* Athens: University of Georgia Press, 1983.

Beard, Charles A., and Beard, Mary R. *The Rise of American Civilization.* Volume II. New York: Macmillan Company, 1930.

Bell, Malcolm, Jr. *Major Butler's Legacy: Five Generations of a Slaveholding Family.* Athens: University of Georgia Press, 1987.

Bickley, R. Bruce, Jr. *Joel Chandler Harris* (1978). Reprinted: Athens: University of Georgia Press, 1987.

———, ed. *Critical Essays on Joel Chandler Harris.* Boston: G. K. Hall and Company, 1981.

Billings, Dwight B. *Planters and the Making of a "New South."* Chapel Hill: University of North Carolina Press, 1979.

Blackett, R. J. M. "Fugitive Slaves in Britain: The Odyssey of William and Ellen Craft." *Journal of American Studies* 12 (1978), 41–62.

Blackstock, Walter. *Corra Harris: An Analytical Study of Her Novels.* Tallahassee: Florida State University, 1955.

Bleser, Carol, ed. *In Joy and Sorrow: Women, Family and Marriage in the Victorian South, 1830–1900.* New York: Oxford University Press, 1991.

Bode, Frederick A. "A Common Sphere: White Evangelicals and Gender in Antebellum Georgia." *Georgia Historical Quarterly* 79 (1995), 775–809.

Boles, John B., ed. *Masters and Slaves in the House of the Lord: Race and Religion in the American South, 1740–1870.* Lexington: University Press of Kentucky, 1988.

Boney, F. Nash. *Southerners All.* Macon: Mercer University Press, 1984.

———. "A British 'Grand Tour' of Crackerland: Basil and Margaret Hall View Frontier Georgia in 1828." *Georgia Historical Quarterly* 74 (1990), 277–92.

Bonner, James C. *A History of Georgia Agriculture, 1732–1860.* Athens: University of Georgia Press, 1964.

Boudon, Raymond. *The Analysis of Ideology.* Translated by Malcolm Slater. Chicago: University of Chicago Press, 1989.

Brookes, Stella Brewer. *Joel Chandler Harris: Folklorist.* Athens: University of Georgia Press, 1950.

Brooks, Robert P. *The Agrarian Revolution in Georgia, 1865–1912.* Madison: University of Wisconsin Press, 1914.

Bruce, Dickson D., Jr. *And They All Sang Hallelujah: Plain Folk Camp-Meeting Religion, 1800–1845.* Knoxville: University of Tennessee Press, 1974.

Brundage, W. Fitzhugh. *Lynching in the New South: Georgia and Virginia, 1880–1930.* Champaign: University of Illinois Press, 1993.

———. "The Varn Mill Riot of 1891: Lynchings, Attempted Lynchings, and Justice in Ware County, Georgia." *Georgia Historical Quarterly* 77 (1994), 257–80.

Bryan, Ferald J. *Henry Grady or Tom Watson?: The Rhetorical Struggle for the New South, 1880–1890.* Macon: Mercer University Press, 1994.

Bryan, T. Conn. *Confederate Georgia.* Athens: University of Georgia Press, 1953.

Bryant, Keith L., Jr. "The Role and Status of the Female Yeomanry in the Antebellum South: The Literary View." *Southern Quarterly* 18 (1980), 73–88.

Buck, Paul. *The Road to Reunion, 1865–1900.* Boston: Little, Brown, 1937.

Burrison, John A. *"The Golden Arm": The Folk Tale and Its Literary Use by Mark Twain and Joel C. Harris.* Research Paper Number 19. Atlanta: Georgia State College, 1968.

Bush, Robert. "Will N. Harben's Northern Georgia Fiction." *Mississippi Quarterly* 20 (1976), 103–17.

Byrne, William A. "'Uncle Billy' Sherman Comes to Town: The Free Winter of Black Savannah." *Georgia Historical Quarterly* 79 (1995), 91–116.

Candler, Allen D., and Evans, Clement A., eds. *Cyclopedia of Georgia* (1906). Volume III. Reprinted: Spartanburg: Reprint Company, 1972.

Cash, Wilbur J. *The Mind of the South* (1941). Reprinted: New York: Vintage Books, 1969.

Cashin, Joan E. *A Family Venture: Men and Women on the Southern Frontier.* Baltimore: Johns Hopkins University Press, 1991.

Cassity, Michael J. "Southern Workers and Social Change: Concepts and Prospects." *Georgia Historical Quarterly* 62 (1978), 200–212.

Chalmers, David M. *Hooded Americanism: The History of the Ku Klux Klan* (1965). Reprinted: Chicago: Quadrangle Paperbacks, 1968.

Cimbala, Paul A. "The Freedmen's Bureau, the Freedmen and Sherman's Grant in Reconstruction Georgia, 1865–1867." *Journal of Southern History* 55 (1989), 597–632.

———. "On the Front Line of Freedom: Freedmen's Bureau Officers and Agents in Reconstruction Georgia, 1865–1868." *Georgia Historical Quarterly* 76 (1992), 577–611.

———. *Under the Guardianship of the Nation: The Freedmen's Bureau and the Reconstruction of Georgia, 1865–1870.* Athens: University of Georgia Press, 1997.

Clare, Virginia. *Thunder and Stars: The Life of Mildred Rutherford.* Atlanta: Oglethorpe University Press, 1941.

Clark, Thomas D. *Travels in the Old South: A Bibliography.* 3 vols. Norman: University of Oklahoma Press, 1956–59.

Clinton, Catherine. *The Plantation Mistress: Woman's World in the Old South.* New York: Pantheon, 1982.

Clinton, Catherine, and Silber, Nina, eds. *Divided Houses: Gender and the Civil War.* New York: Oxford University Press, 1992.

Coclanis, Peter A. *The Shadow of a Dream: Economic Life and Death in the South Carolina Low Country, 1670–1920.* New York: Oxford University Press, 1989.

Coffing, Karen. "Southern Womanhood Preached to a National Audience: Corra Harris, Author and Novelist." Ph.D. dissertation, Kent State University, 1992.

———. "Corra Harris and the *Saturday Evening Post:* Southern Domesticity Conveyed to a National Audience, 1900–1930." *Georgia Historical Quarterly* 79 (1995), 367–93.

Cohen, William. *At Freedom's Edge: Black Mobility and the Southern White Quest for Racial Control, 1861–1915.* Baton Rouge: Louisiana State University Press, 1991.

Coleman, Kenneth, and Gurr, Charles Stephen, eds. *Dictionary of Georgia Biography.* 2 vols. Athens: University of Georgia Press, 1983.

Conway, Alan. *The Reconstruction of Georgia.* Minneapolis: University of Minnesota Press, 1966.

Cooper, Helen M., Anslander, Adrienne, and Squier, Susan Merrill, eds. *War, Gender, and Literary Representation.* Chapel Hill: University of North Carolina Press, 1989.

Coulter, E. Merton. *Auraria: The Story of a Georgia Gold-Mining Town.* Athens: University of Georgia Press, 1956.

Cousins, Paul M. *Joel Chandler Harris, a Biography.* Baton Rouge: Louisiana State University Press, 1968.

Cowdry, Albert E. *This Land, This South: An Environmental History.* Lexington: University Press of Kentucky, 1983.

Crowe, Charles. "Racial Violence and Social Reform: Origins of the Atlanta Race Riot of 1906." *Journal of Negro History* 53 (1968), 234–56.

———. "Racial Massacre in Atlanta, September 22, 1906." *Journal of Negro History* 54 (1969), 150–73.

Daniel, Pete. *Breaking the Land: The Transformation of Cotton, Tobacco, and Rice Cultures since 1880.* Urbana: University of Illinois Press, 1985.

———. *Standing at the Crossroads: Southern Life in the Twentieth Century.* New York: Hill and Wang, 1986.

Davis, Harold E. "Henry Grady, the Atlanta Constitution, and the Politics of Farming in the 1880s." *Georgia Historical Quarterly* 71 (1987), 571–600.

———. *Henry Grady's New South: Atlanta, a Brave and Beautiful City.* Tuscaloosa: University of Alabama Press, 1990.

De Bellis, Jack. *Sidney Lanier.* New York: Twayne Publishers, 1972.

Dick, Everett. *The Dixie Frontier: A Social History* (1948). Reprinted: Norman: University of Oklahoma Press, 1993.

Doyle, Don H. *New Men, New Cities, New South: Atlanta, Nashville, Charleston, Mobile, 1860–1910.* Chapel Hill: University of North Carolina Press, 1990.

Drago, Edmund. "How Sherman's March through Georgia Affected the Slaves." *Georgia Historical Quarterly* 57 (1973), 361–75.

Duncan, Russell. *Freedom's Shore: Tunis Campbell and the Georgia Freedmen.* Athens: University of Georgia Press, 1986.

Dushinberre, William. *Them Dark Days: Slavery in the American Rice Swamps.* New York: Oxford University Press, 1996.

Eagleton, Terry. *Ideology: An Introduction.* London; Verso, 1991.

Eaton, Clement. *The Growth of Southern Civilization, 1790–1860.* New York: Harper and Row Publishers, 1961.

———. *The Waning of the Old South Civilization, 1860–1880's.* Athens: University of Georgia Press, 1968.

Edwards, Corliss H., Jr. "Richard Malcolm Johnston's View of the Old-Field School." *Georgia Historical Quarterly* 50 (1966), 382–90.

Escott, Paul D. "The Context of Freedom: Georgia's Slaves during the Civil War." *Georgia Historical Quarterly* 58 (1974), 79–104.

Farnham, Christie Anne. *The Education of the Southern Belle: Higher Education in the Antebellum South.* New York: New York University Press, 1994.

Faust, Drew Gilpin. *A Sacred Circle: The Dilemma of the Intellectual in the Old South, 1840–1860.* Baton Rouge: Louisiana State University Press, 1977.

———. *The Creation of Confederate Nationalism: Ideology and Identity in the Civil War South.* Baton Rouge: Louisiana State University Press, 1988.

———. *Southern Stories: Slaveholders in Peace and War.* Columbia: University of Missouri Press, 1992.

———. *Mothers of Invention: Women of the Slaveholding South in the American Civil War* (1996). Reprinted: New York: Vintage Books, 1997.

———, ed. *Ideology of Slavery: Proslavery Thought in the Antebellum South, 1830–1860.* Baton Rouge: Louisiana State University Press, 1981.

Ferguson, T. Reed. *The John Couper Family at Cannon's Point.* Macon: Mercer University Press, 1994.

Figh, Margaret Gillis. "Life in Nineteenth-Century Georgia As Reflected in Bill Arp's Works." *Georgia Historical Quarterly* 35 (1951), 16–22.

Fite, Gilbert C. *Cotton Fields No More: Southern Agriculture, 1865–1980.* Lexington: University Press of Kentucky, 1984.

Fitzgerald, O. P. *Judge Longstreet: A Life Sketch.* Nashville: Publishing House of the Methodist Episcopal Church South, 1891.

Flamming, Douglas. *Creating the Modern South: Millhands and Managers in Dalton Georgia, 1884–1984.* Chapel Hill: University of North Carolina Press, 1993.

Flanders, Bertram H. *Early Georgia Magazines: Literary Periodicals to 1865.* Athens: University of Georgia Press, 1944.

Flanders, Ralph B. "Planter Problems in Ante-Bellum Georgia." *Georgia Historical Quarterly* 14 (1930), 17–40.

———. *Plantation Slavery in Georgia.* Chapel Hill: University of North Carolina Press, 1933.

Flynn, Charles L., Jr. *White Land, Black Labor: Caste and Class in Late Nineteenth-Century Georgia.* Baton Rouge: Louisiana State University Press, 1983.

Flynt, J. Wayne. *Dixie's Forgotten People: The South's Poor Whites.* Bloomington: Indiana University Press, 1980.

Fogel, Robert William. *Without Consent or Contract: The Rise and Fall of American Slavery.* New York: W. W. Norton, 1989.

Foner, Eric. *Nothing But Freedom: Emancipation and Its Legacy.* Baton Rouge: Louisiana State University Press, 1983.

———. *Reconstruction: America's Unfinished Revolution, 1863–1877.* New York: Harper and Row, 1988.

Ford, Charlotte A. "Eliza Frances Andrews, Practical Botanist, 1840–1931." *Georgia Historical Quarterly* 70 (1986), 63–80.

Foster, Gaines M. *Ghosts of the Confederacy: Defeat, the Lost Cause, and the Emergence of the New South, 1865–1913.* New York: Oxford University Press, 1987.

Fox-Genovese, Elizabeth. *Within the Plantation Household: Black and White Women of the Old South.* Chapel Hill: University of North Carolina Press, 1988.

Fox-Genovese, Elizabeth, and Genovese, Eugene D. *Fruits of Merchant Capital: Slavery and Bourgeois Property in the Rise and Expansion of Capitalism.* New York: Oxford University Press, 1983.

Frederickson, George M. *The Black Image in the White Mind: The Debate on Afro-American Character and Destiny, 1817–1914.* New York: Harper and Row, 1971.

Friedman, Jean E. *The Enclosed Garden: Women and Community in the Evangelical South, 1830–1900.* Chapel Hill: University of North Carolina Press, 1985.

Furnas, J. C. *Fanny Kemble: Leading Lady of the Nineteenth-Century Stage.* New York: Dial Press, 1982.

Gaither, Gerald H. *Blacks and the Populist Revolt: Ballots and Bigotry in the "New South."* Tuscaloosa: University of Alabama Press, 1977.

Gaston, Paul. *The New South Creed: A Study in Southern Mythmaking.* Baton Rouge: Louisiana State University Press, 1970.

Geertz, Clifford. *The Interpretation of Cultures: Selected Essays.* New York: Basic Books, 1973.

Genovese, Eugene D. *The Political Economy of Slavery: Studies in the Economy and Society of the Slave South* (1964). Reprinted: New York: Vintage Books, 1967.

———. *The World the Slaveholders Made: Two Essays in Interpretation* (1969). Reprinted: New York: Vintage Books, 1971.

———. *Roll, Jordan, Roll: The World the Slaves Made.* New York: Random House, 1974.

———. *"Slavery Ordained of God": The Southern Slaveholders' View of Biblical History and Modern Politics.* Gettysburg: Gettysburg College, 1985.

———. *The Slaveholders' Dilemma: Freedom and Progress in Southern Conservative Thought, 1820–1860.* Columbia: University of South Carolina Press, 1992.

Genovese, Eugene D. and Fox-Genovese, Elizabeth. "The Religious Ideals of Southern Slave Society." *Georgia Historical Quarterly* 70 (1986), 1–16.

Glatthaar, Joseph. *The March to the Sea and Beyond: Sherman's Troops in the Savannah and Carolinas Campaign.* New York: New York University Press, 1985.

Goff, John H. "The Sandtown Trail." *Atlanta Historical Bulletin* 11 (1966), 34–52.

Goodwyn, Lawrence. *Democratic Promise: The Populist Moment in America.* New York: Oxford University Press, 1976.

Gorn, Elliott J. "'Gouge and Bite, Pull Hair and Scratch': The Social Significance of Fighting in the Southern Backcountry." *American Historical Review* 90 (1985), 18–43.

Grantham, Dewey W. *The South in Modern America: A Region at Odds.* New York: HarperCollins Publishers, 1994.

Gray, Lewis C. *History of Agriculture in the Southern United States to 1860.* 2 vols. Washington, D.C.: Carnegie Institution, 1933.

Gray, Richard. *The Life of William Faulkner.* Oxford: Blackwell Publishers, 1994.

Greenberg, Kenneth S. *Honor and Slavery: Lies, Duels, Noses, Masks, Dressing as a Woman, Gifts, Strangers, Baseball, Hunting, and Gambling in the Old South.* Princeton: Princeton University Press, 1996.

Guilds, John Caldwell. *Simms: A Literary Life.* Fayetteville: University of Arkansas Press, 1992.

Gulley, H. E. "Women and the Lost Cause: Preserving a Confederate Identity in the American Deep South." *Journal of Historical Geography* 19 (1993), 125–41.

Gutman, Herbert G. *The Black Family in Slavery and Freedom, 1750–1925* (1976). Reprinted: New York: Vintage Books, 1977.

Gwin, Minrose C. *Black and White Women of the Old South: The Peculiar Sisterhood in American Literature.* Knoxville: University of Tennessee Press, 1985.

Hagler, Harland D. "The Ideal Woman in the Antebellum South: Lady or Farmwife?" *Journal of Southern History* 46 (1980), 405–17.

Hahn, Stephen. *The Roots of Southern Populism: Yeoman Farmers and the Transformation of the Georgia Upcountry, 1850–1890.* New York: Oxford University Press, 1983.

Hair, William I. "Stagecoaches and Public Accommodations in Antebellum Georgia." *Georgia Historical Quarterly* 68 (1984), 323–33.

Harlow, Alvin F. *Joel Chandler Harris: Plantation Storyteller.* New York: Julian Messner, 1941.

Harris, William H. *The Harder We Run: Black Workers since the Civil War.* New York: Oxford University Press, 1982.

Hart, Bertha Sheppard. *Introduction to Georgia Writers.* Macon: J. W. Burke Company, 1929.

Hearden, Patrick J. *Independence and Empire: The New South's Cotton Mill Campaign, 1865–1901.* DeKalb: Northern Illinois University Press, 1982.

Hicks, John D. *The Populist Revolt: A History of the Farmers' Alliance and the People's Party.* Minneapolis: University of Minnesota Press, 1931.

Hill, Samuel S., ed. *Religion in the Southern States: A Historical Study.* Macon: Mercer University Press, 1983.

———, ed. *Varieties of Southern Religious Experience.* Baton Rouge: Louisiana State University Press, 1988.

———, et al. *Religion and the Solid South.* Nashville: Abingdon Press, 1972.

Hitchcock, Bert. *Richard Malcolm Johnston.* Boston: Twayne Publishers, 1978.

Hoare, Quinten, and Smith, Geoffrey Nowell, editors and translators. *Selections from the Prison Notebooks of Antonio Gramsci.* New York: International Publishers, 1971.

Hobsbawm, E. J., and Rudé, George. *Captain Swing: A Social History of the Great English Agricultural Uprising of 1830.* New York: W. W. Norton and Company, 1968.

Hobson, Fred. *Tell about the South: The Southern Rage to Explain.* Baton Rouge: Louisiana State University Press, 1983.

Hoffman, Charles, and Hoffman, Tess. *North by South: The Two Lives of Richard James Arnold.* Athens: University of Georgia Press, 1988.

Holmes, William F. "The Southern Farmers' Alliance: The Georgia Experience." *Georgia Historical Quarterly* 72 (1988), 627–53.

———. "Populism: In Search of Context." *Agricultural History* 64 (1990), 26–58.

———. "The Southern Farmers' Alliance and the Jute Cartel." *Journal of Southern History* 60 (1994), 59–80.

———, ed. *American Populism.* Lexington: D. C. Heath and Company, 1994.

Hoole, William Stanley. "A Note on Simms's Visits to the Southwest." *American Literature* 6 (1934), 334–36.

———. *Alias Simon Suggs: The Life and Times of Johnson Jones Hooper.* Tuscaloosa: University of Alabama Press, 1952.

Hubbell, Jay B. *The South in American Literature, 1607–1900.* Durham: Duke University Press, 1954.

———. *Southern Life in Fiction.* Athens: University of Georgia Press, 1960.

Hunt, Patricia K. "Clothing as an Expression of History: The Dress of African-American Women in Georgia, 1880–1910." *Georgia Historical Quarterly* 76 (1992), 459–71.

Hunter, Tera W. "Domination and Resistance: The Politics of Wage Household Labor in New South Atlanta." *Labor History* 34 (1993), 205–20.

———. *To 'Joy My Freedom: Southern Black Women's Lives and Labors after the Civil War.* Cambridge: Harvard University Press, 1997.

Inge, M. Thomas, ed. *The Frontier Humorists: Critical Views.* Hamden: Archon Books, 1975.

Inscoe, John C. "The Confederate Homefront Sanitized: Joel Chandler Harris' *On the Plantation* and Sectional Reconciliation." *Georgia Historical Quarterly* 76 (1992), 652–74.

Jameson, Fredric. *Postmodernism; or, The Cultural Logic of Late Capitalism.* Durham: Duke University Press, 1991.

Jarrell, Hampton M. "Simms's Visits to the Southwest." *American Literature* 5 (1933), 29–30.

Jaynes, Gerald David. *Branches without Roots: Genesis of the Black Working Class in the American South, 1862–1882.* New York: Oxford University Press, 1986.

Jenkins, William S. *Pro-Slavery Thought in the Old South.* Chapel Hill: University of North Carolina Press, 1935.

Johnson, Paul E., and Wilentz, Sean. *The Kingdom of Matthias: A Story of Sex and Salvation in Nineteenth-Century America.* New York: Oxford University Press, 1994.

Johnston-Miller, Mary M. "Heirs to Paternalism: Elite Women and Their Servants in Alabama and Georgia, 1861–1874." Ph.D. dissertation, Emory University, 1994.

Jones, Anne Goodwyn. *Tomorrow Is Another Day: The Woman Writer in the South, 1859–1936.* Baton Rouge: Louisiana State University Press, 1981.

Jones, Jacqueline. *Soldiers of Light and Love: Northern Teachers and Georgia Blacks, 1865–1873* (1980). Reprinted: Athens: University of Georgia Press, 1992.

———. *Labor of Love, Labor of Sorrow: Black Women, Work and the Family, from Slavery to the Present* (1985). Reprinted: New York: Vintage Books, 1986.

Kennett, Lee B. *Marching through Georgia: The Story of Soldiers and Civilians during Sherman's Campaign.* New York: HarperCollins, 1995.

King, Kimball. *Augustus Baldwin Longstreet.* Boston: Twayne Publishers, 1984.

Kirby, Jack Temple. *Rural Worlds Lost: The American South, 1920–1960.* Baton Rouge: Louisiana State University Press, 1987.

Knight, Lucien Lamar. *Biographical Dictionary of Southern Authors* (1929). Reprinted: Detroit: Gale Research Company, 1978.

Kolchin, Peter. *American Slavery, 1619–1877.* New York: Hill and Wang, 1993.

Kulikoff, Allan. *The Agrarian Origins of American Capitalism.* Charlottesville: University Press of Virginia, 1992.

Kyle, Clason. "Who Was Mary Lennox?" Columbus *Sunday Ledger-Enquirer Magazine,* 28 July 1968, 10–12.

LaCapra, Dominick, and Kaplan, Stephen L., eds. *Modern European Intellectual History: Reappraisals and New Perspectives.* Ithaca: Cornell University Press, 1982.

Lanier, Doris. "Henry W. Grady and the Piedmont Chautauqua [1888–91]." *Southern Studies* 23 (1984), 216–42.

———. "Harry Stillwell Edwards: Chronicler of the South." *Atlanta History: A Journal of Georgia and the South* 31 (1987), 30–41.

Lears, T. J. Jackson. *No Place of Grace: Antimodernism and the Transformation of American Culture, 1880–1920.* New York: Pantheon Books, 1981.

———. "The Concept of Cultural Hegemony: Problems and Possibilities." *American Historical Review* 90 (1985), 567–93.

Levine, Lawrence W. *Black Culture and Black Consciousness: Afro-American Folk Thought from Slavery to Freedom.* New York: Oxford University Press, 1977.

Lichtenstein, Alex. *Twice the Work of Free Labor: The Political Economy of Convict Labor in the New South.* New York: Verso, 1996.

Litwack, Leon F. *Been in the Storm So Long: The Aftermath of Slavery.* New York: Alfred A. Knopf, 1980.

Lorenz, Lincoln. *The Life of Sidney Lanier.* New York: Coward-McMann, 1935.

Loveland, Anne C. *Southern Evangelicals and the Social Order, 1800–1860.* Baton Rouge: Louisiana State University Press, 1988.

MacKethan, Lucinda Hardwick. *The Dream of Arcady: Place and Time in Southern Literature.* Baton Rouge: Louisiana State University Press, 1980.

Mandle, Jay R. *The Roots of Black Poverty: The Southern Plantation Economy after the Civil War.* Durham: Duke University Press, 1978.

———. *Not Slave, Not Free: The African American Economic Experience since the Civil War.* Durham: Duke University Press, 1992.

Marszalek, John F. *Sherman: A Soldier's Passion for Order.* New York: Random House, 1993.

Massey, Mary Elizabeth. *Ersatz in the Confederacy: Shortages and Substitutes on the Southern Homefront.* Columbia: University of South Carolina Press, 1993.

Mathews, Donald G. *Slavery and Methodism: A Chapter in American Morality, 1780–1845.* Princeton: Princeton University Press, 1965.

Mayfield, John. "The Theatre of Public Esteem: Ethics and Values in Longstreet's *Georgia Scenes.*" *Georgia Historical Quarterly* 75 (1991), 566–86.

McCurry, Stephanie. *Masters of Small Worlds: Yeoman Households, Gender Rela-*

tions, and the Political Culture of the Antebellum South Carolina Low Country. New York: Oxford University Press, 1995.

McHugh, Cathy. *The Labor System in the Southern Cotton Textile Industry, 1880–1915.* New York: Oxford University Press, 1988.

McMath, Robert C., Jr. *Populist Vanguard: A History of the Southern Farmers' Alliance* (1975). Reprinted: New York: W. W. Norton and Company, 1977.

———. *American Populism: A Social History, 1877–1898.* New York: Hill and Wang, 1993.

McMillen, Sally G. *Motherhood in the Old South.* Baton Rouge: Louisiana State University Press, 1990.

———. *Southern Women: Black and White in the Old South.* Arlington Heights: Harlan Davidson, 1992.

———. "Antebellum Southern Fathers and the Health Care of Children." *Journal of Southern History* 60 (1994), 513–32.

McPherson, James M. *Battle Cry of Freedom: The Civil War Era.* New York: Ballantine Books, 1988.

Meriwether, James B. "Augustus Baldwin Longstreet: Realist and Artist." *Mississippi Quarterly* 35 (1982), 351–64.

Merrington, John. "Town and Country in the Transition to Capitalism." *New Left Review* 93 (1975), 71–92.

Miller, Henry Prentice. "The Life and Works of Wiliam Tappan Thompson." Ph.D. dissertation, University of Chicago, 1942.

———. "The Background and Significance of Major Jones's Courtship." *Georgia Historical Quarterly* 30 (1946), 267–96.

Mims, Edwin. *Sidney Lanier.* Boston: Houghton, Mifflin and Company, 1905.

Minrose, Gwin C. *Black and White Women of the Old South: The Peculiar Sisterhood in American Literature.* Knoxville: University of Tennessee Press, 1985.

Mixon, Gregory. "'Good Negro-Bad Negro': The Dynamics of Race and Class in Atlanta During the Era of the 1906 Riot." *Georgia Historical Quarterly* 81 (1997), 593–621.

Mixon, Wayne. "Joel Chandler Harris, the Yeoman Tradition, and the New South Movement." *Georgia Historical Quarterly* 61 (1977), 308–17.

———. *Southern Writers and the New South Movement, 1865–1913.* Macon: Mercer University Press, 1980.

———. "The Ultimate Irrelevance of Race: Joel Chandler Harris and Uncle Remus in Their Time." *Journal of Southern History* 56 (1990), 457–80.

———. "Hillbilly Heretic: Will N. Harben's Challenge to the Old-Time Religion." In Charles Reagan Wilson, ed., *Cultural Perspectives on the American South,* vol. V. New York: Gordon and Beach, 1991, 17–29.

Mohr, Clarence L. "Harrison Berry: A Black Pamphleteer in Georgia during Slavery and Freedom." *Georgia Historical Quarterly* 67 (1983), 189–205.

———. *On the Threshold of Freedom: Masters and Slaves in Civil War Georgia.* Athens: University of Georgia Press, 1986.

Moore, Barrington, Jr. *Social Origins of Dictatorship and Democracy: Lord and Peasant in the Making of the Modern World.* Boston: Beacon Press, 1966.

Moss, Elizabeth. *Domestic Novelists in the Old South: Defenders of Southern Culture.* Baton Rouge: Louisiana State University Press, 1992.

Murphy, James K. *Will N. Harben.* Boston: Twayne Publishers, 1979.

Nathans, Elizabeth Studley. *Losing the Peace: Georgia Republicans and Reconstruction.* Baton Rouge: Louisiana State University Press, 1969.

Newby, I. A. *Plain Folk in the New South: Social Change and Cultural Persistence, 1880–1915.* Baton Rouge: Louisiana State University Press, 1989.

Nixon, Raymond B. *Henry W. Grady: Spokesman of the New South.* New York: Alfred Knopf, 1943.

Oakes, James. *The Ruling Race: A History of American Slaveholders.* New York: Alfred A. Knopf, 1982.

———. *Slavery and Freedom: An Interpretation of the Old South.* New York: Alfred A. Knopf, 1990.

Osterweis, Rollin G. *The Myth of the Lost Cause, 1865–1900.* Hamden: Archon Books, 1973.

Owen, Christopher H. *The Sacred Flame of Love: Methodism and Society in Nineteenth-Century Georgia.* Athens: University of Georgia Press, 1998.

Ownby, Ted. *Subduing Satan: Religion, Recreation, and Manhood in the Rural South, 1865–1920.* Chapel Hill: University of North Carolina Press, 1990.

Owsley, Frank L. *Plain Folk of the Old South.* Baton Rouge: Louisiana State University Press, 1949.

Palmer, Bruce. *Man Over Money: The Southern Populist Critique of American Capitalism.* Chapel Hill: University of North Carolina Press, 1980.

Palmer, Bryan D. *Descent into Discourse: The Reification of Language and the Writing of Social History.* Philadelphia: Temple University Press, 1990.

Parker, David B. "Bill Arp and Blacks: The Forgotten Letters." *Georgia Historical Quarterly* 67 (1983), 336–49.

———. "Bill Arp, Joe Brown, and the Confederate War Effort." *Georgia Historical Quarterly* 73 (1989), 79–87.

Parker, David C. *Alias Bill Arp: Charles Henry Smith and the South's "Goodly Heritage."* Athens: University of Georgia Press, 1991.

Parks, Edd Winfield. *Sidney Lanier: The Man, the Poet, the Critic.* Athens: University of Georgia Press, 1968.

Phillips, Robert L., Jr. "The Novel and the Romance in Middle Georgia Humor and Local Color: A Study of Narrative Method in the Works of Augustus Baldwin Longstreet, William Tappan Thompson, Richard Malcolm Johnston, and Joel Chandler Harris." Ph.D. dissertation, University of North Carolina, 1971.

Phillips, Ulrich B. *American Negro Slavery* (1918). Forward by Eugene D. Genovese. Reprinted: Baton Rouge: Louisiana State University Press, 1966.

———. *Life and Labor in the Old South* (1929). Reprinted: Boston: Little, Brown and Company, 1941.

Polanyi, Karl. *The Great Transformation: The Political and Economic Origins of Our Time* (1944). Reprinted: Boston: Beacon Press, 1957.

Pratt, Mary Louise. "Scratches on the Face of the Country; or, What Mr. Barrow Saw in the Land of the Bushmen." In Henry Louis Gates Jr., ed., *"Race," Writing, and Difference.* Chicago: University of Chicago Press, 1986.

Rabinowitz, Howard N. *Race Relations in the Urban South, 1865–1890.* New York: Oxford University Press, 1978.

———. *The First New South, 1865–1920.* Arlington Heights: Harlan Davidson, 1992.

Rable, George C. *But There Was No Peace: The Role of Violence in the Politics of Reconstruction.* Athens: University of Georgia Press, 1984.

———. *Civil Wars: Women and the Crisis of Southern Nationalism.* Urbana: University of Illinois Press, 1989.

Raboteau, Albert J. *Slave Religion: The "Invisible Institution" in the Antebellum South.* New York: Oxford University Press, 1978.

Range, Willard. *A Century of Georgia Agriculture, 1850–1950.* Athens: University of Georgia Press, 1954.

Redkey, Edwin S. *Black Exodus: Black Nationalist and Back-to-Africa Movements, 1890–1910.* New Haven: Yale University Press, 1969.

Regis, Pamela. *Describing Early America: Bartram, Jefferson, Crèvecoeur, and the Rhetoric of Natural History.* Dekalb: Northern Illinois University Press, 1992.

Reidy, Joseph P. *From Slavery to Agrarian Capitalism in the Cotton Plantation South: Central Georgia.* Chapel Hill: University of North Carolina Press, 1992.

Ridgely, Joseph Vincent. *Nineteenth-Century Southern Literature.* Lexington: University Press of Kentucky, 1980.

Roark, James L. *Masters without Slaves: Southern Planters in the Civil War and Reconstruction.* New York: W. W. Norton and Company, 1977.

Robertson, Henry O., Jr. "The Prism of Laughter: Antebellum Humorists in Regional Perspective." Ph.D. dissertation, Louisiana State University, 1997.

Roediger, David R. *The Wages of Whiteness: Race and the Making of the American Working Class.* New York: Verso, 1991.

Rogers, George A., and Saunders, R. Frank, Jr. *Swamp Water and Wiregrass: Historical Sketches of Coastal Georgia.* Macon: Mercer University Press, 1984.

Rose, Alan Henry. *Demonic Vision: Racial Fantasy and Southern Fiction.* Hamden: Archon Books, 1976.

Rubin, Louis D., Jr., ed. *The History of Southern Literature.* Baton Rouge: Louisiana State University Press, 1985.

———, ed. *The Edge of the Swamp: A Study in the Literature and Society of the Old South.* Baton Rouge: Louisiana State University Press, 1989.

Russell, James Michael. *Atlanta, 1847–1890: City Building in the Old South and the New.* Baton Rouge: Louisiana State University Press, 1988.

Saxton, Alexander. *The Rise and Fall of the White Republic: Class Politics and Mass Culture in Nineteenth-Century America.* New York: Verso, 1990.

Schultz, Stanley K. "Temperence Reform in the Antebellum South: Social Control and Urban Order." *South Atlantic Quarterly* 83 (1984), 323–39.

Schwartz, Michael. *Radical Protest and Social Structure: The Southern Farmers' Alliance and Cotton Tenancy, 1880–1890.* New York: Academic Press, 1976.

Scott, Anne Firor. *The Southern Lady: From Pedestal to Politics, 1830–1930.* Chicago: University of Chicago Press, 1970.

Sellers, Charles. *The Market Revolution: Jacksonian America, 1815–1846.* New York: Oxford University Press, 1991.

Shadgett, Olive H. *The Republican Party in Georgia: From Reconstruction through 1900.* Athens: University of Georgia Press, 1964.

Shaw, Barton C. *The Wool-Hat Boys: Georgia's Populist Party.* Baton Rouge: Louisiana State University Press, 1984.

Shields, Johanna Nichol. "A Sadder Simon Suggs: Freedom and Slavery in the Humor of Johnson Hooper." *Journal of Southern History* 56 (1990), 641–64.

———. "White Honor, Black Humor, and the Making of a Southern Style." *Southern Cultures* 1 (1995), 420–30.

Shippey, Herbert Phinehas. "William Tappan Thompson: A Biography and Uncollected Writings." Ph.D. dissertation, University of South Carolina, 1991.

Shore, Laurence. *Southern Capitalists: The Ideological Leadership of an Elite, 1832–1885.* Chapel Hill: University of North Carolina Press, 1986.

Silber, Nina. *The Romance of Reunion: Northerners and the South, 1865–1900.* Chapel Hill: University of North Carolina Press, 1993.

Simms, L. Moody, Jr. "Richard Malcolm Johnston on Rural Life in Middle Georgia." *Georgia Historical Quarterly* 58 (1974), 181–92.

Simpson, Lewis P. *The Brazen Face of History: Studies in the Literary Consciousness in America.* Baton Rouge: Louisiana State University Press, 1980.

Singal, Daniel Joseph. *The War Within: From Victorian to Modernist Thought in the South, 1919–1945.* Chapel Hill: University of North Carolina Press, 1982.

Skaggs, Merrill Maguire. *The Folk of Southern Fiction.* Athens: University of Georgia Press, 1972.

Smith, Frances Foster. *Witnessing Slavery: The Development of Ante-Bellum Slave Narratives.* Second edition. Madison: University of Wisconsin Press, 1994.

Smith, John David. *An Old Creed for the New South: Proslavery Ideology and Historiography, 1865–1918.* Westport: Greenwood Press, 1985.

Smith, Julia F. *Slavery and Rice Culture in Low Country Georgia, 1750–1860.* Knoxville: University of Tennessee Press, 1985.

Smith, Nelle Edwards. *Harry Stillwell Edwards: A Man . . . Not without Honor.* Macon: Eneas Africanus Press, 1969.

Snay, Mitchell. *Gospel of Disunion: Religion and Separatism in the Antebellum South.* New York: Cambridge University Press, 1993.

Stampp, Kenneth M. *The Peculiar Institution: Slavery in the Ante-Bellum South* (1956). Reprinted: New York: Vintage Books, 1989.

Starke, Aubrey Harrison. *Sidney Lanier: A Biographical and Critical Study.* Chapel Hill: University of North Carolina Press, 1933.

Starke, Catherine. *Black Portraiture in American Fiction: Stock Characters, Archetypes, and Individuals.* New York: Basic Books, 1971.

Starobin, Robert S. *Industrial Slavery in the Old South.* New York: Oxford University Press, 1970.

Stephens, Lester D. *Joseph LeConte: Gentle Prophet of Evolution.* Baton Rouge: Louisiana State University Press, 1982.

Stewart, Mart A. *"What Nature Suffers to Groe": Life, Labor, and Landscape on the Georgia Coast, 1680–1920.* Athens: University of Georgia Press, 1996.

Stowe, Steven M. *Intimacy and Power in the Old South: Ritual in the Lives of the Planters.* Baltimore: Johns Hopkins University Press, 1987.

Sundquist, Eric J. *To Wake the Nations: Race in the Making of American Literature.* Cambridge: Belknap Press of Harvard University Press, 1993.

Talmadge, John E. *Rebecca Latimer Felton: Nine Stormy Decades.* Athens: University of Georgia Press, 1960.

———. *Corra Harris, Lady of Purpose.* Athens: University of Georgia Press, 1968.

Taylor, Elizabeth A. "The Origin and Development of the Convict Lease System in Georgia." *Georgia Historical Quarterly* 26 (1942), 113–28.

———. "The Abolition of the Convict Lease System in Georgia." *Georgia Historical Quarterly* 26 (1942), 273–87.

Taylor, William R. *Cavalier and Yankee: The Old South and American National Character.* New York: George Braziller, 1961.

Temin, Peter. "Patterns of Cotton Agriculture in Post-Bellum Georgia." *Journal of Economic History* 43 (1983), 661–74.

Thomas, Emory M. *The Confederate Nation, 1861–1865.* New York: Harper and Row, 1979.

Thompson, C. Mildred. *Reconstruction in Georgia* (1915). Reprinted: Savannah: Beehive Press, 1972.

Thompson, E. P. *The Making of the English Working Class.* New York: Pantheon Books, 1963.

———. "Time, Work Discipline and Industrial Capitalism." *Past and Present* 38 (1967), 56–97.

———. "Patrician Society, Plebeian Culture." *Journal of Social History* 7 (1974), 382–405.

———. *Whigs and Hunters: The Origin of the Black Act.* New York: Pantheon Books, 1975.

———. "Eighteenth-Century English Society: Class Struggle without Class?" *Social History* 3 (1978), 133–65.

———. *Customs in Common: Studies in Traditional Popular Culture.* New York: New Press, 1993.

Tise, Larry E. *Proslavery: A History of the Defense of Slavery in America, 1701–1840.* Athens: University of Georgia Press, 1987.

Toulmin, Harry Aubrey, Jr. *Social Historians.* Boston: Gorham Press, 1911.

Tracy, Susan J. *In the Master's Eye: Representations of Women, Blacks, and Poor Whites in Antebellum Southern Literature.* Amherst: University of Massachusetts Press, 1995.

Tullos, Allen. *Habits of Industry: White Culture and the Transformation of the Carolina Piedmont.* Chapel Hill: University of North Carolina Press, 1989.

Tyrrell, Ian R. *Sobering Up: From Temperance to Prohibition in Antebellum America, 1800–1860.* Westport: Greenwood Press, 1979.

———. "Drink and Temperance in the Old South: An Overview and Interpretation." *Journal of Southern History* 48 (1982), 485–510.

Volosinov, V. N. *Marxism and the Philosophy of Language.* Translated by Ladislav Matejka and I. R. Titunik. Cambridge: Harvard University Press, 1986.

Vovelle, Michel. *Ideologies and Mentalities.* Translated by Eamon O'Flaherty. Chicago: University of Chicago Press, 1990.

Wade, John Donald. *Augustus Baldwin Longstreet: A Study of the Development of Culture in the South.* New York: Macmillan Company, 1924.

Wallerstein, Immanuel. *The Modern World-System: Capitalist Agriculture and the Origins of the European World Economy in the Sixteenth Century.* New York: Academic Press, 1974.

———. *The Modern World-System II: Mercantilism and the Consolidation of the European World-Economy, 1600–1750.* New York: Academic Press, 1980.

———. *The Modern World-System III: The Second Era of Great Expansion of the Capitalist World-Economy, 1730–1840s.* San Diego: Academic Press, 1989.

Watkins, Floyd C., and Watkins, Charles Hubert. *Yesterday in the Hills.* Athens: University of Georgia Press, 1982.

Watson, Charles S. *From Nationalism to Secession: The Changing Fiction of William Gilmore Simms.* Westport: Greenwood Press, 1993.

Watson, Ritchie Devon, Jr. *Yeoman Versus Cavalier: The Old Southwest's Fictional Road to Rebellion.* Baton Rouge: Louisiana State University Press, 1993.

Wetherington, Mark V. *The New South Comes to Wiregrass Georgia, 1860–1910.* Knoxville: University of Tennessee Press, 1994.

Wheeler, Otis B. *The Literary Career of Maurice Thompson.* Baton Rouge: Louisiana State University Press, 1965.

White, Deborah Gray. *Ar'n't I a Woman? Female Slaves in the Plantation South.* New York: W. W. Norton and Company, 1985.

Wieman, David F. "The Economic Emancipation of the Non-Slaveholding Class: Upcountry Farmers in the Georgia Cotton Economy." *Journal of Economic History* 45 (1985), 71–94.

———. "Farmers and the Market in Antebellum America: A View from the Georgia Upcountry." *Journal of Economic History* 47 (1987), 627–47.

Wiener, Jonathan. *Social Origins of the New South: Alabama, 1860–1885.* Baton Rouge: Louisiana State University Press, 1978.

———. "Class Structure and Economic Development in the American South, 1865–1955." *American Historical Review* 84 (1979), 970–92.

Wiggins, Robert Lemuel. *The Life of Joel Chandler Harris: From Obscurity in Boyhood to Fame in Early Manhood.* Nashville: Publishing House Methodist Episcopal Church, South, 1918.

Williams, Jack K. "Georgia As Seen by Ante-Bellum English Travelers." *Georgia Historical Quarterly* 32 (1948), 158–74.

———. "Travel in Ante-Bellum Georgia As Recorded by English Visitors." *Georgia Historical Quarterly* 33 (1949), 191–205.

———. "An Evaluation of Seventeen British Travelers to Ante-Bellum Georgia." *Georgia Historical Quarterly* 35 (1951), 307–18.

Williams, Raymond. *Culture and Society, 1780–1950* (1958). Reprinted: New York: Harper and Row, 1966.

———. *The Country and the City.* London: Chatto and Windus, 1973.

———. *Keywords: A Vocabulary of Culture and Society.* New York: Oxford University Press, 1976.

———. *Marxism and Literature.* New York: Oxford University Press, 1977.

Williamson, Joel. *New People: Miscegenation and Mullattoes in the United States.* New York: Free Press, 1980.

———. *The Crucible of Race: Black-White Relations in the American South since Emancipation.* New York: Oxford University Press, 1984.

Wilson, Charles Reagan. *Baptized in Blood: The Religion of the Lost Cause, 1865–1920.* Athens: University of Georgia Press, 1980.

Wimsatt, Mary Ann. *The Major Fiction of William Gilmore Simms.* Baton Rouge: Louisiana State University Press, 1989.

Wingo, Horace Calvin. "Race Relations in Georgia, 1872–1908." Ph.D. dissertation, University of Georgia, 1969.

Wood, Betty. *Women's Work, Men's Work: The Informal Slave Economies of Georgia.* Athens: University of Georgia Press, 1995.

Woodman, Harold D. *King Cotton and His Retainers: Financing and Marketing the Cotton Crop of the South, 1800–1925.* Lexington: University of Kentucky Press, 1968.

———. *New South, New Law: The Legal Foundations of Credit and Labor Relations in the Postbellum Agricultural South.* Baton Rouge: Louisiana State University Press, 1995.

Woods, James M. "In the Eye of the Beholder: Slavery in the Travel Accounts in the Old South, 1790–1860." *Southern Studies* 1 (1990), 33–59.

Woodward, C. Vann. *Tom Watson: Agrarian Rebel* (1938). Reprinted: New York: Oxford University Press, 1975.

———. *Origins of the New South, 1877–1913* (1951). Reprinted: Baton Rouge: Louisiana State University Press, 1971.

———. *The Burden of Southern History.* Revised edition. Baton Rouge: Louisiana State University Press, 1968.

———. *The Strange Career of Jim Crow.* Third revised edition. New York: Oxford University Press, 1974.

Wright, Gavin. *The Political Economy of the Cotton South.* New York: W. W. Norton, 1978.

———. *Old South, New South: Revolutions in the Southern Economy since the Civil War.* New York: Basic Books, 1986.

Wright, Richard N. "Ambivalent Bastions of Slavery: The 'Peculiar Institution' on College Campuses in Antebellum Georgia." *Georgia Historical Quarterly* 80 (1996), 467–85.

Wyatt-Brown, Bertram. *Southern Honor, Ethics and Behavior in the Old South.* New York: Oxford University Press, 1982.

Wynne, Lewis Nicholas. *The Continuity of Cotton: Planter Politics in Georgia, 1865–1892.* Macon: Mercer University Press, 1986.

Young, Jeffrey R. "Ideology and Death on a Savannah River Rice Plantation, 1833–1867: Paternalism Amidst 'a Good Supply of Disease and Pain.'" *Journal of Southern History* 59 (1993), 673–706.

Zboray, Ronald J. *A Fictive People: Antebellum Economic Development and the American Reading Public.* New York: Oxford University Press, 1993.

INDEX